Fisherman's Bible

The World's Most Comprehensive Angling Reference

Foreword by Kirk Deeter
Edited by Jay Cassell

SKYHORSE PUBLISHING

Skyhorse Publishing books may be purchased in bulk at special discounts for sales promotion, corporate gifts, fund-raising, or educational purposes. Special editions can also be created to specifications. For details, contact the Special Sales Department, Skyhorse Publishing, 307 West 36th Street, 11th Floor, New York, NY 10018 or info@skyhorsepublishing.com.

Skyhorse® and Skyhorse Publishing® are registered trademarks of Skyhorse Publishing, Inc.®, a Delaware corporation.

Visit our website at www.skyhorsepublishing.com.

Library of Congress Cataloging-in-Publication Data is available on file.

10 9 8 7 6 5 4 3 2 1

ISBN: 978-1-61608-837-8

Printed in Canada

Note: Every effort has been made to record specifications and descriptions of rods, reels, lures, and lines accurately, but the Publisher can take no responsibility for errors or omissions. The prices shown for rods, reels, lures, and lines are manufacturers' suggested retail prices and are furnished for information only. These were in effect at press time and are subject to change without notice. Purchasers of the book have complete freedom of choice in pricing for resale.

CONTENTS

INTRODUCTION

Congratulations. You have just purchased the first *Fisherman's Bible* ever published. It is our intention to publish a new, updated, and expanded edition of this compendium every year, starting right now. You are in on the ground level. You have bought the first edition!

To give some background, Skyhorse Publishing publishes many fishing, hunting, shooting, and outdoor books. One of our most popular books, and one of our bestsellers, is the *Shooter's Bible*. The *Shooter's Bible* was first published in 1925 and has been published annually, and in some cases bi-annually, ever since. More than seven million copies have been sold in that time, and it continues to be the ultimate reference book for millions of people who want information on new guns, ammunition, optics, and accessories, as well as up-to-date prices and specs for thousands of firearms.

According to recent statistics, there are approximately 15 million hunters in the United States. That pales in comparison to the number of anglers in the nation. A 2011 survey conducted by the US Fish and Wildlife Service found that there are more than 40 million fresh- and saltwater anglers in the United States—and that doesn't even include the millions of anglers not required to have licenses in many saltwater angling states. It is, as Kirk Deeter notes in his foreword, a $48 billion industry—bigger than golf!

The *Fisherman's Bible* is the result of our editorial team (a tip of the hat to head researcher Lindsey Breuer) gathering information on all fresh- and saltwater rods, reels, lines, and lures that are currently in production. Just as the *Shooter's Bible* provides up-to-date information on in-production firearms, ammunition, optics, and reloading equipment, the

HERE I TRY OUT AN ORVIS HELIOS ROD ON THE WEBER RIVER, EAST OF SALT LAKE CITY, UTAH.

Fisherman's Bible does the same on the angling side. In this tome, you will find specs and figures for everything fishing. The New Products section, in the front of the book, highlights everything new, every rod, reel, line, and lure that has been introduced in the past twelve months. Photos of every piece of gear are included, with the New Product section featuring color photographs.

Products in the *Fisherman's Bible* have been arranged carefully to make it easy for readers to find what they're looking for. As mentioned, new products are featured in the front color section, while the rest are listed in detail in black and white. Each section is organized by Rods, Reels, Lines, and Lures. After that, we classified products to make it easier for, say, a freshwater flyfisherman to find exactly what he or she is looking for with ease. So, Rods, Reels, and Lures are divided by Spinning, Spincasting, Baitcasting,

and Fly. Then, freshwater and saltwater gear are listed separately within those sections.

As we do with the *Shooter's Bible*, next year we will take all of the new products that appear in this edition and incorporate them into the main section of the book. All rods, reels, lines, and lures that are no longer in production will be removed. All prices will then be double-checked and updated. There will be a new New Products section next year, featuring everything that has been introduced by the tackle companies from the date this first edition was published to the date the second edition comes out.

Our research team has made every effort to get all specs and prices correct. We have scoured all of the websites, we have attended ICAST, the trade show of the American Sportfishing Association held annually in either Orlando or Las Vegas, plus we have gone

STEVE BECHARD, OWNER OF THE RISE FISHING COMPANY, SHOWS ME ONE OF HIS COMPANY'S NEWEST RODS, A 9-FOOT, 4-PIECE, 5-WEIGHT IN-STREAM FLY ROD THAT RETAILS FOR $199.

to as many regional angling-related shows as possible. As I write this column at the end of January, I'm still unpacking luggage and brochures after getting back from the 22nd annual Fly Fishing Show held in Somerset, New Jersey. It was there, for example, where I had the opportunity to examine some new graphite rods being offered by the up-and-coming Rise Fishing Company.

As you thumb through the pages of this *Fisherman's Bible*, please understand that we have made every effort to include every tackle company on the planet. If anything is missing, and I'm guessing we may have missed some, we want to know about it. Please contact us at www.skyhorsepublishing.com, and we'll make sure to include any missing information in next year's edition.

Good fishing!

Jay Cassell
Editorial Director
Skyhorse Publishing
New York, New York
January 26, 2014

FOREWORD

Sportfishing is many things to many people. It's a pastime, a hobby, a culture, and—at least in name—it is also a sport (although I've often wondered if something you can do while seated, at the same time you're eating a sandwich, actually really should be called a "sport").

One thing cannot be argued, and that is that sportfishing also supports a very large, sustained industry. By most recent estimates, there are nearly 40 million licensed anglers in the United States alone, accounting for over $40 billion in retail product sales. The larger impact of fishing on the American economy is projected at $115 billion, and well over 800,000 people depend on the sportfishing industry for employment. Anglers also are the stewards of the world's natural waters. License fees, as well as taxes paid on sportfishing products, are used to conserve, protect, and restore the oceans, lakes, rivers, and streams that support sportfishing (and various other forms of recreation), not only in the United States but around the planet.

The important thing to note, in this context, is that this entire world revolves on an axis of product.

When you boil it all down, anglers are obsessed with three concerns—where to go, what to use, and how to use it. The "what to use" part supports the "where to go." And without the "what to use," there

KIRK DEETER WITH A LINEUP OF NEW RODS, READY FOR TESTING. © TIM ROMANO

wouldn't be a whole lot to talk about on the "how to use it" side at all, would there?

From rods and reels to lines, lures, flies, and myriad other things that go into the angler's "arsenal," it's hard to imagine a realm where innovation is more delicately balanced with tradition than recreational fishing. The "fair chase" ethic is the root of sportfishing (and hence, the real meaning of "sport"), and yet anglers are also consumed and captivated by performance.

To cast farther . . . to fight stronger . . . to tease and trick the most fickle quarry . . . those are the things that keep us interested, right? It might all have started with a simple tug you felt while fishing a worm and bobber with your granddad. But it's the continuous puzzle solving—and, by connection, the tools we use to get those puzzles solved—that keeps us hooked for years. That's why grown men and women still melt like little kids at the sight of a shiny new fishing rod propped in the window display of their favorite tackle shop.

There has never been a more exciting time to follow and understand products made for recreational fishing than right now. The technologies have never been better: aerospace graphites and resins now used to make lighter, faster rods; composite materials used in the brakes of Formula 1 racing cars being designed into the disc drags of fly-fishing reels; medical grade materials used to make lines and lures; laser-sharpened hooks; and on, and on, and on. . . .

And yet, if you are a cane-pole "purist" or a "minimalist," you haven't been forgotten. The beauty of the current array of fishing products is that there are more choices to fit more personal interests than ever before. What fits your interests and how you choose to use it is up to you.

There's never been a wider array of product specifically designed for different fish species than there is

A NORTHERN PIKE TAKEN ON A CRANKBAIT, READY FOR RELEASE. © TIM ROMANO

THE RING OF THE RISE: WHAT DID THAT TROUT JUST EAT?

right now. Yes indeed, most of the ink and attention in the fishing world has traditionally revolved around largemouth bass, and striped bass, and billfish, and trout, and pike, and walleyes, and (overseas at least) carp. But now you see more tackle for sharks, and fly rigs for panfish, and so on. I'll concede that a lot of product is designed to catch anglers as much as it is really designed to catch fish. And a classic Panther Martin lure or a black woolly bugger fly, in the right angler's hands, can catch many different things. But you have more choices now. How you make them is up to you.

There's now more product specifically designed for women anglers than there ever has been before. And by "designed for women," I do not mean "painted pink." There should be more of this, and there inevitably will be. But there are more choices available. How you make them is up to you.

There are more products specifically designed for youth than there have been in the past. Again, this is

CATCH AND RELEASE ENSURES THAT OTHER ANGLERS MAY ALSO ENJOY GOOD FISHING.

DEETER WRITING ON FISHING, ABOVE THE BANKS OF A TRIBUTARY OF MICHIGAN'S PERE MARQUETTE. © TIM ROMANO

an important focus. I learned to fish with my grandfather's rod, and there's no doubt that many youngsters are doing the same (learning with "adult" tackle) now. At least I hope so. But there are more options and choices available. How you make these choices is up to you.

And lastly, there are more affordable fishing products these days than there ever have been. Granted, this is largely the result of many tackle companies moving manufacturing operations offshore. One can argue against imports and question their effect on the fishing economy in America. But there is no denying that this phenomenon is yielding lower-price-point products that eventually wind up in the hands of many aspiring anglers. And there will always, in my mind, be some level of value associated with classic "made in America" tackle for certain anglers. How you feel in this regard, and the choices you make, well, those things are up to you.

The purpose of this book is, quite simply, to get a handle on many of the options that are out there now, so that you can be better informed to make the choices that are completely up to you. Whether you are in the market, or simply want to behold an incredible array of fishing product, there's never been anything this comprehensive or detailed to help anglers, and there's never been a time when a resource like this has been more relevant.

Enjoy it. I hope it answers your questions. I hope it prompts you to ask more. Most important I hope it prompts you to expand your own fishing horizons.

Kirk Deeter
Editor, *Trout Magazine*
Editor, *Angling Trade News*
Editor-at-Large, *Field & Stream*

HOW ONE FISH CHANGED THE TACKLE INDUSTRY

—Steve Price

The bass that changed the entire fishing tackle industry was not the world record 22-pound, 4-ounce giant George Perry caught in 1932. Instead, it was a little 2 ½-pounder an angler named Bill Dance caught just after daybreak on June 6, 1967, throwing a 7 ¼-inch blue Fliptail plastic worm to a sunken roadbed on Beaver Lake in Arkansas.

It was Dance's first cast of the morning and is widely acknowledged as the very first cast by anyone in the All-American Bass Tournament taking place on the lake that week. The All-American, in turn, was the first event conducted by what would soon become the Bass Anglers Sportsman Society, a fledgling fishing tournament organization that quickly became the unifying voice for millions of American bass fishermen.

Just as importantly, that unification led to the most rapid expansion the fishing tackle industry had ever experienced. Fishing lures, as well as rods, reels, and other equipment, were already being manufactured, of course, in some cases for more than sixty years; the first patent for a fishing lure was actually issued in 1848. But Dance's fish, along with those caught and weighed in by his fellow competitors—another fisherman named Stan Sloan won the three-day event with 37 pounds, 8 ounces—created a wave of excitement that continued to build and grow for decades to come.

GEORGE PERRY CAUGHT HIS 22-POUND, 4-OUNCE WORLD RECORD LARGEMOUTH ON A RAINY JUNE MORNING IN MONTGOMERY LAKE, GEORGIA, A RECORD THAT STOOD FOR MORE THAN 75 YEARS. PERRY WAS RELUCTANT TO TALK ABOUT HIS RECORD CATCH, AND EVEN FAMILY MEMBERS KNEW LITTLE ABOUT IT.

More changes took place in the tackle industry during the next twenty-five years than in all previous years combined, because anglers like Dance, Sloan, and the others were not only learning new techniques, they were teaching those techniques to others. That led to the formation of new manufacturing companies, as well as competition between them, which spurred growth and development even faster. The new industry followed the new tournaments, and more than one competitive fisherman started his own tackle company, either because he needed an item not then available, or if it was, he thought he could make it better.

This is not to detract in any way from James Heddon, who is rightly credited with creating the first American fishing lure manufacturing company in 1902, James Heddon & Son. The business was located in southwestern Michigan in the town of Dowagiac, which, incidentally, translates into "many fishes" in the language of the nearby Potawatomi Indian tribe. Heddon had already been extremely successful in the beekeeping business, but he suffered from asthma; his father and grandfather had both enjoyed fishing occasionally, so he was no stranger to the sport himself. Besides, he felt being on the water helped him feel better.

On one such excursion in 1898, Heddon is said to have whittled a stick down to a small size as he waited for his fishing companions to arrive there at the millpond in Dowagiac, and then absently tossed the carving into the water where it was immediately hit by a bass. Heddon, who had long been intrigued by topwater fishing, then began carving additional lures, attaching hooks, and selling them to his friends. These "frogs" resembled little more than a section of broomstick and included a bottle cap at the head of the stick to create action as the lure was retrieved, but they caught fish.

This crude, stick-like lure evolved into the Dowagiac Perfect Casting Bait and became Heddon's first commercial lure. Although he initially made them in his home, with the paint baked in his wife's

TRIG LUND, SHOWN WITH SOME OF THE FIBERGLASS RODS HE HELPED DESIGN DURING HIS YEARS WORKING WITH HEDDON. LUND WAS HIRED BY JOHN HEDDON IN 1945 AND REMAINED WITH THE FIRM FOR THE NEXT 23 YEARS, EVENTUALLY SERVING AS VICE PRESIDENT. *PHOTO COURTESY HEDDON MUSEUM.*

oven, in 1902 the first permanent lure factory was set up on the second floor of a clothing store in downtown Dowagiac.

Other fishing companies began about this same time, and some actually preceded Heddon. What is known for certain is that the beginning of the fishing tackle industry gradually emerged during the next two decades. Firms like Creek Chub, Hildebrandt, Shakespeare, Pflueger, and South Bend opened their doors, but none could have possibly imagined the future of what, to that point, was still only a casual pastime.

Surprisingly, perhaps, some lures from this long-ago era are still being manufactured and used regularly by today's bass fishermen. Without question, one of the most famous is the Zara Spook, a topwater lure Heddon introduced in 1922 as the Zaragossa Minnow. The lure had been designed by Heddon's son, Will, at their family home in Florida, and named for a well-known street in the red-light district of Pensacola where ladies of the night regularly walked the sidewalks.

The lure became an instant success because of its side-to-side action, which soon became known as "walking the dog." This term also refers to those creative ladies on Zaragossa Street, who, after being forbidden to approach potential customers on the sidewalk, simply began walking their pets on leashes along the same route.

Some lures were named for famous personalities, such as the Little George, produced by Eufaula, Alabama, angler Tom Mann, who fished against Dance in that first Beaver Lake tournament. Mann had been a game warden, and one day while on a stakeout along a stream he whittled a lure that immediately caught bass. Mann named the lure after Alabama's governor at the time, George Wallace.

One lure, the Gilmore Jumper, was even sold with a snakeskin covering. As the story goes, a bass fisherman was having a fabulous day on the Buffalo River in Arkansas catching bass with a brown-painted Jumper, but lost the lure when his line broke. On his way back to town to purchase a new brown lure, he ran over a snake on the road, and seeing the snake's brown coloration, the angler immediately skinned it, glued the skin on another lure, and started fishing again.

In many instances, other lure changes came in bits and pieces over the years, especially in the decades of the 1970s and '80s. Spinnerbaits, for

TOM MANN GAINED LASTING FAME AS AN EARLY LURE MANUFACTURER BY CREATING, AMONG OTHERS, THE FAMOUS SOFT PLASTIC JELLY WORMS, WHICH HE SOLD IN VARIOUS "FLAVORS." MANN WAS A HIGHLY SUCCESSFUL TOURNAMENT ANGLER IN THE EARLY DAYS OF ORGANIZED COMPETITIVE FISHING AS WELL AS A TIRELESS PROMOTER OF HIS OWN LURES.

example, were popular before Dance caught his Beaver Lake bass. The basic safety pin design still in use today was patented on June 28, 1966, by Chicago inventor Jesse M. Shannon, but it was improved on in March, 1970, by John R. Hudson, who patented his design of placing the spinner blade on the wire so it would help make the lure snag-proof. Alabama angler Bill Huntley added ball bearing swivels to the lures, as well as made the change from steel piano wire to satin, stainless wire. Skirts eventually evolved from plastic to rubber, and blades began to change shape from round to long, narrow, and pointed.

In fact, the winner of that first Beaver Lake tournament, Stan Sloan, used his expertise and name recognition to launch his Zorro Spinnerbaits. Don Butler, another competitor in that same tournament, started his Okiebug Spinnerbait company. And Charles Spence and Ray Murski, who also competed at Beaver Lake (Murski finished fourth), were poised to take Spence's fledgling spinnerbait company to heights undreamed of by either of them.

The previous year, Spence had purchased a small, garage-based lure company in west Tennessee and immediately re-named it Strike King. Spinnerbait blades were punched out by a single machine that simply dropped the blades into a cardboard box on the floor, and the wire frames were created by bending a piece of wire around pegs on a small board. In 1968, Murski started selling them across the southern United States—he was one of Sam Walton's original salesmen—and the rest really is history.

Murski was a huge supporter of bass fishing in general and of Ray Scott's professional tournament idea specifically. He fished eleven of Scott's events and earned a check in all of them; he not only knew how to fish, he knew what fishermen wanted, and they wanted spinnerbaits, as well as anything else that would fool a bass. In 1995, Murski bought Strike King from Spence and added additional tournament anglers to his Pro Staff. He didn't just pay them to wear his logo at tournaments, however; the anglers played a very active role in designing Strike King's lures and then winning with them. Today, Strike King is regarded as one of the world's foremost lure manufacturers, with a lineup that includes dozens of baits in both hard and soft plastic designs

Although a spinnerbait blade design known as the willow leaf had been around for several years, it hit national prominence in 1984, when several anglers won national tournaments using it, including a Florida-based pro named Roland Martin, who had done his best to keep the long, narrow, pointed-end blade a secret. Once Martin's secret lure was discovered, no one helped fishermen learn how to use it more than Martin himself, and today the willow leaf spinnerbait blade is the standard blade of choice among bass fishermen everywhere.

While many lure changes were small and incremental, others were sometimes monumental, such as what happened to crankbaits in 1972. Prior to that year, these types of lures, which had been around for half a century, looked remarkably similar. Most featured generally elongated bodies and a front diving lip, most often made of metal. There were other styles, but in 1972 a lure named the Big O changed everything.

The Big O was a hand-carved balsa diving plug, created by Fred Young of Maynardville, Tennessee, and named after his 6-foot, 6-inch football-playing brother Odis. The lure incorporated several features never before combined so successfully in a single plug: it dived quickly on retrieve and swam with a strong side-to-side wobble, then floated right to the surface if the retrieve was stopped. Until then, most crankbaits had a very slow, lazy action. The Big O also featured a short, squared-off bill, so it deflected off cover well, and instead of being long and skinny, it was short and squatty, almost fat. One writer of the time described it as a pregnant guppy.

NO SINGLE INDIVIDUAL HAS DESIGNED AND PRODUCED AS MANY BASS FISHING LURES AS COTTON CORDELL. AMONG HIS BEST-KNOWN CREATIONS ARE THE SPOT, A RATTLING, VIBRATING MINNOW IMITATION, WHICH HE CARVED FROM A PIECE OF PINE BARK WHILE SITTING ON A DEER STAND.

At the June 1972 Tennessee Invitational tournament conducted on Watts Bar Lake by the Bass Anglers Sportsman Society, a professional fisherman named Billy Westmorland (who had been using the Big O secretly for months) accidentally let the lure be seen by his competition, and a virtual stampede to find Big O lures started. At that tournament, the lure rented for five dollars a day but cost twenty-five dollars if you lost it. A new one, if you could locate one, sold for as much as fifty dollars.

In Hot Springs, Arkansas, a leading lure manufacturer of the time, Cotton Cordell, secured the manufacturing rights to the Big O from Young and began producing them in plastic; during the next twelve months he sold more than a million of them. Helping the Big O's reputation during this time was the fact that a tournament fisherman, Larry Hill, caught more than sixty pounds of bass in an hour with the lure en route to winning a national bass tournament competition in Florida.

That type of success led other manufacturers to bring out their own similar-looking lures, and practically overnight the age of the "alphabet plugs" was born. Companies like Bagley, Norman, and others called their creations the Balsa B, Big N, and similar names. The most important legacy the Big O created was that practically every crankbait made today includes some of that lure's same original design and offers the same basic action Fred Young carved into his original lure. Many are thinner, and others will dive much deeper, but all have a distinct wobble.

Plastic worms, widely used today, have been around since the early 1950s. Imitation worms made of rubber and designed for fishing had been tried nearly a century earlier, and later models impregnated with special scents appeared in the 1930s. In the years immediately following World War II, however, as bass fishing continued to grow as a sport, a number of individuals developed worms from plastic. Among them were Dave DeLong, Nick Creme, and Charles Burke.

During this time, as competition between manufacturers began to increase, worm designs started to change. Although the worm itself remained straight, body styles varied considerably. Bing McClellan of Burke introduced the Buckshot Worm that looked like just that, a string of beads or "buckshot" with a floppy tail. Others concentrated on color and length, with DeLong producing worms more than twelve inches in length.

In 1973, however, the plastic worm grew a new tail that changed the lure forever. This change started during the summer of 1973, when R. J. Benson, president of a Rockaway, New Jersey, firm named Generic Systems, showed a French lure named the Sosy Eel at the American Fishing Tackle Manufacturers Show in Chicago. The lure featured a thin, flat, curving tail that produced a dramatic swimming action when retrieved, and, cried Benson, several American firms were illegally copying it.

Indeed, the swimming tail concept was so revolutionary, it was quickly adopted by other manufacturers. The first to bring their own such worm to market was Carver Plastisols Co. (later to become Mister Twister, Inc.) of Minden, Louisiana, and after its introduction in early 1974, more than three million had been shipped by April. They re-tooled their manufacturing facility to be able to produce half a million worms a day.

The impact on the industry was so stunning that nearly all the major manufacturers had curly-tail or swimming-tail worms on the market within weeks. Included were Cordell's Pigtail, Mann's Jelly Twister, Burke's Wig-Wag, Bagley's Screw Tail, Lindy's Swirltail, and Pico's Streaker. A Cordell rep reportedly sold nine thousand dollars worth of their worms by demonstrating one in a toilet bowl.

Although several of these firms are no longer in business, this particular design continues to be one of the most popular and is offered by all of today's manufacturers. The overall concept remains unchanged, though the design has been altered slightly over the years and is now incorporated in plastic lizards, grubs, minnows, and other creatures.

If the curled, swimming tails created a more realistic look for soft plastic lures, then colors and new paints did the same for hard plastic and wood lures. Realism was the catchword of the day, as manufacturers tried different techniques to make their lures appear as natural as possible. Photo-imprintation became popular for a short while, and others kept adding more and more coats of paint. In Bagley's case, each lure received a total of seventeen coats as it moved down the assembly line.

Not all developments in the fledgling fishing industry were lures, of course. Realizing the growing legion of anglers also required rods, reels, and fishing lines in order to use their new lures, various firms entered this new arena specializing with those products. The first "multiplying" reel, a forerunner of today's popular baitcasting reels, had been introduced as far back as 1770 by Onesimus Ustonson of Britain. It was not until 1896, when William Shakespeare Jr. of Kalamazoo, Michigan, created the first true level-wind reel, that these types of reels started to grow in popularity. Level-wind allows line to be wound back evenly on a reel after a cast, and is standard on all baitcasting reels today.

Shakespeare started his own reel-making company the following year, and by 1902, as James Heddon moved his young lure business from his home to a dedicated factory, Shakespeare's company already had a dozen employees. For more than a century the firm, now headquartered in Columbia, South Carolina, has continued to introduce new and innovative reels as well as rods and fishing line. In 1947, Shakespeare introduced the first fiberglass rod, the Wonderod, revolutionizing the market and making bamboo and steel rods all but obsolete.

Shakespeare entered the fishing industry by design; others, like the little company that would eventually become a giant in the sport and one of Shakespeare's strongest competitors, Zebco, moved into the fishing world completely by coincidence.

In 1948, still nearly twenty years before Dance caught that Beaver Lake bass, the Tulsa-based firm was known as the Zero Hour Bomb Company, making time-detonated bombs for use in oil exploration and drilling. By 1948, however, with their patent on bombs about to expire and new technology threatening to make their explosives obsolete, the company began looking for new products to manufacture.

They found it in fishing, when a West Texas angler/watch repairman/inventor named R. D. Hull walked in with something none of them had seen before—a reel that would not backlash. Actually, Hull didn't show them a fishing reel because he hadn't made one; what he did show his future bosses, Harold Binford and Marion Parry, was a Folger's coffee can lid fastened to a piece of plywood. However crude it was, the concept—a fixed spool from which line came off on demand (casting) but was controlled, and could then be "reeled" back onto that spool—impressed Binford and Parry enough to invite Hull back with an actual prototype model.

Hull built his prototype in less than a month and returned to Zebco to show his new creation. Hull's reel was not the first fixed-spool "spinning" reel; British angler Alfred Holden received a patent for

one in 1905, and others had been imported and even built in the United States since the 1930s. While certainly easier for the casual fisherman to use than the revolving-spool baitcasting reels of the day, these early spinning reels still had problems, namely line spilling freely off the spool. That's what Hull's coffee lid stopped; he put a cap over the spool and controlled line flow by use of a pin located inside that cap.

Hull was hired on the spot, and on May 7, 1949, the Zero Hour Bomb Company's first closed-face reel, the Standard, came off the production line. The firm soon shortened its name to Zebco as improvements in their new product, which became known as a spincast reel, continued. In 1954, Zebco introduced the Model 33, featuring a push-button spool control, and during the next thirty-two years

BILL DANCE, FISHING HERE WITH DR. LOREN HILL, HAS OFTEN BEEN DESCRIBED AS "AMERICA'S FAVORITE FISHERMAN," DUE TO HIS LONG CAREER AS A SUCCESSFUL TOURNAMENT ANGLER AND TELEVISION PERSONALITY. HE HAS TAUGHT LITERALLY MILLIONS OF PEOPLE HOW TO FISH THROUGH HIS TELEVISION SHOWS, VIDEOS, AND MAGAZINE ARTICLES.

more than 185 million had been sold, and the reels continue to be sold today. This decision by Harold Binford and Marion Parry, neither of whom knew anything about fishing, has to be considered one of the most fortuitous in the entire history of sport fishing, because Hull's plywood board and coffee can lid literally opened up the world of fishing to the masses.

His invention offered an alternative to the revolving spool reel, which had been around in various forms for well over a century. A Kentucky fisherman named George Snyder invented what is considered the first reel that actually paid out line during a cast; the term "baitcaster," still in use today, arose because virtually all fishing at that time was done with live bait, since there were no artificial lures.

At Beaver Lake in 1967, Dance fished with a baitcaster made by the Swedish firm of Abu, which by that time pretty much controlled the revolving spool reel market. Their signature reel was painted red and designated the 5000. By today's standards, the 5000 would be considered primitive, since it was fairly big and heavy, featured a 5:1 gear ratio, and had no adjustable spool braking system. Once tournament fishing truly became the moving force spurring tackle development, changes in reels came quickly.

Today, baitcasters continue to evolve as bass fishing continues to grow and thrive. Braking systems, usually with a set of tiny internal magnets, have all but made these reels backlash-proof. Gearing varies from 4.7:1 to higher than 7:1, a range that allows a great deal of variation in lure retrieve speed that was never available in Dance's red 5000. The gears are stronger, too; the overall size is smaller and more streamlined; and numerous companies like Shimano, Shakespeare, Pure Fishing, and Ardent compete for angler dollars. Abu reels themselves have changed dramatically as well and are part of the Pure Fishing Company lineup.

Another reel, the open-face, fixed spool spinning reel, had been introduced from Europe into the United States in 1935 but had not gained a following until the years following World War II. This particular design permitted the weight of the lure to pull line off the stationary spool, a feature that allowed the use of extremely light lures. Changes in these reels were also gradual, until 1963 when the Japanese company, Matsui Manufacturing, under its American umbrella, Daiwa Corporation, began importing its first fishing reels.

In 1970, just three years after Dance's tournament on Beaver Lake, Daiwa imported an open-face spinning reel with a skirted spool, a feature that provided far greater line control than previous models, and by 1971 virtually every company making these types of reels offered this feature, which continues to be the standard design of today.

Most of the anglers in that first Beaver Lake event also used 5 ½-foot, hollow fiberglass rods with short pistol-grip handles, but practically no one offers models like this today. The first pistol grip had been whittled out of wood by Cotton Cordell and taken to Japan by Cordell and another rod maker friend from Alabama, Lew Childre. The Japanese produced a handle for them overnight, which Childre then began using on his own rods, known as Speed Sticks, and which quickly became the most popular handle style in America.

One of Childre's employees at the time was a former football player named Shag Shahid, who had traded in his pads for fishing gear. He designed Childre's Speed Stick rods, and as early as 1960 had made a V-shaped spool for baitcasting reels, a design to help reduce backlashes as the line speed slowed automatically during each cast. Childre introduced the reel in the mid–1970s, and while it did not become an overnight success, it led to the emergence of one of today's industry giants, Shimano, the world's largest bicycle component manufacturer. They were the company who did the original manufacturing of Shahid's reel, the Speed Spool.

In 1976, Shimano introduced its own reel, the Bantam 100, which was the first true, small, lightweight baitcaster. Additional baitcasters, spinning reels, and rods followed—all of it starting just nine years after Dance and Sloan had fished that first major tournament and basically shown the world new ways to catch largemouth bass. Today Shimano is one of the foremost rod and reel manufacturing companies in the world.

Cordell had also been experimenting with a lighter, stronger, more sensitive material with which to build his rods, and by 1971 he'd found it: graphite. He wanted to enter that Beaver Lake tournament, but wasn't allowed to, since he'd been making fishing tackle for more than 20 years at that time and was considered a "pro."

During the mid–1970s, Cordell decided to get out of the rod business so he could concentrate on lures, so he called another rod-making friend in Washington state to come get all his equipment if he wanted it. That friend was a man named Gary Loomis, who accepted Cordell's offer and hauled everything back to Woodlands. There he established the G. Loomis rod company, which today is one of the most highly respected rod companies in the world and is now owned by the aforementioned Shimano Corporation.

Another West Coast company, Fenwick, introduced their own graphite rods in 1972, and through their highly successful marketing program, quickly established themselves as a leader in the field. Graphite is available in many different grades, often measured in a modulus, or strength, and during the next two decades Fenwick, G. Loomis, and other rod companies raced each other to see who could create rods with the highest modulus rating. This type of research and development cost hundreds of thousands of dollars, but by then demand from the nation's bass fishermen for lighter, stronger, more sensitive rods could support it.

Another segment of the rapidly growing bass fishing industry—electronics—was, at the same time, growing nearly as fast as the rod, reel, and lure businesses. Fishermen had been using sonar-type equipment prior to 1967, much of it produced by Carl Lowrance, who was using his Navy electronics experience now in fresh water. In 1957, Lowrance introduced what is generally called his "blue box" unit, since most of his equipment was fairly boxy looking and all was painted blue. A year later he produced the "gray box." Basically, these units told fishermen how deep the water was, but not much more.

In 1959, Lowrance introduced his "green box," and suddenly anglers could begin to see not only the bottom but also a clearer view of the bottom contour as well as objects on the bottom. Thus,

the concepts of fishing "cover" (those objects) and "structure" (the contour) became realities. The tournament anglers had already figured out the rudiments of both concepts, but now they began to refine them in an ever-growing circle of knowledge. In 1972, tournament pro and lure maker Tom Mann, who had also started his own depth finder company, Allied Sports (later to become Techsonic Industries), did a quick survey of twenty-five top tournament anglers to determine what they regarded as their most important tool for catching bass; nineteen said it was a depth finder.

By 1973, Lowrance had introduced paper chart recorders that literally graphed the bottom, and after a decade they introduced the first computerized model, the X-15. Two years later, paper units were already on the way out, replaced by liquid crystal recorders. Today, bass fishermen can look at objects in the water and on the bottom far to either side of their boats, not just in a small area underneath them, and they can tell exactly how far away it is so they can fish it that much more efficiently.

The overall concept—showing water depth, bottom contour and cover, and fish above it—is still the same. The visual information is simply being presented in new and more exciting ways, and Dance, still an active fisherman and teacher, admits amazement at all that has happened not only in electronics but also rods, reels, and lures since that remarkable morning on Beaver Lake.

He did not originate the sport of bass fishing when he caught that little 2 ½-pounder. What he, Sloan, and the others did was far more important. Symbolically speaking, they opened the curtain on a brand new world. They were like explorers seeing another continent for the very first time; everything they did was new and fresh and exciting, and the fishing public embraced them because they could feel and experience that very same excitement.

This chapter was excerpted from the soon-to-be-released book, The Fish That Changed America, *by Steve Price. To order a copy of this new book, which traces the history of bass fishing in America from the past to 2014, go to www.skyhorsepublishing.com.*

10 Rods

30 Reels

58 Lures

92 Lines

NEW Products: Rods, Freshwater Spinning

ABU GARCIA VENDETTA 2-PIECE
Model: VNTS662-5, VNTS662-6, VNTS692-4, VNTS702-5
Length: 6'6''; 6'6''; 6'9''; 7'
Power: M; MH; ML; M
Action: MF; F; XF; F
Pieces: 2
Line Weight: 6-12 lbs; 8-14 lbs; 6-10 lbs; 6-12 lbs
Guide Count: 7+tip
Lure Weight: 1/8-1/2 oz; 1/4-3/4 oz; 1/8-1/2 oz; 3/16-5/8 oz

Features: 30-Ton graphite for a lightweight balanced design; one-piece aluminum screw-down hood creates a secure connection; high-density EVA gives greater sensitivity and durability; Texas rigged hook keeper for all bait applications; stainless steel guides with Zirconium inserts; Abu-designed extreme exposure reel seat for increased blank contact and sensitivity; IntraCarbon technology provides a lightweight barrier to improve durability without adding weight.
Price:.....................................**$79.95**

ABU GARCIA VENDETTA
Model: VNTS63-5, VNTS66-5, VNTS66-6, VNTS69-4, VNTS70-5, VNTS70-6, VNTS74-5
Length: 6'3''; 6'6''; 6'6''; 6'9''; 7'; 7'; 7'4''
Power: M; M; MH; ML; M; MH; M
Action: F; MF; F; XF; F; F; F
Pieces: 1
Line Weight: 6-12 lbs; 6-12 lbs; 8-14 lbs; 6-10 lbs; 6-12 lbs; 8-14 lbs; 8-14 lbs
Guide Count: 7+tip

Lure Weight: 1/8-1/2 oz; 1/8-1/2 oz; 1/4-3/4 oz; 1/8-1/2 oz; 3/16-5/8 oz; 1/4-3/4 oz; 1/2-1 oz
Features: 30-Ton graphite for a lightweight balanced design; one-piece aluminum screw-down hood creates a secure connection; high-density EVA gives greater sensitivity and durability; Texas rigged hook keeper for all bait applications; stainless steel guides with Zirconium inserts; Abu-designed extreme exposure reel seat for increased blank contact and sensitivity; IntraCarbon technology provides a lightweight barrier to improve durability without adding weight.
Price:.....................................**$79.95**

ACTION	POWER	
M=Moderate	UL=Ultra Light	H=Heavy
MF=Moderate Fast	L=Light	MH=Medium-Heavy
F=Fast	ML=Medium-Light	XH=Extra Heavy
XF=Extra Fast		

ABU GARCIA VOLATILE

Model: VOLS70-4, VOLS70-5, VOLS70-6, VOLS76-5
Length: 7'; 7'; 7'; 7'6"
Power: M; M; MH; M
Action: F
Pieces: 1
Line Weight: 6-12 lbs; 8-17 lbs; 10-20 lbs; 8-17 lbs
Guide Count: 7+tip

Lure Weight: 1/16-3/8 oz; 1/4-5/8 oz; 3/8-1 oz; 1/4-5/8 oz
Features: 30-Ton graphite with NanoTechnology for decreased weight and increased impact resistance; high-density EVA gives greater sensitivity and durability; Texas-rigged hook keeper for all bait applications; stainless steel guides with Zirconium inserts; Fuji IPS (spinning) and Fuji EPS (casting) reel seat for greater comfort; split grip design.
Price: **$99.95**

BASS PRO SHOPS JOHNNY MORRIS CARBONLITE

Model: CL66MSF, CL66MHSF, CL68MSXF, 69MLSDS, CL70MSF, CL70MHSF, CL72MSDS, CL90MLSM-2PC, CL56ULS, CL60LS, CL66MLS, CL66MSF-2, CL70MHSF-2
Length: 6'6"; 6'6"; 6'8"; 6'9"; 7'; 7'; 7'2"; 9'; 5'6"; 6'; 6'6"; 6'6"; 7'
Power: M; MH; M; ML; M; MH; M; ML; UL; L; ML; M; MH
Action: F; F; XF; F; F; F; F; F; F; F; F; F; F
Pieces: 1; 1; 1; 1; 1; 1; 1; 2; 1; 1; 1; 2; 2
Line Weight: 4-12 lbs; 6-17 lbs; 4-12 lbs; 4-10 lbs; 4-12 lbs; 6-17 lbs; 4-12 lbs; 4-10 lbs; 1-6 lbs; 2-8 lbs; 4-10 lbs; 4-12 lbs; 6-17 lbs

Lure Weight: 1/8-1/2 oz; 1/4-5/8 oz; 1/8-1/2 oz; 1/16-3/8 oz; 1/8-1/2 oz; 1/4-5/8 oz; 1/8-1/2 oz; 1/16-3/8 oz; 1/32-1/4 oz; 1/16-1/4 oz; 1/16-3/8 oz; 1/8-1/2 oz; 1/4-5/8 oz
Features: 85 million modulus carbon fiber blank; Pac Bay DLC stainless steel framed guides; works great with mono, fluoro, or superlines; almost weightless space-age P-Tec polyfoam grips; two-piece soft-touch reel seat with maximum blank exposure.
Price: **$99.99**

ACTION	POWER	
M=Moderate	UL=Ultra Light	H=Heavy
MF=Moderate Fast	L=Light	MH=Medium-Heavy
F=Fast	ML=Medium-Light	XH=Extra Heavy
XF=Extra Fast		

CABELA'S TOURNEY TRAIL SB

Model: TTS664-2
Length: 6'6''
Power: M
Action: F
Pieces: 2
Line Weight: 6-12 lbs

Lure Weight: 1/4-5/8 oz
Features: IM7 construction; graphite reel seat; aluminum oxide guides; high-quality cork handle; steel-blue blank color.
Price: **$64.99**

CABELA'S XML

Model: XMLS601-2, XMLS602-1, XMLS604-1, XMLS663-1, XMLS663-2, XMLS664-1, XMLS664XF-1, XMLS664-2, XMLS665-1, XMLS702-2, XMLS703-1, XML703-2, XMLS704-1, XMLS704-2, XMLS705-1, XMLS705-2
Length: 6'; 6'; 6'; 6'6''; 6'6''; 6'6''; 6'6''; 6'6''; 6'6''; 7'; 7'; 7'; 7'; 7'; 7'; 7'
Power: UL; ML; M; ML; ML; M; M; M; MH; L; ML; ML; M; M; MH; MH
Action: F; F; F; F; F; F; XF; F; F; F; F; F; F; F; F; F
Pieces: 2; 1; 1; 1; 2; 1; 1; 2; 1; 2; 1; 2; 1; 2; 1; 2
Line Weight: 2-6 lbs; 4-8 lbs; 6-12 lbs; 4-8 lbs; 4-8 lbs; 6-12 lbs; 6-12 lbs; 6-12 lbs; 8-20 lbs; 2-8 lbs; 4-8 lbs; 4-8 lbs; 6-12 lbs; 6-12 lbs; 8-20 lbs; 8-20 lbs
Lure Weight: 1/16-3/8 oz; 1/8-3/8 oz; 1/4-5/8 oz; 1/8-3/8 oz; 1/8-3/8 oz; 1/4-5/8 oz; 1/4-5/8 oz; 1/4-5/8 oz; 3/8-1 oz; 1/16-3/8 oz; 1/8-3/8 oz; 1/8-3/8 oz; 1/4-5/8 oz; 1/4-5/8 oz; 3/8-1 oz; 3/8-1 oz

Features: These updated rods are built on our legendary XML 64 million-modulus, spiral-core-technology graphite blanks. They feature lightweight, super-durable SS316 stainless steel Alps guides, double-coated with black chrome for maximum corrosion resistance. Precise guide spacing compacts the distance between guides from the middle to the tip of the rod. This increases sensitivity and decreases line drag. Rods have a palm-swell American Tackle Aero reel seat. Grips are made of premium cork and have thread-covering downlocking fore grips. Butts are compatible with our Weight-Balancing System, available separately.
Price: **$149.99**

ACTION	POWER	
M=Moderate	UL=Ultra Light	H=Heavy
MF=Moderate Fast	L=Light	MH=Medium-Heavy
F=Fast	ML=Medium-Light	XH=Extra Heavy
XF=Extra Fast		

DAIWA CROSSFIRE CFE

Model: CFE562ULFS, CFE602MFS, CFE661MHFS, CFE662MFS, CFE701MHFS, CFE701MLFS, CFE702MFS
Length: 5'6''; 6'; 6'6''; 6'6''; 7'; 7'; 7'
Power: UL; M; MH; M; MH; ML; M
Action: F
Pieces: 2; 2; 1; 2; 1; 1; 2

Line Weight: 1-4 lbs; 6-15 lbs; 8-17 lbs; 6-15 lbs; 8-17 lbs; 4-12 lbs; 6-15 lbs
Guide Count: 5; 5; 6; 6; 6; 6; 6
Lure Weight: 1/32-1/8 oz; 1/8-3/4 oz; 1/4-3/4 oz; 1/8-3/4 oz; 1/4-3/4 oz; 1/8-1/2 oz; 1/8-3/4 oz
Features: 26-ton IM-6 graphite blank construction; aluminum oxide guides; stainless hooded reel seat; split-design foam grip; hook keeper.
Price: **$24.95**

ACTION	POWER	
M=Moderate	UL=Ultra Light	H=Heavy
MF=Moderate Fast	L=Light	MH=Medium-Heavy
F=Fast	ML=Medium-Light	XH=Extra Heavy
XF=Extra Fast		

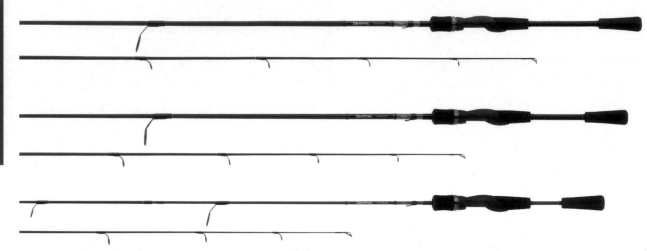

DAIWA EXCELER EXE

Model: EXE562ULFS, EXE602MFS, EXE661MLXS, EXE661MXS, EXE662MFS, EXE661MHXS, EXE702MFS, EXE701MLXS, EXE701MHXS
Length: 5'6''; 6'; 6'6''; 6'6''; 6'6''; 6'6''; 7'; 7'; 7'
Power: UL; M; ML; M; M; MH; M; ML; MH
Action: F; F; XF; XF; F; XF; F; XF; XF
Pieces: 2; 2; 1; 1; 2; 1; 2; 1; 1
Line Weight: 1-4 lbs; 6-15 lbs; 4-12 lbs; 6-15 lbs; 6-15 lbs; 8-17 lbs; 6-15 lbs; 4-12 lbs; 8-17 lbs

Guide Count: 6; 7; 8; 7; 7; 7; 7; 7; 7
Lure Weight: 1/32-1/8 oz; 1/8-3/4 oz; 1/8-1/2 oz; 1/8-3/4 oz; 1/8-3/4 oz; 1/4-1 oz; 1/8-3/4 oz; 1/8-1/2 oz; 1/4-1 oz
Features: 26-ton IM-6 graphite blank with woven carbon accent; aluminum oxide guides; Daiwa custom reel seat; split-design foam grip; hook keeper
Price: **$44.95**

DAIWA LEXA

Model: LEXA721MLFS, LEXA671MXS, LEXA711MXS, LEXA731MHXS
Length: 7'2''; 6'7''; 7'1''; 7'3''
Power: ML; M; M; MH
Action: F; XF; XF; XF
Pieces: 1
Line Weight: 4-12 lbs; 6-15 lbs; 6-15 lbs; 8-17 lbs
Guide Count: 9; 8; 9; 9
Lure Weight: 1/16-3/8 oz; 1/4-3/4 oz; 1/4-3/4 oz; 1/4-3/4 oz

Features: 30-ton IM-7 graphite blank construction; micro pitch blank finish; Minima Zirconia ring guides; three new Micro Guide trigger rods; Fuji (ACS casting & VSS spinning) reel seat EVA foam split grip; woven carbon & stainless steel reel clamp; blank-through-handle construction; hook keeper; five-year limited warranty
Price: **$99.99**

ACTION	POWER	
M=Moderate	UL=Ultra Light	H=Heavy
MF=Moderate Fast	L=Light	MH=Medium-Heavy
F=Fast	ML=Medium-Light	XH=Extra Heavy
XF=Extra Fast		

DAIWA TATULA BASS

Model: TAT701MFS, TAT711MLXS, TAT721MHXS
Length: 7'; 7'1''; 7'2''
Power: M; ML; MH
Action: F; XF; XF
Pieces: 1
Line Weight: 6-14 lbs; 4-12 lbs; 8-17 lbs
Guide Count: 8
Lure Weight: 1/8-3/4 oz; 1/16-3/8 oz; 1/4-3/4 oz

Features: Daiwa's exclusive SVF (Super Volume Fiber) graphite technology; graphite fiber construction for flexibility, strength and virtually zero blank twist; micro pitch blank finish; Daiwa custom reel seat & machined aluminum reel clamp nut; Fuji Alconite ring guides; split grip design with EVA foam; hook keeper; blank-through-handle construction
Price:..................................**$149.95**

FENWICK AETOS

Model: A631MHXFS, A631MXFS, A661MFS, A662MFS, A671MHFS, A681MHXFS, A701MFS, A701MHFS, A702MFS, A721MXFS, A741MHXFS, A761MHFS, A761MLXFS
Length: 6'3''; 6'3''; 6'6''; 6'6''; 6'7''; 6'8''; 7'; 7'; 7'; 7'2''; 7'4''; 7'6''; 7'6''
Power: MH; M; M; M; MH; MH; M; MH; M; M; MH; MH; ML
Action: XF; XF; F; F; F; XF; F; F; F; XF; XF; F; XF
Pieces: 1; 1; 1; 2; 1; 1; 1; 1; 2; 1; 1; 1; 1

Line Weight: 8-17 lbs; 4-12 lbs; 6-14 lbs; 6-14 lbs; 8-17 lbs; 10-17 lbs; 6-14 lbs; 6-14 lbs; 6-14 lbs; 6-14 lbs; 10-17 lbs; 12-20 lbs; 4-10 lbs
Guide Count: 8; 8; 8; 8; 8; 8; 8; 8; 8; 8; 8; 9; 9
Lure Weight: 1/4-3/4 oz; 1/8-5/8 oz; 1/8-5/8 oz; 1/8-5/8 oz; 1/4-3/4 oz; 1/4-3/4 oz; 1/8-5/8 oz; 3/8-1 oz; 1/8-5/8 oz; 1/8-5/8 oz; 3/8-1 oz; 3/8-1 oz; 1/16-1/2 oz
Features: Fuji Skeleton reel seats for a reduced weight and increase in sensitivity; combination of TAC and cork split grip handle constructions; titanium framed guides with lightweight titanium inserts
Price:..................................**$179.95**

ACTION	POWER	
M=Moderate	UL=Ultra Light	H=Heavy
MF=Moderate Fast	L=Light	MH=Medium-Heavy
F=Fast	ML=Medium-Light	XH=Extra Heavy
XF=Extra Fast		

FENWICK ELITETECH ICE

Model: ETI23UL, ETI24ML, ETI25UL, ETI26ML, ETI27M, ETI28MH, ETI28ML
Length: 23''; 24''; 25''; 26''; 27''; 28''; 28''
Power: UL; ML; UL; ML; M; MH; ML
Action: F
Pieces: 1

Line Weight: 2-4 lbs; 2-6 lbs; 2-4 lbs; 2-6 lbs; 4-8 lbs; 6-10 lbs; 2-6 lbs
Guide Count: 4; 4; 4; 5; 5; 5; 5
Features: High-modulus graphite blanks; TAC handles delivers increased grip and durability in even the most rigid conditions; twist-lock reel seat with stainless steel hood
Price: **$29.95**

FENWICK ELITETECH RIVER RUNNER

Model: ESMS632MH-F, ESMS63M-F, ESMS63MH-F, ESMS692M-XF, ESMS69M-XF, ESMS69ML-F, ESMS74M-F
Length: 6'3''; 6'3''; 6'3''; 6'9''; 6'9''; 6'9''; 7'4''
Power: MH; M; MH; M; M; ML; M
Action: F; F; F; XF; XF; F; F
Pieces: 2; 1; 1; 2; 1; 1; 1
Line Weight: 10-17 lbs; 6-12 lbs; 10-17 lbs; 6-12 lbs; 6-12 lbs; 4-10 lbs; 6-12 lbs
Guide Count: 7; 7; 7; 8; 8; 8; 9

Lure Weight: 1/4-3/4 oz; 1/8-3/4 oz; 1/4-3/4 oz; 1/8-3/4 oz; 1/8-3/4 oz; 1/16-5/8 oz; 1/8-3/4 oz
Features: Titanium framed guides with lightweight zirconium inserts reduce overall blank weight and line wear with extreme heat dispersion; TAC inlay reel seat allows function and comfort to coexist; outstanding control with minimum weight not seen on the market today; high-modulus graphite blank designed specifically for smallmouth applications
Price: **$129.95**

ACTION	POWER	
M=Moderate	UL=Ultra Light	H=Heavy
MF=Moderate Fast	L=Light	MH=Medium-Heavy
F=Fast	ML=Medium-Light	XH=Extra Heavy
XF=Extra Fast		

LAMIGLAS X-11

Model: LX 562 ULS, LX 602 LS, LX 622 LS, LX 702 ULS
Length: 5'6''; 6'; 6'6''; 7'
Action: MF
Pieces: 2
Line Weight: 2-8 lbs; 4-8 lbs; 4-8 lbs; 2-8 lbs
Lure Weight: 1/8-1/4 oz; 1/8-3/8 oz; 1/8-1/2 oz; 1/8-1/2 oz
Features: All the value and performance of our new X-11 Series for salmon and steelhead are paired down to specialty applications for smaller species like trout, bass, walleye, panfish, and kokanee. These fast-action blanks feature our durable IM graphite and deep pressed guides with zirconia inserts. The darker maroon color sets a very nice contrast between the reel seat and premium cork handles (one-year limited warranty.)
Price: **$100.00**

LEW'S AMERICAN HERO IM6 SPEED STICK

Model: AH66MS, AH70MS, AH70MHS
Length: 6'6''; 7'; 7'
Power: M; M; MH
Action: F
Pieces: 1
Line Weight: 4-12 lbs; 4-12 lbs; 8-14 lbs
Guide Count: 8; 9; 10
Lure Weight: 1/8-½ oz; 1/8-½ oz; 3/8-¾ oz

Features: Premium IM6 one-piece graphite blanks; multilayer, multidirectional graphite construction for structural strength; rugged gunsmoke stainless steel guide frames with stainless steel inserts; lightweight graphite reel seats with cushioned stainless steel hoods; great hand/reel stability and comfort; exposed blank for instant vibration transmission; premium, durable high-density EVA split grips; split grip lightweight EVA handles; exclusive "No Foul" hook keeper; Lew's limited one-year warranty.
Price: **$69.99**

LEW'S SPEED STICK 365 CARBON NANOLAR

Model: SFS66M, SFS70ML, SFS70M, SFS70MH
Length: 6'6''; 7'; 7'; 7'
Power: M; ML; M; MH
Action: MF
Pieces: 1
Line Weight: 6-12 lbs; 6-10 lbs; 6-12 lbs; 8-14 lbs
Guide Count: 9; 10; 10; 10
Lure Weight: 3/16-5/8 oz; 1/8-1/2 oz; 1/8-5/16 oz; 3/8-3/4 oz

Features: Proprietary multilayer, multidirectional Carbon Nanolar premium HM50; rugged gunsmoke stainless steel guide frames with stainless steel inserts; great hand/reel stability and comfort; exposed blank for instant vibration transmission; Lew's exclusive lightweight graphite skeletal casting reel seat with ceramic hook holder in trigger; premium high-density EVA split grips; Lew's limited one-year warranty.
Price: **$99.99**

ACTION	POWER	
M=Moderate	UL=Ultra Light	H=Heavy
MF=Moderate Fast	L=Light	MH=Medium-Heavy
F=Fast	ML=Medium-Light	XH=Extra Heavy
XF=Extra Fast		

NEW Products: Rods, Freshwater Spinning

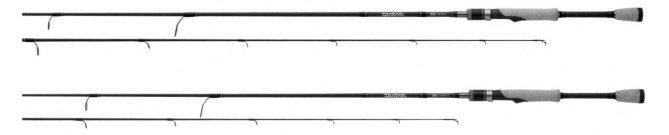

ST. CROIX TROUT SERIES

Model: TSS54ULF, TSS56ULF2, TSS60ULF2, TSS64LF2, TSS70LXF2
Length: 5'4''; 5'6''; 6'; 6'4''; 7'
Power: UL; UL; UL; L; L
Action: F; F; F; F; XF
Pieces: 1; 2; 2; 2; 2
Line Weight: 2-6 lbs; 2-6 lbs; 2-6 lbs; 4-8 lbs; 4-8 lbs
Lure Weight: 1/32-3/16 oz; 1/32-3/16 oz; 1/32-3/16 oz; 1/16-1/4 oz; 1/16-1/4 oz

Features: To paraphrase Theodore Roosevelt, it's not the size of the fish in the fight, but the size of the fight in the fish. You have to figure Teddy would have had his eyes keenly focused on our new Trout Series spinning rods. Like the popular Panfish Series, our new Trout rods offer the perfect blend of weight, sensitivity, and balance. Both series serve up incredibly dialed-in, specialized performance for fish that require the utmost finesse and delicacy.
Price:. . . . . $110.00–$130.00

Saltwater Spinning

DAIWA DXI INSHORE

Model: DXI661MLFS, DXI661MFS, DXI701MLFS, DXI701MFS, DXI761MLFS, DXI761MFS
Length: 6'6''; 6'6''; 7'; 7'; 7'6''; 7'6''
Power: ML; M; ML; M; ML; M
Action: F
Pieces: 1
Line Weight: 8-17 lbs; 8-20 lbs; 8-17 lbs; 8-20 lbs; 8-17 lbs; 8-20 lbs

Guide Count: 8; 8; 8; 8; 9; 9
Lure Weight: 1/8-3/4 oz; 1/4-1 oz; 1/8-3/4 oz; 1/4-1 oz; 1/8-3/4 oz; 1/4-1 oz
Features: IM-6 graphite blank construction; Minima Zirconia ring guides; Fuji (ACS casting & VSS spinning) reel seat; split-design natural cork grip; woven carbon & stainless steel reel clamp; hook keeper; five-year limited warranty
Price:. . . . . $89.95–$99.95

ACTION	POWER	
M=Moderate	UL=Ultra Light	H=Heavy
MF=Moderate Fast	L=Light	MH=Medium-Heavy
F=Fast	ML=Medium-Light	XH=Extra Heavy
XF=Extra Fast		

LOOMIS NRX INSHORE

Model: NRX 804S XMR, NRX 803S XMR, RX 842S MR, NRX 843S MR, NRX 882S MR, NRX 883S MR, NRX 921S MR, NRX 922S MR, NRX 923S MR

Length: 6'8''; 6'8''; 7'; 7'; 7'4''; 7'4''; 7'8''; 7'8''; 7'8''

Power: MH; M; M; MH; M; MH; ML; M; MH

Action: XF; XF; F; F; F; F; F; F; F

Pieces: 1

Line Weight: 10-20 lbs; 8-15 lbs; 8-15 lbs; 10-20 lbs; 8-15 lbs; 10-20 lbs; 6-12 lbs; 8-15 lbs; 10-20 lbs

Lure Weight: 1/2-1 1/2 oz; 3/8-1 oz; 3/16-5/8 oz; 3/16-3/4 oz; 3/16-5/8 oz; 3/16-3/4 oz; 1/8-3/8 oz; 3/16-5/8 oz; 3/16-3/4 oz

Features: Most inshore fishing is done on the flats or in shallow bays around docks or mangroves where getting a bait to the fish and then getting that fish to the boat is a real challenge. You need everything on your side. It's about the tide and the affect it has on the flats, the reeds, the rocks, and the mangroves. It's about being in the right place at the right time and making the right presentation. Basically, it's about NRX "Mag Rod" Inshore spinning rods . . . a series of fast and extra-fast, magnum power spinning rods featuring the new nano-silica resin system that allows us to use less material without losing strength. Rods that are very light, incredibly—no—insanely sensitive and stronger than any high-performance, high-modulus rod we've ever made. These rods are rated for braid. It's the ultimate connection for sensitivity, fish-fighting control, and taking vegetation and heavy cover out of the equation. Another great feature on these new rods is the hybrid guide train. We use titanium-framed, SIC K-frame stripper guides that are designed to keep braided line from tangling on the frames at the stiffest point of the rod. After the first three K-frame guides, we've added nickle-titanium RECOIL guides to reduce weight and increase the rate of recovery for the tip, creating unequaled casting distance! All feature split-grip handle configurations and are backed with a limited-lifetime warranty!

Price: . . . . **$610.00–$675.00**

ST. CROIX LEGENDXTREME INSHORE

Model: XIS70MLF, XIS70MF, XIS70MHF

Length: 7'

Power: ML; M; MH

Action: F

Pieces: 11

Line Weight: 6-12 lbs; 8-17 lbs; 10-20 lbs

Lure Weight: 1/8-1/2 oz; 3/8-3/4 oz; 1/2-1 1/4 oz

Features: The middle school hallway. The Red Zone. The checkout line at Costco. There are places that test your wherewithal—but none as decisively as the inshore saltwater arena. Venture in there and you better be ready to man-up. It might also be a good idea to carry one of our new LegendXtreme Inshore rods. Hyper-performance rods for intense inshore fishing. Loaded with proprietary technologies, built on high-modulus SCVI and SCV graphite blanks and finished with cutting edge fittings, these are the rods you go to when you're intensity level hits high tide.

Price: . . . . **$380.00–$390.00**

NEW Products: **Rods, Freshwater Baitcasting**

ABU GARCIA VERACITY

Model: VERC66-6, VERC69-6, VERC70-5, VERC70-6, VERC73-6, VERC76-6, VERC76-7, VERC79-7
Length: 6'6''; 6'6''; 7'; 7'; 7'3''; 7'6''; 7'6''; 7'9''
Power: MH; MH; M; MH; MH; MH; H; H
Action: MF; F; MF; F; F; F; F; F
Pieces: 1
Line Weight: 12-20 lbs; 12-20 lbs; 8-17 lbs; 12-20 lbs; 12-20 lbs; 12-25 lbs; 14-30 lbs; 14-30 lbs
Guide Count: 10; 10; 10; 10; 11; 11; 11; 10

Lure Weight: 1/4-1 oz; 1/4-1 oz; 1/4-5/8 oz; 1/4-1 oz; 1/4-1 oz; 3/8-1 1/2 oz; 1/2-2 oz; 5/8-3 oz
Features: 36-ton graphite with NanoTechnology for decreased weight and increased impact resistance; titanium alloy guides with Ti inserts allow for a super lightweight guide giving the ultimate in rod performance; high-density EVA gives greater sensitivity and durability; Micro Guide system provides improved balance and sensitivity; Texas rigged hook keeper for all bait applications.
Price: **$149.95**

BASS PRO SHOPS JOHNNY MORRIS CARBONLITE TRIGGER

Model: CL66MTF, CL66MHTF, CL69MHTXF, CL70MTF, CL70MTM, CL70MHTF, CL70HTXF, CL76HTXF, CL76MHTF, CL66MLTF, CL66MTF-2, CL70MHTF-2
Length: 6'6''; 6'6''; 6'9''; 7'; 7'; 7'; 7'; 7'6''; 7'6''; 6'6''; 6'6''; 7'
Power: M; MH; MH; M; M; MH; H; H; MH; ML; M; MH
Action: F; F; XF; F; M; F; XF; XF; F; F; F; F
Pieces: 1; 1; 1; 1; 1; 1; 1; 1; 1; 1; 2; 2

Line Weight: 8-17 lbs; 10-20 lbs; 10-20 lbs; 8-17 lbs; 8-17 lbs; 10-20 lbs; 12-30 lbs; 12-30 lbs; 10-20 lbs; 6-14 lbs; 8-17 lbs; 10-20 lbs
Lure Weight: 1/4-5/8 oz; 3/8-1 oz; 3/8-1 oz; 1/4-5/8 oz; 1/4-5/8 oz; 3/8-1 oz; 3/8-1 1/2 oz; 3/8-2 oz; 3/8-1 1/2 oz; 1/16-1/2 oz; 1/4-5/8 oz; 3/8-1 oz
Features: 85 million modulus carbon fiber blank; Pac Bay DLC stainless steel–framed guides; almost weightless spaceage P-Tec polyfoam grips; two-piece Soft Touch reel seat with maximum blank exposure
Price: . . . .**$99.99–$119.99**

ACTION	POWER	
M=Moderate	UL=Ultra Light	H=Heavy
MF=Moderate Fast	L=Light	MH=Medium-Heavy
F=Fast	ML=Medium-Light	XH=Extra Heavy
XF=Extra Fast		

CABELA'S XML

Model: XMLC624-1, XMLC664-1, XMLC665-1, XMLC665-2, XMLC704-1, XMLC704-2, XMLC705-1, XMLC705-2, XMLC706-1, XMLC706-2
Length: 6'2''; 6'6''; 6'6''; 6'6''; 7'; 7'; 7'; 7'; 7'; 7'
Power: M; M; MH; MH; M; M; MH; MH; H; H
Action: F
Pieces: 1; 1; 1; 2; 1; 2; 1; 2; 1; 2
Line Weight: 8-17 lbs; 8-17 lbs; 8-17 lbs; 8-17 lbs; 8-17 lbs; 8-17 lbs; 8-17 lbs; 8-17 lbs; 10-20 lbs; 10-20 lbs
Lure Weight: 1/4-5/8 oz; 1/4-5/8 oz; 1/4-1 oz; 1/4-1 oz; 1/4-5/8 oz; 1/4-5/8 oz; 1/4-1 oz; 1/4-1 oz; 3/8-2 1/4 oz; 3/8-2 1/4 oz

Features: These updated rods are built on our legendary XML 64 million-modulus, spiral-core-technology graphite blanks. They feature lightweight, super-durable SS316 stainless steel Alps guides, double coated with black chrome for maximum corrosion resistance. Precise guide spacing compacts the distance between guides from the middle to the tip of the rod. This increases sensitivity and decreases line drag. Exposed-blank MagTouch reel seats. Grips are made of premium cork and have thread-covering down-locking fore grips. Butts are compatible with our Weight-Balancing System, available separately.
Price: **$149.99**

CABELA'S TOURNAMENT ZX BASS

Model: TZXC-71MH (Spinnerbait/Swim Jig), TZXC-79H (Swimbait/Umbrella Rig), TZXC-69M (Jerkbait/Topwater), TZXC-76HXF (Flippin), TZXC-72MH (Jig & Worm), TZXC-73H (Topwater Frog), TZXC-71M (Crankbait)
Length: 7'1''; 7'9''; 6'9''; 7'6''; 7'2''; 7'3''; 7'1''
Power: MH; H; M; H; MH; H; M
Action: F; MF; F; XF; XF; F; MF
Lure Weight: 1/4-5/8 oz; 1-4 oz; 1/4-3/8 oz; 1/2-1 1/2 oz; 3/16-5/8 oz; 1/4-1 1/4 oz; 1/4-5/8 oz
Features: Built with technique-specific actions, these bass fishing rods are constructed using HM64 graphite rod

blanks. The result is the optimum balance of power, light weight, and responsiveness. Black Pac Bay stainless steel–framed guides with Hialoy ceramic guide inserts virtually eliminate line friction without tacking extra weight on the blank. Split-grip handles with MagTouch reel seats for all day fishing comfort. Down-locking woven carbon-fiber hood eliminates exposed reel-seat threads. EVA grips with Winn Grip overlays provide a custom, secure grip even when wet. Each technique is clearly displayed on the exposed portion of the split-grip handle for easy identification in the rod locker.
Price: **$99.99**

ACTION	POWER	
M=Moderate	UL=Ultra Light	H=Heavy
MF=Moderate Fast	L=Light	MH=Medium-Heavy
F=Fast	ML=Medium-Light	XH=Extra Heavy
XF=Extra Fast		

LAMIGLAS X-11

Model: LX 702 ULC
Length: 7'
Action: MF
Pieces: 2
Line Weight: 2-8 lbs
Lure Weight: 1/8-1/2 oz
Features: All the value and performance of our new X-11 Series for salmon and steelhead are paired down to specialty applications for smaller species like trout, bass, walleye, panfish, and kokanee. These fast-action blanks feature our durable IM graphite and deep pressed guides with zirconia inserts. The darker maroon color sets a very nice contrast between the reel seat and premium cork handles (one-year limited warranty).
Price:. **$100.00**

LEW'S AMERICAN HERO IM6 SPEED STICK

Model: AH66MHC, AH70MC, AH70MHC, AH76HC
Length: 6'6''; 7'; 7'; 7'6''
Power: MH; M; MH; H
Action: F
Pieces: 1
Line Weight: 10-20 lbs; 8-17 lbs; 10-20 lbs; 20-40 lbs
Guide Count: 9; 9; 10; 10
Lure Weight: 3/8-1 oz; 1/4-5/8 oz; 3/8-1 1/2 oz; 3/4-6 oz
Features: Premium IM6 one-piece graphite blanks; multilayer, multidirectional graphite construction for structural strength; rugged gunsmoke stainless steel guide frames with stainless steel inserts; lightweight graphite reel seats with cushioned stainless steel hoods; great hand/reel stability and comfort; exposed blank for instant vibration transmission; premium, durable high-density EVA split grips; split-grip lightweight EVA handles; exclusive "No Foul" hook keeper; Lew's limited one-year warranty.
Price:. **$69.99**

ACTION		POWER
M=Moderate	UL=Ultra Light	H=Heavy
MF=Moderate Fast	L=Light	MH=Medium-Heavy
F=Fast	ML=Medium-Light	XH=Extra Heavy
XF=Extra Fast		

LEW'S SPEED STIC 365 CARBON NANOLAR

Model: SFC66M, SFC66MH, SFC70ML, SFC70M, SFC70MH, SFC72XH, SFC76H
Length: 6'6''; 6'6''; 7'; 7'; 7'; 7'2''; 7'6''
Power: M; MH; ML; M; MH; XH; H
Action: MF
Pieces: 1
Line Weight: 10-14 lbs; 10-20 lbs; 6-10 lbs; 10-17 lbs; 12-20 lbs; 17-30 lbs; 14-30 lbs
Guide Count: 9; 9; 9; 9; 9; 9; 10

Lure Weight: 1/4-5/8 oz; 3/8-1 oz; 1/8-1/2 oz; 1/4-5/8 oz; 3/8-1 oz; 1/2-2 1/2 oz; 1/2-2 oz
Features: Proprietary multilayer, multidirectional Carbon Nanolar premium HM50; rugged gunsmoke stainless steel guide frames with stainless steel inserts; great hand/reel stability and comfort; exposed blank for instant vibration transmission; Lew's exclusive lightweight graphite skeletal casting reel seat with ceramic hook holder in trigger; premium high-density EVA split grips; Lew's limited one-year warranty
Price: **$99.99**

ST. CROIX PREMIER

Model: PC56MF, PC60MF, PC60MHF, PC66MF, PC66MF2, PC66MHF, PC66MHF2, PC70MLF, PC70MF, PC70MHF, PC70HF, PC70HF2
Length: 5'6''; 6'; 6'; 6'6''; 6'6''; 6'6''; 6'6''; 7'; 7'; 7'; 7'; 7'
Power: M; M; MH; M; M; MH; MH; ML; M; MH; H; H
Action: F
Pieces: 1; 1; 1; 1; 2; 1; 2; 1; 1; 1; 1; 2
Line Weight: 8-14 lbs; 10-17 lbs; 10-20 lbs; 10-17 lbs; 10-17 lbs; 10-20 lbs; 10-20 lbs; 8-14 lbs; 10-17 lbs; 10-20 lbs; 12-25 lbs; 12-25 lbs
Lure Weight: 1/4-5/8 oz; 1/4-3/4 oz; 3/8-1 oz; 1/4-3/4 oz; 1/4-3/4 oz; 3/8-1 oz; 3/8-1 oz; 3/16-5/8 oz; 1/4-3/4 oz; 3/8-1 oz; 1/2-1 1/2 oz; 1/2-1 1/2 oz

Features: Let's take a moment and thank genetics. And, because it's a well-known fact musky fishermen possess above average intelligence, combined with a knack for vanishing for long lengths of time, it's nice for us all that genetics does the work of passing that intelligence down. You'll still have to do the honors of handing down the intelligence on the premium SCII graphite blanks and top-grade components that make up the Premier casting rods. Be sure to let them know they are not only fast, light, and loaded with genuine fortitude—but have earned a bit of their own honor over the years, too.
Price: . . . . **$120.00–$160.00**

ACTION	POWER	
M=Moderate	UL=Ultra Light	H=Heavy
MF=Moderate Fast	L=Light	MH=Medium-Heavy
F=Fast	ML=Medium-Light	XH=Extra Heavy
XF=Extra Fast		

ST. CROIX WILD RIVER

Model: WRC80HF2, WRC86MF2, WRC86MHF2, WRC86HF2, WR90MF2, WRC90MLF2, WRC90MHF2, WRC90HF2, WRC90HM2, WRC90XHM2, WRC96HM2, WRC96XHM2, WRC106MF2, WRC106MHM2, WRC106HM2, WRC106XHM2

Length: 8'; 8'6''; 8'6''; 8'6''; 9'; 9'; 9'; 9'; 9'; 9'; 9'6''; 9'6''; 10'6''; 10'6''; 10'6''; 10'6''

Power: H; M; MH; H; ML; M; MH; H; H; XH; H; XH; M; MH; H; XH

Action: F; F; F; F; F; F; F; F; M; M; M; M; F; M; M; M

Pieces: 2

Line Weight: 15-40 lbs; 8-12 lbs; 10-17 lbs; 12-25 lbs; 6-10 lbs; 8-12 lbs; 10-17 lbs; 12-25 lbs; 15-30 lbs; 15-40 lbs; 15-30 lbs; 15-40 lbs; 8-12 lbs; 10-17 lbs; 12-25 lbs; 15-40 lbs

Lure Weight: 3/4-3 oz; 1/4-3/4 oz; 3/8-1 oz; 1/2-2 oz; 1/8-5/8 oz; 1/4-3/4 oz; 3/8-1 oz; 1/2-2 oz; 1-6 oz; 4-12 oz; 1-6 oz; 4-12 oz; 1/4-3/4 oz; 3/8-1 oz; 1/2-2 oz; 4-12 oz

Features: Salmon and steelhead fishing is not the NBA. It doesn't just go on and on, day after day with no end. When the fish are running, it's time to hit it—and preferably with a St. Croix Wild River rod. Thirty-eight unique, specialized lengths, actions, and powers to cover any situation, Wild River rods are built on rich gold dust green metallic finish blanks and are even available in Downrigging and Kokanee categories. Remember, there's no shame in letting a little dust collect around the house.

Price: . . . . **$170.00–$220.00**

Saltwater Baitcasting

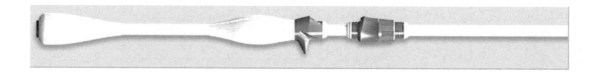

ST. CROIX LEGENDXTREME INSHORE

Model: XIC70MHF

Length: 7'

Power: MH

Action: F

Pieces: 1

Line Weight: 10-20 lbs

Lure Weight: 1/2-1 1/4 oz

Features: The middle school hallway. The Red Zone. The checkout line at Costco. There are places that test your wherewithal—but none as decisively as the inshore saltwater arena. Venture in there and you better be ready to man-up. It might also be a good idea to carry one of our new LegendXtreme Inshore rods. Hyper-performance rods for intense inshore fishing. Loaded with proprietary technologies, built on high-modulus SCVI and SCV graphite blanks and finished with cutting edge fittings, these are the rods you go to when you're intensity level hits high tide.

Price: **$380.00**

ACTION		POWER	
M=Moderate	UL=Ultra Light		H=Heavy
MF=Moderate Fast	L=Light		MH=Medium-Heavy
F=Fast	ML=Medium-Light		XH=Extra Heavy
XF=Extra Fast			

NEW Products: Rods, Freshwater Fly Fishing

LAMIGLAS INFINITY SI

Model: ISI 904, ISI 905, ISI 906, ISI 907, ISI 908, ISI 909, ISI 910, ISI 1178 SW
Length: 9'; 9'; 9'; 9'; 9'; 9'; 9'; 11'
Action: F
Pieces: 1; 1; 1; 2; 2; 2; 2; 2
Line Weight: 4 W–10 W
Features: Endless opportunity awaits with our new Infinity Fly series. Fifteen state-of-the-art new blanks, with lighter faster actions, including 4 ultra long casting models. Of special note, the 1178 is the first ever "switch" rod in our collection. A unique new hybrid cross of traditional casting and spey casting design. Its balance and handle design accommodates both methods to confidently swing steelhead flies on large rivers in the morning and work the brushy shores in the evening. Finished with exotic machined aluminum and carbon fiber reel seats.
Price: . . . . **$310.00–$400.00**

LAMIGLAS X-11

Model: LX 905, LX 906, LX 908, LX 909, LX 910
Length: 9'
Action: MF
Pieces: 2
Line Weight: 5 W–9 W
Features: Our new X-11 Series teaches another valuable lesson: high performance doesn't have to come with a high price tag. These moderate/fast action blanks feature our durable IM graphite and deep pressed guides with zirconia inserts. You'll have years, and likely decades, of exceptional casting and catches. The darker maroon color sets a very nice contrast between the reel seat and premium cork handles (one-year limited warranty).
Price: **$160.00**

ACTION	POWER	
M=Moderate	UL=Ultra Light	H=Heavy
MF=Moderate Fast	L=Light	MH=Medium-Heavy
F=Fast	ML=Medium-Light	XH=Extra Heavy
XF=Extra Fast		

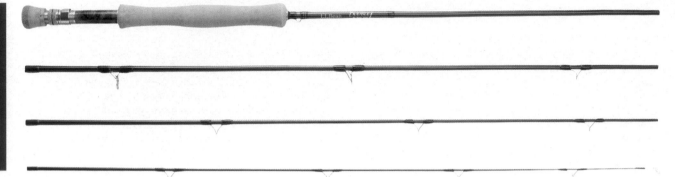

L.L.BEAN DOUBLE L

Model: 8'6'', 4 wt; 8'6'', 5 wt; 8'6'', 6 wt; 9', 4 wt; 9', 5 wt; 9', 6 wt; 9', 7 wt; 9', 8 wt
Length: 8'6''; 8'6''; 8'6''; 9'; 9'; 9'; 9'; 9'
Pieces: 4
Line Weight: 4W–8W

Features: The fastest, lightest, and strongest Double L Rod ever offered; perfect blend of tradition and performance; fluid, medium action for ease of casting and delicate presentations.
Price:. . . . .**$245.00–$275.00**

G. LOOMIS PRO4X TROUT

Model: PRO4x 963-4, PRO4x 964-4, PRO4x 1084-4, PRO4x 1085-4, PRO4x 1086-4, PRO 4X 1146-4 FR, PRO 4X 1147-4 FR, PRO 4X 1148-4 FR, PRO 4X 1203-4 FR, PRO 4X 1204-4 FR
Length: 8'; 8'; 9'; 9'; 9'; 9'6''; 9'6''; 9'6''; 10'; 10'
Power: M; M; MS; MS; MS; MS; MS; MS; MS; MS
Action: MF; MF; F; F; F; F; F; F; F; F
Pieces: 4
Line Weight: 3 W–8 W
Features: We took a page from our NRX blank technology to develop a new series of fly rods that "new-to-the-sport"

and intermediate flyfishers will learn to appreciate and will have expert anglers wondering how this much performance gets packed into such an affordable package. A new taper design along with a noticeable weight-reduction in the upper half of the blank allows us to make a fly rod that is incredibly light, recovers quickly, and casts with unbelievable precision. It's the G.Loomis way . . . reduce as much weight as possible, take total advantage of the materials, and create a taper that is dynamic, efficient, and user-friendly. They are as beautiful to look at as they are to cast. A rod any flyfisher would be proud to own!
Price:. . . . .**$345.00–$375.00**

ACTION	POWER	
M=Moderate	UL=Ultra Light	H=Heavy
MF=Moderate Fast	L=Light	MH=Medium-Heavy
F=Fast	ML=Medium-Light	XH=Extra Heavy
XF=Extra Fast		

LAMIGLAS BUG SLINGER

Model: BS908, BS909, BS910, BS911, BS912
Length: 9'
Action: F
Pieces: 1
Line Weight: 8 W–12 W
Features: We'll place our new Bug Slinger Fly rods up against anything and be highly confident of the outcome.

Smooth, long, effortless casts with perfect balance and control. These are powerful, 1-piece, saltwater specialty fly rods with a backbone tough enough for big tarpon and wily bonefish. A custom machined aluminum reel seat with woven carbon fiber insert anchors the natural black polished graphite blank.

Price: . . . . **$425.00–$495.00**

LOOMIS NRX PRO-1

Model: NRX 1068-1 PRO-1, NRX 1068-1 PRO-1 G, NRX 1069-1 PRO-1, NRX 1069-1 PRO-1 G, NRX 10610-1 PRO-1, NRX 10610-1 PRO-1 G, NRX 10611-1 PRO-1, NRX 10611-1 PRO-1 G, NRX 10612-1 PRO-1, NRX 10612-1 PRO-1 G

Length: 8'10''
Power: S
Action: XF
Pieces: 1
Line Weight: 8 W–12 W
Price: . . . . **$725.00–$815.00**

ACTION	POWER	
M=Moderate	UL=Ultra Light	H=Heavy
MF=Moderate Fast	L=Light	MH=Medium-Heavy
F=Fast	ML=Medium-Light	XH=Extra Heavy
XF=Extra Fast		

NEW Products: Rods, Saltwater Fly Fishing

REDINGTON CLASSIC TROUT

Model: 276-4, 376-4, 386-4, 480-4, 486-4, 490-4, 586-4, 590-4, 690-4, 380-6, 590-6
Length: 7'6''; 7'6''; 8'6''; 8'; 8'6''; 9'; 8'6''; 9'; 9'; 8'; 9'
Action: M
Pieces: 4; 6
Line Weight: 2W–6W

Features: Medium action. Offered in 4 piece and 6 piece configurations. 6 piece offers extreme packability for the backpacking and traveling angler. Titanium oxide stripping guides. Dark clay brown blank with matching Rosewood reel seat insert. Custom machined reel seat components. Alignment dots for easy rod set up. Divided brown ballistic Nylon rod tube.
Price:.............................$149.95–$169.95

REDINGTON CROSSWATER

Model: 476-2, 580-2, 586-2, 590-2, 690-2, 890-2, 990-2; 590-4; 890-4
Length: 7'6''; 8'; 8'6''; 9'; 9'; 9'; 9'; 9'; 9'
Action: MF
Pieces: 2; 4
Line Weight: 4W–9W

Features: Medium-Fast Action Attractive trim details and cosmetics. Alignment dots for easy rod set up. Weights available from 4wt to 9wt for multiple fishing needs. Durable anodized aluminum reel seat, ideal for all fresh- and saltwater applications. Rod comes with black cloth rod sock. Outfits come complete and ready to fish with a Crosswater reel that's prespooled with backing, RIO Mainstream WF fly line, and knotless leader.
Price:.............................$69.95–$89.95

REDINGTON VOYANT

Model: 376-4, 486-4, 490-4, 586-4, 590-4, 596-4, 5100-4, 690-4, 696-4, 6100-4, 790-4, 7100-4, 890-4, 990-4, 1090-4
Length: 7'6''; 8'6''; 9'; 8'6''; 9'; 9'6''; 10'; 9'; 9'6''; 10'; 9'; 10'; 9'; 9'; 9'
Action: F
Pieces: 4

Line Weight: 3W–10W
Features: Fast action. Alignment dots for easy rod set up. Half-wells grip (3wt - 6wt). Full-wells models (7wt - 10wt). Durable anodized aluminum and wood reel seat. Comes in a cloth tube with zippered closure and a black cloth rod bag. Lifetime warranty.
Price:..................................$189.95

ACTION		POWER	
M=Moderate	UL=Ultra Light	H=Heavy	
MF=Moderate Fast	L=Light	MH=Medium-Heavy	
F=Fast	ML=Medium-Light	XH=Extra Heavy	
XF=Extra Fast			

REDINGTON PREDATOR

Model: 6710-4, 690-4, 790-4, 8710-4, 890-4, 983-4, 990-4, 1083-4, 1090-4, 1190-4, 1290-4, 1480-4
Length: 7'10''; 9'; 9'; 7'10''; 9'; 8'3''; 9'; 8'3''; 9'; 9'; 9'; 9'
Action: F
Pieces: 4
Line Weight: 6W–14W
Features: Fast action; power for picking up line and fighting large fish; carbon fiber weave in butt section and at ferrules for improved strength and durability; 54 and 42 million modulus; red; core blank; anodized machined aluminum reel seat, ideal for all saltwater applications; durable oversized guides, titanium oxide ring, robust for salt water and for shooting line for extra distance; gun smoke frame snake and stripping guides; comes with fabric rod tube with dividers.
Price: **$249.95**

SAGE MOTIVE

Model: 890-4, 990-4, 1090-4, 1190-4, 1290-4
Length: 9'
Action: F
Pieces: 4
Line Weight: 8 W–12 W
Features: Saltwater series; fast action; new taper design; bluefin blue color blank; blue primary thread wraps with royal blue and black trim wraps; aluminum reel seat with hidden hook keepers; full-wells grip; blue steel divided ballistic nylon rod tube with divided liner.
Price: **$425**

ST. CROIX LEGEND X SALTWATER

Model: LXF907.4, LXF908.4, LXF909.4, LXF9010.4
Length: 9'
Action: MF
Pieces: 4
Line Weight: 7 W–10 W
Features: To the gentle readers who still think fly fishing is nothing more than the quiet pastime of stately figures in tweed, we have someone we'd like you to meet. Yeah, that's right, the guy over there with the musky on his line, a buzz from the action, and a brand new St. Croix Legend X fly rod in his hand. This revolutionary fly rod series is just what the counter-fly-culture crowd has been craving. A beefy, multi-dynamic blend of four carbon materials capable of getting big flies out to the meanest predatory fish—bass, pike and musky. Loaded with IPC and ART, these bad boys put it all right there, and then some. Wrap your hands around the grip of a Legend X and hang on.
Price: . . . . **$480.00–$490.00**

ACTION	POWER	
M=Moderate	UL=Ultra Light	H=Heavy
MF=Moderate Fast	L=Light	MH=Medium-Heavy
F=Fast	ML=Medium-Light	XH=Extra Heavy
XF=Extra Fast		

NEW Products: **Reels, Freshwater Spinning**

CABELA'S FISH EAGLE UL

Model: 500ULX, 2000X, 2500X, 3000X
Gear Ratio: 5.2:1
Spool Cap. (M): 6 lbs/110 yds; 8 lbs/140 yds; 12 lbs/180 yds; 4 lbs/100 yds.
Weight: 6.8 oz; 8.8 oz; 10 oz; 6.3 oz
Hand Retrieve: R or L
Reel Bearings: 4+1

Features: 4+1 bearings for ultrasmooth retrieves. Instant anti-reverse with on/off switch. Everlast oversized bail system. Aluminum spool and Stealth Oscillation for even line lay. Aluminum handle with soft-touch paddle knob. Adjustable for left- or right-hand retrieve. Graphite body and rotor.
Price: **$29.99**

CABELA'S VERANO

Model: 2000VRN, 2500VRN, 3500VRN
Gear Ration: 6.0:1; 6.0:1; 6.2:1
Inches/Turn: 31.1; 35; 41.3
Spool Cap. (M): 6 lbs/135 yds; 8 lbs/170 yds; 16 lbs/220 yds
Weight: 7.6 oz; 8.5 oz; 17.6 oz
Hand Retrieve: R or L

Max Drag: 8.8 lbs; 15.4 lbs; 17.6 lbs
Reel Bearings: 9+1
Features: Engineered by Daiwa Lightweight; corrosion-resistant Zaion body; spool's rearward taper helps prevent tangles; waterproof drag with click adjustment.
Price: **$149.99**

LEW'S GOLD SPIN HIGH SPEED SPIN
Model: 1000H, 2000H, 3000H, 4000H
Gear Ratio: 5.6:1; 6.1:1; 6.1:1; 6.1:1
Inches/Turn: 25; 31; 34; 38
Spool Cap. (M): 6 lbs/150 yds; 8 lbs/140 yds; 10 lbs/140 yds; 12 lbs/160 yds
Weight: 6.3 oz; 7.3 oz; 7.4 oz; 8.5 oz

Hand Retrieve: R or L
Reel Bearings: 9+1
Features: The high-speed Gold series features the lightweight high-strength C40 carbon body and side cover to meet anglers' most demanding expectations for spinning reels that are lighter, faster, and stronger.
Price: **$129.99**

LEW'S LASER SPEED SPIN

Model: 100, 200, 300, 400
Gear Ratio: 5.2:1
Inches/Turn: 22; 26; 31; 33
Spool Cap. (M): 6 lbs/170 yds; 6 lbs/150 yds; 10 lbs/180 yds; 12 lbs/195 yds.
Weight: 8.7 oz; 8.9 oz; 9.9 oz; 10.4 oz
Hand Retrieve: R or L
Reel Bearings: 9+1
Features: Quality ten-bearing system; rugged graphite body and rotor with metallic paint; double-anodized aluminum spool with holes and gold accent lines; larger diameter spool for longer casting and faster line retrieve; strong and balanced thick aluminum bail; thin compact gear box; zero-reverse one-way clutch bearing; aluminum handle with performance handle knob; adjustable for right- or left-hand retrieve; speed lube for exceptional smoothness and performance in all temperatures.
Price:. **$39.99**

LEW'S TOURNAMENT HIGH-SPEED SPEED SPIN

Model: 100H; 200H; 300H; 400H
Gear Ratio: 5.6:1; 6.1:1; 6.1:1; 6.1:1
Inches/Turn: 25; 31; 34; 38
Spool Cap. (M): 6 lbs/150 yds; 8lbs/140 yds; 10 lbs/140 yds; 12 lbs/160 yds
Weight: 6.9 oz; 8.3 oz; 8.4 oz; 9.6 oz
Hand Retrieve: R or L
Reel Bearings: 9+1
Features: Premium ten stainless steel bearing system; zero-reverse one-way clutch bearing; rugged graphite body and side cover; Digi-balanced graphite rotor with stainless; durable stainless steel main shaft; external stainless steel screws; machine-cut aluminum handle; smooth carbon Teflon multi-disc sealed drag system; quality solid brass pinion gearing; durable stainless steel main shaft; parallel line lay oscillation system; oversized titanium line roller to reduce line twist; double-anodized ported aluminum spool; external stainless steel; screws; adjustable right- or left-hand retrieve; speed lube for exceptional smoothness and performance in all temperatures; designed for use in fresh and salt water.
Price: **$79.99**

PENN Z SERIES

Model: 704Z; 706Z (bail-less)
Gear Ratio: 3.8:1
Inches/Turn: 30; 33
Spool Cap. (M): 15 lbs/345 yds; 20 lbs/295 yds
Spool Cap. (B): 30 lbs/465 yds; 50 lbs/400 yds
Weight: 23.5 oz; 22.8 oz
Hand Retrieve: L

Max Drag: 15 lbs
Reel Bearings: 1; 3
Features: Full metal body with graphite sideplate; HT-100 carbon fiber drag washers; machine-cut brass main gear with stainless steel pinion gear; machined and anodized aluminum spool.
Price: **$199.99**

PFLUEGER TRION

Model: 20X; 25X; 30X; 35X; 40X
Gear Ratio: 5.2:1
Inches/Turn: 20.8; 23; 25.9; 28.5; 31.9
Spool Cap. (M): 4 lbs/100 yds; 4 lbs/110 yds; 6 lbs/145 yds; 8 lbs/185 yds; 10 lbs/230 yds
Spool Cap. (B): 6 lbs/125 yds; 6 lbs/140 yds; 8 lbs/190 yds; 10 lbs/220 yds; 14 lbs/280 yds
Weight: 5.9 oz; 7.1 oz; 8.6 oz; 10.4 oz; 11.4 oz
Hand Retrieve: R or L

Max Drag: 6 lbs; 6 lbs; 9 lbs; 10 lbs; 12 lbs
Reel Bearings: 5; 7; 7; 7; 7
Features: 6+1 bearings (4+1 bearings on TRI20B); double-anodized aluminum spool; on/off instant anti-reverse bearing; lightweight graphite body and rotor; long-cast aluminum spool with titanium lip; smooth multi-disc drag system with stainless steel and oiled felt washer; sure-click bail provides an audible signal when bail is fully opened and ready to cast; anti-twist titanium line roller; aluminum handle with soft-touch knob.
Price: . . . .$29.99–$39.99

QUANTUM CATALYST PTI

Model: 15, 25, 30
Gear Ratio: 5.3:1; 5.2:1; 5.2:1
Inches/Turn: 26; 28; 31
Spool Cap. (M): 6 lbs/140 yds; 8 lbs/150 yds; 10 lbs/150 yds
Weight: 7.5 oz; 8.6 oz; 8.9 oz
Hand Retrieve: R or L
Max Drag: 8 lbs; 19 lbs; 19 lbs
Reel Bearings: 10

Features: ThinLine aluminum body and side cover; TiMag titanium bail with magnetic trip; polymer-stainless hybrid PT bearings; line management system; extra-hard PT gears; lightweight, machined aluminum crank handle; MAGLOK magnetic continuous anti-reverse; aluminum long stroke spool design; smooth front-adjustable drag system.
Price: $119.99

NEW Products: **Reels, Freshwater Spinning**

SHIMANO STELLA FE

Model: 1000, 2500, 3000, 4000
Gear Ratio: 25; 35; 35; 38
Spool Cap. (M): 4 lbs/140 yds; 8 lbs/140 yds; 8 lbs/170 yds; 10 lbs/200 yds
Spool Cap. (B): 15 lbs/85 yds; 15 lbs/145 yds; 20 lbs/140 yds; 30 lbs/170 yds
Weight: 6.0 oz; 8.0 oz; 8.1 oz; 9.5 oz
Hand Retrieve: R or L
Max Drag: 7 lbs; 20 lbs; 20 lbs; 24 lbs

Reel Bearings: 14+1
Features: A fresh/salt hybrid that is both lightweight and incredibly smooth, with plenty of power for finessing large fish on light line; features Paladin gear durability enhancement and propulsion line management system; Aero Wrap II worm gear oscillation; cold-forged machined aluminum spool with titanium lip; Power Roller III with diamond-like carbon coating.
Price: . . . . **$699.99–$749.99**

Saltwater Spinning

CABELA'S SALT STRIKER SURF

Model: 6000
Gear Ratio: 4.6:1
Inches/Turn: 37.2
Spool Cap. (M): 30 lbs/240 yds
Weight: 24.6 oz
Hand Retrieve: R or L
Max Drag: 33 lbs
Reel Bearings: 7+1

Features: Smooth, eight-bearing system and anodized aluminum surf-casting spool offer long-line control for deep casts and retrieves; one-way clutch instant anti-reverse bearing eliminates back-play for responsive hooksetting power; super-tough, titanium-coated line roller resists abrasion from sand and debris; corrosion-resistant aluminum body and graphite rotor; high-strength aluminum handle with a soft-touch grip.
Price: **$69.99**

DAIWA ISLA

Model: 4000H, 5000H, 7000H, 7000HBULL
Gear Ratio: 5.7:1; 5.7:1; 5.7:1; 4.3:1
Inches/Turn: 39.9; 47.6; 54.7; 40.9
Spool Cap. (M): 12 lbs/260 yds; 17 lbs/310 yds; 25 lbs/350 yds; 25 lbs/350 yds
Spool Cap. (B): 40 lbs/320 yds; 55 lbs/440 yds; 80 lbs/550yds; 80 lbs/550 yds
Weight: 15.2 oz; 21.2 oz; 29.4 oz; 29.4 oz
Hand Retrieve: R or L
Max Drag: 22 lbs; 33 lbs; 66 lbs; 66 lbs
Reel Bearings: 8+1

Features: The spool-to-rotor seam is Mag Sealed—permanently sealed via magnetic oil in conjunction with powerful magnets which bar entry to water and debris while maintaining nearly friction-free rotation; the Zaion air rotor is 15 percent lighter than normal rotor designs, better balanced, and extraordinarily strong; features a protrusion-free air bail; forged aluminum spool; Digigear gear design; ultra-smooth nine-bearing system (2 CRBB, 6 BB, 1 RB); ultimate tournament drag; oversized soft-touch handle knob.
Price:. . . . . **$699.99–$899.99**

LEW'S GOLD SPIN HIGH SPEED SPIN

Model: 1000H, 2000H, 3000H, 4000H
Gear Ratio: 5.6:1; 6.1:1; 6.1:1; 6.1:1
Inches/Turn: 25; 31; 34; 38
Spool Cap. (M): 6 lbs/150 yds; 8 lbs/140 yds; 10 lbs/140 yds; 12 lbs/160 yds
Weight: 6.3 oz; 7.3 oz; 7.4 oz; 8.5 oz

Hand Retrieve: R or L
Reel Bearings: 9+1
Features: The high-speed Gold series features the lightweight high strength C40 carbon body and side cover to meet anglers' most demanding expectations for spinning reels that are lighter, faster, and stronger.
Price:. **$129.99**

LEW'S SPEED SPIN INSHORE

Model: 3000, 4000, 5000
Gear Ratio: 6.1:1; 6.1:1; 5.6:1
Inches/Turn: 34; 38; 40
Spool Cap. (M): 12 lbs/170 yds; 14 lbs/220 yds; 17 lbs/220 yds
Weight: 9.6 oz; 10.0 oz; 15.8 oz
Hand Retrieve: R or L
Reel Bearings: 5+1
Features: Solid aluminum body and sideplate; includes sealed body engineering design; lightweight graphite rotor; premium six stainless steel bearing system; sealed zero-reverse anti-reverse clutch bearing, plus three sealed ball bearings in key locations; oversized hard chrome-plated line roller to reduce line twist; stainless steel, lightweight hollow bail wire; double-anodized aluminum spool; smooth carbon Teflon multi-disc sealed drag system; quality solid brass pinion gearing; high-strength zinc alloy drive gear; durable stainless steel main shaft; external stainless steel screws; machine-cut aluminum handle; power knob on model INS5000; adjustable right- or left-hand retrieve; designed for salt water.
Price:. **$99.99**

NEW Products: **Reels, Saltwater Spinning**

QUANTUM BOCA PTS

Model: 40, 50, 60, 80
Gear Ratio: 5.3:1; 5.3:1; 4.9:1; 4.9:1
Inches/Turn: 33; 36; 37; 41
Spool Cap. (M): 10 lbs/230 yds; 12 lbs/225 yds; 14 lbs/300 yds; 20 lbs/330 yds
Weight: 13.9 oz; 14.1 oz; 24 oz; 25 oz
Hand Retrieve: R or L
Max Drag: 25 lbs; 28 lbs; 30 lbs; 45 lbs

Reel Bearings: 6+1
Features: TiMag titanium bail with magnetic trip; polymer-stainless hybrid PT bearings; extra-hard PT gears; MAGLOK magnetic continuous anti-reverse; SaltGuard seven-layer corrosion protection finish; forged aluminum concave spool; Magnum ceramic drag; aluminum long stroke spool design; smooth front-adjustable drag system; machined aluminum handle.
Price: . . . . $139.95–$179.95

NEW Products: **Reels, Saltwater Spinning**

LEW'S TOURNAMENT HIGH-SPEED SPEED SPIN

Model: 100H; 200H; 300H; 400H
Gear Ratio: 5.6:1; 6.1:1; 6.1:1; 6.1:1
Inches/Turn: 25; 31; 34; 38
Spool Cap. (M): 6 lbs/150 yds; 8lbs/140 yds; 10 lbs/140 yds; 12 lbs/160 yds.
Weight: 6.9 oz; 8.3 oz; 8.4 oz; 9.6 oz
Hand Retrieve: R or L
Reel Bearings: 9+1
Features: Premium ten stainless steel bearing system; zeroreverse one-way clutch bearing; rugged graphite body and side cover; Digi-balanced graphite rotor with stainless; durable stainless steel main shaft; external stainless steel screws; machine-cut aluminum handle; smooth carbon Teflon multi-disc sealed drag system; quality solid brass pinion gearing; durable stainless steel main shaft; parallel line lay oscillation system; oversized titanium line roller to reduce line twist; double-anodized ported aluminum spool; external stainless steel screws; adjustable right- or left-hand retrieve; speed lube for exceptional smoothness and performance in all temperatures; designed for use in fresh and saltwater.

Price: **$79.99**

PENN CONFLICT

Model: 1000; 2000; 2500; 3000; 4000; 5000; 6000; 8000
Gear Ratio: 5.2:1; 6.2:1; 6.2:1; 6.2:1; 6.2:1; 5.6:1; 5.6:1; 5.3:1
Inches/Turn: 22; 30; 33; 35; 37; 36; 41; 44
Spool Cap. (M): 4 lbs/135 yds; 6 lbs/180 lbs; 8 lbs/175 yds; 10 lbs/165 yds; 10 lbs/220 yds; 15 lbs/200 yds; 20 lbs/230 yds; 25 lbs/310 yds.
Spool Cap. (B): 8 lbs/130 yds; 10 lbs/180 yds; 15 lbs/220 yds; 20 lbs/180 yds; 20 lbs/260 yds; 30 lbs/300 yds; 40 lbs/390 yds; 65 lbs/390 yds
Weight: 7.8 oz; 9.5 oz; 9.8 oz; 11.3 oz; 12 oz; 19 oz; 21.5 oz; 28.1 oz
Hand Retrieve: R or L
Max Drag: 9 lbs; 10 lbs; 12 lbs; 15 lbs; 15 lbs; 25 lbs; 25 lbs; 30 lbs
Reel Bearings: 7+1
Features: HT-100 carbon fiber drag washers; full metal body and sideplate; sealed stainless steel ball bearings; line capacity rings; Superline spool; infinite anti-reverse; Techno-Balanced rotor gives smooth retrieves; heavy-duty aluminum bail wire.

Price: . . . . **$139.99–$159.99**

SHIMANO SARAGOSA
Model: 5000, 6000, 8000, 10000, 20000, 25000
Gear Ratio: 5.7:1; 5.7:1; 5.6:1; 4.9:1; 4.4:1; 4.4:1
Inches/Turn: 38.2; 40.6; 42.2; 40; 41; 45
Spool Cap. (M): 12 lbs/195 yds; 12 lbs/265 yds; 14 lbs/270 yds; 16 lbs/300 yds; 20 lbs/380 yds; 50 lbs/230 yds
Spool Cap. (B): 20 lbs/255 yds; 30 lbs/245 yds; 40 lbs/300 yds; 50 lbs/405 yds; 65 lbs/525 yds; 80 lbs/520 yds
Weight: 20 oz; 21 oz; 24 oz; 24 oz; 29 oz; 30 oz
Hand Retrieve: R or L
Max Drag: 22 lbs; 22 lbs; 27 lbs; 33 lbs; 44 lbs; 44 lbs
Reel Bearings: 5+1; 5+1; 5+1; 5+1; 6+1; 6+1
Features: SW concept design with X-ship and X-tough drag; durable cam oscillation system for better drag performance; rigid support drag on 20000 and 25000 sizes; Paladin gear durability enhancement; propulsion line management system; S A-RB shielded ball bearings; 5+1 bearings (6+1 on 20000 & 25000); high-speed retrieves; Stopperless design (no anti-reverse switch); aluminum frame; graphite rotor (aluminum on 10000, 20000 & 25000); Power Roller III line roller; S-arm cam; Super Stopper II anti-reverse; direct drive mechanism; machined aluminum handle shank; Dyna-Balance; Fluidrive II; cold-forged aluminum spool; titanium spool lip; waterproof drag; easy-access drag washers; Dartainium drag (6000-25000); Septon handle grips; rated for use with mono, fluoro, and braided lines.
Price: . . . . **$239.99–$399.99**

SHIMANO STELLA FE
Model: 1000, 2500, 3000, 4000
Gear Ratio: 5.0:1; 6.0:1; 6.0:1; 6.2:1
Inches/Turn: 25; 35; 35; 38
Spool Cap. (M): 4 lbs/140 yds; 8 lbs/140 yds; 8 lbs/170 yds 10 lbs/200 yds
Spool Cap. (B): 15 lbs/85 yds; 15 lbs/145 yds; 20 lbs/140 yds; 30 lbs/170 yds
Weight: 6.0 oz; 8.0 oz; 8.1 oz; 9.5 oz
Hand Retrieve: R or L
Max Drag: 7 lbs; 20 lbs; 20 lbs; 24 lbs
Reel Bearings: 14+1
Features: Paladin gear durability enhancement; X-ship double-bearing supported pinion gear; ultra-light handle rotation; increased gearing efficiency and power propulsion line management system: propulsion spool lip, SR one-piece bail wire, Power Roller III with diamond-like carbon coating; EI surface treatment for extreme corrosion protection on spool; Aero Wrap II oscillation; SR-concept: SR 3D gear, SR handle, SR 3BB oscillation, SR balanced body, SR floating shaft, SR boltless magnesium body, SR one-piece bail wire, SR slider; shielded A-RB bearings; magnesium frame and sideplate; aluminum rotor (1000 size is magnesium); cold-forged and machined aluminum spool with titanium lip; S-concept: S-rotor, S-guard, S-shield roller clutch, S-arm cam; rigid support system: rigid support drag, SR slider; machined aluminum handle; direct drive mechanics (thread in handle attachment); Septon handle grips; waterproof drag; maintenance port; Fluidrive II; Dyna-Balance; Super Stopper II; repairable clicker; approved for use in saltwater; rated for use with mono, fluorocarbon, and PowerPro lines.
Price: . . . . **$699.99–$749.99**

NEW Products: Reels, Saltwater Spinning

SHIMANO STELLA SW

Model: 5000, 6000, 8000, 10000, 14000, 18000, 20000
Gear Ratio: 6.2:1; 5.7:1; 5.6:1; 4.9:1; 6.2:1; 5.7:1; 4.4:1
Inches/Turn: 41; 41; 42; 40; 53; 51; 41
Spool Cap. (M): 12 lbs/195 yds; 16 lbs/170 yds; 12 lbs/325 yds; 20 lbs/220 yds; 16 lbs/360 yds; 20 lbs/415 yds; 20 lbs/460 yds
Spool Cap. (B): 20 lbs/245 yds; 30 lbs/290 yds; 40 lbs/340 yds; 50 lbs/360 yds; 65 lbs/315 yds; 50 lbs/600 yds; 80 lbs/445 yds
Weight: 15.3 oz; 15.5 oz; 23.8 oz; 24.2 oz; 24.3 oz; 30.9 oz; 31.2 oz
Hand Retrieve: R or L
Max Drag: 28.7 lbs; 28.7 lbs; 61.7 lbs; 55.1 lbs; 55.1 lbs; 55.1 lbs; 55.1 lbs
Reel Bearings: 14+1

Features: X-touch drag to handle big, fast, fish; X-ship enhances power transmission through the gear; X-shield and X-protect combine to provide extreme water resistance; power aluminum body, X-rigid rotor, X-rigid body and X-rigid handle; propulsion line management system; propulsion spool lip; SR one-piece bail wire; Power Roller IV oversized roller with over-flange; redesigned bail trip; S-arm cam; Aero Wrap II oscillation; Paladin gear durability enhancement; low wear rate pinion gear; cold-forged aluminum spool; ceramic coating on entire spool; diamond-like carbon line roller coating; shielded A-RB bearings; Super Stopper II; Stopperless design (no anti-reverse switch); Septon handle grip (models 10000 and up); direct drive mechanism (thread-in handle attachment); Fluidrive II; Dyna-Balance; approved for use in salt water; rated for use with PowerPro, fluorocarbon, and mono lines.
Price:......................... $1059.99–$1259.99

PFLUEGER TRION
Model: CSCX, SSCX, 6SCB, USCB, 0SCX, 10USCB
Gear Ratio: 4.1:1; 4.1:1; 3.4:1; 3.4:1; 3.8:1; 3.8:1;
Inches/Turn: 14; 14; 14.5; 14.5; 18.5; 18.5
Spool Cap. (M): 2 lbs/90 yds; 2 lbs/90 yds; 4 lbs/110 yds; 4 lbs/110 yds; 8 lbs/90 yds; 8 lbs/90 yds
Hand Retrieve: R or L

Reel Bearings: 2
Features: Two ball bearings; ported machined aluminum front cone; aluminum handle with soft-touch handle knob; titanium pick-up pins; heavy-duty metal gears; convertible left- and right-hand retrieve; pre-spooled with line.
Price: **$29.99**

ZEBCO 33 AUTHENTIC
Model: 33
Gear Ration: 3.6:1
Inches/Turn: 19
Spool Cap. (M): 10 lbs/110 yds
Weight: 8.5 oz
Hand Retrieve: R or L
Reel Bearings: 2+1

Features: Three-bearing drive; industrial-grade stainless steel covers; reversible for right- or left-hand retrieve; quick-set multi-stop anti-reverse; micro-fine adjustment drag control; improved line management system; TPR over-molded rubber knobs.
Price: **$26.99**

NEW Products: **Reels, Freshwater Spincasting**

ZEBCO 33 AUTHENTIC LADIES
Model: 33 Lady
Gear Ration: 3.6:1
Inches/Turn: 19
Spool Cap. (M): 10 lbs/110 yds
Weight: 8.5 oz
Hand Retrieve: R or L

Reel Bearings: 1
Features: Ball bearing drive; quick-set multi-stop anti-reverse; industrial-grade stainless steel covers; reversible for right- or left-hand retrieve; micro-fine adjustment drag control; improved line management system; PVC rubber knobs.
Price:. **$21.99**

Freshwater Baitcasting

ABU-GARCIA REVO MGXTREME
Model: MGXTREME, MGXTREME-L
Gear Ratio: 7.1:1
Inches/Turn: 28
Retrieve Speed: Std
Spool Cap. (M): 12 lbs/115 yds
Spool Cap. (B): 30 lbs/130 yds
Weight: 4.9 oz
Hand Retrieve: R; L
Max Drag: 12 lbs

Reel Bearings: 10
Features: Ten-bearing system; seven stainless high-performance corrosion-resistant bearings plus one roller bearing; two additional CeramiLite spool bearings; one-piece X-Mag alloy frame; aircraft-grade aluminum main gear; Carbon Matrix drag system; C6 carbon sideplates; infinitely variable centrifugal brake; Infini II spool design; compact bent carbon handle; round EVA knob.
Price:. **$499.99**

ABU-GARCIA REVO STX

Model: STX, STX-HS, STX-HS-L, STX-L, STX-SHS
Gear Ratio: 6.4:1; 7.1:1; 7.1:1; 6.4:1; 8.0:1
Inches/Turn: 26; 29; 29; 26; 33
Retrieve Speed: Std; High; High; Std; Super High
Spool Cap. (M): 12 lbs/145 yds
Spool Cap. (B): 30 lbs/140 yds
Weight: 6.35 oz
Hand Retrieve: R; R; L; L; R
Max Drag: 20 lbs
Reel Bearings: 10+1
Features: Ten high-performance corrosion-resistant bearings plus one roller bearing provides increased corrosion protection; X2-Cräftic alloy frame for increased corrosion resistance; C6 carbon sideplates provide significant weight reduction without sacrificing strength and durability; Carbon Matrix drag system provides smooth, consistent drag pressure across the entire drag range; D2 gear design provides a more efficient gear system while improving gear durability; Infini brake system allows almost limitless adjustability to handle any fishing situation; Infini II spool design for extended castability and extreme loads; compact bent handle and star provide a more ergonomic design; titanium-coated line guide reduces friction and improves durability.
Price: **$199.95**

NEW Products: **Reels, Freshwater Baitcasting**

BASS PRO SHOPS VIPER
Model: 10HB
Gear Ratio: 6.3:1
Inches/Turn: 28
Spool Cap. (M): 12 lbs/130 yds
Weight: 8 oz
Hand Retrieve: R

Max Drag: 12 lbs
Reel Bearings: 9+1
Features: Lightweight, strong graphite frame; durable and smooth brass gearing; aluminum recurve drag star and handle; ten-position external magnetic brake; ten-bearing system; Powerlock instant anti-reverse; 6.3:1 gear ratio; twelve pounds max drag power.
Price: **$39.87**

DAIWA EXCELER EXE
Model: 100HA, 100HSA, 100HLA, 100HSLA, 100PA
Gear Ratio: 6.3:1; 7.3:1; 6.3:1; 7.3:1; 4.9:1
Inches/Turn: 25.7; 30.6; 25.7; 30.6; 20.6
Spool Cap. (M): 14 lbs/120 yds
Spool Cap. (B): 40 lbs/140 yds
Weight: 7.9 oz
Hand Retrieve: R; R; L; R; R
Max Drag: 11 lbs

Reel Bearings: 5+1
Features: Aluminum frame and sideplate; gear ratios from 4.9 power cranking to 7.3:1 hyper speed; ultimate tournament drag with 11-pound drag max; Magforce cast control; oversized, I-shape grips; infinite, dual anti-reverse; cut-away swept handle for greater power, less wobble, lighter weight.
Price: **$99.99**

DAIWA LEXA HIGH CAPACITY

Model: 100H, 400HS-P, 300HS-P, 300HS, 100HS, 300H, 400HL, 400HSL, 400HSL-P, 300PWRL, 300HSL-P, 300HSL, 300HL, 100HSL, 100HL, 100PL, 300PWR, 100P, 400H, 400HS, 400PWR-P

Gear Ratio: 6.3:1; 7.1:1; 7.1:1; 7.1:1; 7.1:1; 6.3:1; 6.3:1; 7.1:1:1; 7.1:1:1 5.1:1; 7.1:1; 7.1:1; 6.3:1; 7.1:1; 6.3:1; 4.9:1; 5.1:1; 4.9:1; 6.3:1; 7.1:1; 5.1:1

Inches/Turn: 25.7; 37.7; 32.4; 32.4; 30.0; 28.8; 33.4; 37.7; 37.7; 23.3; 32.4; 32.4; 28.8; 30.0; 25; 20.6; 23.3; 20.6; 33.4; 37.7; 27.1

Spool Cap. (M): 14 lbs/120 yds; 17 lbs/245 yds; 12 lbs/240 yds; 12 lbs/240 yds; 14 lbs/120 yds; 12 lbs/240 yds; 17 lbs/245 yds; 17 lbs/245 yds; 17 lbs/245 yds; 12 lbs/240 yds; 12 lbs/240 yds; 12 lbs/240 yds; 12 lbs/240 yds; 14 lbs/120 yds; 14 lbs/120 yds; 14 lbs/120 yds; 12 lbs/240 yds; 14 lbs/120 yds; 17 lbs/245 yds; 17 lbs/245 yds; 17 lbs/245 yds

Spool Cap. (B): 40 lbs/140 yds; 44 lbs/300 yds; 40 lbs/240 yds; 40 lbs/240 yds; 40 lbs/140 yds; 55 lbs/140 yds; 40 lbs/140 yds; 40 lbs/140 yds; 40 lbs/240 yds; 40 lbs/240 yds; 55 lbs/300 yds; 55 lbs/300 yds; 55 lbs/300 yds; 40 lbs/240 yds; 40 lbs/240 yds; 40 lbs/240 yds; 40 lbs/240 yds; 40 lbs/140 yds; 55 lbs/300 yds; 55 lbs/300 yds; 55 lbs/300 yds

Weight: 8 oz; 16.2 oz; 11.3 oz; 10.5 oz; 8 oz; 10.5 oz; 15.3 oz; 15.3 oz; 16.2 oz; 10.5 oz; 11.3 oz; 10.5 oz; 10.5 oz; 8 oz; 8 oz; 8 oz; 10.5 oz; 8 oz; 15.3 oz; 15.3 oz; 16.2 oz

Hand Retrieve: R; R; R; R; R; R; L; L; L; L; L; L; L; L; L; L; R; R; R; R; R

Max Drag: 11 lbs; 25 lbs; 22 lbs; 22 lbs; 11 lbs; 22lbs; 25 lbs; 25 lbs; 25 lbs; 22 lbs; 22 lbs; 22 lbs; 22 lbs; 11 lbs; 11 lbs; 11 lbs; 22 lbs; 11 lbs; 25 lbs; 25 lbs; 25 lbs

Reel Bearings: 7+1

Features: Aluminum frame and sideplate (gear side); seven-bearing system (2CRBB, 4BB+1RB); Magforce cast control; infinite anti-reverse; swept handle with weight-reducing cutouts; counter-balanced power handle on P models; super-leverage 120mm handle on 400 size models; A7075 aluminum spool, super lightweight and extra strong (100 size); extra line capacity for strong lines; ultimate tournament carbon drag.

Price:. . . . .$129.99–$249.99

DAIWA TATULA
Model: 100HL, 100HSL, 100H, 100HS, R100H, R100XS, R100HL, R100XSL, 100P
Gear Ratio: 6.3:1; 7.3:1; 6.3:1; 7.3:1; 6.3:1; 8.1:1; 6.3:1; 8.1:1; 5.4:1
Inches/Turn: 26.3; 30.5; 26.3; 30.5; 26.3; 33.9; 26.3; 33.9; 22.9
Spool Cap. (M): 14 lbs/120 yds
Spool Cap. (B): 40 lbs/140 yds
Weight: 7.9; 7.9; 7.9; 7.9; 7.6; 7.6; 7.6; 7.6; 7.9
Hand Retrieve: L; L; R; R; R; R; L; L; R

Max Drag: 13.2 lbs
Reel Bearings: 7+1
Features: New T-wing system; rugged, lightweight aluminum frame and sideplate (gear side); air rotation; ultimate tournament carbon drag with 13.2-pound drag max; Magforce-Z cast control; 5.4:1, 6.3:1, and 7.3:1 gear ratios; seven ball bearings plus roller bearing; infinite anti-reverse; corrosion-resistant clutch mechanism; large, 90mm swept power handle with cutouts for reduced weight; new I-shape handle knob.
Price: **$199.95**

LEW'S BB1 PRO SPEED SPOOL
Model: PS1; PS1HZ, PS1SHZ, PS1HZL, PS1SHZL
Gear Ratio: 5.1:1; 6.4:1; 7.1:1; 6.4:1; 7.1:1
Inches/Turn: 21; 28; 31; 28; 31
Spool Cap. (M): 12 lbs/160 yds
Weight: 6.5 oz
Hand Retrieve: R; R; R; L; L
Max Drag: 14 lbs
Reel Bearings: 9+1
Features: Premium ten-bearing system with double-shielded stainless steel ball bearings; available in multi-stop (PS1) and zero-reverse anti-reverse models (PS1HZ, PS1SHZ, PS1HLZ, PS1SHLZ); one-piece die-cast aluminum

frame with graphite sideplates; braid-ready machined forged double-anodized; aircraft-grade machine-forged Duralumin spools and drive train; externally adjustable SpeedCast centrifugal braking system; right-side aluminum spool tension knob with audible clicker; carbon composite metal star drag system with 14 pounds of drag power; audible click bowed metal star drag; bowed lightweight carbon fiber reel handle with custom paddle knobs; oversized titanium line guide positioned farther from the spool to minimize line friction and maximize casting performance; quick release sideplate mechanism provides easy access to spool; external lube port.
Price: **$199.99**

Reels, Freshwater Baitcasting

LEW'S BB2 WIDE SPEED SPOOL

Model: 2HZ, 2SHZ, 2SHZL
Gear Ratio: 6.4:1; 7.1:1; 7.1:1
Inches/Turn: 28; 31; 31
Spool Cap. (M): 14 lbs/190 yds
Weight: 7.4 oz
Hand Retrieve: R; R; L
Max Drag: 14 lbs
Reel Bearings: 9+1
Features: Premium ten-bearing system with double-shielded ball bearings and zero-reverse anti-reverse; one-piece die-cast aluminum frame; machine-forged aluminum double-anodized U-shaped large capacity spool; external lube port; quick release sideplate mechanism provides easy access to spool and centrifugal brake system; positive on/off SmartPlus; six-pin, positive on/off centrifugal braking system; right-side aluminum spool tension knob with audible clicker; rugged carbon composite drag system provides up to 14 pounds of drag power; audible click bowed metal star drag; 95mm bowed aluminum cranking handle with soft-touch paddles.
Price: **$169.99**

LEW'S TEAM LEW'S PRO SPEED SPOOL

Model: 1HZ, 1SHZ, 1HZL, 1SHZL
Gear Ratio: 6.4:1; 7.1:1; 6.4:1; 7.1:1
Inches/Turn: 28; 31; 28; 31
Spool Cap. (M): 12 lbs/120 yds
Weight: 6.1 oz
Hand Retrieve: R; R; L; L
Max Drag: 14 lbs
Reel Bearings: 10+1
Features: One-piece die-cast aluminum frame and sideplates; titanium deposition finish on sideplates for ultimate durability; double-anodized gold detail finishing; aircraft-grade Duralumin; twelve-hole drilled U-style spool, drive gear, crank shaft, and worm shaft; premium, double-shielded, stainless steel, eleven-bearing system with zero-reverse anti-reverse; frictionless titanium-coated zirconia line guide; multi-setting brake utilizing both an external click dial to adjust the magnetic brake system, and an internal four-pin positive on/off centrifugal brake system; anodized aluminum spool tension adjustment with audible click; rugged carbon composite drag system, provides up to 14 pounds of drag power, audible click metal star drag; premium bowed light weight 85mm carbon handle with custom soft-touch contoured paddles.
Price: **$299.99**

NEW Products: **Reels, Freshwater Baitcasting**

OKUMA HELIOS 2013
Model: 273VA, 273VLXA
Gear Ratio: 7.3:1
Inches/Turn: 31.5
Spool Cap. (M): 10 lbs/160 yds
Weight: 6.3 oz
Hand Retrieve: R; L
Max Drag: 14 lbs
Reel Bearings: 8+1
Features: Rigid die-cast aluminum frame and sideplates; corrosion-resistant coating process; A6061-T6 machined aluminum, anodized spool; heavy duty, aluminum gears and shafts; multi-disc carbonite drag system; micro-click drag star for precise drag settings; 8BB+1RB stainless steel bearing drive system; precision Japanese ABEC-5 spool bearings; quick-set anti-reverse roller bearing; new lightweight seven-position velocity control system; ergonomic handle design allows cranking closer to body; easy change left side plate access port; lightweight at only 6.3 ounces; zirconium line guide inserts for use with braided line; available in both right- and left-hand retrieve; three-year warranty.
Price: **$199.99**

SHIMANO ANTARES
Model: 100, 101, 100HG, 101HG
Gear Ratio: 5.6:1; 5.6:1; 7.4:1; 7.4:1
Inches/Turn: 26; 26; 34; 34
Spool Cap. (M): 8 lbs/140 yds
Weight: 7.9 oz
Hand Retrieve: R; L; R; L
Reel Bearings: 10+1
Features: Micro module gear; SVS infinity brake system; X-ship; shielded S-ARB ball bearings; Super Stopper II roller bearing; gear ratios of 5.6:1 and 7.4:1; cross carbon drag washers; escape hatch; cold-forged aluminum handle shank; Septon grips; recessed reel seat foot; magnesium frame with aluminum sideplates; G Free-Spool III magnesium spool; not recommended for salt water.
Price: **$599.99**

NEW Products: **Reels, Freshwater Baitcasting**

SHIMANO METANIUM
Model: 100, 101, 100HG, 101HG, 100XG, 101XG
Gear Ratio: 6.2:1; 6.2:1; 7.4:1; 7.4:1; 8.5:1; 8.5:1
Inches/Turn: 26; 26; 31; 31; 36; 36
Spool Cap. (M): 8 lbs/140 yds
Weight: 6.0 oz; 6.0 oz; 6.0 oz; 6.0 oz; 6.2 oz; 6.2 oz
Hand Retrieve: R; L; R; L; R; L
Reel Bearings: 9+1
Features: Micro module gear; SVS infinity; X-ship; shielded S-ARB ball bearings; gear ratios of 6.2:1, 7.4:1, and 8.5:1;

Super Stopper II roller clutch bearing; Dartanium 2 drag washers; MET XG 96mm handle with PV paddle grips; tapered line guide; escape hatch; cold-forged aluminum drag star; Septon handle grip; aluminum cast control knob; recessed reel seat foot; lightweight aluminum drive gear; ultra lightweight magnesium frame; magnesium handle sideplate; carbon onside sideplate; approved for use in salt water.
Price: **$419.99**

Saltwater Baitcasting

ABU GARCIA ORRA 2 SX
Model: SX, SX-HS, SX-L
Gear Ratio: 6.4:1; 7.1:1; 6.4:1
Inches/Turn: 26; 29; 26
Retrieve Speed: Std; High; Std
Spool Cap. (M): 12 lbs/145 yds
Spool Cap. (B): 30 lbs/140 yds
Weight: 7.3 oz
Hand Retrieve: R; R; L
Max Drag: 15 lbs
Reel Bearings: 8

Features: Seven stainless steel ball bearings plus one roller bearing provides smooth operation; X-Cräftic alloy frame for increased corrosion resistance; graphite sideplates; Power Disk drag system gives smooth drag performance; MagTrax brake system gives consistent brake pressure throughout the cast; compact bent handle and star provide a more ergonomic design; Duragear brass gear for extended gear life.
Price: **$99.99**

NEW Products: **Reels, Saltwater Baitcasting**

ABU GARCIA REVO INSHORE

Model: Revo Inshore
Gear Ratio: 7.1:1
Inches/Turn: 29
Retrieve Speed: High
Spool Cap. (M): 12 lbs/180 yds
Spool Cap. (B): 30 lbs/180 yds
Weight: 8.7 oz
Hand Retrieve: R
Max Drag: 20 lbs
Reel Bearings: 6+1
Features: Six high-performance corrosion-resistant bearings plus one roller bearing provides increased corrosion protection; X2-Cräftic alloy frame for increased corrosion resistance; C6 carbon sideplates provide significant weight reduction without sacrificing strength and durability; Carbon Matrix drag system provides smooth, consistent drag pressure across the entire drag range; D2 gear design provides a more efficient gear system while improving gear durability; pitch centrifugal brake system; large EVA knobs provide improved grip; extended bent handle for increased cranking power; titanium-coated line guide reduces friction and improves durability; dual anti-reverse provides additional backup for high-pressure situations.
Price: **$249.95**

ABU GARCIA REVO ROCKET

Model: ROCKET, ROCKET-L
Gear Ratio: 9.0:1
Inches/Turn: 37
Retrieve Speed: Super High
Spool Cap. (M): 12 lbs/145 yds
Spool Cap. (B): 30 lbs/140 yds
Weight: 6.75 oz
Hand Retrieve: R; L
Max Drag: 20 lbs
Reel Bearings: 10+1
Features: Ten stainless steel high-performance corrosion-resistant bearings plus one roller bearing provides increased corrosion protection; rocket fast gear ratio of 9.0:1 provides superfast line retrieve of 37 inches per turn, for picking up line quickly; X-Cräftic alloy frame and sideplates for increased corrosion resistance; Carbon Matrix drag system provides smooth, consistent drag pressure across the entire drag range; D2 gear design provides a more efficient gear system while improving gear durability; Infini brake system allows almost limitless adjustability to handle any fishing situation; Infini II spool design for extended castability and extreme loads; extended bent carbon handle for increased cranking power; large EVA knobs provide improved grip; titanium-coated line guide reduces friction and improves durability.
Price:. **$299.99**

NEW Products: **Reels, Saltwater Baitcasting**

DAIWA EXCELER EXE

Model: 100HA, 100HSA, 100HLA, 100HSLA, 100PA
Gear Ratio: 6.3:1; 7.3:1; 6.3:1; 7.3:1; 4.9:1
Inches/Turn: 25.7; 30.6; 25.7; 30.6; 20.6
Spool Cap. (M): 14 lbs/120 yds
Spool Cap. (B): 40 lbs/140 yds
Weight: 7.9 oz
Hand Retrieve: R; R; L; R; R
Max Drag: 11 lbs

Reel Bearings: 5+1
Features: Aluminum frame and sideplate; gear ratios from 4.9 power cranking to 7.3:1 hyper speed; ultimate tournament drag with 11-pound drag max; Magforce cast control; oversized, I-shape grips; infinite, dual anti-reverse; cut-away swept handle for greater power, less wobble, lighter weight.
Price: **$99.99**

DAIWA LEXA HIGH CAPACITY

Model: 100H, 400HS-P, 300HS-P, 300HS, 100HS, 300H, 400HL, 400HSL, 400HSL-P, 300PWRL, 300HSL-P, 300HSL, 300HL, 100HSL, 100HL, 100PL, 300PWR, 100P, 400H, 400HS, 400PWR-P

Gear Ratio: 6.3:1; 7.1:1; 7.1:1; 7.1:1; 7.1:1; 6.3:1; 6.3:1; 7.1:1; 7.1:1; 5.1:1; 7.1:1; 7.1:1; 6.3:1; 7.1:1; 6.3:1; 4.9:1; 5.1:1; 4.9:1; 6.3:1; 7.1:1; 5.1:1

Inches/Turn: 25.7; 37.7; 32.4; 32.4; 30.0; 28.8; 33.4; 37.7; 37.7; 23.3; 32.4; 32.4; 28.8; 30.0; 25; 20.6; 23.3; 20.6; 33.4; 37.7; 27.1

Spool Cap. (M): 14 lbs/120 yds; 17 lbs/245 yds; 12 lbs/240 yds; 12 lbs/240 yds; 14 lbs/120 yds; 12 lbs/240 yds; 17 lbs/245 yds; 17 lbs/245 yds; 17 lbs/245 yds; 12 lbs/240 yds; 12 lbs/240 yds; 12 lbs/240 yds; 12 lbs/240 yds; 14 lbs/120 yds; 14 lbs/120 yds; 14 lbs/120 yds; 12 lbs/240 yds; 14 lbs/120 yds; 17 lbs/245 yds; 17 lbs/245 yds; 17 lbs/245 yds

Spool Cap. (B): 40 lbs/140 yds; 55 lbs/300 yds; 40 lbs/240 yds; 40 lbs/240 yds; 40 lbs/140 yds; 40 lbs/240 yds; 55 lbs/300 yds; 55 lbs/300 yds; 55 lbs/300 yds; 40 lbs/240 yds; 40 lbs/240 yds; 40 lbs/240 yds; 40 lbs/240 yds; 40 lbs/140 yds; 40 lbs/140 yds; 40 lbs/140 yds; 40 lbs/240 yds; 40 lbs/140 yds; 55 lbs/300 yds; 55 lbs/300 yds; 55 lbs/300 yds

Weight: 8 oz; 16.2 oz; 11.3 oz; 10.5 oz; 8 oz; 10.5 oz; 15.3 oz; 15.3 oz; 16.2 oz; 10.5 oz; 11.3 oz; 10.5 oz; 10.5 oz; 8 oz; 8 oz; 8 oz; 10.5 oz; 8 oz; 15.3 oz; 15.3 oz; 16.2 oz

Hand Retrieve: R; R; R; R; R; R; L; L; L; L; L; L; L; L; L; L; R; R; R; R; R

Max Drag: 11 lbs; 25 lbs; 22 lbs; 22 lbs; 11 lbs; 22lbs; 25 lbs; 25 lbs; 25 lbs; 22 lbs; 22 lbs; 22 lbs; 22 lbs; 11 lbs; 11 lbs; 11 lbs; 22 lbs; 11 lbs; 25 lbs; 25 lbs; 25 lbs

Reel Bearings: 7+1

Features: Aluminum frame and sideplate (gear side); seven-bearing system (2CRBB, 4BB+1RB); Magforce cast control; infinite anti-reverse; swept handle with weight-reducing cutouts; counter-balanced power handle on P models; super-leverage 120mm handle on 400 size models; A7075 aluminum spool, super lightweight and extra strong (100 size); extra line capacity for strong lines; ultimate tournament carbon drag.

Price: . . . . **$129.99–$249.99**

DAIWA TATULA

Model: 100HL, 100HSL, 100H, 100HS, R100H, R100XS, R100HL, R100XSL, 100P

Gear Ratio: 6.3:1; 7.3:1; 6.3:1; 7.3:1; 6.3:1; 8.1:1; 6.3:1; 8.1:1; 5.4:1

Inches/Turn: 26.3; 30.5; 26.3; 30.5; 26.3; 33.9; 26.3; 33.9; 22.9

Spool Cap. (M): 14 lbs/120 yds

Spool Cap. (B): 40 lbs/140 yds

Weight: 7.9; 7.9; 7.9; 7.9; 7.6; 7.6; 7.6; 7.6; 7.9

Hand Retrieve: L; L; R; R; R; R; L; L; R

Max Drag: 13.2 lbs

Reel Bearings: 7+1

Features: New T-wing system; rugged, lightweight aluminum frame and sideplate (gear side); air rotation; ultimate tournament carbon drag with 13.2-pound drag max; Magforce-Z cast control; gear ratios of 5.4:1, 6.3:1, and 7.3:1; seven ball bearings plus roller bearing; infinite anti-reverse; corrosion resistant clutch mechanism; large, 90mm swept power handle with cutouts for reduced weight; new I-shape handle knob.

Price: $199.95

NEW Products: **Reels, Saltwater Baitcasting**

LEW'S BB1 INSHORE SPEED SPOOL
Model: 1H, 1SH
Gear Ratio: 6.4:1; 7.1:1
Inches/Turn: 28; 31
Spool Cap. (M): 12 lbs/160 yds
Weight: 7.8 oz
Hand Retrieve: R
Max Drag: 14 lbs
Reel Bearings: 7+1
Features: Premium eight-bearing system with double-shielded stainless steel ball bearings; sturdy one-piece all aluminum frame, handle, and sideplate with three external drain ports on frame; braid-ready machined double-anodized deep-capacity aluminum spool; high-strength brass gearing for durability zero-reverse anti-reverse; multi-setting brake features an external-adjust magnetic braking system and an internal four-pin positive on/off centrifugal brake system; double-anodized aluminum spool tension knob with audible clicker; rugged carbon composite drag system that provides up to 14 pounds of drag power; audible click bowed metal star drag; bowed 95mm aluminum cranking handle with soft-touch paddles; oversized silver titanium line guide positioned farther from the spool to minimize line friction and maximize casting performance; quick release sideplate mechanism provides easy access to spool and centrifugal brake system.
Price: **$199.99**

QUANTUM SMOKE INSHORE
Model: 100HPTs, 101HPTs
Gear Ratio: 7.0:1
Inches/Turn: 28
Spool Cap. (M): 12 lbs/135 yds
Weight: 6.2 oz
Hand Retrieve: R; L
Reel Bearings: 7+1
Features: New and improved SCR base alloy aluminum body and side covers protected by our exclusive SaltGaurd 2.0 multilayer corrosion protection.
Price: **$219.95**

SHIMANO METANIUM

Model: 100, 101, 100HG, 101HG, 100XG, 101XG
Gear Ratio: 6.2:1; 6.2:1; 7.4:1; 7.4:1; 8.5:1; 8.5:1
Inches/Turn: 26; 26; 31; 31; 36; 36
Spool Cap. (M): 8 lbs/140 yds
Weight: 6.0 oz; 6.0 oz; 6.0 oz; 6.0 oz; 6.2 oz; 6.2 oz
Hand Retrieve: R; L; R; L; R; L
Reel Bearings: 9+1
Features: Micro module gear; SVS infinity; X-ship; shielded
S-ARB ball bearings; gear ratios of 6.2:1, 7.4:1, and 8.5:1;

Super Stopper II roller clutch bearing; Dartanium 2 drag
washers; MET XG 96mm handle with PV paddle grips;
tapered line guide; escape hatch; cold-forged aluminum
drag star; Septon handle grip; aluminum cast control knob;
recessed reel seat foot; lightweight aluminum drive gear;
ultra lightweight magnesium frame; magnesium handle
sideplate; carbon onside sideplate; approved for use in salt
water.
Price:. **$419.99**

Freshwater Fly Fishing

ORVIS BATTENKILL

Model: I, II, III
Gear Ratio: 2.75; 3; 3.25
Inches/Turn: 2.8 oz; 2.9 oz; 3.2 oz
Weight: 2.8 oz; 2.9 oz; 3.2 oz
Hand Retrieve: R or L
Features: Simple design and flawless construction make
this the perfect click-and-pawl fly reel for nearly any
freshwater fishing situation; features a classically styled, yet
technically enhanced, four-position click-and-pawl drag

system that is adjusted internally and is designed to work in
tandem with the palm of your hand; constructed with a
narrow spool for less line stacking on retrieve and a larger
spool diameter for higher line retrieval rates; the ultra-
lightweight fly reel design balances perfectly on shorter
rods; machined from heavy-duty bar-stock aluminium for
added durability; easily adjustable left- or right-hand
retrieve; highlighted by laser-engraved logos; black nickel;
imported.
Price:. **$98.00**

BANDIT LURES B-SHAD

Type: Crankbait
Color/Pattern: Chartreuse/Black Stripe, Red Chartreuse, Chrome/Black Back, Chrome/Blue Back, Popsicle, Khaki/Brown
Size: 3-1/2in
Weight: 1/4 oz

Running Depth: 8 ft–10 ft
Features: Great for trolling the flats for walleye or working the shoreline to draw wary largemouths from the weeds; runs true right out of the package.
Price: **$6.19**

BASS PRO SHOPS XPS LAZER EYE

Type: Floating
Color/Pattern: Orange Pearl, Chrome Clown, Pink Lemonade, Orange Shad, Chartreuse Pearl, Perch, Purple Pearl, Natural Perch, Sultry Shad, Black Gold, Purple Tiger, Purple Dawn, Hollywood, XXX Shad, Psycho Perch, Spectrum, Blue Tiger, Purple Haze, Dyno-Mite, Copper Minnow, Blue Gill, Ghost Norman Flake, Blue Sparks, Green Ghost, Lime Blue Pearl, Pumpkinseed, Natural Bream
Size: 2 1/4 in, 2 7/8 in, 3 in
Weight: 3/16 oz., 3/8 oz., 1/3 oz
Running Depth: 5 ft, 6 ft, 7 ft
Features: Naturally shaped body design; lifelike 3D laser eyes; extra-loud rattles; hot finishes; equipped with premium, extra-sharp hooks.
Price: **$4.49**

BASS PRO SHOPS XPS POP-N-TOP
Type: Popper
Color/Pattern: Bone Orange Belly, Bleeding Tennessee Shad, Chrome Black Back, Chartreuse Shad, XXX Shad
Size: 5 1/4 in
Weight: 7/8 oz

Running Depth: Topwater
Features: Weight transfer system for increased casting distance; weight balance system for "walk-the-dog" action; cupped mouth to "spit" water; dressed treble tail hook.
Price: **$5.99**

BASS PRO SHOPS XPS Z9R PERCH
Type: Swimbait
Color/Pattern: Neon Bluegill, Shad, Green Perch, Bluegill
Size: 3 1/2 in
Weight: 3/4 oz

Features: High-quality construction and hardware; deeper-bodied perch profile; extreme realism, down to intricate gill, fin, and eye detail; precisely reproduced natural coloration.
Price: **$11.99**

BERKLEY FLICKER SHAD PRO SERIES
Type: Crankbait
Color/Pattern: Slick Purple Candy, Slick Purple Bengal, Slick Sunset, Slick Chartreuse Purple, Slick Firetiger, Slick Mouse, Flashy Clown, Flashy Ghost, Flashy Perch, Flashy Purple Tiger
Size: 1 5/8 in, 2 in 1/2 in 3/4 in

Weight: 1/8 oz., 3/16 oz., 1/4 oz., 5/16 oz.
Running Depth: 6 ft–8 ft, 9 ft–11 ft, 10 ft–12 ft, 11 ft–13 ft
Features: Wobbly action and unique rattle imitates a wounded baitfish to trigger strikes; flashy color patterns feature a translucent body with foil interior for a natural baitfish flash; slick colors sport an oil-slick pattern for maximum reflection; ideal for trolling or cast and retrieve.
Price: **$3.99**

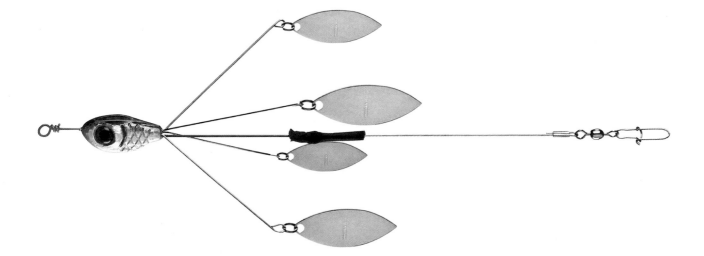

BOOYAH BOO FLEX RIG

Type: Umbrella rig
Color/Pattern: Alpine
Weight: 1/4 oz, 3/8 oz, 1/2 oz

Features: Fish any lure at any depth; attach spinnerbaits, crankbaits, or any other lure; add casting distance to ultralight lures.
Price: **$3.99**

BOOYAH BOO RIG

Type: Umbrella rig
Color/Pattern: Alpine
Weight: 1/4 oz, 3/8 oz, 1/2 oz
Features: Four willow-leaf blades perfectly mimic a school of fish and a flexible arm lets you attach a crankbait, jig, or any other lure, making this setup deadly on any game fish; weight and design provide excellent castability, giving you the versatility to cast or troll; spinnerbait-style head is available in multiple sizes to match your quarry.
Price: **$6.99**

BOOYAH BOO SPIN RIG — WILLOW

Type: Umbrella rig
Color/Pattern: Alpine
Weight: 1/4 oz, 3/8 oz, 1/2 oz

Features: Irresistible bait-chase presentation; attach a crankbait, spinnerbait, or any other lure; easily snake through wood and other cover.
Price: **$6.99**

BOOYAH BOO TEASER RIG

Type: Umbrella rig
Color/Pattern: Alpine
Weight: 1/4 oz, 3/8 oz, 1/2 oz
Features: Add the highly effective bait-chase characteristic to any lure presentation; flexible arm lets crankbaits swim naturally, enticing more fish to strike; four stiff outer arms come with curtail grub teasers that imitate a school of baitfish, a mouthwatering sight to large game fish; can be fished shallow or deep; spinnerbait-style head.
Price: **$6.99**

CABELA'S DEATH ROLL SPINNER RIGS

Type: Bait rig
Color/Pattern: Glow, Chartreuse, Red
Features: A new twist on traditional walleye rigs with the introduction of the Death Roll spinner rigs. Thread the crawler on the hook and it spins as it's pulled through the water, enticing bites from lethargic walleye. Each comes fully rigged with a barrel swivel to prevent line twists, a 5mm bead, and one size 1 or one size 1/0 hook on a 36 in-long, 12 lb monofilament leader.
Price:. **$3.99/6**

CABELA'S FISHERMAN SERIES BIG WATER WALLEYE RIG

Type: Bait rig
Color/Pattern: Watermelon, Emerald, Purple, Pink, Chartreuse, Firetiger, Clown
Blade size: 4, 5, 6

Features: Oversized, deep-cup blades come complete with larger hooks and heavier monofilament line than standard spinners and boast time-tested and proven big-water colors; rigged with 72 in, 17 lb test monofilament and size 2 hooks.
Price:. **$3.99**

NEW Products: **Lures, Hardbait**

CABELA'S FISHERMAN SERIES JOINTED SUSPENDING SHAD

Type: Crankbait
Color/Pattern: Glass Blue Shad, Firetiger, Glass Perch, Red Craw, Glass Black Shad, Glass Road Crew, Flasher, Glass Chartreuse Growler
Size: 2 1/8 in
Weight: 1/4 oz

Running Depth: 6 ft–10 ft
Features: The jointed design, rattling, and suspending action make this bait an optimum baitfish imitator that lures in walleye, bass, and oversized panfish; especially effective around submerged structures and can be cast or trolled; suspends at rest.
Price: **$3.99**

CABELA'S HDS ESOX MINNOW

Type: Stick bait
Color/Pattern: Northern Pike, Musky, Tiger Musky
Size: 4 3/4 in
Weight: 1/2 oz
Features: With Cabela's innovative High-Definition Series (HDS) technology for unsurpassed realism you have to see to believe, a special printing process transfers an actual

image of a live baitfish onto the lure, resulting in color and detail only a real fish can match. Modeled after the juvenile northern pike, one of the most sought-after forage fish in the lake; draws ferocious strikes from trophy bass, pike, musky, and walleye; rigged with quality Matzuo hooks.
Price: **$5.99**

CABELA'S HOT METAL SHAD
Type: Crankbait
Color/Pattern: Glass Purple Demon, Glass/Blue Back, Chrome Black Back, Flasher, Blue Racer, Perch, Purple Haze, Firetiger
Size: 2 3/8 in, 2 3/4 in

Weight: 1/4 oz, 3/8 oz
Features: Metallic, depth-control lip; mimics popular forage fish; rigged with quality Matzuo hooks; ideal for trolling for feeding walleye.
Price: **$4.99**

CREEK CHUB CHUG-A-LUG
Type: Topwater bait
Color/Pattern: Bunker, Squid, Mackerel, Funny Bone, Sweet Purple, Red Head, Blue Flyer
Size: 7 1/4 in
Weight: 4 oz
Features: Hydro-Ribs amplify vibration, which, combined with lifelike colors and large pupil eyes, draw aggresive fish

from a distance; stainless steel through-wire construction and hard wood body are built to withstand hard strikes from large fish; 300 lb test heavy belly hook swivel and triple split rings keep fish hooked; 3X salt water-grade hooks withstand corrosion from harsh saltwater, providing multiple seasons of use.
Price: **$24.99**

NEW Products: **Lures, Hardbait**

GARY YAMAMOTO CHIKARA CRANKBAIT

Type: Crankbait
Color/Pattern: Black Red Flake, Pumpkin Black Flake, Silver Black Back, Silver Blue Back, Sexy Shad, Crawfish Green, Crawfish Red, Chartreuse Black Back, Olive Green Shad
Size: 2 in

Weight: 1/2 oz
Running Depth: 3 ft–4 ft, 6 ft–8 ft, 8 ft–10 ft
Features: The innovative design outperforms other lures when fishing in cover or open water; fish-enticing colors draw the wariest lunkers out of hiding.
Price: **$8.99**

GARY YAMAMOTO SHIBUKI POPPER

Type: Topwater bait
Color/Pattern: Silver Black Back, Silver Blue Back, White Bone, Black Bone, Green Frog
Size: 2 3/8in, 3 1/8 in
Weight: 1/4 oz, 7/16 oz

Features: A small concave-faced popper that can either move a lot of water or a little; premium color schemes drive fish crazy and sharp hooks catch them when they strike; ideal for imitating a fleeing baitfish of any species or drawing cautious fish out of cover.
Price: **$8.99**

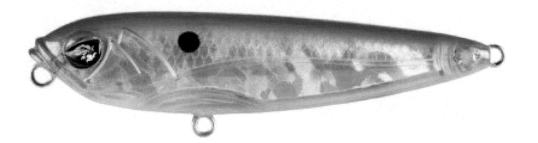

GARY YAMAMOTO TATE' PENCIL BAIT
Type: Crankbait
Color/Pattern: Silver Black Back, Silver Blue Back,
Chartreuse Blue Back, White Bone, Black Bone, Green Frog
Size: 3 in, 4 in
Weight: 7/16 oz, 9/16 oz

Features: Tate', which means "dance" in Japanese, is a classic walk-the-dog topwater pencil bait with more character and zip than its counterparts. Even the most disinterested bass cannot help but take notice of this quivering lure. Whether it's mere inches from the surface or well into the depths, big fish will be suckered in.
Price: **$8.99**

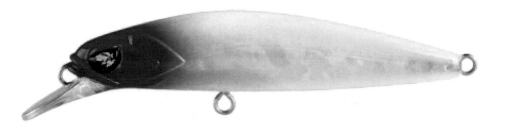

GARY YAMAMOTO TENKUU JERKBAIT
Type: Stick bait
Color/Pattern: Silver Black Back, Silver Blue Back,
Crawfish Green, Crawfish Red, Chartreuse Black Back,
Gold Fish, Olive Green Shad, Albino Shad
Size: 3 in, 4 in, 4 1/4 in

Weight: 1/3 oz, 1/2 oz, 3/4 oz
Running Depth: 4 ft, 8 ft, 10 ft
Features: Excellent for large, pre-spawn fish; can be fished successfully year-round; three sizes represent common baitfish.
Price: **$8.99**

NEW Products: **Lures, Hardbait**

LUCKY CRAFT LV RTO 150 LIPLESS CRANKBAIT

Type: Crankbait
Color/Pattern: Chrome Blue, TO Gill, FF Male Gill, Ghost Minnow, Chartreuse Shad, MS American Shad
Size: 5.2 in

Weight: 1/2 oz
Running Depth: 3 ft–4 ft
Features: Shimmy action irresistible to bass; flat head for a strong wobbling action; perfect in weedy areas and near structure.
Price: **$17.99**

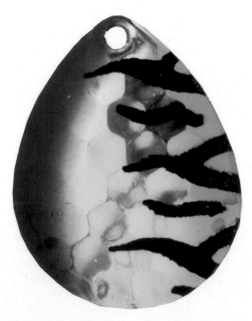

NORTHLAND CRAWLER HAULER SPEED SPINNER

Type: Bait rig
Color/Pattern: Silver Shiner, Gold Shiner, Gold Perch, Sunrise
Blade Size: 3, 4

Features: Life-like Holographic Baitfish-Image spinner blade rigged on a double stainless steel wire harness that is highly visible to fish; VMC Crawler Hauler Hook has a frantic action that induces strikes; molded Snap-Back-Barb bait keeper keeps bait firmly on your hook.
Price: **$3.29**

NORTHLAND FLOAT'N CRAWLER HAULER

Type: Bait rig
Color/Pattern: Shrimp, Crawdad, Moonlight, Firetiger
Size: Hook #2

Features: Combines the original Gum-Drop foam floater with the innovative Crawler Hauler hook; perfect for fishing live and soft baits over moss, weeds, and rocks; molded snap-back-barbed bait keeper prevents nightcrawlers, minnows, and soft baits from sliding the hook shank.
Price: **$3.99**

NORTHLAND IMPULSE RIGGED NIGHTCRAWLER

Type: Bait rig
Color/Pattern: Silver Shiner, Gold Shiner, Gold Perch, Sunrise

Size: 6 in
Blade Size: 3
Features: ActionCup tail; baitfish-Image spinner harness; mirrors swimming action of a live nightcrawler.
Price: **$3.99**

NEW Products: **Lures, Hardbait**

PANTHER MARTIN FISHSEEUV SALMON AND STEELHEAD SPINNERS

Type: InLine Spinner
Color/Pattern: UV Red Tiger, UV Pink Tiger, UV Chartreuse Lime Orange, UV Firetiger, UV Red White
Weight: 7/16 oz, 1/2 oz, 3/4 oz
Features: FishSeeUV paint on these Panther Martin Salmon and Steelhead Spinners adds to their already proven fish-catching ability and also increases their effectiveness on cloudy days or in murky waters; unique blades send an enticing vibration through the water that's irresistible to predatory fish; a great choice for salmon, steelhead, pike, and musky.
Price: . . . . **$4.79–$5.49**

PANTHER MARTIN HAMMERED SPINNERS

Type: InLine Spinner
Color/Pattern: Silver, Gold, UV Salmon Black, UV Lime Chartreuse, Yellow Red
Weight: 1/16 oz, 1/8 oz, 1/4 oz
Features: The awesome vibration of the original Panther Martin spinner with the added flash of a hammered blade; classic color options or fish-enticing FishSeeUV colors; effective on everything from panfish to pike.
Price: . . . . **$3.99–$4.19**

PANTHER MARTIN TAILWAGGER

Type: Tail-spinning
Color/Pattern: Super Shad, Albino, Chrome/Black, Chartreuse, Silver/Blue, UV Firetiger, UV Red/White
Weight: 3/8 oz, 1/2 oz
Features: New Super Shad color naturally attracts bass and trout; easiest and fastest spinning action in the world; sends out sonic vibrations that are irresistable to all gamefish; concave mouth to increase wobbling swimming action of the body; super sharp premium quality hooks keep fish caught!
Price: . . . . **$4.49–$4.99**

PANTHER MARTIN VIBRANT IMAGE SPINNER

Type: InLine Spinner
Color/Pattern: Firetiger, Bullfrog, Camo
Weight: 1/16 oz, 1/8 oz, 1/4 oz
Features: UV-enhanced iridescent pearl-base finish and colorful graphics for maximum underwater visibility; color graphics are digitally applied into the paint so they won't peel or fade; classic color options or fish-enticing FishSeeUV colors; effective on everything from panfish to pike.
Price: **$4.49**

NEW Products: **Lures, Hardbait**

PANTHER MARTIN MUSKIE MARABUCK
Type: InLine Spinner
Color/Pattern: Electric Chicken, Gold/Black/Red, Gold/Firetiger, Silver/Red/Black, Silver/White/Red, White/Purple/Blue
Weight: 1 oz, 1 1/2 oz

Features: Genuine natural hand-tied marabou and bucktail; our famous convex/concave blades in gold and silver; super sharp and strong eagle claw treble hooks; oversized heavy weighted brass bodies; can be used as a true countdown lure.
Price:. . . . .$19.99–$21.99

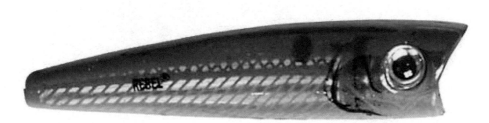

REBEL SALTWATER SUPER POP-R
Type: Topwater bait
Color/Pattern: Blue Stripe Mullet, Red Fish, Red Head, Speckled Trout, Barfish
Size: 3 1/8 in
Weight: 5/16 oz

Features: Produces an erratic, splashing action that induces bone-crushing topwater hits from large saltwater fish such as red fish and ocean speckled trout; two #4 Permasteel treble hooks resist corrosion, even after 1,000 hours of saltwater exposure, maintaining a sharp point for deep hooksets; a variety of colors allow you to catch fish nearly anywhere, no matter what baitfish inhabit your target water.
Price:. $6.99

SÉBILE ACTION FIRST BULL CRANK

Type: Crankbait
Color/Pattern: Black Chrome Gold Head, Smokin' Black Shad, Greenback Ghost, Smokin' Purple Pearl, Yellow Shad, Blue Red Craw
Size: 2 in, 2 1/2 in
Weight: 1/4 oz, 1/2 oz
Running Depth: 4 ft–7 ft, 8 ft–12 ft

Features: Engineered with intricate precision to be an exceptional swimmer, a square bill gives the bait a wider wobble and deflects off cover erratically; Xternal Weight System keeps the bait on a strike-inducing track and positions hooks for sure sets; near silent action prevents spooking and entices the most wary hogs in the school.
Price:.................................... **$6.99**

SÉBILE ACTION FIRST LIPLESS SEEKER

Type: Lipless bait
Color/Pattern: Greenback Ghost, Dark Blue Chrome, Lime Ghost, Black Gold, Black Chrome, Red Orange Craw, Firetiger
Size: 3 in

Weight: 1/2 oz
Features: Xternal Weight System creates optimal swim action; casts far and sinks fast; heavy bass beads cause a high-pitch rattle.
Price:.................................... **$5.99**

NEW Products: **Lures, Hardbait**

SÉBILE ACTION FIRST SQUAREBILL SUNFISH

Type: Crankbait
Color/Pattern: Greenback Ghost, Yellow Shad, Warmouth, Black Chrome Gold Head, Breeding Bluegill, Golden Ghost
Size: 2 1/2 in
Weight: 3/8 oz
Running Depth: 2 ft–6 ft

Features: A square bill gives the bait a wider wobble and deflects off cover erratically; the flat sides of the crank resemble a sunnie when viewed from above, below, or behind and give it a natural sunfish swimming action; Xternal Weight System keeps the bait on a strike-inducing track and positions hooks for sure sets; one internal free bead creates a knocking sound that could only be a sunfish encroaching on the bass' turf.
Price: **$6.99**

SÉBILE ACTION FIRST STAR SHINER

Type: Stick bait
Color/Pattern: Greenback Ghost, Smokin' Purple Pearl, Lime Perch, Spotted Mess, Black Chrome Gold Head, Golden Ghost, Red Gold, Ghost and Bones
Size: 3 1/2 in, 4 1/4 in
Weight: 1/4 oz, 1/2 oz
Running Depth: 2 ft–5 ft, 3 ft–6 ft

Features: One internal free bead makes a knocking sound, resembling an injured baitfish when jerked; Xternal Weight System works with the free bead to suspend the bait in perfect position when still; each minnow has two diving depths to cover the water column in the pivotal strike zones.
Price: **$7.99**

STORM ARASHI RATTLING DEEP

Type: Crankbait
Color/Pattern: Baby Bass, Black Silver Shad, Blue Back Herring, Bluegill, Crappie, Hot Blue Shad, Hot Chartreuse Shad, Mossy Chartreuse Craw, Parrot, Red Craw, Rusty Craw, Wakasagi
Size: 2 3/8 in
Weight: 9/16 oz

Running Depth: 10 ft
Features: Swims with a moderate rolling action for the right amount of search with loads of tail kick; multi-ball rattle for loud, variable pitch and a long-cast design for increased distance with accuracy; premium Black Nickel VMC hooks, size 4.
Price: **$8.99**

STORM ARASHI RATTLING FLAT

Type: Crankbait
Color/Pattern: Baby Bass, Black Silver Shad, Blue Back Herring, Bluegill, Crappie, Hot Blue Shad, Hot Chartreuse Shad, Mossy Chartreuse Craw, Parrot, Red Craw, Rusty Craw, Wakasagi
Size: 2 1/8 in

Weight: 7/16 oz
Running Depth: 7 ft
Features: Swims with a tight wiggling action creating maximum flash and vibration; multi-ball rattle for loud, variable pitch and a long-cast design for increased distance with accuracy; premium black Nickel VMC hooks, size 4.
Price: **$8.9**

STORM ARASHI SILENT SQUARE
Type: Crankbait
Color/Pattern: Baby Bass, Black Silver Shad, Blue Back Herring, Bluegill, Crappie, Hot Blue Shad, Hot Chartreuse Shad, Mossy Chartreuse Craw, Parrot, Red Craw, Rusty Craw, Wakasagi
Size: 2 1/8 in, 2 3/8 in
Weight: 1/2 oz, 5/8 oz
Running Depth: 3 ft, 5 ft

Features: Runs with a lively rolling action and a pronounced tail kick; buoyancy to back out of cover and square lip design for increased deflection are a perfect match for contacting structure; non-rattling for a silent approach to wary or pressured fish in shallow water; premium black Nickel VMC hooks, sizes 4 and 2.
Price: **$8.99**

TSUNAMI COCKTAIL SPINNERS
Type: InLine spinner
Color/Pattern: Black, White, Yellow, Firetiger, Chrome/White, Chartreuse
Weight: 1/16 oz, 1/8 oz, 1/6 oz, 1/4 oz

Features: Highly reflective blades spin with minimal movement; holographic bodies add flash for a larger bait profile; feather dressed, premium treble hook doesn't let them get off.
Price: **$2.99**

YO-ZURI 3DB JERKBAIT

Type: Stick bait
Color/Pattern: Prism Clown, Prism Gold Black, Prism Ghost Shad, Prism Silver Blue, Prism Silver Black, Prism Tennessee Shad
Size: 3 1/2 in
Weight: 7/16 oz
Running Depth: 2 ft

Features: Patent-pending 3D internal prism creates an unparalleled flash in the water, enticing fish to bite; patented wave-motion belly sends vibrations through the water that fish can detect with their lateral lines, bringing in lunkers from distances beyond what they can see; black-nickel hooks.
Price: **$9.99**

YO-ZURI 3DB MID CRANK

Type: Crankbait
Color/Pattern: Prism Shad, Prism Tennessee Shad, Prism Crawfish, Prism Firetiger, Prism Bluegill, Prism Parrot
Size: 2 3/4 in
Weight: 1/2 oz

Running Depth: 4 ft–6 ft
Features: 3D internal prism creates enticing flash; dives 4–6 ft on retrieve; floats when paused; patented wave-motion ribs send out irresistible vibrations.
Price: **$9.99**

YO-ZURI 3DB MINNOW

Type: Stick bait
Color/Pattern: Prism Gold Black, Prism Ghost Shad, Prism Silver Blue, Prism Silver Black, Prism Shad, Prism Tennessee Shad
Size: 3 1/2 in

Weight: 3/8 oz
Running Depth: 2 ft
Features: 3D internal prism creates enticing flash; patented wave-motion ribs send irresistible vibrations; mimics wobbly, wounded baitfish.
Price: **$9.99**

YO-ZURI 3DB POPPER

Type: Topwater bait
Color/Pattern: Prism Clown, Prism Frog, Prism Gold Black, Prism Ghost Shad, Prism Silver Blue, Prism Silver Black, Prism Shad
Size: 3 in
Weight: 3/8 oz
Running Depth: Floating

Features: The patented wave-motion belly sends vibrations through the water that fish can detect with their lateral lines, bringing in lunkers from distances beyond what they can see; a small, secondary popper cup throws water spray on the retrieve; lure rests in a horizontal position, perfectly mimicking a baitfish.
Price: **$9.99**

BERKLEY GULP! ALIVE! LEECH HALF-PINT

Type: Leech
Color/Pattern: Black
Size: 3 in, 5 in
Quantity: 15, 10

Features: Artificial bait proven to outfish and outlast live bait; Alive! attractant is 20 percent more effective than the original; baits keep their natural shapes; recharge baits by placing them back into the attractant.
Price:. **$9.95**

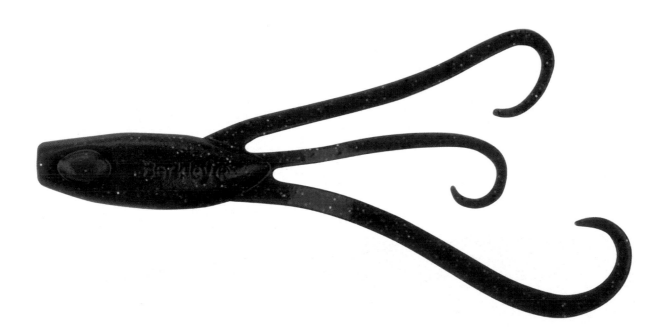

BERKLEY GULP! ALIVE! 6-IN SQUIDO

Type: Soft plastic
Color/Pattern: Glow, New Penny, Pink, Pearl White, Root Beer Fleck, Chartreuse, Camo, Watermelon Red Glitter
Size: 6 in
Quantity: 8
Features: Squido has a versatile body design for nearly unlimited rigging options; three legs kick and squirm in the water, delivering enticing looks that fish can't resist; absorbs 20 percent more Gulp! scent; durable and long-lasting, they look, smell, and feel like live squid; especially effective when used with heavy jigs to pull bottom dwellers out of structure.
Price:. **$19.99**

NEW Products: **Lures, Softbait**

BERKLEY GULP! ALIVE! MINNOW GRUB HALF-PINT

Type: Jerk bait
Color/Pattern: Chartreuse, Pearl White
Size: 3 in

Quantity: 13
Features: 100 percent biodegradeable; absorbs up to 20 percent more fish attractant by weight; great for jigs, drop-shot, and live-bait rigs; delivers natural action, scent, and taste.
Price: **$9.95**

BERKLEY GULP! ALIVE! MINNOW HALF-PINT

Type: Jerk bait
Color/Pattern: Black Shad, Emerald Shiner, Smelt
Size: 2 1/2 in, 3 in, 4 in

Quantity: 25, 15, 10
Features: Gulp! Minnow is ideal for drifting or jigging; it is 100 percent biodegradable.
Price: **$9.95**

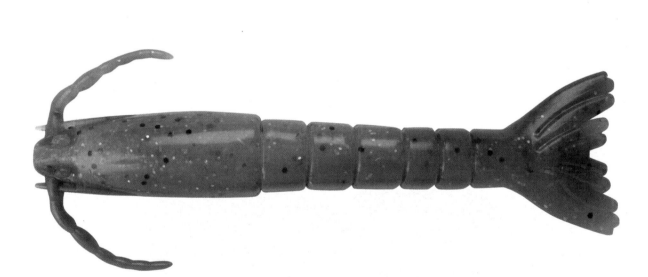

BERKLEY GULP! ALIVE! NIGHTCRAWLER HALF-PINT

Type: Worm
Color/Pattern: Natural
Size: 6 in
Quantity: 12

Features: Looks, smells and tastes like the real thing; 34 percent better swimming action than original Gulp!; made of water-soluble, natural ingredients; releases over 400 times more scent than other plastics.
Price: **$9.95**

BERKLEY GULP! ALIVE! SHRIMP HALF-PINT

Type: Shrimp bait
Color/Pattern: Nuclear Chicken, Pearl White, Natural, New Penny
Size: 3 in, 4 in

Quantity: 7, 5
Features: Whether you're fishing expansive flats, a wreck, or oil rig, the fact that saltwater fish love shrimp remains the same; durable and long-lasting, they look, smell, and feel like live shrimp.
Price: **$9.95**

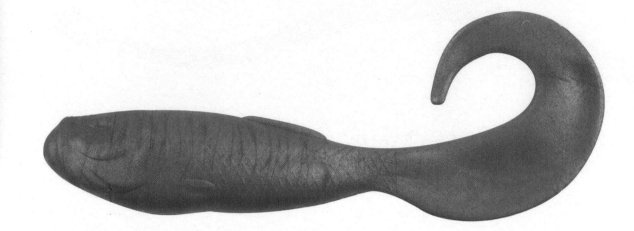

BERKLEY GULP! ALIVE! SWIMMING MULLET HALF-PINT

Type: Soft plastic
Color/Pattern: Pearl White, Glow Chartreuse, Chartreuse, Pink
Size: 4 in
Quantity: 14

Features: Baits come floating in "Magic Gravy," enabling you to recharge your baits by putting them back in the bucket; swimming tail action of the Mullet is irresistible to all saltwater species; environmentally safe 100 percent biodegradable plastic-free construction; highly durable and can stand up to multiple strikes.
Price: **$9.95**

BIG BITE BAITS REAL DEAL CRAW

Type: Craw
Color/Pattern: Green Pumpkin, Watermelon Red Flake, Black Neon/Watermelon Red, HD Black/Red Craw, HD Crawdad, HD Blue Craw
Size: 4 in
Quantity: 7, 3 for HD

Features: Designed by Bassmaster Elite Series pro, Russ Lane; built with an extra-realistic craw profile; bursting with detail and covered in a texture that bass won't want to let go of; works great as a jig trailer or on a Texas-rig; can be fished with the claws together for a smooth, gliding movement, or with the claws cut for a lively swimming action.
Price: . . . . **$3.99–$5.99**

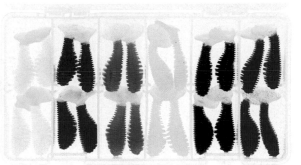

CABELA'S 25-PIECE SWIMMING SHAD KIT

Type: Kit
Color/Pattern: White/Chartreuse, Red/White, Blue/White, Chartreuse, Black/Chartreuse, Red/Chartreuse
Size: 1 3/4 in
Quantity: 24

Features: Filled with grubs known to be deadly on large crappies, bass, walleye, and a variety of other freshwater fish, the 25-Piece Swimming Shad Kit is a must-have for any avid angler; includes a Plano 3500 utility box filled with 24 1 3/4 in swimming grubs in six attention-grabbing colors; each grub sports a fat-body design with an oversized boot tail that renders a pronounced thumping action.
Price: **$9.95**

CABELA'S ACTION TAIL 2-INCH FAT GRUB

Type: Grub
Color/Pattern: White, Chartreuse Sparkle, Black/Blue/Chartreuse, Lemon Meringue, Tennessee Shad, Bad Blood, Bubble Gum/Chartreuse, Firetiger, Pink/Yellow/Pearl, Orange/Chartreuse, Blue Shiner, Chartreuse/Shad, Junebug/Chartreuse, Red/Chartreuse, Purple Glitter/Opaque Chartreuse
Size: 2 in
Quantity: 25
Features: Fast-flitting tails; subtle, lifelike movements; ideal for large crappies and panfish.
Price: **$2.99**

CABELA'S ACTION-TAIL MINNOW

Type: Jerk bait
Color/Pattern: Firecracker, Blue Pearl Pepper, Black/Chartreuse, Junebug/Chartreuse, Tennessee Shad, Purple Glitter/Opaque Chartreuse, Silver Glitter/Pearl, Black/Red/Chartreuse, Electric Chicken, Red/Chartreuse, Orange/Chartreuse, Black Neon/Pearl/Silver, Lemon Meringue, Alewife, Chartreuse Sparkle
Size: 1 3/4 in
Quantity: 15
Features: Darting action of a minnow in distress; thin-tail design seems to come to life; ideal for crappies and other panfish.
Price: **$2.49**

CABELA'S FISHERMAN SERIES 48-PIECE FINESSE TUBE KIT

Type: Kit
Color/Pattern: White Illusion Pepper, Smoke Pepper, Green Pumpkin Pepper, Chartreuse Pepper, Melon Pepper, Smoke Blue Green Flake
Size: 3 1/2 in
Quantity: 48
Features: Finesse tubes mimic a variety of prey including baitfish and crawfish; slender tube design has a small profile, perfect for lighter presentations; each tube is salted; kit comes in a reusable box; includes eight each of the colors.
Price: **$14.99**

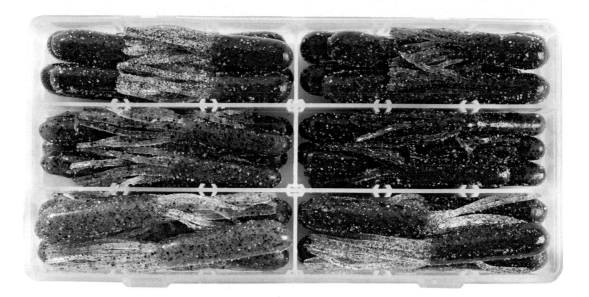

CABELA'S FISHERMAN SERIES ASSORTED 44-PIECE BASS TUBE KIT
Type: Kit
Color/Pattern: Variable
Size: 2 ¾ in, 3 ½ in, 4 in

Quantity: 44
Features: Perfectly sized tube baits for bass; ideal for using in shallow or deep water; salted for a realistic sinking rate; two colors per size.
Price:................................. **$10.99**

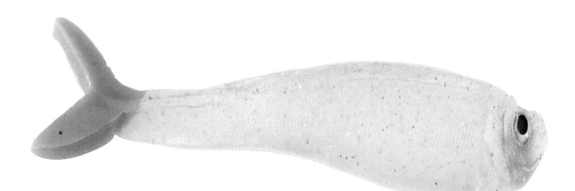

CABELA'S GO-TO HAND-POUR SPLIT TAIL MINNNOW
Type: Jerk bait
Color/Pattern: Chartreuse Silver Glitter, Chartreuse Silver/Orange Tail, Amber Black Pearl, Clear Silver/Orange Tail, Emerald Shad, Firetiger

Size: 3 in
Quantity: 6
Features: Super-soft for an extremely lifelike action that entices fish to strike; realistic minnow profile can be fished on a jig or as a drop bait.
Price:................................. **$3.99**

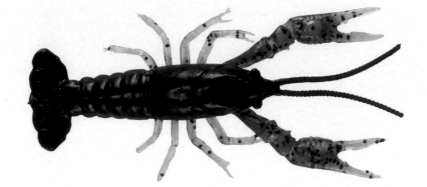

SAVAGE GEAR 3D CRAW

Type: Craw
Color/Pattern: Summer Craw, Spring Craw, Red, Black & Blue, PB&J
Size: 3 in, 4 3/4 in
Weight: 1/5 oz, 1/2 oz
Quantity: 4, 3
Features: Air-filled claws and head cavity on the 3D Craw deliver flotation and natural underwater movement, imitating crawfish, a favorite meal of many game fish; iodine makes crawfish a staple meal for a big female bass' egg development; lures come infused with iodine, salt, and crawfish scents; excellent for Carolina rigging, stand-up jigheads or fishing weedless on a weighted hook over heavy weed mats and then paused in openings for a slow, enticing fall; exaggerated antennae and legs add lifelike action on either a forward drag or tail-first retrieve.
Price: **$9.99**

SAVAGE GEAR 3D MANIC SHRIMP

Type: Shrimp bait
Color/Pattern: Brown, Red, Natural, Blue Pearl, Avocado, Gold
Size: 2 1/2 in, 4 in
Weight: 3/25 oz, 3/11 oz
Quantity: 1
Features: Molded using 3D scanning of a real shrimp, Savage Gear's Manic Shrimp wreaks havoc on a wide variety of saltwater sport fish; soft-plastic construction, lifelike paint scheme, and strike-inducing kicking action, make this realistic underwater bait one you'll never want to leave home without; exaggerated legs and antennae create attractive swimming movements on both the fall and the retrieve; pre-rigged with a weighted EWG hook; tail section is infused with nylon mesh to help prevent tearing on the hookset.
Price: **$5.99**

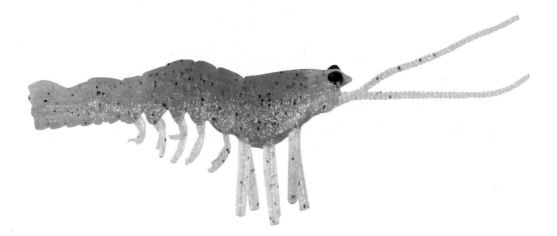

SAVAGE GEAR 3D SHRIMP
Type: Shrimp bait
Color/Pattern: Blue Pearl, Magic Brown, Krill Pink, Glow, Olive Brown, Golden
Size: 2 1/2 in, 4 in
Weight: 1/8 oz, 1/3 oz

Quantity: 6, 4
Features: Created using 3D scans of real shrimp; exaggerated legs and antenna create realistic underwater actions; use under a popping cork, on a jighead, or in thick weeds.
Price: **$5.99**

STORM WILDEYE LIVE BABY BASS
Type: Rigged plastic swimbait
Color/Pattern: Baby Bass
Size: 4 in
Weight: 1/2 oz

Quantity: 3
Features: Internally weighted bodies for lifelike action; 3D holographic WildEye eyes; holographic flash foil; durable soft outer body.
Price: **$5.99**

STORM WILDEYE LIVE BLUEGILL

Type: Rigged plastic swimbait
Color/Pattern: Bluegill
Size: 2 in, 3 in
Weight: 1/4 oz, 5/16 oz
Quantity: 3

Features: So realistic you will want to keep them in your livewell; internally weighted bodies give them a lifelike action that makes fish strike; 3D holographic WildEye eyes add to the successful imitation; holographic flash foil is highly visible to fish; soft outer body is durable for long-term use, hit after hit.
Price:. . . . . **$5.29–$5.99**

Z-MAN DIEZEL MINNOWZ

Type: Unrigged plastic swimbait
Color/Pattern: Smoky Shad, Pearl, Bad Shad, Opening Night, Redbone, Houdini, Mulletron, Pinfish
Size: 4 in

Quantity: 5
Features: Best for fresh- or saltwater applications; ElaZtech is 10 times stronger than traditional soft plastic; boasts one of the highest fish-per-bait ratings.
Price:. **$3.99**

Z-MAN HARD LEG FROGZ

Type: Frog bait
Color/Pattern: White, Watermelon/Chartreuse, Watermelon Red, Green Pumpkin, Redbone, Mud Minnow
Size: 4 in
Quantity: 3

Features: Get lively paddle-foot swimming action with the Z-Man Hard Leg FrogZ; made of ElaZtech, which is 10 times stronger than traditional soft plastic; resists nicks, cuts, and tears; boasts one of the highest fish-per-bait ratings in the industry at an affordable price; naturally buoyant; 100 percent nontoxic.
Price:. **$3.99**

NEW Products: **Lures, Softbait**

Z-MAN MINNOWZ

Type: Swimbait
Color/Pattern: Smoky Shad, Pearl, New Penny, Opening Night, Redbone, Houdini, Mood Ring, Pinfish
Size: 3 in
Quantity: 8
Features: Z-Man MinnowZ are an effective, universal baitfish imitation; popular inshore saltwater bait for redfish, trout, snook, and flounder due to durability and action; superior smaller swimbait for rigging on a jighead, as a swim jig trailer, on a Fish Head Spin or on an umbrella rig; made of ElaZtech, which is ten times stronger than traditional soft plastic; resists nicks, cuts, and tears.
Price: **$3.99**

Z-MAN SCENTED POGYZ

Type: Unrigged plastic swimbait
Color/Pattern: Pearl, Root Beer/Chartreuse, New Penny, Pinfish
Size: 3 in
Quantity: 5
Features: Ultrarealistic profile, natural swimming action; irresisitable to bass and game fish; mimics pinfish, threadfin, and pilchards.
Price: **$4.99**

Z-MAN TURBO CRAWZ

Type: Craw
Color/Pattern: Green Pumpkin, Green Pumpkin/Orange, Pearl, Watermelon Candy, Okeechobee Craw, Bluegill, Sprayed Grass, Silver Shadow
Size: 4 in
Quantity: 6

Features: The ultimate in durability, buoyancy, and action, this soft-bodied jig trailer is perfect for grabbing the attention of hungry bass; thick, eye-catching body, six legs, and flapping claws provide realistic movement on the retrieve that no largemouth will be able to resist.
Price: **$3.99**

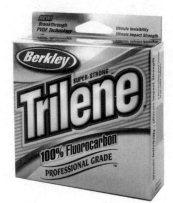

BERKLEY TRILENE 100% FLUOROCARBON - PROFESSIONAL GRADE

Color: Clear, green tint
Type: Fluorocarbon
Length: 110 yd, 200 yd
Lb. Test: 4, 6, 8, 10, 12, 15, 17, 20, 25

Diameter: 0.007 in–0.019 in
Features: Invisible fluorocarbon; proprietary 100 percent PVDF formula specially processed for the ultimate in impact strength; lower memory for superior casting; available in green tint for reduced sparkle and flash.
Price: . . . .**$10.99–$25.99**

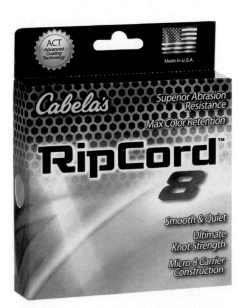

CABELA'S RIPCORD 8 BRAIDED

Color: Green, yellow
Type: Braid
Length: 150 yd, 300 yd
Lb. Test: 6, 8, 10, 15, 20, 30, 40, 50, 65, 80, 100, 130

Features: Unique bi-axial braid construction that realigns fibers to provide a smooth exterior; quieter through the rod guides and creates less friction for longer casts; realignment of the fibers also gives greater knot strength than traditional braided lines; Advanced Coating Technology adds superior abrasion resistance and increased color.
Price: . . . .**$19.99–$39.99**

CABELA'S RIPCORD PRO

Color: Frost, green, yellow
Type: Braid
Length: 150 yd, 300 yd, 600 yd, 1200 yd
Lb. Test: 6, 8, 10, 15, 20, 30, 40, 50, 65, 80, 100, 130

Features: Advanced Coating Technology penetrates on the molecular level; increased abrasion resistance and color retention; unparalleled knot strength and virtually no-stretch feel; superior strength equated to a rounded, smaller diameter.
Price:............................**$14.99–$184.99**

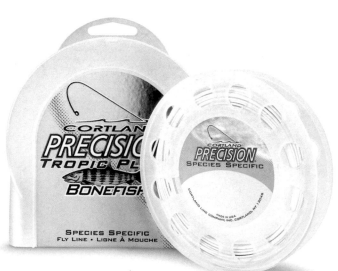

CORTLAND PRECISION TROPIC PLUS FL

Color: Light yellow
Type: Saltwater braid
Length: 90 ft
Lb. Test: 6, 7, 8, 9, 10, 12

Features: This all-purpose tropical line features a slick, abrasion-resistant coating to withstand harsh saltwater elements in warm-weather climates; braided mono core reduces line memory, and its long body taper provides quick loading and smooth, accurate casts.
Price:...................................**$72.00**

DAIWA SALTIGA BOAT BRAIDED

Color: Multi
Type: Saltwater braid
Length: 1800m
Lb. Test: 40, 55, 70, 80, 100, 120, 150
Features: Designed for deep drop fishing with Dendoh Style power assist reels; eight woven braids make it super-strong yet one of the finest diameter braids available; less affected by currents for a straighter, more accurate drop; smooth surface means less friction and noise from guides on the retrieve; color changes every ten meters, with five and one meter indicators, shows depth and line movement; coded for quick programming into Dendoh reel memory for maximum readout accuracy.
Price: . . . . **$249.95–$379.95**

DAIWA SAMURAI BRAIDED

Color: Green
Type: Braid
Length: 150 yd, 300 yd, 1500 yd
Lb. Test: 15, 20, 30, 40, 55, 70, 80, 100, 150
Diameter: 0.007 in–0.024 in
Features: Strong and sensitive; noticeably thinner, softer, smoother, and more flexible than ordinary braids; less friction for better casts; reduced line noise on the retrieve; faster sink rate due to less current resistance; available in 150-yard, 300-yard, and 1500-yard spools.
Price: . . . . **$24.95–$249.95**

DAIWA STEEZ FLUOROCARBON

Color: Green
Type: Fluorocarbon
Length: 125 yd
Lb. Test: 5, 6, 8, 10, 12, 16, 20
Diameter: 0.007 in–0.016 in

Features: Super soft, super strong 100 percent fluorocarbon line with the flexibility and castability of regular monofilament; formulated exclusively for Steez spinning and casting reels, it is highly resistant to abrasion and offers a faster sink rate than monofilament; parallel winding on the filler spool prevents dents and inconsistency in roundness that can reduce casting efficiency.
Price: . . . .**$19.99–$26.99**

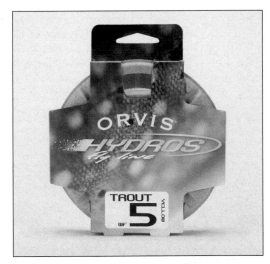

ORVIS HYDROS WF TROUT

Color: Olive dun, yellow
Type: Freshwater fly
Length: 90 ft
Lb. Test: 3, 4, 5, 6, 7, 8
Features: Versatile weight-forward classic trout fly-line taper, now in the new Hydros configuration; fly line incorporates five new technological advances, including Hy-Flote Tip, Orvis Line ID, and Wonderline Coating;

enhanced welded loop; innovative weight forward taper combined with slightly larger line diameters produce a line that is ideal at close to medium range, but still capable of delivering at distance; longer head than traditional weight-forward lines; braided multifilament core.
Price: **$79.00**

POWERPRO ZERO IMPACT MICROFILAMENT BRAIDED

Color: Aqua green, yellow hi-viz
Type: Braid
Length: 150 yd, 300 yd
Lb. Test: 20, 30, 50, 80

Diameter: 0.009 in–0.017 in
Features: 50 percent stronger Termination Zones; high-strength zones marked black; added strength without sacrificing line capacity.
Price:. . . . .**$24.99–$42.99**

RIO AQUALUX MIDGETIP

Color: Clear, yellow
Type: Freshwater fly
Length: 90 ft, 100 ft
Features: The most effective fish-catching zone in the majority of lakes is within the top 6 feet of the water column. RIO's Sub-surface lake series fly lines are deadly effective on windy days and when fishing in shallow bays, close to lake shores and over the top of weed beds. Each line is built with a supple coldwater core and coating and features a welded loop in the front for fast rigging. One metre (39 inches) clear intermediate tip; perfect for fishing nymphs, emergers, and chironomids (buzzers) in the top twelve inches of the water column; great for shallow shorelines, sub-surface on windy days and over the top of weed beds.
Price:. **$79.95**

RIO CONNECTCORE SHOOTING LINE

Color: Orange, teal
Type: Fly—Spey
Length: 100 ft
Features: RIO's new ConnectCore shooting line is the very best coated shooting line on the market with tremendous assets for the Spey fly fisher. Built on RIO's ConnectCore the shooting line has virtually no stretch, allowing anglers to stay perfectly in touch with their fly throughout the swing and feel every slight touch. A thicker diameter handling section prolongs the life of the line and ensures it is very easy to grip the line in cold conditions, while the highly visible front section makes it very easy to see when to stop stripping and make the cast; unique core also ensures the most perfect coils of line when stripping in, resulting in far fewer tangles and snarls; neat eight-inch welded loop at the front end allows for fast and efficient head changes, while the super slick XS Technology coating floats high and shoots far; ultra-low stretch ConnectCore allows anglers to feel every single touch; thick, highly visible handling section for durability and visibility.

Price: **$59.95**

RIO PERCEPTION

Color: Camo, gray, green, tan
Type: Freshwater fly
Length: 80 ft, 90 ft, 100 ft
Features: Built with ultra-low stretch ConnectCore Technology, Perception lines provide groundbreaking levels of sensitivity for intuitively better cast timing, easier line lift, and sharp, precise mends; lack of stretch also means enhanced detection of subtle takes and faster reaction time when setting the hook; exclusive SureFire color system (RIO's uniquetri-color distance measure) improves casting accuracy by making it easy to gauge exact distances with a quick glance; unique three-color SureFire system ensures deadly accurate distance control; ConnectCore improves casting timing, hook set, and mending; EasyID tag to quickly identify fly line; winner of best New Fly Line for 2014 at EFTTEX and IFTD shows.

Price: **$89.95**

NEW Products: **Lines**

RIO SHORT HEAD SPEY

Color: Blue, straw
Type: Fly—Spey
Length: 100 ft
Features: Very easy casting, traditional style Spey line, which is ideal for Spey casters moving up from easier casting Scandi and Skagit heads; head length varies between forty feet and fifty feet, depending on line size, and it is a great choice of traditional Spey line for anglers using shorter rods and when fishing in tight quarters; longer head lengths (when compared to Skagit and Scandi heads) allow for less stripping in time at the end of each cast, which means more fishing time, and less loose line to handle and shoot with each cast; short head loads quickly and makes it simple to cast in tight quarters; rear-loaded weight distribution loads rods easily and ensures effortless, efficient Spey casts.

Price: **$89.95**

SEAGUAR FLUOROCARBON SALMON STS LEADER

Type: Fluorocarbon
Length: 100 yd
Lb. Test: 20, 25, 30, 40, 50
Diameter: 0.016 in–0.026 in

Features: Genuine 100 percent fluorocarbon leader material delivers incredible abrasion resistance and maximum impact and knot strength, all with a smaller line diameter than monofilament.

Price: . . . . **$15.99–$24.99**

SEAGUAR FLUOROCARBON STEELHEAD/ TROUT STS LEADER

Type: Fluorocarbon
Length: 100 yd
Lb. Test: 4, 6, 8, 10, 12, 15, 17
Diameter: 0.007 in–0.015 in

Features: Incredible abrasion resistance and 30 percent better knot strength at a smaller diameter than monofilament; fast-sinking line gets you in the strike zone quicker; with a lower refractive index than monofilament, it is significantly less visible to fish underwater.
Price: . . . .**$11.99–$13.99**

SEAGUAR SMACKDOWN SLEEK, ULTRA-STRONG 8-STRAND BRAID

Color: Green, yellow
Type: Braid
Length: 150 yd
Lb. Test: 10, 15, 20, 30, 40, 50, 65
Diameter: 0.005 in–0.016 in

Features: This next generation Seaguar braid is so thin that 20 lb test has the diameter of 6 lb monofilament; Smackdown Braid is made with 8 ultra-thin, micro-weave strands in a round, smooth-casting profile with extra sensitivity; it provides exceptional knot and tensile strength with unparalleled abrasion resistance.
Price: . . . .**$19.99–$24.99**

SEAGUAR THREADLOCK ULTRA-STRONG 16-STRAND HOLLOW-CORE BRAID

Color: Blue, green, white, yellow
Type: Braid
Length: 600 yd, 2500 yd
Lb. Test: 50, 60, 80, 100, 130, 200
Diameter: 0.015 in–0.030 in

Features: Designed for offshore saltwater anglers who are targeting pelagic species and looking for solid connections in structure and kelp; in smaller pound test sizes, Threadlock is also a perfect line choice for certain heavy cover freshwater applications like Flippin' and Punchin'.
Price: 600 yd: $130.00–$180.00; 2500 yd: $545.00–$815.00

ABU GARCIA VENGEANCE

Model: VNGS56-3, VNGS66-4, VNGS66-5, VNGS66-6, VNGS70-5, VNGS70-6
Length: 5'6''; 6'6''; 6'6''; 6'6''; 7'; 7'
Power: L; ML; M; MH; M; MH
Action: MF; F; MF; F; F; F
Pieces: 1
Line Weight: 2-10 lbs; 6-10 lbs; 6-12 lbs; 8-14 lbs; 6-12 lbs; 6-14 lbs
Guide Count: 6+tip; 7+tip; 7+tip; 7+tip; 7+tip; 7+tip

Lure Weight: 1/16-5/16 oz; 1/8-1/2 oz; 1/8-1/2 oz; 1/4-3/4 oz; 3/16-5/8 oz; 1/4-3/4 oz
Features: 24-ton graphite construction for a lightweight and balanced design; high-density EVA handles are more durable and comfortable; soft-touch sea guide reel seats for increased comfort; zirconium coated guides are perfect for braided line usage; Texas-rigged hook keeper for all bait applications; one-piece rod.
Price: **$49.99**

ABU GARCIA VENGEANCE 2PC

Model: VNGS662-4, VNGS662-5, VNGS662-6, VNGS702-5
Length: 6'6''; 6'6''; 6'6''; 7'
Power: ML; M; MH; M
Action: F; MF; F; F
Pieces: 2
Line Weight: 6-10 lbs; 6-12 lbs; 8-14 lbs; 6-12 lbs
Guide Count: 7+tip
Lure Weight: 1/8-1/2 oz; 1/8-1/2 oz; 1/4-3/4 oz; 3/16-5/8 oz

Features: 24-ton graphite construction for a lightweight and balanced design; high-density EVA handles are more durable and comfortable; soft-touch sea guide reel seats for increased comfort; zirconium coated guides are perfect for braided line usage; Texas-rigged hook keeper for all bait applications.
Price: **$49.99**

ACTION	POWER	
M=Moderate	UL=Ultra Light	H=Heavy
MF=Moderate Fast	L=Light	MH=Medium-Heavy
F=Fast	ML=Medium-Light	XH=Extra Heavy
XF=Extra Fast		

ABU GARCIA VERACITY–MICRO-GUIDE

Model: VERS69-4, VERS70-5, VERS70-6, VERS76-5
Length: 6'9''; 7'; 7'; 7'6''
Power: ML; M; MH; M
Action: F
Line Weight: 6-10 lbs; 8-14 lbs; 8-14 lbs; 6-12 lbs
Guide Count: 6+tip; 7+tip; 7+tip; 8+tip
Lure Weight: 1/8-1/2 oz; 3/16-5/8 oz; 1/4-3/4 oz; 3/16-5/8 oz
Features: 36-ton graphite with nanotechnology for decreased weight and increased impact resistance; titanium alloy guides with titanium inserts allow for a super lightweight guide giving the ultimate in rod performance; high-density EVA gives greater sensitivity and durability; micro-guide system provides improved balance and sensitivity; Texas-rigged hook keeper for all bait applications.
Price: **$149.95**

ABU GARCIA VERACITY–WINCH MODEL

Model: VERSW70-5
Length: 7'
Power: M
Action: M
Line Weight: 8-14 lbs
Guide Count: 7+tip
Lure Weight: 3/16-5/8 oz
Features: 36-ton graphite with nanotechnology for decreased weight and increased impact resistance; titanium alloy guides with titanium inserts allow for a super lightweight guide giving the ultimate in rod performance; high-density EVA gives greater sensitivity and durability; micro-guide system provides improved balance and sensitivity; Texas-rigged hook keeper for all bait applications.
Price: **$149.95**

ACTION	POWER	
M=Moderate	UL=Ultra Light	H=Heavy
MF=Moderate Fast	L=Light	MH=Medium-Heavy
F=Fast	ML=Medium-Light	XH=Extra Heavy
XF=Extra Fast		

ABU GARCIA VERITAS SPINNING

Model: VRS66-5, VRS66-6, VRS69-4, VRS70-5, VRS70-6
Length: 6'6''; 6'6''; 6'9''; 7'; 7'
Power: M; MH; ML; M; MH
Action: XF; F; MF; F; F
Pieces: 1
Line Weight: 6-12 lbs; 8-14 lbs; 6-10 lbs; 6-12 lbs; 8-14 lbs
Guide Count: 7+tip
Lure Weight: 1/8-1/2 oz; 1/4-3/4 oz; 1/8-1/2 oz; 3/16-5/8 oz; 1/4-3/4 oz
Features: 30-ton graphite construction with

nanotechnology for decreased weight and increased compression strength; one-piece double-anodized aluminum screw down creates a secure connection with the reel; high-density EVA handles are more durable and comfortable; Abu-designed extreme exposure reel seats provide direct finger to rod contact for increased sensitivity; titanium alloy guides with SiC inserts create a lightweight, balanced rod design; Texas-rigged hook keeper for all bait applications; one-piece rod.
Price: **$99.95**

ABU GARCIA VERITAS SPINNING 2PC

Model: VRS662-5, VRS662-6, VRS702-5
Length: 6'6''; 6'6''; 7'
Power: M; MH; M
Action: F; F; XF
Pieces: 2
Line Weight: 6-12 lbs; 8-14 lbs; 6-12 lbs
Guide Count: 7+tip
Lure Weight: 1/8-1/2 oz; 1/4-3/4 oz; 3/16-5/8 oz
Features: 30-ton graphite construction with nanotechnology for decreased weight and increased compression strength;

one-piece double-anodized aluminum screw down creates a secure connection with the reel; high-density EVA handles are more durable and comfortable; Abu-designed extreme exposure reel seats provide direct finger to rod contact for increased sensitivity; titanium alloy guides with SiC inserts create a lightweight, balanced rod design; Texas-rigged hook keeper for all bait applications.
Price: **$99.95**

ACTION	POWER	
M=Moderate	UL=Ultra Light	H=Heavy
MF=Moderate Fast	L=Light	MH=Medium-Heavy
F=Fast	ML=Medium-Light	XH=Extra Heavy
XF=Extra Fast		

ABU GARCIA VILLAIN–MICRO-GUIDE SPINNING

Model: VLSM610-5, VLSM69-4, VLSM71-5
Length: 6'10''; 6'9''; 7'1''
Power: M; ML; M
Action: MF; F; F
Pieces: 1
Line Weight: 6-12 lbs; 6-10 lbs; 6-12 lbs
Guide Count: 7+tip

Lure Weight: 3/16-5/8 oz; 1/8-1/2 oz; 3/16-5/8 oz
Features: Titanium alloy guides, with titanium inserts allow for a super lightweight guide, giving the ultimate in rod performance; C6 total exposure reel seat gives complete contact to the rod for the ultimate sensitivity; high-density EVA gives greater sensitivity and durability; carbon-wrapped guides reduce weight; Texas-rigged hook keeper for all bait applications; split-grip design; one-piece rod.
Price: **$179.95**

ABU GARCIA VILLAIN–SPINNING

Model: VLS610-5, VLS66-6, VLS69-4, VLS71-5, VLS71-6
Length: 6'10''; 6'6''; 6'9''; 7'1''; 7'1''
Power: M; MH; ML; M; MH
Action: MF; F; F; F; F
Pieces: 1
Line Weight: 6-12 lbs; 8-14 lbs; 6-10 lbs; 6-12 lbs; 8-14 lbs
Guide Count: 7+tip
Lure Weight: 3/16-5/8 oz; 1/4-3/4 oz; 1/8-1/2 oz; 3/16-5/8 oz; 1/4-3/4 oz

Features: Titanium alloy guides with titanium inserts allow for a super lightweight guide, giving the ultimate in rod performance; C6 total exposure reel seat gives complete contact to the rod for the ultimate sensitivity; high-density EVA gives greater sensitivity and durability; carbon-wrapped guides reduce weight; Texas-rigged hook keeper for all bait applications; split-grip design; one-piece rod.
Price: **$179.95**

ACTION	POWER	
M=Moderate	UL=Ultra Light	H=Heavy
MF=Moderate Fast	L=Light	MH=Medium-Heavy
F=Fast	ML=Medium-Light	XH=Extra Heavy
XF=Extra Fast		

ABU GARCIA VILLAIN–SPINNING 2PC
Model: VLS6102-5, VLS662-6
Length: 6'10''; 6'6''
Power: M; MH
Action: MF; F
Pieces: 2
Line Weight: 6-12 lbs; 8-14 lbs
Guide Count: 7+tip
Lure Weight: 3/16-5/8 oz; 1/4-3/4 oz

Features: Titanium alloy guides with titanium inserts allow for a super lightweight guide giving the ultimate in rod performance; C6 total exposure reel seat gives complete contact to the rod for the ultimate sensitivity; high-density EVA gives greater sensitivity and durability; carbon wrapped guides reduce weight; Texas-rigged hook keeper for all bait applications; split grip design.
Price: **$179.95**

BASS PRO SHOPS 3' GRAPHITE
Model: 3' Graphite
Length: 3'
Power: M
Action: F
Pieces: 1
Line Weight: 6–12 lb
Lure Weight: 1/8-1/2 oz

Features: An excellent rod for pitching lures under docks, working areas with thick brush, kayak fishing, and ice fishing for larger fish; great for children; features high-performing IM6 graphite blanks for the strength and sensitivity you need to take your limit; complete with aluminum oxide guides and our comfortable cork handles with a graphite reel seat.
Price: **$19.99**

ACTION	POWER	
M=Moderate	UL=Ultra Light	H=Heavy
MF=Moderate Fast	L=Light	MH=Medium-Heavy
F=Fast	ML=Medium-Light	XH=Extra Heavy
XF=Extra Fast		

RODS

BASS PRO SHOPS JOHNNY MORRIS SIGNATURE SERIES II
Model: 68MS, 68MHS, 72MS, 72MHS
Length: 6'8"; 6'8''; 7'2''; 7'2''
Power: M; MH; M; MH
Action: XF; XF; F; F
Pieces: 1
Line Weight: 4–12 lbs; 6–17 lbs; 4-12 lbs; 6-17 lbs
Lure Weight: 1/8-½ oz; ¼-5/8 oz; 1/8-½ oz; ¼-5/8 oz

Features: Super-high-grade 85 million modulus graphite blank; industry leading Type 1 slit carbon powerwall construction; exclusive carbon cloth butt wrap for unprecedented strength; Fuji new concept stainless steel K-guides with Alconite rings; premium molded split handles with ultra-comfortable P-Tec polyfoam grips; our super-low-profile two-piece exposed-blank reel seat with a soft-touch finish.
Price: **$139.99**

ACTION	POWER	
M=Moderate	UL=Ultra Light	H=Heavy
MF=Moderate Fast	L=Light	MH=Medium-Heavy
F=Fast	ML=Medium-Light	XH=Extra Heavy
XF=Extra Fast		

BASS PRO SHOPS MICRO LITE GRAPHITE

Model: ML36/4-T, 46ULS, 50ULS, 56ULS-2, 56LS, 60ULS-2, 60LS, 60MLS, 66ULS-2, 66LS-2, 66MLS-2, 70ULS-2, 70LS-2, 70MLS-2, 76ULS-2
Length: 3'6"; 4'6"; 5'; 5'6"; 5'6"; 6'; 6'; 6'; 6'6"; 6'6"; 6'6"; 7'; 7'; 7'; 7'6"
Power: L; UL; UL; UL; L; UL; L; ML; UL; L; ML; UL; L; ML; UL
Action: Fast
Pieces: 1; 1; 1; 2; 1; 2; 1; 1; 2; 2; 2; 2; 2; 2; 2
Line Weight: 2-8 lbs; 1-6 lbs; 1-6 lbs; 1-6 lbs; 2-8 lbs; 1-6 lbs; 2-8 lbs; 4-10 lbs; 1-6 lbs; 2-8 lbs; 4-10 lbs; 2-6 lbs; 2-8 lbs; 4-10 lbs; 2-6 lbs

Lure Weight: 1/32-1/4 oz; 1/64-1/8 oz; 1/32-1/4 oz; 1/32-1/4 oz; 1/16-1/4 oz; 1/32-1/4 oz; 1/16-1/4 oz; 1/16-3/8 oz; 1/32-1/4 oz; 1/16-1/4 oz; 1/16-3/8 oz; 1/16-1/4 oz; 1/16-1/4 oz; 1/16-3/8 oz; 1/16-1/4 oz
Features: Another excellent rod for light tackle; features IM6 graphite blanks with real solid carbon tip sections for incredible sensitivity and toughness; ultra-thin, lightweight guides that balance almost weightlessly on the spline and deliver a truly awesome feel; complete with gold anodized reel seats; contoured cork handles.
Price: **$49.99**

BASS PRO SHOPS MICRO LITE GRAPHITE FLOAT 'N' FLY

Model: 80MLS-2, 86MLS-2, 96MLS-2
Length: 8'; 8'6"; 9'6"
Power: ML
Action: F
Pieces: 2
Line Weight: 4-10 lbs
Lure Weight: 1/16–3/8 oz

Features: A perfect rod for light tackle; features IM6 graphite blanks with real solid carbon tip sections for incredible sensitivity and toughness; ultra-thin, lightweight guides balance almost weightlessly on the spline and deliver a truly awesome feel; complete with gold anodized reel seats; contoured cork handles; pre-equipped for use with balance kit (sold separately).
Price: **$54.99**

ACTION	POWER	
M=Moderate	UL=Ultra Light	H=Heavy
MF=Moderate Fast	L=Light	MH=Medium-Heavy
F=Fast	ML=Medium-Light	XH=Extra Heavy
XF=Extra Fast		

BERKLEY AIR IM8

Model: A94-8-6M, A94-9MH, A94-9L, A94-9M, A94-9-6M, A94-99ML, A94-10-6XL, A94-109ML
Length: 8'6''; 9'; 9'; 9'; 9'6''; 9'9''; 10'6''; 10'6''
Power: M; MH; L; M; M; ML; XL; ML
Pieces: 2
Line Weight: 8-12 lbs; 10-20 lbs; 6-10 lbs; 8-14 lbs; 8-12 lbs; 6-10 lbs; 4-10 lbs; 6-10 lbs
Guide Count: 9; 9; 9; 9; 10; 10; 10; 10
Lure Weight: 3/8-3/4 oz; 1/2-1 1/2 oz; 1/8-1/2 oz; 3/8-3/4 oz; 3/8-3/4 oz; 1/8-1/2 oz; 1/8-1/2 oz; 1/8-1/2 oz

Features: Constructed of IM8 advanced-modulus graphite; air IM8 rods are lightweight and have a sensitive blank that provides the ultimate in feel with enough power to land big fish with ease; titanium-coated SS304 guides for increased durability and abrasion resistance when fishing with braided line; perfect for casting to big steelhead or trolling for giant lake trout; concept guide spacing improves sensitivity and maximizes blank strength; air IM8 gives anglers the length, power, and performance they need for demanding conditions.
Price:............................ **$99.95–$109.95**

BERKLEY AMP

Model: AS562L, AS601M, AS662ML, AS661M, AS662M, AS701M, AS702M
Length: 5'6''; 6'; 6'6''; 6'6''; 6'6''; 7'; 7'
Power: L; M; ML; M; M; M; M
Pieces: 2; 1; 2; 1; 2; 1; 2
Line Weight: 2-8 lbs; 4-12 lbs; 4-10 lbs; 4-12 lbs; 4-12 lbs; 4-12 lbs; 4-12 lbs
Guide Count: 4; 4; 5; 5; 5; 5; 5

Lure Weight: 1/16-3/8 oz; 1/8-3/4 oz; 1/8-5/8 oz; 1/8-3/4 oz; 1/8-3/4 oz; 1/8-3/4 oz; 1/8-3/4 oz
Features: Lighter, faster, and more sensitive than the average rod; features X-posed reel seats and split-grip cork handles on both spinning and casting models, allowing the hand to remain in constant contact with the rod blank and taking sensitivity and light weight to a new level; comes with an armadillo hide finish that eliminates cut fibers and ensures the blank is free from imperfections.
Price:............................ **$29.95–$29.99**

ACTION	POWER	
M=Moderate	UL=Ultra Light	H=Heavy
MF=Moderate Fast	L=Light	MH=Medium-Heavy
F=Fast	ML=Medium-Light	XH=Extra Heavy
XF=Extra Fast		

BERKLEY CHERRYWOOD HD

Model: CWD461ULS, CWD501ULS, CWD561ULS, CWD562LS, CWD601MS, CWD601MHS, CWD662MLS, CWD661MS, CWD662MS, CWD701MS, CWD702MS, CWD702MHS
Length: 4'6''; 5'; 5'6''; 5'6''; 6'; 6'; 6'6''; 6'6''; 6'6''; 7'; 7'; 7'
Power: UL; UL; UL; L; M; MH; ML; M; M; M; M; MH
Pieces: 1; 1; 1; 2; 1; 1; 2; 1; 2; 1; 2; 2
Line Weight: 1-4 lbs; 1-4 lbs; 2-6 lbs; 2-6 lbs; 6-14 lbs; 8-17 lbs; 4-12 lbs; 6-14 lbs; 6-14 lbs; 6-14 lbs; 6-14 lbs; 8-17 lbs

Guide Count: 4; 4; 5; 5; 5; 5; 6; 6; 6; 6; 6; 6
Lure Weight: 1/32-1/8 oz; 1/32-1/8 oz; 1/32-1/8 oz; 1/16-1/4 oz; 1/8-3/4 oz; 1/4-1 oz; 1/8-5/8 oz; 1/8-3/4 oz; 1/8-3/4 oz; 1/8-3/4 oz; 1/8-3/4 oz; 1/4-1 oz
Features: Graphite technology; remarkable value; offers a balanced graphite composition blank and quality construction for excellent responsiveness and durability; comes with a chromium guide system that is 20 times tougher and up to 55 percent lighter than conventional oxide guides.
Price: **$24.99**

BERKLEY C-SERIES

Model: BCS902L, BCS1002L, BCS1102L, BCS1202L, BCS1403L
Length: 9'; 10'; 11'; 12'; 14'
Power: L
Pieces: 2
Line Weight: 4-12 lbs
Guide Count: 9; 9; 10; 10; 11

Features: Solid carbon fiber tip allows for quick reaction on even the lightest bite; 24-ton carbon fiber blank creates a lightweight and sensitive feeling rod; EVA power grip ergonomically designed for more control and less hand fatigue; durable, high strength-to-weight titanium oxide insert; stainless steel guides; bell-shaped tapered rear handle for secure rod holder placement.
Price: **$44.99**

ACTION	POWER	
M=Moderate	UL=Ultra Light	H=Heavy
MF=Moderate Fast	L=Light	MH=Medium-Heavy
F=Fast	ML=Medium-Light	XH=Extra Heavy
XF=Extra Fast		

BERKLEY GLOWSTIK
Model: GSS702M, GSS802MH, GSS902MH, GSS1002MH
Length: 7'; 8'; 9'; 10'
Power: M; MH; MH; MH
Pieces: 2
Line Weight: 10-20 lbs; 10-25 lbs; 10-30 lbs; 10-30 lbs
Guide Count: 5; 5; 6; 7

Lure Weight: 1/2-3 oz; 1-4 oz; 1-5 oz; 1-5 oz
Features: The right rod for any nighttime fishing adventure; features super strong, super tough E-glass technology, making it nearly indestructible; exclusive lighted blank design can be activated to glow continuously for great night bite detection.
Price: . . . . **$39.95–$49.95**

BERKLEY LIGHTNING ROD–ICE
Model: LR24ULS, LR28MLS, LR28MS, LR32MHS, LR32HS, LR32MHC
Length: 2'; 2'4''; 2'4''; 2'8''; 2'8''; 2'8''
Power: UL; ML; M; MH; H; MH
Pieces: 1
Line Weight: 1-6 lbs; 2-6 lbs; 4-8 lbs; 6-10 lbs; 8-14 lbs
Guide Count: 3; 4; 4; 4; 4; 4

Features: Fore-grip uses hidden thread technology to reduce wear and tear on your fingers; skeleton reel seat provides increased sensitivity and reduces overall weight; guides are 20X tougher and 55 percent lighter than traditional aluminum oxide guides and are factory tested for dependability.
Price: . . . . **$14.99–$19.99**

ACTION	**POWER**	
M=Moderate	UL=Ultra Light	H=Heavy
MF=Moderate Fast	L=Light	MH=Medium-Heavy
F=Fast	ML=Medium-Light	XH=Extra Heavy
XF=Extra Fast		

RODS: Freshwater Spinning

BERKLEY LIGHTNING ROD IM6

Model: LR502ULS, LR562LS, LR601MHS, LR601MLS, LR602MLS, LR601MS, LR662MLS, LR661MS, LR662MS, LR701MS, LR702MS
Length: 5'; 5'6''; 6'; 6'; 6'; 6'; 6'6''; 6'6''; 6'6''; 7'; 7'
Power: UL; L; MH; ML; ML; ML; ML; M; M; M; M
Pieces: 2; 2; 1; 1; 2; 1; 2; 1; 2; 1; 2
Line Weight: 2-6 lbs; 4-8 lbs; 10-17 lbs; 6-12 lbs; 6-12 lbs; 8-14 lbs; 6-12 lbs; 8-14 lbs; 8-14 lbs; 8-14 lbs; 8-14 lbs
Guide Count: 5; 5; 6; 6; 6; 6; 6; 6; 6; 6; 6

Lure Weight: 1/32-1/4 oz; 1/16-3/8 oz; 3/8-3/4 oz; 1/16-1/2 oz; 1/16-1/2 oz; 1/4-5/8 oz; 1/16-1/2 oz; 1/4-5/8 oz; 1/4-5/8 oz; 1/4-5/8 oz; 1/4-5/8 oz
Features: #1 selling graphite rod; unique combination of strength and sensitivity; the fastest, strongest, and lightest rod in its class; features chrome-plated SS304 guides.
Price: **$39.99**

BERKLEY LIGHTNING ROD SHOCK

Model: SHS601M, SHS662ML, SHS661M, SHS701ML, SHS701M, SHS761ML
Length: 6'; 6'6''; 6'6''; 7'; 7'; 7'6''
Power: M; ML; M; ML; M; ML
Pieces: 1; 2; 1; 1; 1; 1
Line Weight: 4-12 lbs; 4-10 lbs; 4-12 lbs; 4-10 lbs; 4-12 lbs; 4-10 lbs
Guide Count: 5
Lure Weight: 1/8-3/4 oz; 1/8-5/8 oz; 1/8-3/4 oz; 1/8-5/8 oz; 1/4-3/4 oz; 1/8-5/8 oz
Features: Near zero-stretch line with plenty of strength in a small diameter; designed specifically for superline fishing; aluminum oxide guides are diamond polished to a rich, black surface for strength, durability, and reduced friction; downsized guides help decrease wind knots while remaining lightweight and tough; strike-amplifying tip blends fiberglass with graphite to produce a slower-reacting tip; split-grip design delivers more sensitivity and better balance with less weight; suspended reel seat dampens reel vibration, ensuring maximum sensitivity; 1K power helix construction produces extra strength in the backbone while remaining light weight, to handle the stress loads inherent to fishing with superline.
Price: . . . . **$49.95–$54.95**

ACTION	POWER	
M=Moderate	UL=Ultra Light	H=Heavy
MF=Moderate Fast	L=Light	MH=Medium-Heavy
F=Fast	ML=Medium-Light	XH=Extra Heavy
XF=Extra Fast		

BERKLEY TROUT DOUGH

Model: TDS461UL, TDS501UL, TDS562UL, TDS602UL, TDS662UL, TDS702UL, TDS702L, TDS762UL, TDS802UL
Length: 4'6''; 5'; 5'6''; 6'; 6'6''; 7'; 7'; 7'6''; 8'
Power: UL; UL; UL; UL; UL; UL; L; UL; UL
Pieces: 1; 1; 2; 2; 2; 2; 2; 2; 2
Line Weight: 1-4 lbs; 1-4 lbs; 1-6 lbs; 1-6 lbs; 1-6 lbs; 1-6 lbs; 2-8 lbs; 1-6 lbs; 1-6 lbs
Guide Count: 5; 6; 7; 7; 8; 8; 8; 9; 10

Lure Weight: 1/32-1/8 oz; 1/32-1/8 oz; 1/32-3/16 oz; 1/32-3/16 oz; 1/32-1/4 oz; 1/32-1/4 oz; 1/16-3/8 oz; 1/32-1/4 oz; 1/32-1/4 oz
Features: Engineered specifically to cast farther and with more accuracy without losing your bait; cork split-grip handle construction helps to reduce overall weight; unidirectional fiberglass technology delivers the strength required to fish for trout without compromising the diameter or weight of the rod.
Price: **$39.99**

CABELA'S FISH EAGLE 50

Model: S583-1, S664-1, S704-1, S706-2, S703-1, S703-2, S601-2, S705-2, S763-1, S663-2, S664-2, S662-2, S663-1, S603-1, S762-2, S705-1, S702-2, S604-1, S665-2, S665-1, S561-2, S704-2
Length: 5'8''; 6'6''; 7'; 7'; 7'; 7'; 6'; 7'; 7'6''; 6'6''; 6'6''; 6'6''; 6'6''; 6'; 7'6''; 7'; 7'; 6'; 6'6''; 6'6''; 5'6''; 7'
Power: ML; M; M; H; ML; ML; UL; MH; ML; ML; M; L; ML; ML; L; MH; L; ML; MH; MH; UL; M
Action: F; F; F; F; F; F; F; F; XF; F; F; F; F; F; F; F; F; F; F; F; F; F
Pieces: 1; 2; 2; 1; 1; 2; 1; 2; 2; 2; 1; 2; 2; 1; 1; 2; 1; 2; 1; 2; 1; 2
Line Weight: 4-8 lbs; 6-12 lbs; 8-12 lbs; 10-25 lbs; 4-10 lbs; 4-10 lbs; 2-6 lbs; 8-20 lbs; 4-10 lbs; 4-10 lbs; 6-12 lbs; 2-8 lbs; 4-10 lbs; 4-10 lbs; 4-10 lbs; 8-20 lbs; 2-8 lbs; 6-12 lbs; 8-20 lbs; 8-20 lbs; 2-6 lbs; 8-12 lbs
Lure Weight: 1/8-3/8 oz; 1/4-5/8 oz; 1/4-3/4 oz; 1/2-1 1/2 oz; 1/8-5/8 oz; 1/8-5/8 oz; 1/32-1/4 oz; 3/8-1 oz; 1/8-5/8 oz; 1/8-5/8 oz; 1/4-5/8 oz; 1/16-3/8 oz; 1/8-5/8 oz; 1/8-5/8 oz; 1/8-1/2 oz; 3/8-1 oz; 1/16-3/8 oz; 1/4-5/8 oz; 3/8-1 oz; 3/8-1 oz; 1/32-1/4 oz; 1/4-3/4 oz
Features: High-quality HM50 graphite, 50 million-PSI modulus blanks; Pacific Bay stainless steel guide frames with durable wear-resistant Hialoy ceramic inserts, to reduce line friction for consistently longer casts and smoother retrieves; down-locking fore grips for flawless security, eliminating exposed reel seat threads; cork grips with rubberized accents for a better grasp; pearl gray-green color has a matte finish.
Price: **$89.99**

ACTION	POWER	
M=Moderate	UL=Ultra Light	H=Heavy
MF=Moderate Fast	L=Light	MH=Medium-Heavy
F=Fast	ML=Medium-Light	XH=Extra Heavy
XF=Extra Fast		

CABELA'S FISH EAGLE 50 TRAVEL
Model: FE50S704-4
Length: 7'
Power: M
Action: F
Pieces: 4
Line Weight: 8-12 lbs
Lure Weight: 1/4-3/4 oz
Features: High-quality HM50 graphite, 50 million-PSI modulus blanks; Pacific Bay stainless steel guide frames with durable wear-resistant Hialoy ceramic inserts, to reduce line friction for consistently longer casts and smoother retrieves; down-locking fore grips for flawless security, eliminating exposed reel seat threads; cork grips with rubberized accents for a better grasp; pearl gray-green color has a matte finish; travel rods break down into four pieces for easy portability (case sold separately).
Price: **$99.99**

CABELA'S KING KAT
Model: CKKS702, CKKS802, CKKS102, CKKS602-M, CKKS662-M
Length: 7'; 8'; 10'; 6'; 6'6''
Power: MH; MH; MH; M; M
Pieces: 2
Line Weight: 12-25 lbs; 14-30 lbs; 14-30 lbs; 6-15 lbs; 6-15 lbs

Features: This rod stands up to the long fights big flatheads and blues are known for; constructed from ultratough E-glass; bright tip to help you detect nighttime bites; rugged double-foot ceramic guides and stainless steel hoods on the reel seats add to the performance and durability of our King Kat rods; sure-grip EVA handles offer no-slip confidence during long fights in bad weather.
Price: **$29.99**

ACTION	POWER	
M=Moderate	UL=Ultra Light	H=Heavy
MF=Moderate Fast	L=Light	MH=Medium-Heavy
F=Fast	ML=Medium-Light	XH=Extra Heavy
XF=Extra Fast		

CABELA'S PLATINUM ZX

Model: PZXS663-1, PZXS663-2, PZXS664-1, PZXS664-2, PZXS693-1, PZXS702-2, PZXS703-1, PZXS703-2, PZXS704-1, PZXS704-2, PZXS705-2, PZXS763-2
Length: 6'6''; 6'6''; 6'6''; 6'6''; 6'9''; 7'; 7'; 7'; 7'; 7'; 7'; 7'6''
Power: ML; ML; M; M; M; L; ML; ML; M; M; MH; ML
Action: F
Pieces: 1; 2; 1; 2; 1; 2; 1; 2; 1; 2; 2; 2

Line Weight: 4-8 lbs; 4-8 lbs; 6-12 lbs; 6-12 lbs; 6-12 lbs; 2-8 lbs; 4-8 lbs; 4-8 lbs; 6-12 lbs; 6-12 lbs; 8-20 lbs; 4-8 lbs
Lure Weight: 1/8-3/8 oz; 1/8-3/8 oz; 1/4-5/8 oz; 1/4-5/8 oz; 1/4-5/8 oz; 1/16-3/8 oz; 1/8-3/8 oz; 1/8-3/8 oz; 1/4-5/8 oz; 1/4-5/8 oz; 3/8-1 oz; 1/8-3/8 oz
Features: 3M Powerlux matrix resin; Fuji's tangle-eliminating K-Series guides; up to 30 percent stronger and 15 percent lighter; diamond-polished SiC inserts; palm-swell seats.
Price: **$199.99**

CABELA'S PRO GUIDE

Model: PGS501-1, PGS604-1, PGS604-2, PGS664-1, PGS664-2, PGS704-2, PGS593-1, PGS663-1, PGS663-2, PGS703-1, PGS703-2
Length: 5'; 6'; 6'; 6'6''; 6'6''; 7'; 5'9''; 6'6''; 6'6''; 7'; 7'
Power: UL; M; M; M; M; M; ML; ML; ML; ML; ML
Pieces: 1; 1; 2; 1; 2; 2; 1; 1; 2; 1; 2
Line Weight: 2-6 lbs; 6-12 lbs; 6-12 lbs; 6-12 lbs; 6-12 lbs; 8-12 lbs; 4-8 lbs; 4-10 lbs; 4-10 lbs; 4-10 lbs; 4-10 lbs

Lure Weight: 1/16-3/8 oz; 1/4-5/8 oz; 1/4-5/8 oz; 1/4-5/8 oz; 1/4-5/8 oz; 1/4-3/4 oz; 1/8-3/8 oz; 1/8-1/2 oz; 1/8-1/2 oz; 1/8-5/8 oz; 1/8-5/8 oz
Features: Fast-action tips for precise casting and rapid hooksets; graphite reel seats with padded hoods; field-tested IM6 graphite blanks; Portuguese cork handles; aluminum-oxide guide inserts.
Price: **$44.99**

ACTION	POWER	
M=Moderate	UL=Ultra Light	H=Heavy
MF=Moderate Fast	L=Light	MH=Medium-Heavy
F=Fast	ML=Medium-Light	XH=Extra Heavy
XF=Extra Fast		

CABELA'S WHUPPIN' STICK

Model: WSSM60-2, WSSH72-2, WSSH80-2, WSSM10-2, WSSL56-2, WSSMH60-1, WSSMH90-2, WSSM90-2, WSSM66-2, WSSM80-2, WSSM70-2, WSSML66-2
Length: 6'; 7'2''; 8'; 10'; 5'6''; 6'; 9'; 9'; 6'6''; 8'; 7'; 6'6''
Power: M; H; H; M; L; MH; MH; M; M; M; M; M
Pieces: 2; 2; 2; 2; 2; 1; 2; 2; 2; 2; 2; 2
Line Weight: 6-15 lbs; 12-50 lbs; 14-50 lbs; 4-20 lbs; 4-10 lbs; 6-15 lbs; 14-30 lbs; 4-20 lbs; 6-15 lbs; 4-20 lbs; 6-15 lbs; 4-12 lbs

Features: This rod is known for its nearly indestructible, advanced polymer fiberglass blanks; graphite reel seats securely lock reel in place without adding significant weight to the rod; blank-through-handle construction makes it easy to feel even the light biters; stainless steel frame guides with ceramic inserts will stand up to the toughest fish; cork grips ensure all-day comfort.
Price:. . . . . **$24.99–$29.99**

CABELA'S XML TRAVEL

Model: XMLS603-4, XMLS665XF-4, XMLS663-4, XMLS703-4, XMLS704-4
Length: 6'; 6'6''; 6'6''; 7'; 7'
Power: ML; M; ML; ML; M
Action: F; XF; F; F; F
Pieces: 4
Line Weight: 4-8 lbs; 6-12 lbs; 4-8 lbs; 4-8 lbs; 6-12 lbs
Lure Weight: 1/8-3/8 oz; 1/4-5/8 oz; 1/8-3/8 oz; 1/8-3/8 oz; 1/4-5/8 oz

Features: Four-piece rods are built on the legendary XML 64 million-modulus, spiral-core-technology graphite blanks; features lightweight, super-durable stainless steel Alps guides, double-coated with black chrome for maximum corrosion resistance; concept spacing increases sensitivity while decreasing line drag; palm-swell Aero reels seats; premium cork grips and thread-covering downlocking fore grips; butts are compatible with the XML weight-balance system (sold separately); Cordura nylon case and nylon storage sleeve included.
Price:. **$159.99**

ACTION	POWER	
M=Moderate	UL=Ultra Light	H=Heavy
MF=Moderate Fast	L=Light	MH=Medium-Heavy
F=Fast	ML=Medium-Light	XH=Extra Heavy
XF=Extra Fast		

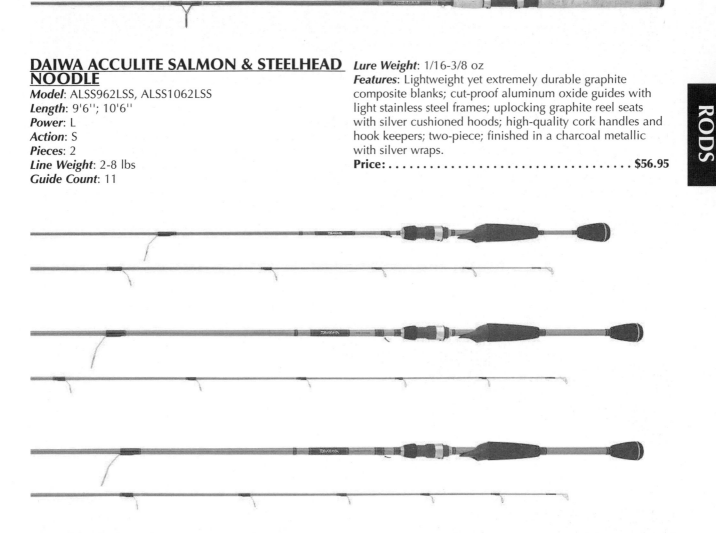

DAIWA ACCULITE SALMON & STEELHEAD NOODLE

Model: ALSS962LSS, ALSS1062LSS
Length: 9'6''; 10'6''
Power: L
Action: S
Pieces: 2
Line Weight: 2-8 lbs
Guide Count: 11

Lure Weight: 1/16-3/8 oz
Features: Lightweight yet extremely durable graphite composite blanks; cut-proof aluminum oxide guides with light stainless steel frames; uplocking graphite reel seats with silver cushioned hoods; high-quality cork handles and hook keepers; two-piece; finished in a charcoal metallic with silver wraps.
Price: **$56.95**

DAIWA AIRD

Model: AIRD562ULFS, AIRD602MXS, AIRD661MHXS, AIRD662MXS, AIRD701MXS
Length: 5'6''; 6'; 6'6''; 6'6''; 7'
Power: UL; M; MH; M; M
Action: F; XF; XF; XF; XF
Pieces: 2; 2; 1; 2; 1
Line Weight: 1-4 lbs; 4-10 lbs; 8-17 lbs; 6-15 lbs; 6-15 lbs
Guide Count: 6; 7; 8; 8; 8

Lure Weight: 1/32-1/2 oz; 1/8-1/2 oz; 1/4-1 oz; 1/4-3/4 oz; 1/4-3/4 oz
Features: IM6 graphite blank; minimized, direct contact reel seat for reduced weight and greater sensitivity with stainles steel hood; lightweight split-grip design with non-slip, high-density EVA foam; stainless steel guides; folding hook keeper.
Price: . . . . **$44.95–$54.95**

ACTION	POWER	
M=Moderate	UL=Ultra Light	H=Heavy
MF=Moderate Fast	L=Light	MH=Medium-Heavy
F=Fast	ML=Medium-Light	XH=Extra Heavy
XF=Extra Fast		

DAIWA CIELO BASS
Model: CEL6101MLXS, CEL711MFS, CEL721MLFS, CEL731MHFS
Length: 6'10"; 7'1"; 7'2"; 7'3"
Power: ML; M; ML; MH
Action: XF; F; F; F
Pieces: 1
Line Weight: 4-12 lbs; 6-14 lbs; 4-12 lbs; 8-17 lbs
Guide Count: 8

Lure Weight: 1/16-3/8 oz; 1/8-3/4 oz; 1/16-3/8 oz; 1/4-3/4 oz
Features: 3D cross reinforced Bias Graphite or GlaTech construction; unsanded blank with micro pitch taping pattern; Fuji skeleton pipe reel seat for lighter weight and greater sensitivity; machined aluminum reel clamp with graphite insert; Minima black ring guides; 20 percent to 30 percent lighter than ceramics split-grip design with natural cork and EVA foam; hook keeper; five-year limited warranty.
Price:............................$129.95–$139.95

ACTION	POWER	
M=Moderate	UL=Ultra Light	H=Heavy
MF=Moderate Fast	L=Light	MH=Medium-Heavy
F=Fast	ML=Medium-Light	XH=Extra Heavy
XF=Extra Fast		

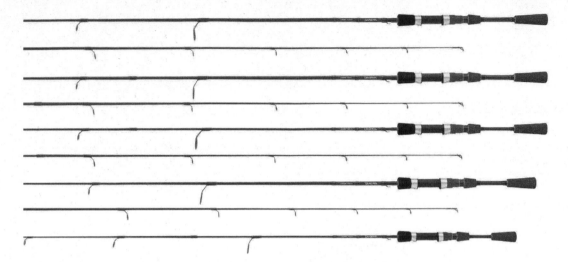

DAIWA LAGUNA

Model: LAG601MFS, LAG661MLXS, LAG661MFS, LAG661MXS, LAG662MFS, LAG701MLXSM, LAG701MXS, LAG701MHFS, LAG702MFS, LAG761MXS, LAG562ULFS, LAG602ULFS, LAG662ULFS, LAG702ULFS
Length: 6'; 6'6''; 6'6''; 6'6''; 6'6''; 7'; 7'; 7'; 7'; 7'6''; 5'6''; 6'; 6'6''; 7'
Power: M; ML; M; M; M; ML; M; MH; M; M; UL; UL; UL; UL
Action: F; XF; F; XF; F; XF; XF; F; F; XF; F; F; F; F
Pieces: 1; 1; 1; 1; 2; 1; 1; 1; 2; 1; 2; 2; 2; 2
Line Weight: 6-15 lbs; 4-12 lbs; 6-15 lbs; 6-15 lbs; 6-15 lbs; 4-12 lbs; 6-15 lbs; 8-17 lbs; 6-15 lbs; 6-15 lbs; 1-4 lbs; 1-4 lbs; 1-4 lbs; 1-4 lbs

Guide Count: 7; 7; 7; 7; 7; 7; 7; 7; 7; 8; 6; 7; 7; 7
Lure Weight: 1/8-3/4 oz; 1/8-1/2 oz; 1/8-3/4 oz; 1/8-3/4 oz; 1/8-3/4 oz; 1/8-1/2 oz; 1/8-3/4 oz; 1/4-3/4 oz; 1/8-3/4 oz; 1/8-3/4 oz; 1/32-1/8 oz; 1/32-1/8 oz; 1/32-1/8 oz; 1/32-1/8 oz
Features: IM6 graphite with woven carbon construction; stainless steel hooded reel seat; aluminum oxide guides; lightweight, split-foam grip; strong, blank-through-handle construction; convenient hook keeper.
Price:. **$39.99**

ACTION	POWER	
M=Moderate	UL=Ultra Light	H=Heavy
MF=Moderate Fast	L=Light	MH=Medium-Heavy
F=Fast	ML=Medium-Light	XH=Extra Heavy
XF=Extra Fast		

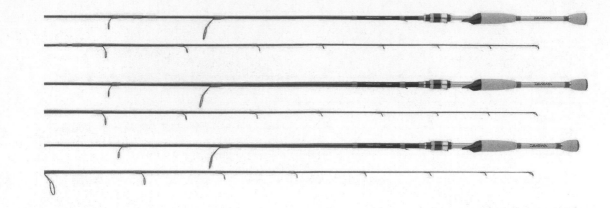

DAIWA PROCYON

Model: PRCN661MLXS, PRCN701MLXS, PRCN601MXS, PRCN661MXS, PRCN701MXS, PRCN661MHXS, PRCN701MHXS, PRCN662MFS, PRCN602MHFS, PRCN702MHFS
Length: 6'6"; 7'; 6'; 6'6"; 7'; 6'6"; 7'; 6'6"; 6'; 7'
Power: ML; ML; M; M; M; MH; MH; M; MH; MH
Action: XF; XF; XF; XF; XF; XF; XF; F; F; F
Pieces: 1; 1; 1; 1; 1; 1; 1; 2; 2; 2
Line Weight: 4-12 lbs; 4-12 lbs; 6-15 lbs; 6-15 lbs; 6-15 lbs; 8-17 lbs; 8-17 lbs; 8-17 lbs; 6-14 lbs; 8-17 lbs

Guide Count: 8; 9; 7; 8; 9; 9; 9; 7; 8; 9
Lure Weight: 1/8-1/2 oz; 1/8-1/2 oz; 1/4-3/4 oz; 1/4-3/4 oz; 1/4-3/4 oz; 1/4-1 oz; 1/4-1 oz; 1/4-1 oz; 1/8-3/4 oz; 1/4-1 oz
Features: IM7 graphite construction; micro pitch blank taping; Minima reel seat with machined clamp nut; woven graphite insert; Minima black ring guides; lightweight split-grip cork handles; hook keeper; five-year limited warranty.
Price: . . . . **$59.95–$69.95**

ACTION		**POWER**	
M=Moderate	UL=Ultra Light		H=Heavy
MF=Moderate Fast	L=Light		MH=Medium-Heavy
F=Fast	ML=Medium-Light		XH=Extra Heavy
XF=Extra Fast			

DAIWA TRIFORCE-E

Model: TFE562ULFS, TFE562LFS, TFE602ULFS, TFE602LFS, TFE602MFS, TFE662MFS, TFE702MFS, TFE501ULFS, TFE601MFS, TFE661MFS, TFE661MHFS, TFE701MFS

Length: 5'6''; 5'6''; 6'; 6'; 6'; 6'6''; 7'; 5'; 6'; 6'6''; 6'6''; 7'

Power: UL; L; UL; L; M; M; M; UL; M; M; MH; M

Action: F

Pieces: 2; 2; 2; 2; 2; 2; 2; 1; 1; 1; 1; 1

Line Weight: 1-4 lbs; 2-6 lbs; 1-4 lbs; 2-6 lbs; 6-14 lbs; 6-14 lbs; 6-14 lbs; 1-4 lbs; 6-14 lbs; 6-14 lbs; 8-17 lbs; 8-17 lbs

Guide Count: 6; 6; 7; 7; 7; 7; 7; 6; 7; 7; 7; 7

Lure Weight: 1/32-1/8 oz; 1/16-3/8 oz; 1/32-1/8 oz; 1/16-3/8 oz; 1/8-3/4 oz; 1/8-3/4 oz; 1/8-3/4 oz; 1/32-1/8 oz; 1/8-3/4 oz; 1/8-3/4 oz; 1/4-1 oz; 1/4-3/4 oz

Features: High-quality graphite blank; strong, blank-through-handle construction; cut-proof aluminum oxide guides; custom thread wrap with durable multi-coat finish; protective foam butt cap and grip check.

Price: **$29.95**

ACTION		POWER	
M=Moderate	UL=Ultra Light	H=Heavy	
MF=Moderate Fast	L=Light	MH=Medium-Heavy	
F=Fast	ML=Medium-Light	XH=Extra Heavy	
XF=Extra Fast			

RODS: Freshwater Spinning

FENWICK AETOS ICE
Model: AICE18LXFS, AICE21LXFS, AICE25MXFS, AICE25ULXFS, AICE28MLXFS, AICE29MXFTS, AICE30MHXFS
Length: 18''; 21''; 25''; 25''; 28''; 28''; 30''
Power: L; L; M; UL; ML; M; MH
Action: XF
Pieces: 1

Line Weight: 2-4 lbs; 2-4 lbs; 4-8 lbs; 2-4 lbs; 2-6 lbs; 4-8 lbs; 6-10 lbs
Guide Count: 4; 4; 5; 5; 6; 6; 6
Features: High-modulus solid graphite blanks; hidden handle design reel seats with carbon fiber hoods; combination of TAC and cork handle construction; stainless steel guides with stainless steel inserts.
Price:. **$49.95**

FENWICK ELITETECH WALLEYE
Model: EWS63M-XF, EWS66M-F, EWS66ML-F, EWS69ML-F, EWS72M-F, EWS72ML-F, EWS592MH-MF, EWS662M-F, EWS692MH-MF, EWS722M-F
Length: 6'3''; 6'6''; 6'6''; 6'9''; 7'2''; 7'2''; 5'9''; 6'6''; 6'9''; 7'2''
Power: M; M; ML; ML; M; ML; MH; M; MH; M
Action: XF; F; F; F; F; F; MF; F; MF; F
Pieces: 1; 1; 1; 1; 1; 1; 1; 2; 2; 2
Line Weight: 4-12 lbs; 4-12 lbs; 4-10 lbs; 4-10 lbs; 4-12 lbs; 4-10 lbs; 6-12 lbs; 4-10 lbs; 6-12 lbs; 4-10 lbs
Guide Count: 8; 8; 8; 10; 10; 10; 8; 8; 10; 10

Lure Weight: 1/8-3/4 oz; 1/8-3/4 oz; 1/8-5/8 oz; 1/8-5/8 oz; 1/8-3/4 oz; 1/8-5/8 oz; 1/8-1 oz; 1/8-3/4 oz; 1/8-1 oz; 1/8-3/4 oz
Features: Fuji Alconite guides and Fuji reel seat TAC handles provide increased grip in all fishing conditions, are more durable than cork, and provide enhanced grip when wet; FDS graphite-crafted from multi-laminate lay-up for lightweight strength and increased sensitivity; tips soft enough to cast your ultra-light jigs or feel the lightest tap when you go vertical.
Price:. **$149.95**

ACTION	POWER	
M=Moderate	UL=Ultra Light	H=Heavy
MF=Moderate Fast	L=Light	MH=Medium-Heavy
F=Fast	ML=Medium-Light	XH=Extra Heavy
XF=Extra Fast		

FENWICK HMG

Model: HMG60L-MS-2, HMG60M-FS, HMG60M-FS-2, HMG60ML-FS, HMG66L-MFS-2, HMG66M-FS, HMG66M-FS-2, HMG66MH-FS, HMG69ML-FS, HMG69ML-FS-2, HMG70M-FS, HMG70M-FS-2, HMG70MH-FS, HMG70ML-FS, HMG70UL-MS-2, HMG76L-MS-2, HMG76ML-FS
Length: 6'; 6'; 6'; 6'; 6'6''; 6'6''; 6'6''; 6'6''; 6'9''; 6'9''; 7'; 7'; 7'; 7'; 7'; 7'6''; 7'6''
Power: L; M; M; ML; L; M; M; MH; ML; ML; M; M; MH; ML; UL; L; ML
Action: M; F; F; F; MF; F; F; F; F; F; F; F; F; F; M; M; F
Pieces: 2; 1; 2; 1; 2; 1; 2; 1; 1; 2; 1; 2; 1; 1; 2; 2; 1
Line Weight: 4-8 lbs; 8-14 lbs; 8-14 lbs; 6-12 lbs; 4-8 lbs; 8-14 lbs; 8-14 lbs; 10-17 lbs; 6-12 lbs; 6-12 lbs; 8-14 lbs; 8-14 lbs; 10-17 lbs; 6-12 lbs; 2-6 lbs; 4-8 lbs; 6-12 lbs

Guide Count: 7; 7; 7; 7; 8; 8; 8; 8; 8; 8; 9; 9; 9; 9; 9; 9; 9
Lure Weight: 1/16-3/8 oz; 1/4-3/4 oz; 1/4-3/4 oz; 1/8-5/8 oz; 1/16-3/8 oz; 1/4-3/4 oz; 1/4-3/4 oz; 3/8-1 oz; 1/8-5/8 oz; 1/8-5/8 oz; 1/4-3/4 oz; 1/4-3/4 oz; 3/8-1 oz; 1/8-5/8 oz; 1/32-1/4 oz; 1/16-3/8 oz; 1/8-5/8 oz
Features: Blanks spiraled with carbon thread creating unparalleled strength and precise action; sculpted TAC and EVA-blended handle combine for a feeling of outstanding control, while keeping weight to an absolute minimum; deep pressed titanium guides help eliminate insert pop-out and are virtually bullet proof; soft-touch Fuji reel sat designs.
Price:. **$99.95**

LEW'S LASER LG GRAPHITE

Model: LGA56ULFS, LGA56LFS, LGA60MLFS, LGA60MFS, LGA66MFS, LGA66MHFS, LGA70MLFS, LGA70MFS
Length: 5'6''; 5'6''; 6'; 6'; 6'6''; 6'6''; 7'; 7'
Power: UL; L; ML; M; M; MH; ML; M
Action: F
Pieces: 1
Line Weight: 1-6 lbs; 2-8 lbs; 4-10 lbs; 4-12 lbs; 4-12 lbs; 6-17 lbs; 4-10 lbs; 4-12 lbs
Guide Count: 7; 7; 7; 7; 8; 8; 9; 9
Lure Weight: 1/32-1/4 oz; 1/16-1/2 oz; 1/16-5/16 oz; 1/8-3/8 oz; 1/8-1/2 oz; 1/4-5/8 oz; 1/16-5/16 oz; 1/8-1/2 oz

Features: Premium IM6 graphite blank; multi layer, multidirectional graphite one-piece blanks reinforced with premium resins; Lew's proprietary advanced performance technology blank construction; black-coated stainless steel frame with titanium oxide guide rings; lightweight graphite reel seat with cushioned stainless steel hoods; great hand/reel stability and comfort; exposed blank for instant vibration transmission on casting models; natural cork split-grip handles offer reduced weight without compromising rod control; limited one-year warranty.
Price:. **$49.99**

ACTION	POWER	
M=Moderate	UL=Ultra Light	H=Heavy
MF=Moderate Fast	L=Light	MH=Medium-Heavy
F=Fast	ML=Medium-Light	XH=Extra Heavy
XF=Extra Fast		

LEW'S TOURNAMENT SL MICRO GUIDE

Model: TS66MFS, TS66MHFS, TS70MLFS, TS70MFS
Length: 6'6''; 6'6''; 7'; 7'
Power: M; MH; ML; M
Action: F
Pieces: 1
Line Weight: 6-12 lbs; 8-14 lbs; 6-14 lbs; 8-14 lbs
Guide Count: 9
Lure Weight: 3/16-5/8 oz; 3/16-3/4 oz; 1/8-5/8 oz; 1/4-5/8 oz
Features: Premium HM60 graphite blanks; multilayer, multidirectional 60 million-modulus graphite blank reinforced with premium resins; Lew's proprietary advanced performance technology blank construction; black-coated stainless steel frames with hard aluminum oxide micro guides, which reduce rod weight, enhance casting distance, and increase sensitivity; lightweight skeletal graphite reel seats with cushioned black stainless steel hoods; great hand/reel stability and comfort; exposed blank for instant vibration transmission; high-density EVA foam split-grip handles reduce weight without sacrificing control; limited lifetime warranty.
Price: **$119.99**

G LOOMIS CLASSIC SPIN JIG

Model: SJR 6400 IMX, SJR 642 IMX, SJR 700 GL3, SJR 720 IMX, SJR 721 GLX, SJR 721 IMX, SJR 721 GL3, SJR 722 GLX, SJR 722 IMX, SJR 722 GL3, SJR 723 IMX, SJR 724 IMX, SJR 781 IMX, SJR 782 GLX, SJR 782 IMX, SJR 782 GL3, SJR 783 GLX, SJR 783 IMX, SJR 783 GL3, SJR 783-2 GLX, SJR 783-2 GL3, SJR 842 GL3, SJR 843 IMX, SJR 843 GL3, SJR 844 IMX, SJR 902 IMX
Length: 5'4''; 5'4''; 5'10''; 6'; 6'; 6'; 6'; 6'; 6'; 6'; 6'; 6'; 6'6''; 6'6''; 6'6''; 6'6''; 6'6''; 6'6''; 6'6''; 6'6''; 6'6''; 7'; 7'; 7'; 7'; 7'6''
Power: ML; M; ML; ML; L; L; L; M; M; M; MH; H; L; M; M; M; MH; MH; MH; MH; MH; M; MH; MH; H; M
Action: XF; F; XF; XF; F; F; F; F; F; F; F; F; F; F; F; F; F; F; F; F; F; F; F; F; F; F
Pieces: 1; 1; 1; 1; 1; 1; 1; 1; 1; 1; 1; 1; 1; 1; 1; 1; 1; 1; 1; 1; 2; 2; 1; 1; 1; 1; 1
Line Weight: 2-6 lbs; 6-12 lbs; 4-8 lbs; 4-8 lbs; 6-10 lbs; 6-10 lbs; 6-10 lbs; 6-12 lbs; 6-12 lbs; 6-12 lbs; 8-15 lbs; 10-17 lbs; 6-10 lbs; 6-12 lbs; 6-12 lbs; 6-12 lbs; 8-15 lbs; 8-15 lbs; 8-15 lbs; 8-15 lbs; 8-15 lbs; 6-12 lbs; 8-15 lbs; 8-15 lbs; 10-17 lbs; 8-17 lbs
Lure Weight: 1/64-1/8 oz; 1/8-3/8 oz; 1/32-1/4 oz; 1/32-1/4 oz; 1/16-5/16 oz; 1/16-5/16 oz; 1/16-5/16 oz; 1/8-3/8 oz; 1/8-3/8 oz; 1/8-3/8 oz; 3/16-5/8 oz; 1/4-1 oz; 1/16-5/16 oz; 1/8-3/8 oz; 1/8-3/8 oz; 1/8-3/8 oz; 3/16-5/8 oz; 3/16-5/8 oz; 3/16-5/8 oz; 3/16-5/8 oz; 3/16-5/8 oz; 1/8-3/8 oz; 3/16-3/4 oz; 1/4-1 oz; 1/4-5/8 oz
Features: These are special, fast-action rods designed to give warm-water spin fishermen the power and performance of a casting rod in a spinning configuration; rated for slightly lighter line because spinning reels traditionally don't handle heavier line as well as a casting reel, even with oversized guides; originally developed for fishing soft plastics for bass, but have since been discovered by walleye anglers for vertical jigging as well as grubs and light bottom-bounce rigs; many of these rods are suitable for light saltwater use; light, sensitive, and extremely accurate; the more popular models are available in GLX, IMX, and GL3.
Price: . . . .**$210.00–$450.00**

ACTION		POWER	
M=Moderate	UL=Ultra Light	H=Heavy	
MF=Moderate Fast	L=Light	MH=Medium-Heavy	
F=Fast	ML=Medium-Light	XH=Extra Heavy	
XF=Extra Fast			

G LOOMIS GL2 JIG & WORM
Model: GL2 802S JWR, GL2 803S JWR, GL2 804S JWR, GL2 852S JWR, GL2 853S JWR, GL2 854S JWR
Length: 6'8''; 6'8''; 6'8''; 7'1''; 7'1''; 7'1''
Power: MW; MH; H; M; MH; H
Action: XF
Pieces: 1
Line Weight: 6-12 lbs; 8-14 lbs; 12-20 lbs; 6-12 lbs; 8-14 lbs; 12-20 lbs

Lure Weight: 1/8-3/8 oz; 3/16-5/8 oz; 5/16-3/4 oz; 1/8-3/8 oz; 3/16-5/8 oz; 5/16-3/4 oz
Features: These rods are most effective for really big bass; nice tip to give smooth, accurate casts and a powerful butt-section to help set the hook and land the fish; handles feature split grips; uniquely comfortable reel seat; Fuji concept guides.
Price: . . . .**$200.00–$205.00**

G LOOMIS GLX JIG & WORM
Model: GLX 722S JWR, GLX 782S JWR, GLX 783S JWR, GLX 801S JWR, GLX 802S JWR, GLX 803S JWR, GLX 852S JWR, GLX 853S JWR, GLX 902S JWR
Length: 6'; 6'6''; 6'6''; 6'8''; 6'8''; 6'8''; 7'1''; 7'1''; 7'6''
Power: M; M; MH; ML; M; MH; M; MH; M
Action: F; F; F; XF; XF; XF; XF; XF; F
Pieces: 1
Line Weight: 6-12 lbs; 6-12 lbs; 8-14 lbs; 6-10 lbs; 6-12 lbs; 8-14 lbs; 6-12 lbs; 8-14 lbs; 6-12 lbs

Lure Weight: 1/8-3/8 oz; 1/8-3/8 oz; 3/16-5/8 oz; 1/16-3/16 oz; 1/8-3/8 oz; 3/16-5/8 oz; 1/8-3/8 oz; 3/16-5/8 oz; 1/8-3/8 oz
Features: Designed specifically for fishing jigs and soft plastics; feature a split-grip handle with our unique cork comfort grip; Fuji titanium SIC guides and tip-top; legendary for their sensitivity; extra-fast actions, allowing accurate, low trajectory casts with plenty of power to handle even the biggest bass; made with a gorgeous dark green blank.
Price: . . . .**$410.00–$450.00**

ACTION	POWER	
M=Moderate	UL=Ultra Light	H=Heavy
MF=Moderate Fast	L=Light	MH=Medium-Heavy
F=Fast	ML=Medium-Light	XH=Extra Heavy
XF=Extra Fast		

RODS: **Freshwater Spinning**

G LOOMIS NRX JIG & WORM

Model: NRX 802S JWR, NRX 802S JWR G, NRX 803S JWR, NRX 803S JWR G, NRX 852S JWR, NRX 852S JWR G, NRX 872S JWR, NRX 872S JWR G, NRX 901S JWR, NRX 901S JWR G, NWR 902S JWR, NRX 902S JWR G
Length: 6'8''; 6'8''; 6'8''; 6'8''; 7'1''; 7'1''; 7'3''; 7'3''; 7'6''; 7'6''; 7'6''; 7'6''
Power: M; M; MH; MH; M; M; M; M; ML; ML; M; M
Action: XF; XF; XF; XF; XF; XF; XF; XF; F; F; F; F
Pieces: 1
Line Weight: 6-10 lbs; 6-10 lbs; 8-14 lbs; 8-14 lbs; 6-12 lbs; 6-12 lbs; 6-12 lbs; 6-12 lbs; 4-10 lbs; 4-10 lbs; 6-12 lbs; 6-12 lbs

Lure Weight: 1/8-1/4 oz; 1/8-1/4 oz; 1/8-5/16 oz; 1/8-5/16 oz; 1/8-3/8 oz; 1/8-3/8 oz; 1/8-3/8 oz; 1/8-3/8 oz; 1/16-5/16 oz; 1/16-5/16 oz; 1/8-3/8 oz; 1/8-3/8 oz
Features: Designed specifically for fishing jigs and soft plastics; insanely light, unbelievably sensitive, and strong; feature split-grip cork handles; Fuji titanium SIC stripper guides, with the ultra-lite, ultra-strong RECOIL guides the rest of the way.
Price:.............................$500.00–$575.00

OKUMA C3-40X

Model: C3x-S-6101L, C3x-S-661M, C3x-S-661MH, C3x-S-691ML, C3x-S-701M, C3x-S-701MH, C3x-S-701ML, C3x-S-741ML, C3x-S-761M
Length: 6'10''; 6'10''; 6'6''; 6'6''; 6'9''; 7'; 7'; 7'; 7'4''; 7'6''
Power: L; MH; M; MH; ML; M; MH; ML; ML; M
Action: F
Pieces: 1
Line Weight: 4-8 lbs; 6-14 lbs; 8-17 lbs; 10-20 lbs; 6-10 lbs; 8-17 lbs; 10-20 lbs; 6-12 lbs; 6-12 lbs; 8-17 lbs
Guide Count: 8; 8; 7; 7; 8; 8; 8; 8; 8; 9
Lure Weight: 3/8-3/4 oz; 3-12 oz; 1/8-3/8 oz; 1/16-5/8 oz; 1/4-5/8 oz; 1/4-5/8 oz; 1/4-1 oz; 1/8-3/8 oz; 1/8-3/8 oz; 3/8-3/4 oz

Features: 40-ton carbon, ultra-sensitive blank construction; custom 1K woven carbon cone grip configuration; customized ported Fuji reel seats for reduced weight; ultra-hard zirconium guide inserts for braided line; titanium guide frames on all spinning models; titanium guide frames on all double foot casting guides; ALPS low profile frames on all single foot casting guides; split-grip butt for reduced weight and improved balance; C3 rods are backed by a limited lifetime warranty.
Price:............................$154.99–$174.99

ACTION		POWER	
M=Moderate	UL=Ultra Light		H=Heavy
MF=Moderate Fast	L=Light		MH=Medium-Heavy
F=Fast	ML=Medium-Light		XH=Extra Heavy
XF=Extra Fast			

OKUMA CITRIX

Model: Ci-S-661M, Ci-S-661MH, Ci-S-661ML, Ci-S-662M, Ci-S-691ML, Ci-S-701M, Ci-S-701MH
Length: 6'6''; 6'6''; 6'6''; 6'6''; 6'9''; 7'; 7
Power: M; MH; ML; M; ML; M; MH
Action: F
Pieces: 1; 1; 1; 2; 1; 1; 1
Line Weight: 8-17 lbs; 10-20 lbs; 6-12 lbs; 8-17 lbs; 6-10 lbs; 8-17 lbs; 10-20 lbs
Guide Count: 8

Lure Weight: 1/4-1 oz; 1/8-3/8 oz; 1/4-5/8 oz; 1/8-1/2 oz; 1/4-5/8 oz; 1/4-1 oz
Features: IM8 graphite blank construction; lightweight EVA split grips for reduced weight; zero foregrip design for improved balance and weight reduction; ALPS stainless steel guide frames; zirconium line guide inserts for use with braid or mono lines; Pacific Bay Minima reel seat for reduced weight; custom anodized aluminum reel seat threads for strength and balance; stainless steel hook keeper; citrix rods are backed by a limited lifetime warranty.
Price:. **$119.99**

OKUMA CRAPPIE HIGH PERFORMANCE

Model: CHP-S-501L, CHP-S-561L, CHP-S-601L, CHP-S-661L
Length: 5'; 5'6''; 6'; 6'6''
Power: L
Action: M
Pieces: 1
Line Weight: 4-8 lbs
Guide Count: 6; 6; 7; 7

Lure Weight: 1/16-5/16 oz
Features: Premium IM8 graphite rod blanks; crappie-specific rod actions; low-profile stainless steel guide frames; split-grip butt design reduces weight and improves balance; premium cork fore and rear grips; custom skeleton reel seat design on spinning models; one-year limited warranty.
Price:. **$64.99**

ACTION	POWER	
M=Moderate	UL=Ultra Light	H=Heavy
MF=Moderate Fast	L=Light	MH=Medium-Heavy
F=Fast	ML=Medium-Light	XH=Extra Heavy
XF=Extra Fast		

OKUMA HELIOS

Model: HS-CM-701H, HS-CM-701M, HS-CM-701MH, HS-CM-761H, HS-CM-761XH, HS-SKR-701M, HS-SKR-701MH, HS-SKR-701ML
Length: 7'; 7'; 7'; 7'6"; 7'6"; 7'; 7'; 7'
Power: H; M; MH; H; XH; M; MH; ML
Action: F
Pieces: 1
Line Weight: 12-25 lbs; 8-17 lbs; 10-20 lbs; 12-25 lbs; 15-30 lbs; 8-17 lbs; 10-20 lbs; 6-10 lbs
Guide Count: 10; 10; 10; 11; 11; 8; 8; 8
Lure Weight: 3/8-1 1/4 oz; 1/4-5/8 oz; 1/4-1 oz; 3/8-1 1/4 oz; 1/2-2 oz; 1/4-5/8 oz; 1/4-1 oz; 1/8-1/2 oz

Features:
40-ton carbon, ultra-sensitive blank construction; rods starting in the 3.6 oz range; designed with ALPS mini guide system; ultra-hard zirconium inserts for braided line; zero foregrip design for improved balance and weight reduction; machined aluminum reel seat thread with Fuji hood; durable, lightweight Pacific Bay Minima reel seat and trigger; split-grip butt design for reduced weight and improved balance; comfortable EVA rear grips; Fuji movable hook keeper for precise keeper placement; helios rods are backed by a limited lifetime warranty.
Price:. . . . .**$174.99–$179.99**

OKUMA TARVOS

Model: TV-S-601M, TV-S-602M, TV-S-661M, TV-S-661ML, TV-S-662M, TV-S-662ML, TV-S-701M, TV-S-701MH, TV-S-702M
Length: 6'; 6'; 6'6"; 6'6"; 6'6"; 6'6"; 7'; 7'; 7'
Power: M; M; M; ML; M; ML; M; MH; M
Action: M/MF
Pieces: 1; 2; 1; 1; 2; 2; 1; 1; 2
Line Weight: 6-15 lbs; 6-15 lbs; 6-15 lbs; 4-10 lbs; 6-15 lbs; 4-10 lbs; 6-15 lbs; 6-15 lbs; 6-15 lbs

Guide Count: 7
Lure Weight: 1/8-5/8 oz; 1/8-5/8 oz; 1/8-5/8 oz; 1/8-5/16 oz; 1/8-5/8 oz; 1/8-5/16 oz; 1/4-3/4 oz; 1/4-3/4 oz; 1/4-3/4 oz
Features: Graphite composite rod blank construction; stainless steel guide frames; titanium oxide guide inserts; stainless steel hooded reel seat; split-grip butt design; comfortable EVA fore and rear grips; stainless steel hook keeper; one-year limited warranty.
Price:. **$42.99**

ACTION		POWER	
M=Moderate	UL=Ultra Light	H=Heavy
MF=Moderate Fast	L=Light	MH=Medium-Heavy
F=Fast	ML=Medium-Light	XH=Extra Heavy
XF=Extra Fast		

SHIMANO CLARUS

Model: CSSW60MLB, CSSWX60MLB, CSSW60MB, CSSWX60MB, CSSW66MLB, CSSWX66MLB, CSSWX66ML2B, CSSW66MB, CSSWX66MB, CSSWX66M2B, CSSW70MLB, CSSW70MB, CSSW76MLB, CSSW76MB

Length: 6'; 6'; 6'; 6'; 6'6''; 6'6''; 6'6''; 6'6''; 6'6''; 6'6''; 7'; 7'; 7'6''; 7'6''

Power: ML; ML; M; M; ML; ML; ML; M; M; M; ML; M; ML; M

Action: F; XF; F; XF; F; XF; XF; F; XF; XF; F; F; F; F

Pieces: 1; 1; 1; 1; 1; 1; 2; 1; 1; 2; 1; 1; 1; 1

Line Weight: 4-10 lbs; 4-10 lbs; 6-10 lbs; 6-10 lbs; 4-10 lbs; 4-10 lbs; 4-10 lbs; 6-10 lbs; 6-10 lbs; 6-12 lbs; 4-10 lbs; 6-10 lbs; 4-12 lbs; 6-12 lbs

Guide Count: 7; 7; 7; 7; 8; 8; 8; 8; 8; 8; 9; 9; 9; 9

Lure Weight: 1/16-5/16 oz; 1/16-5/16 oz; 3/16-5/8 oz; 3/16-5/8 oz; 1/16-3/8 oz; 1/16-3/8 oz; 1/16-3/8 oz; 3/16-5/8 oz; 3/16-5/8 oz; 3/16-5/8 oz; 1/16-3/8 oz; 3/16-5/8 oz; 1/16-5/8 oz; 3/16-5/8 oz

Features: IM8 graphite construction; Fuji aluminum oxide guides; custom reel seats.

Price: . . . . **$79.99–$99.99**

SHIMANO COMPRE

Model: CPSW60MLC, CPSWX60MLC, CPSW60MC, CPSWX60MC, CPSW66MLC, CPSWX66MLC, CPSW66MC, CPSWX66MC, CPSW70MLC, CPSW70MC, CPSW70M2C, CPSW76MLC, CPSW76MC

Length: 6'; 6'; 6'; 6'; 6'6''; 6'6''; 6'6''; 6'6''; 7'; 7'; 7'; 7'6''; 7'6''

Power: ML; ML; M; M; ML; ML; M; M; ML; M; M; ML; M

Action: F; XF; F; XF; F; XF; F; XF; F; F; F; F; F

Pieces: 1

Line Weight: 4-10 lbs; 4-10 lbs; 6-10 lbs; 6-10 lbs; 4-10 lbs; 4-10 lbs; 6-10 lbs; 6-10 lbs; 4-10 lbs; 6-10 lbs; 6-12 lbs; 4-12 lbs; 6-12 lbs

Guide Count: 7; 7; 7; 7; 8; 8; 8; 8; 9; 9; 9; 9; 9

Lure Weight: 1/16-5/16 oz; 1/16-5/16 oz; 3/16-5/8 oz; 3/16-5/8 oz; 1/16-3/8 oz; 1/16-3/8 oz; 3/16-5/8 oz; 3/16-5/8 oz; 1/16-3/8 oz; 3/16-5/8 oz; 3/16-5/8 oz; 1/16-5/8 oz; 3/16-5/8 oz

Features: IM9 graphite construction; Fuji aluminum oxide guides; custom reel seats.

Price: **$119.99**

ACTION		POWER	
M=Moderate		UL=Ultra Light	H=Heavy
MF=Moderate Fast		L=Light	MH=Medium-Heavy
F=Fast		ML=Medium-Light	XH=Extra Heavy
XF=Extra Fast			

RODS: **Freshwater Spinning**

SHIMANO CUMARA

Model: CUS68MA, CUS68MHA, CUS72MA, CUS72MHA, CUS76MA, CUSX76MA, CUSDX68MA, CUSCX72MA, CUSS71MLA, CUSS71MA
Length: 6'8''; 6'8''; 7'2''; 7'2''; 7'6''; 7'6''; 6'8''; 7'2''; 7'1''; 7'1''
Power: M; MH; M; MH; M; M; M; M; ML; M
Action: F; F; F; F; F; XF; XF; XF; F; F
Line Weight: 6-12 lbs; 8-14 lbs; 6-12 lbs; 8-14 lbs; 8-16 lbs; 8-17 lbs; 5-10 lbs; 5-10 lbs; 6-10 lbs; 8-12 lbs

Lure Weight: 1/8-3/8 oz; 3/16-5/8 oz; 1/8-3/8 oz; 3/16-5/8 oz; 1/4-5/8 oz; 1/4-5/8 oz; 1/8-3/8 oz; 1/8-3/8 oz; 1/16-1/4 oz; 1/8-5/16 oz
Features: Convenient hook keeper; Fuji KR-concept Alconite guides; custom Shimano reel seat; shaped EVA foam grips; micro guides; technique specific actions; laser-etched badge.
Price: **$259.99**

SHIMANO FX

Model: FXS50ULB2, FXS56ULB2, FXS56MB2, FXS60MB2, FXS66MB2, FXS70MB2, FXS70MHB2, FXS66MHB2, FXS80MHB2, FXS90MHB2
Length: 5'; 5'6''; 5'6''; 6'; 6'6''; 6'6''; 7'; 7'; 8'; 9'
Power: UL; UL; M; M; M; MH; M; MH; MH; MH
Action: F
Pieces: 2
Line Weight: 1-4 lbs; 2-6 lbs; 6-14 lbs; 6-14 lbs; 6-14 lbs; 8-17 lbs; 6-14 lbs; 12-25 lbs; 12-25 lbs; 14-25 lbs

Guide Count: 5; 5; 5; 5; 5; 6; 6; 7; 7; 7
Lure Weight: 1/32-3/16 oz; 1/32-3/16 oz; 1/8-1/2 oz; 1/8-1/2 oz; 1/4-5/8 oz; 1/4-3/4 oz; 1/4-5/8 oz; 1/2-3 oz; 3/4-4 oz; 3/4-4 oz
Features: Durable aeroglass blank construction; features reinforced aluminum oxide guides; solid locking graphite reel seat; comfortable EVA handles.
Price: **$19.99**

ACTION	POWER	
M=Moderate	UL=Ultra Light	H=Heavy
MF=Moderate Fast	L=Light	MH=Medium-Heavy
F=Fast	ML=Medium-Light	XH=Extra Heavy
XF=Extra Fast		

SHIMANO SOJOURN

Model: SJS50UL2A, SJS56UL2A, SJS60MA, SJS60M2A, SJS60ML2A, SJS66MA, SJS66M2A, SJS66MHA, SJS70HA, SJS70MA, SJS70M2A, SJS70MHA
Length: 5'; 5'6''; 6'; 6'; 6'; 6'6''; 6'6''; 6'6''; 7'; 7'; 7'; 7'
Power: UL; UL; M; M; ML; M; M; MH; H; M; M; MH
Action: F
Pieces: 2; 2; 1; 2; 2; 1; 2; 1; 1; 1; 2; 1
Line Weight: 1-4 lbs; 2-6 lbs; 6-12 lbs; 6-12 lbs; 4-10 lbs; 6-14 lbs; 6-14 lbs; 8-17 lbs; 12-25 lbs; 6-14 lbs; 6-14 lbs; 10-20 lbs

Lure Weight: 1/32-3/16 oz; 1/32-3/16 oz; 1/8-1/2 oz; 1/8-1/2 oz; 1/16-3/8 oz; 1/8-5/8 oz; 1/8-5/8 oz; 1/4-3/4 oz; 1/2-3 oz; 1/4-3/4 oz; 1/4-3/4 oz; 1/4-1 oz
Features: Graphite composite blank; low-profile aluminum oxide guides; custom reel seat; custom-shaped cork handle; EVA butt cap; multi-purpose hook keeper.
Price: . . . . **$29.99–$34.99**

ACTION	POWER	
M=Moderate	UL=Ultra Light	H=Heavy
MF=Moderate Fast	L=Light	MH=Medium-Heavy
F=Fast	ML=Medium-Light	XH=Extra Heavy
XF=Extra Fast		

RODS

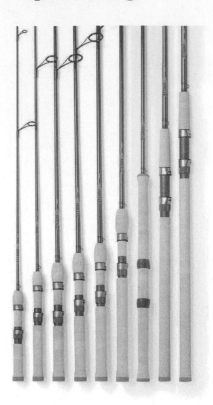

ST. CROIX AVID SERIES

Model: AVS46ULF, AVS50ULF, AVS56ULF2, AVS59MXF, AVS60ULF, AVS60ULF2, AVS60LF, AVS60MLF, AVS60MF, AVS63MLXF, AVS63MXF, AVS66ULF, AVS66ULF2, AVS66LF, AVS66LF2, AVS66MLF, AVS66MLF2, AVS66MF, AVS66MF2, AVS66MHF, AVS66MHF2, AVS68MXF, AVS69MLXF, AVS70ULF, AVS70ULM2, AVS70MLF, AVS7070MLF2, AVS70MF, AVS70MF2, AVS70MHF; AVS76MLXF, AVS76MLXF2, AVS80MLM2

Length: 4'6''; 5'; 5'6''; 5'9''; 6'; 6'; 6'; 6'; 6'; 6'3''; 6'3''; 6'6''; 6'6''; 6'6''; 6'6''; 6'6''; 6'6''; 6'6''; 6'6''; 6'6''; 6'6''; 6'8''; 6'9''; 7'; 7'; 7'; 7'; 7'; 7'; 7'; 7'6''; 7'6''; 8'

Power: UL; UL; UL; M; UL; UL; L; ML; M; ML; M; UL; UL; L; L; ML; ML; M; M; MH; MH; M; ML; UL; UL; ML; ML; M; M; MH; ML; ML; ML

Action: F; F; F; XF; F; F; F; F; F; XF; XF; F; F; F; F; F; F; F; F; F; F; XF; XF; F; M; F; F; F; F; F; XF; XF; M

Pieces: 1; 1; 2; 1; 1; 2; 1; 1; 1; 1; 1; 1; 2; 1; 2; 1; 2; 1; 2; 1; 2; 1; 1; 1; 2; 1; 2; 1; 1; 1; 1; 2; 2

Line Weight: 2-6 lbs; 2-6 lbs; 2-6 lbs; 6-10 lbs; 2-6 lbs; 2-6 lbs; 4-8 lbs; 4-10 lbs; 6-12 lbs; 4-8 lbs; 6-10 lbs; 2-6 lbs; 2-6 lbs; 4-8 lbs; 4-8 lbs; 4-10 lbs; 4-10 lbs; 6-12 lbs; 6-12 lbs; 8-14 lbs; 8-14 lbs; 6-12 lbs; 6-10 lbs; 2-6 lbs; 2-6 lbs; 4-10 lbs; 4-10 lbs; 6-12 lbs; 6-12 lbs; 8-14 lbs; 4-10 lbs; 4-10 lbs; 4-8 lbs

Lure Weight: 1/32-3/16 oz; 1/32-3/16 oz; 1/32-3/16 oz; 1/8-1/2 oz; 1/32-3/16 oz; 1/32-3/16 oz; 1/16-1/4 oz; 1/8-3/8 oz; 3/16-5/8 oz; 1/16-3/8 oz; 1/8-1/2 oz; 1/32-3/16 oz; 1/32-3/16 oz; 1/16-1/4 oz; 1/16-1/4 oz; 1/8-3/8 oz; 1/8-3/8 oz; 3/16-5/8 oz; 3/16-5/8 oz; 3/8-3/4 oz; 3/8-3/4 oz; 3/16-5/8 oz; 1/8-1/2 oz; 1/32-3/16 oz; 1/32-3/16 oz; 1/8-3/8 oz; 1/8-3/8 oz; 3/16-5/8 oz; 3/16-5/8 oz; 3/8-3/4 oz; 1/8-3/8 oz; 1/8-3/8 oz; 1/16-5/16 oz

Features: Integrated Poly Curve tooling technology; premium, high-modulus SCIII graphite; superb sensitivity, extreme strength and durability, incredibly light, and an outstanding value; specialized, technique-specific, and species-specific designs; slim-profile ferrules; Fuji Alconite concept guide system with black frames; Fuji SKM reel seat/gunsmoke hoods; Fuji DPS reel seat/gunsmoke hoods on carp models; select-grade cork handle; two coats of Flex Coat slow-cure finish; lifetime limited warranty.

Price:. . . . .$140.00–$210.00

ACTION	POWER	
M=Moderate	UL=Ultra Light	H=Heavy
MF=Moderate Fast	L=Light	MH=Medium-Heavy
F=Fast	ML=Medium-Light	XH=Extra Heavy
XF=Extra Fast		

ST. CROIX LEGEND ELITE

Model: LES60ULF2, LES60MLF, LES60MF, LES63MXF, LES66LF, LES66LF2, LES66MLF, LES66MLF2, LES66MF, LES66MF2, LES66MHF, LES68MXF, LES70ULM2, LES70LF, LES70LF2, LES70MLF, LES70MLF2, LES70MF, LES70MF2, LES70MHF, LES70MHF2, LES76MLXF, LES76MLXF2, LES76MF, LES76MF2

Length: 6'; 6'; 6'; 6'3''; 6'6''; 6'6''; 6'6''; 6'6''; 6'6''; 6'6''; 6'6''; 6'8''; 7'; 7'; 7'; 7'; 7'; 7'; 7'; 7'; 7'; 7'6''; 7'6''; 7'6''; 7'6''

Power: UL; ML; M; M; L; L; ML; ML; M; M; MH; M; UL; L; L; ML; ML; M; M; MH; MH; ML; ML; M; M

Action: F; F; F; XF; F; F; F; F; F; F; F; XF; M; F; F; F; F; F; F; F; F; XF; XF; F; F

Pieces: 2; 1; 1; 1; 1; 2; 1; 2; 1; 2; 1; 1; 2; 1; 2; 1; 2; 1; 2; 1; 2; 1; 2; 1; 2

Line Weight: 2-6 lbs; 4-10 lbs; 6-12 lbs; 6-10 lbs; 4-8 lbs; 4-8 lbs; 4-10 lbs; 4-10 lbs; 6-12 lbs; 6-12 lbs; 8-14 lbs; 6-12 lbs; 2-6 lbs; 4-8 lbs; 4-8 lbs; 4-10 lbs; 4-10 lbs; 6-12 lbs; 6-12 lbs; 8-14 lbs; 8-14 lbs; 4-10 lbs; 4-10 lbs; 6-12 lbs; 6-12 lbs

Lure Weight: 1/32-3/16 oz; 1/8-3/8 oz; 3/16-5/8 oz; 1/8-1/2 oz; 1/16-1/4 oz; 1/16-1/4 oz; 1/8-3/8 oz; 1/8-3/8 oz; 3/16-5/8 oz; 3/16-5/8 oz; 3/8-3/4 oz; 3/16-5/8 oz; 1/32-3/16 oz; 1/16-1/4 oz; 1/16-1/4 oz; 1/8-3/8 oz; 1/8-3/8 oz; 3/16-5/8 oz; 3/16-5/8 oz; 3/8-3/4 oz; 3/8-3/4 oz; 1/8-3/8 oz; 1/8-3/8 oz; 3/16-5/8 oz; 3/16-5/8 oz

Features: Integrated Poly Curve tooling technology; Advanced Reinforcing Technology; super high-modulus SCVI graphite with FRS in lower section for maximum power and strength with reduced weight; high-modulus/high-strain SCV graphite with FRS and carbon-matte scrim for unparalleled strength and durability; slim-profile ferrules; phenomenally sensitive, light, and smooth casting; Fuji SiC Concept Guide System with titanium-finished frames; Fuji VSS reel seat/frosted silver hood on spinning models; Fuji ACS reel seat/frosted silver hood on casting models; machined-aluminum wind check; super-grade cork handle; two coats of Flex Coat slow-cure finish; includes deluxe rod sack; lifetime limited warranty.

Price:............................**$320.00–$370.00**

ACTION	POWER	
M=Moderate	UL=Ultra Light	H=Heavy
MF=Moderate Fast	L=Light	MH=Medium-Heavy
F=Fast	ML=Medium-Light	XH=Extra Heavy
XF=Extra Fast		

ST. CROIX LEGENDXTREME

Model: LXS59MXF, LXS63MXF, LXS68MXF, LXS610MLXF, LXS610MXF, LXS70LF, LXS70LF2, LXS70MLF, LXS70MLF2, LXS70MF, LXS70MF2, LXS70MHF, LXS70MHF2, LXS76MLXF, LXS76MLXF2, LXS76MF, LXS76MF2

Length: 5'9''; 6'3''; 6'8''; 6'10''; 6'10''; 7'; 7'; 7'; 7'; 7'; 7'; 7'; 7'; 7'6''; 7'6''; 7'6''; 7'6''

Power: M; M; M; ML; M; L; L; ML; ML; M; M; MH; MH; ML; ML; M; M

Action: XF; XF; XF; XF; XF; F; F; F; F; F; F; F; F; XF; XF; F; F

Pieces: 1; 1; 1; 1; 1; 1; 2; 1; 2; 1; 2; 1; 2; 1; 2; 1; 2

Line Weight: 6-10 lbs; 6-10 lbs; 6-12 lbs; 6-10 lbs; 6-12 lbs; 4-8 lbs; 4-8 lbs; 4-10 lbs; 4-10 lbs; 6-12 lbs; 6-12 lbs; 8-14 lbs; 8-14 lbs; 4-10 lbs; 4-10 lbs; 6-12 lbs; 6-12 lbs

Lure Weight: 1/8-1/2 oz; 1/8-1/2 oz; 3/16-5/8 oz; 1/8-1/2 oz; 1/8-5/16 oz; 1/16-1/4 oz; 1/16-1/4 oz; 1/8-3/8 oz; 1/8-3/8 oz; 3/16-5/8 oz; 3/16-5/8 oz; 3/8-3/4 oz; 3/8-3/4 oz; 1/8-3/8 oz; 1/8-3/8 oz; 3/16-5/8 oz; 3/16-5/8 oz

Features: Integrated Poly Curve tooling technology; Taper Enhancement Technology blank design provides curved patterns for improved action with increased sensitivity; Advanced Reinforcing Technology; super high-modulus SCVI graphite with FRS in lower section for maximum power and strength with reduced weight; high-modulus/high-strain SCV graphite with FRS and carbon-matte scrim for unparalleled strength, durability, and sensitivity; slim-profile ferrules; Fuji K-R Concept Tangle Free guides with SiC rings and exclusive E-color finish frames. Ideal for super braid, mono, and fluorocarbon lines, the sloped frame and ring shed tangles before they become a problem; Fuji SK2 split reel seat for the ultimate in light weight and sensitivity; Xtreme-Skin handle repels water, dirt, and fish slime and cleans up easily; manufactured by St. Croix to provide outstanding angler comfort, casting efficiency, and sensitivity; machined-aluminum wind check, handle trim pieces and butt cap with logo badge; two coats of Flex Coat slow-cure finish; includes protective rod sack; lifetime limited warranty.

Price: . . . .**$350.00–$420.00**

ACTION	POWER	
M=Moderate	UL=Ultra Light	H=Heavy
MF=Moderate Fast	L=Light	MH=Medium-Heavy
F=Fast	ML=Medium-Light	XH=Extra Heavy
XF=Extra Fast		

ST. CROIX PREMIER SPINNING

Model: PS46ULM, PS50ULM, PS56ULF2, PS56LF, PS56MF, PS60ULF, PS60ULF2, PS60LF, PS60MLF, PS60MLF2, PS60MF, PS60MF2, PS60MHF, PS66ULF, PS66ULF2, PS66LF, PS66LF2, PS66MLF, PS66MLF2, PS66MF, PS66MF2, PS66MHF, PS66MHF2, PS70ULF2, PS70MLF, PS70MLF2, PS70MF, PS70MF2, PS70MHF, PS70HF, PS70HF2, PS70XHF, PS76MLF, PS76MLF2, PS76MF, PS76MF2, PS86LM2

Length: 4'6''; 5'; 5'6''; 5'6''; 5'6''; 6'; 6'; 6'; 6'; 6'; 6'; 6'; 6'; 6'6''; 6'6''; 6'6''; 6'6''; 6'6''; 6'6''; 6'6''; 6'6''; 6'6''; 6'6''; 7'; 7'; 7'; 7'; 7'; 7'; 7'; 7'; 7'; 7'6''; 7'6''; 7'6''; 7'6''; 8'6''

Power: UL; UL; UL; L; M; UL; UL; L; ML; ML; M; M; MH; UL; UL; L; L; ML; ML; M; M; MH; MH; UL; ML; ML; M; M; MH; H; H; XH; ML; ML; M; M; L

Action: M; M; F; F; F; F; F; F; F; F; F; F; F; F; F; F; F; F; F; F; F; F; F; F; F; F; F; F; F; F; F; F; F; F; F; F; M

Pieces: 1; 1; 2; 1; 1; 1; 2; 1; 1; 2; 1; 2; 1; 1; 2; 1; 2; 1; 2; 1; 2; 1; 2; 2; 1; 2; 2; 1; 2; 1; 2; 1; 1; 2; 1; 1; 2; 1; 2; 2

Line Weight: 2-6 lbs; 2-6 lbs; 2-6 lbs; 4-8 lbs; 6-12 lbs; 2-6 lbs; 2-6 lbs; 4-8 lbs; 4-10 lbs; 4-10 lbs; 6-12 lbs; 6-12 lbs; 8-14 lbs; 2-6 lbs; 2-6 lbs; 4-8 lbs; 4-8 lbs; 4-10 lbs; 4-10 lbs; 6-12 lbs; 6-12 lbs; 8-14 lbs; 8-17 lbs; 2-6 lbs; 4-10 lbs; 4-10 lbs; 6-12 lbs; 6-12 lbs; 8-14 lbs; 10-20 lbs; 10-20 lbs; 12-25 lbs; 4-10 lbs; 4-10 lbs; 6-12 lbs; 6-12 lbs; 4-8 lbs

Lure Weight: 1/16-1/4 oz; 1/16-1/4 oz; 1/32-3/16 oz; 1/16-5/16 oz; 1/4-5/8 oz; 1/32-3/16 oz; 1/32-3/16 oz; 1/16-5/16 oz; 1/8-1/2 oz; 1/8-1/2 oz; 1/4-5/8 oz; 1/4-5/8 oz; 3/8-3/4 oz; 1/32-3/16 oz; 1/32-3/16 oz; 1/16-5/16 oz; 1/16-5/16 oz; 1/8-1/2 oz; 1/8-1/2 oz; 1/4-5/8 oz; 1/4-5/8 oz; 3/8-1/4 oz; 1/2-1 oz; 1/32-3/16 oz; 1/8-1/2 oz; 1/8-1/2 oz; 1/4-5/8 oz; 1/4-5/8 oz; 3/8-3/4 oz; 1/2-1 1/2 oz; 1/2-1 1/2 oz; 3/4-2 oz; 1/8-1/2 oz; 1/8-1/2 oz; 1/4-5/8 oz; 1/4-5/8 oz; 1/16-5/16 oz

Features: Premium-quality SCII graphite; outstanding strength, sensitivity and hook-setting power; finely tuned actions and tapers for superior performance; Kigan Master Hand 3D guides featuring slim, strong aluminum-oxide rings with black frames; Fuji DPS reel seat/frosted silver hoods; premium-grade cork handle; two coats of Flex Coat slow-cure finish; five-year warranty.
Price: . . . .**$100.00–$160.00**

ACTION	POWER	
M=Moderate	UL=Ultra Light	H=Heavy
MF=Moderate Fast	L=Light	MH=Medium-Heavy
F=Fast	ML=Medium-Light	XH=Extra Heavy
XF=Extra Fast		

RODS: Freshwater Spinning

ST. CROIX RAGE SERIES
Model: RS68MXF, RS610MLXF, RS610MXF, RS71MF, RS71MHF
Length: 6'8''; 6'10''; 6'10''; 7'1''; 7'1''
Power: M; ML; M; M; MH
Action: XF; XF; XF; F; F
Pieces: 1
Line Weight: 6-12 lbs; 6-10 lbs; 6-12 lbs; 6-12 lbs; 8-14 lbs
Lure Weight: 3/16-5/8 oz; 1/8-1/2 oz; 1/8-5/16 oz; 3/16-5/8 oz; 3/8-3/4 oz
Features: Integrated Poly Curve (IPC) tooling technology; premium, high-modulus SCIII graphite; incredibly lightweight and sensitive with superb balance and extreme strength; Pac Bay Minima micro guide configuration for high performance and improved durability by eliminating insert failure, plus 20 percent to 30 percent weight savings compared to ceramic guides; Pacific Bay Minima casting reel seat/black hood provides maximum rod blank exposure and is 30 percent lighter than conventional trigger reel seats; Pacific Bay Minima spinning reel seat/black hood provides maximum rod blank exposure and is 10 percent to 20 percent lighter than conventional spinning reel seats; contoured handle provides split-grip performance; featuring a precision-shaped core wrapped with a neoprene skin for maximum comfort and sensitivity; EVA trim pieces provide additional refinement; two coats of Flex Coat slow-cure finish; five-year warranty.
Price: **$150.00**

Saltwater Spinning

DAIWA SALTIGA INSHORE COAST-TO-COAST
Model: CC701HFS, CC701XHFS, CC761MFS, CC761MHFS
Length: 7'; 7'; 7'6''; 7'6''
Power: H; XH; M; MH
Action: F
Pieces: 1
Line Weight: 15-25 lbs; 17-30 lbs; 10-17 lbs; 12-20 lbs
Guide Count: 8; 8; 7; 7
Lure Weight: 1/2-1 1/2 oz; 1/2-2 oz; 3/8-3/4 oz; 1/4-1 oz
Features: Bias construction high-modulus graphite blank; tough Fuji Alconite guides; Fuji SiC tip-top (Northeast models only); genuine Fuji reel seat; high-quality cork grip; convenient hook keeper; protective rubber butt cap; limited lifetime warranty.
Price: **$149.95**

ACTION	POWER	
M=Moderate	UL=Ultra Light	H=Heavy
MF=Moderate Fast	L=Light	MH=Medium-Heavy
F=Fast	ML=Medium-Light	XH=Extra Heavy
XF=Extra Fast		

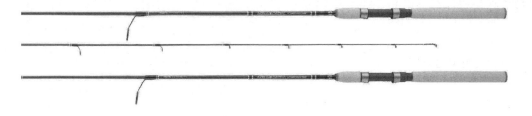

DAIWA SALTIGA INSHORE GULF COAST

Model: GC661MFS, GC701MFS, GC701MLXS, GC761MLXS, GC801MLXS
Length: 6'6''; 7'; 7'; 7'6''; 8'
Power: M; M; ML; ML; ML
Action: F; F; XF; XF; XF
Pieces: 1
Line Weight: 8-20 lbs; 8-20 lbs; 8-17 lbs; 8-17 lbs; 8-17 lbs
Guide Count: 8; 9; 9; 9; 10

Lure Weight: 1/4-1 oz; 1/4-1 oz; 1/8-3/4 oz; 1/8-3/4 oz; 1/8-3/4 oz
Features: Bias construction high-modulus graphite blank; tough Fuji Alconite guides; Fuji SiC tip-top (Northeast models only); genuine Fuji reel seat; high-quality cork grip; convenient hook keeper, protective rubber butt cap; limited lifetime warranty.
Price: **$149.95**

LAMIGLAS BLACK SALT

Model: BS 722 S, BS 723 S, BS 724 S, BS 725 S, BS 773 S, BS 774 S, BS 775 S, BS 806 TARPON
Length: 7'2''; 7'2''; 7'2''; 7'2''; 7'7''; 7'7''; 7'7''; 8'
Action: F; F; F; F; F; F; MF
Pieces: 1
Line Weight: 4-10 lbs; 6-15 lbs; 8-17 lbs; 10-20 lbs; 6-15 lbs; 8-17 lbs; 10-20 lbs; 15-40 lbs

Lure Weight: 1/8-3/8 oz; 1/4-1/2 oz; 3/8-3/4 oz; 3/8-1 oz; 1/4-1/2 oz; 3/8-3/4 oz; 3/8-1 oz; 1-3 oz
Features: These rods offer the smooth agility to cast accurately and the raw power to pull fish to the boat; deep pressed guides with zirconia inserts; AmTack Areo reel seats; graphite handles; made in the USA.
Price: **$270.00**

ACTION	POWER	
M=Moderate	UL=Ultra Light	H=Heavy
MF=Moderate Fast	L=Light	MH=Medium-Heavy
F=Fast	ML=Medium-Light	XH=Extra Heavy
XF=Extra Fast		

RODS: Saltwater Spinning

LAMIGLAS EXCEL INSHORE

Model: XLS 702 S, XLS 703 S, XLS 704 S, XLS 763 S, XLS 764 S, XLS 7114 S, XLS 823 S
Length: 7'; 7'; 7'; 7'6''; 7'6''; 7'11''; 8'2''
Action: MF; F; F; F; F; MF; F
Pieces: 1
Line Weight: 6-10 lbs; 8-12 lbs; 8-17 lbs; 8-12 lbs; 8-17 lbs; 8-17 lbs; 8-17 lbs

Lure Weight: 1/8-3/8 oz; 1/4-1/2 oz; 3/8-3/4 oz; 1/4-1/2 oz; 3/8-3/4 oz; 3/8-3/4 oz; 3/8-3/4 oz
Features: Lightweight blanks with deep pressed stainless guides are ideal for all inshore species; lighter models feature split-grip handles; finished in a metallic copper tone; made in USA.
Price:...................................$230.00

LAMIGLAS TRI-FLEX GRAPHITE

Model: TFX 6015 S, TFX 6615 S
Length: 6'; 6'6''
Action: F
Pieces: 1
Line Weight: 8-17 lbs
Lure Weight: 1/4-1 oz
Features: Cork handles immediately categorize these rods as inshore, but don't overlook these nine highly capable models wherever the need for refined power of tri-flex graphite exists (specifically, the new TFX 6015 C, TFX 6015 S, and TRX 6615 S); latest editions are precision-balanced rods for throwing bucktails for striped bass, fluke, and bluefish; others are equally at home casting swim baits to tuna as they are throwing eels to stripers or crabs to tarpon; easy handling and can-do nature.
Price:...................................$220.00

ACTION	POWER	
M=Moderate	UL=Ultra Light	H=Heavy
MF=Moderate Fast	L=Light	MH=Medium-Heavy
F=Fast	ML=Medium-Light	XH=Extra Heavy
XF=Extra Fast		

OKUMA CRUZ POPPING

Model: CRP-S-762M, CRP-S-792H, CRP-S-792MH
Length: 7'6''; 7'9''; 7'9''
Power: M; H; MH
Action: M
Pieces: 1
Line Weight: 30-65 lbs; 65-150 lbs; 50-100 lbs
Guide Count: 7; 8; 7
Lure Weight: 1-5 1/2 oz; 5 1/2-11 1/2 oz; 3-7 oz
Features: Extremely durable carbon and glass blank mixture for ultimate strength; ALPS 316-grade stainless steel double-footed guide frames; smaller diameter guide inserts allow line to shoot out of rod for longer cast; ALPS hard zirconium guide inserts, perfect for braided line; custom ALPS machined aluminum, two-tone anodized reel seats; EVA fore and rear grips for all day casting comfort; one-piece rod blank construction, butted into handle for uninterrupted rod tapers; machined tapered hood transitions above and below reel seat; low-profile butt cap design for unobstructed fishing; heavy model features a machined aluminum gimbal; all Cruz popping rods are one-piece blanks plus the handle configuration; limited lifetime warranty.
Price: . . . .**$179.99–$189.99**

ACTION	POWER	
M=Moderate	UL=Ultra Light	H=Heavy
MF=Moderate Fast	L=Light	MH=Medium-Heavy
F=Fast	ML=Medium-Light	XH=Extra Heavy
XF=Extra Fast		

RODS: Saltwater Spinning

OKUMA PEZ VELA

Model: PV-S-661MH, PV-S-701M, PV-S-701MH
Length: 6'6''; 7'; 7'
Power: MH; M; MH
Action: MF
Pieces: 1
Line Weight: 15-30 lbs; 15-25 lbs; 20-30 lbs
Guide Count: 6; 7; 7

Features: Extremely durable carbon and glass rod blank mixture; EVA fore and rear grips on spinning models; casting models feature EVA fore grip and a graphite butt; double-footed stainless steel guide frames; polished titanium oxide guide inserts; cushioned stainless steel hooded reel seat; durable non-skid, rubber gimbals on all models; all Pez Vela rods are one-piece blank construction; one-year warranty.
Price: **$69.99**

OKUMA SARASOTA

Model: Sr-S-661M, Sr-S-661ML, Sr-S-701M, Sr-S-701ML
Length: 6'6''; 6'6''; 7'; 7'
Power: M; ML; M; ML
Action: MF
Pieces: 1
Line Weight: 20-40 lbs; 15-30 lbs; 20-40 lbs; 15-30 lbs
Guide Count: 6; 6; 7; 7

Features: Durable E-glass blank construction; glass fiber outer wrap increases hoop strength; double-footed stainless steel guide frames HD model uses heavy duty-style guide frames; use Pacific Bay roller stripper and tip guides; polished titanium oxide guide inserts; stainless steel hooded reel seats; heavy duty aluminum hooded reel seat on HD/T models; graphite gimbals on all models; custom epoxy-wrapped foregrip transition cone; one-year warranty.
Price: **$49.99**

ACTION	POWER	
M=Moderate	UL=Ultra Light	H=Heavy
MF=Moderate Fast	L=Light	MH=Medium-Heavy
F=Fast	ML=Medium-Light	XH=Extra Heavy
XF=Extra Fast		

SHIMANO SAGUARO

Model: SGS66M, SGS66MH, SGS70ML, SGS70M, SGS70MH, SGS70H, SGS80MH2, SGS90MH2
Length: 6'6''; 6'6''; 7'; 7'; 7'; 7'; 8'; 9'
Power: M; MH; ML; M; MH; H; MH; MH
Action: F
Pieces: 1; 1; 1; 1; 1; 1; 2; 2

Line Weight: 14-30 lbs; 20-40 lbs; 8-14 lbs; 12-20 lbs; 14-30 lbs; 20-40 lbs; 14-30 lbs; 14-30 lbs
Guide Count: 7; 7; 7; 7; 7; 7; 8; 8
Features: Aluminum O ring; T-glass; graphite reel seat with stainless steel hoods; comfortable EVA handles; one-year warranty.
Price: **$54.99**

SHIMANO TALAVERA

Model: TES66MH, TES66H, TES70ML, TES70M, TES70MH, TES70H
Length: 6'6''; 6'6''; 7'; 7'; 7'; 7'
Power: MH; H; ML; M; MH; H
Action: F
Pieces: 1
Line Weight: 14-30 lbs; 20-40 lbs; 8-14 lbs; 12-20 lbs; 14-30 lbs; 20-40 lbs

Guide Count: 7
Features: Graphite reel seat; Fuji aluminum oxide guides; EVA grip; AFTCO roller stripper; tip with Fuji heavy duty aluminum oxide boat guides (trolling models only); graphite gimbal with cap (on selected models); black aluminum reel seat (trolling models only).
Price: . . . . **$79.99–$89.99**

ACTION	**POWER**	
M=Moderate	UL=Ultra Light	H=Heavy
MF=Moderate Fast	L=Light	MH=Medium-Heavy
F=Fast	ML=Medium-Light	XH=Extra Heavy
XF=Extra Fast		

RODS: Saltwater Spinning

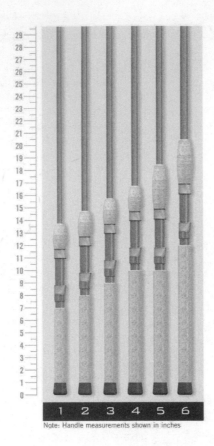

Note: Handle measurements shown in inches

ST. CROIX AVID SERIES INSHORE

Model: AIS66MF, AIS66MHF, AIS70LM, AIS70MLF, AIS70MF, AIS70MM, AIS70MHF, AIS70HF, AIS76MLF, AIS76MF, AIS76MHF, AIS76HF, AIS80MLF, AIS80MF, AIS80MHF, AIS80HF

Length: 6'6''; 6'6''; 7'; 7'; 7'; 7'; 7'; 7'; 7'6''; 7'6''; 7'6''; 7'6''; 8'; 8'; 8'; 8'

Power: M; MH; L; ML; M; M; MH; H; ML; M; MH; H; ML; M; MH; H

Action: F; F; M; F; F; M; F; F; F; F; F; F; F; F; F; F

Pieces: 1

Line Weight: 8-17 lbs; 10-20 lbs; 6-12 lbs; 6-12 lbs; 8-17 lbs; 8-17 lbs; 10-20 lbs; 15-30 lbs; 6-12 lbs; 8-17 lbs; 10-20 lbs; 15-30 lbs; 6-12 lbs; 8-17 lbs; 14-30 lbs; 17-40 lbs

Lure Weight: 3/8-3/4 oz; 1/2-1 1/4 oz; 1/8-3/8 oz; 1/8-1/2 oz; 3/8-3/4 oz; 1/4-5/8 oz; 1/2-1 1/4 oz; 3/4-2 oz; 1/8-1/2 oz; 3/8-3/4 oz; 1/2-1 1/4 oz; 3/4-2 oz; 1/8-1/2 oz; 3/8-3/4 oz; 1/2-2 oz; 3/4-3 oz

Features: Integrated Poly Curve tooling technology; premium, high-modulus SCIII graphite; designed specifically for inshore saltwater angling; ALPS zirconium guides with 316 stainless steel frames for outstanding protection from saltwater corrosion; Fuji DPS reel seat/frosted silver hoods on spinning models; ECS or TCS reel seat/frosted silver hood on casting models; machined-aluminum wind check; super-grade cork handle; two coats of Flex Coat slow-cure finish; lifetime limited warranty.

Price:. . . . .**$200.00–$260.00**

ACTION	POWER	
M=Moderate	UL=Ultra Light	H=Heavy
MF=Moderate Fast	L=Light	MH=Medium-Heavy
F=Fast	ML=Medium-Light	XH=Extra Heavy
XF=Extra Fast		

ST. CROIX LEGEND INSHORE

Model: LIS70MLF, LIS70MF, LIS70MHF, LIS76MLF, LIS76MF
Length: 7'; 7'; 7'; 7'6''; 7'6''
Power: ML; M; MH; ML; M
Action: F
Pieces: 1
Line Weight: 6-12 lbs; 8-17 lbs; 10-20 lbs; 6-12 lbs; 8-17 lbs
Lure Weight: 1/8-1/2 oz; 3/8-3/4 oz; 1/2-1 1/4 oz; 1/8-1/2 oz; 3/8-3/4 oz
Features: Integrated Poly Curve tooling technology; Advanced Reinforcing Technology; high-modulus/high-strain SCIV graphite with FRS for unparalleled strength and durability; designed specifically for inshore saltwater angling; Kigan Master Hand Zero Tangle guides with zirconia rings and titanium frames for the ultimate protection against saltwater corrosion; the sloped, wide-leg design prevents line tangles with mono, fluorocarbon, and super braid lines; Fuji SK2 split reel seat for the ultimate in light weight and sensitivity; super-grade cork handle on spinning models; split-grip/super-grade cork handle on casting models; corrosion-proof wind check and reel seat trim pieces; two coats of Flex Coat slow-cure finish; lifetime limited warranty.
Price:............................$340.00–$370.00

ACTION	POWER	
M=Moderate	UL=Ultra Light	H=Heavy
MF=Moderate Fast	L=Light	MH=Medium-Heavy
F=Fast	ML=Medium-Light	XH=Extra Heavy
XF=Extra Fast		

RODS: Saltwater Spinning

ST. CROIX MOJO INSHORE

Model: MIS70MLF, MIS70MF, MIS70MHF, MIS70HF, MIS76MLF, MIS76MF, MIS76MHF, MIS76HF
Length: 7'; 7'; 7'; 7'; 7'6''; 7'6''; 7'6''; 7'6''
Power: ML; M; MH; H; ML; M; MH; H
Action: F
Pieces: 1
Line Weight: 6-14 lbs; 8-17 lbs; 10-20 lbs; 15-30 lbs; 6-14 lbs; 8-17 lbs; 10-20 lbs; 15-30 lbs
Lure Weight: 1/8-1/2 oz; 3/8-3/4 oz; 1/2-1 1/4 oz; 3/4-2 oz; 1/8-1/2 oz; 3/8-3/4 oz; 1/2-1 1/4 oz; 3/4-2 oz

Features: Premium-quality SCII graphite; specialized inshore saltwater series designed and built for superior performance; Batson Forecast hard aluminum-oxide guides with 316 stainless-steel frames for dramatically improved corrosion resistance compared to 304 stainless-steel frames; Fuji DPS reel seat/black hoods on spinning models; Fuji ECS reel seat/black hood on casting models; split-grip/premium-grade cork handle; two coats of Flex Coat slow-cure finish; five-year warranty.
Price:............................$130.00–$150.00

ACTION	POWER	
M=Moderate	UL=Ultra Light	H=Heavy
MF=Moderate Fast	L=Light	MH=Medium-Heavy
F=Fast	ML=Medium-Light	XH=Extra Heavy
XF=Extra Fast		

ST. CROIX TRIUMPH SURF

Model: TSR70M, TSRS80M2, TSRS90M2, TSRS100M2, TSRS106MH2
Length: 7'; 8'; 9'; 10'; 10'6''
Power: M; M; M; M; MH
Action: MF
Pieces: 1; 2; 2; 2; 2
Line Weight: 8-17 lbs; 8-17 lbs; 8-20 lbs; 8-20 lbs; 10-25 lbs

Lure Weight: 1/2-2 oz; 1/2-2 oz; 1/2-2 1/2 oz; 3/4-4 oz; 2-6 oz
Features: Premium-quality SCII graphite; designed for long-distance casting; lightweight, hard aluminum-oxide surf guides; Fuji DPS reel seat/frosted silver hoods; custom cork tape handle; two coats of Flex Coat slow-cure finish; five-year warranty.
Price: . . . .**$110.00–$180.00**

ACTION	POWER	
M=Moderate	UL=Ultra Light	H=Heavy
MF=Moderate Fast	L=Light	MH=Medium-Heavy
F=Fast	ML=Medium-Light	XH=Extra Heavy
XF=Extra Fast		

RODS

EAGLE CLAW BRAVE EAGLE
Model: BRV100-3, BRV100-4, BRV100-5
Length: 3'; 4'; 5'
Power: M
Pieces: 1; 1; 2
Line Weight: 4-15 lbs
Guide Count: 3

Lure Weight: 1/4-5/8 oz; 3/16-1/2 oz; 1/8-3/8 oz
Features: Available in spinning and spincast models; durable, solid glass construction for years of trouble free fishing; soft foam handles for all day comfort; stainless steel guides; one-year warranty.
Price: **$19.99**

Freshwater Baitcasting

ABU GARCIA VENDETTA
Model: VNTC63-5, VNTC66-5, VNTC66-6, VNTC69-6, VNTC70-5, VNTC70-6, VNTC73-6, VNTC73-7, VNTC76-6, VNTC76-7
Length: 6'3"; 6'6"; 6'6"; 6'9"; 7'; 7'; 7'3"; 7'3"; 7'6"; 7'6"
Power: M; M; MH; M; M; MH; MH; H; MH; H
Action: F; F; XF; F; MF; F; XF; M; F; F
Pieces: 1
Line Weight: 8-17 lbs; 8-17 lbs; 12-20 lbs; 12-20 lbs; 8-17 lbs; 12-20 lbs; 12-20 lbs; 14-30 lbs; 12-25 lbs; 14-30 lbs
Guide Count: 8; 8; 8; 8; 8; 8; 9; 8; 8; 8

Lure Weight: 1/4-5/8 oz; 1/4-5/8 oz; 1/4-1 oz; 1/4-2 oz; 1/4-5/8 oz; 1/4-1 oz; 1/4-1 oz; 3/8-1 1/2 oz; 3/8-1 1/4 oz; 3/8-1 1/2 oz
Features: 30-ton graphite for a lightweight balanced design; one-piece aluminum screw down hood creates a secure connection; high-density EVA gives greater sensitivity and durability; Texas-rigged hook keeper for all bait applications; stainless steel guides with zirconium inserts; Abu designed extreme exposure reel seat for increased blank contact and sensitivity; IntraCarbon technology provides a lightweight barrier to improve durability without adding weight.
Price: **$79.95**

ACTION	POWER	
M=Moderate	UL=Ultra Light	H=Heavy
MF=Moderate Fast	L=Light	MH=Medium-Heavy
F=Fast	ML=Medium-Light	XH=Extra Heavy
XF=Extra Fast		

ABU-GARCIA VENDETTA 2PC
Model: VNTC662-6
Length: 6'6"
Power: MH
Action: XF
Pieces: 2
Line Weight: 12-20 lbs
Guide Count: 8
Lure Weight: 1/4-1 oz

Features: 30-ton graphite for a lightweight balanced design; one-piece aluminum screw down hood creates a secure connection; high-density EVA gives greater sensitivity and durability; Texas-rigged hook keeper for all bait applications; stainless steel guides with zirconium inserts; Abu-designed extreme exposure reel seat for increased blank contact and sensitivity; IntraCarbon technology provides a lightweight barrier to improve durability without adding weight.
Price:.................................... **$79.95**

ABU-GARCIA VENGEANCE
Model: VNGC66-5, VNGC66-6, VNGC70-5, VNGC70-6, VNGC76-7
Length: 6'6"; 6'6"; 7'; 7'; 7'6"
Power: M; MH; M; MH; H
Action: MF; F; MF; F; XF
Pieces: 1
Line Weight: 8-17 lbs; 12-20 lbs; 8-17 lbs; 12-20 lbs; 14-30 lbs
Guide Count: 8; 8; 8; 8; 9

Lure Weight: 1/4-5/8 oz; 1/4-1 oz; 1/4-5/8 oz; 1/4-1 oz; 3/8-1 1/2 oz
Features: 24-ton graphite construction for a lightweight and balanced design; high-density EVA handles are more durable and comfortable; soft-touch sea guide reel seats for increased comfort; zirconium-coated guides are perfect for braided line usage; Texas-rigged hook keeper for all bait applications; one-piece rod.
Price:............................... **$49.99–$59.99**

ABU-GARCIA VENGEANCE 2PC
Model: VNGC662-5
Length: 6'6"
Power: M
Action: F
Pieces: 1
Line Weight: 8-17 lbs
Guide Count: 8

Lure Weight: 1/4-5/8 oz
Features: 24-ton graphite construction for a lightweight and balanced design; high-density EVA handles are more durable and comfortable; soft-touch sea guide reel seats for increased comfort; zirconium-coated guides are perfect for braided line usage; Texas-rigged hook keeper for all bait applications; one-piece rod.
Price:.................................... **$49.99**

ACTION	POWER	
M=Moderate	UL=Ultra Light	H=Heavy
MF=Moderate Fast	L=Light	MH=Medium-Heavy
F=Fast	ML=Medium-Light	XH=Extra Heavy
XF=Extra Fast		

ABU-GARCIA VERITAS

Model: VRC66-5, VRC66-6, VRC69-6, VRC70-5, VRC70-6, VRC70-7, VRC711-7, VRC73-6, VRC76-6
Length: 6'6''; 6'6''; 6'9''; 7'; 7'; 7'; 7'11''; 7'3''; 7'6''
Power: M; MH; MH; M; MH; H; H; MH; MH
Action: F; F; XF; MF; F; XF; MF; F; F
Pieces: 1
Line Weight: 8-17 lbs; 12-20 lbs; 12-20 lbs; 8-17 lbs; 12-20 lbs; 12-25 lbs; 12-25 lbs; 12-20 lbs; 12-25 lbs
Guide Count: 10
Lure Weight: 1/4-5/8 oz; 1/4-1 oz; 1/4-1 oz; 1/4-5/8; 1/4-1 oz; 3/8-1 1/2 oz; 3/8-1 1/2 oz; 1/4-1 oz; 3/8-1 1/4 oz

Features: 30-ton graphite construction with nanotechnology for decreased weight and increased compression strength; one-piece double-anodized aluminum screw down creates a secure connection with the reel; high-density EVA handles are more durable and comfortable; Abu-designed extreme exposure reel seats provide direct finger to rod contact for increased sensitivity; titanium alloy guides with SiC inserts create a lightweight, balanced rod design; Texas-rigged hook keeper for all bait applications; one-piece rod.
Price:. . . . . $99.95–$119.94

ABU-GARCIA VILLAIN

Model: VLC66-5, VLC66-6, VLC69-4, VLC69-6, VLC71-5, VLC71-6, VLC73-7, VLC76-6, VLC80-7
Length: 6'6''; 6'6''; 6'9''; 6'9''; 7'1''; 7'1''; 7'3''; 7'6''; 8'
Power: M; MH; ML; MH; M; MH; H; MH; H
Action: F; F; MF; F; M; F; F; F; MF
Pieces: 1
Line Weight: 8-17 lbs; 12-20 lbs; 6-10 lbs; 12-20 lbs; 8-17 lbs; 12-20 lbs; 14-30 lbs; 12-25 lbs; 14-30 lbs
Guide Count: 10

Lure Weight: 1/4-5/8 oz; 1/4-1 oz; 1/8-1/2 oz; 1/4-1 oz; 1/4-5/8 oz; 1/4-1 oz; 3/4-1 1/2 oz; 3/8-1 1/4 oz; 3/8-1 1/2 oz
Features: Titanium alloy guides with titanium inserts allow for a super lightweight guide giving the ultimate in rod performance; C6 total exposure reel seat gives complete contact to the rod for the ultimate sensitivity; high-density EVA gives greater sensitivity and durability; carbon-wrapped guides reduces weight; Texas-rigged hook keeper for all bait applications; split-grip design; one-piece rod.
Price:. $179.95

ACTION	POWER	
M=Moderate	UL=Ultra Light	H=Heavy
MF=Moderate Fast	L=Light	MH=Medium-Heavy
F=Fast	ML=Medium-Light	XH=Extra Heavy
XF=Extra Fast		

ABU-GARCIA VOLATILE
Model: VOLC69-4, VOLC70-5, VOLC70-6, VOLC72-5, VOLC79-5, VOLC80-6, VOLC80-7
Length: 6'9''; 7'; 7'; 7'2''; 7'9''; 8'; 8'
Power: ML; M; MH; M; M; MH; H
Action: XF; F; F; M; F; F; F
Pieces: 1
Line Weight: 6-12 lbs; 8-17 lbs; 12-20 lbs; 8-17 lbs; 10-20 lbs; 12-25 lbs; 15-30 lbs
Guide Count: 9; 9; 8; 9; 10; 10; 11

Lure Weight: 1/16-3/8 oz; 1/4-5/8 oz; 1/2-1 oz; 3/8-3/4 oz; 3/8-2 oz; 1/2-3 oz; 3/4-4 oz
Features: 30-ton graphite with nanotechnology for decreased weight and increased impact resistance; high-density EVA gives greater sensitivity and durability; Texas-rigged hook keeper for all bait applications; stainless steel guides with zirconium inserts; Fuji IPS (spinning) and Fuji EPS (casting) reel seat for greater comfort; split-grip design.
Price:. . . . . **$99.95–$139.95**

ABU-GARCIA VOLATILE MUSKIE
Model: VOLCMU79-6, VOLCMU80-6, VOLCMU80-7, VOLCMU86-8
Length: 7'9''; 8'; 8'; 8'6''
Power: MH; MH; H; XH
Action: F
Pieces: 1
Line Weight: 25-30 lbs; 30-60 lbs; 40-60 lbs; 50-100 lbs
Guide Count: 10; 11; 11; 12

Lure Weight: 1/4-1 oz; 2-6 oz; 4-10 oz; 6-16 oz
Features: 30-ton graphite with nanotechnology for decreased weight and increased impact resistance; high-density EVA gives greater sensitivity and durability; Texas-rigged hook keeper for all bait applications; stainless steel guides with zirconium inserts; Fuji IPS (spinning) and Fuji EPS (casting) reel seat for greater comfort; split-grip design.
Price:. . . . .**$129.95–$149.95**

RODS

ACTION	POWER	
M=Moderate	UL=Ultra Light	H=Heavy
MF=Moderate Fast	L=Light	MH=Medium-Heavy
F=Fast	ML=Medium-Light	XH=Extra Heavy
XF=Extra Fast		

BASS PRO SHOPS BIONIC BLADE XPS MICRO GUIDE TRIGGER

Model: BBM66MT, BBM66MHT, BBM70MT, BBM70MHT, BBM70HT

Length: 6'6''; 6'6''; 7'; 7'; 7'

Power: M; MH; M; MH; H

Action: F

Pieces: 1

Line Weight: 8-17 lbs; 10-20 lbs; 8-17 lbs; 10-20 lbs; 12-30 lbs

Lure Weight: 1/4-5/8 oz; 3/8-3/4 oz; 1/4-5/8 oz; 3/8-3/4 oz; 3/8-2 oz

Features: Engineered for sensitivity and feature Pacific Bay micro guides for smooth casting and virtually friction-free line flow; revolutionary IM8 blank is created with innovative ArmorCore Technology—a stronger-than-steel aramid fiber core that is wrapped with ultra-light, superpowerful IM8 graphite to make this one of the most powerful, lightweight rods; EVA split grips add to control and fishing comfort.

Price: **$79.99**

BASS PRO SHOPS CLASSIC 200

Model: BPCL-205, BPCL-207, BPCL-208

Length: 5'6''; 6'; 6'6''

Power: L; M; M

Pieces: 2

Line Weight: 4-8 lbs; 6-12 lbs; 6-12 lbs

Lure Weight: 1/16–1/2 oz; 1/8-1/2 oz; 1/8-1/2 oz

Features: Durable, strong, and very affordable fiberglass rods; two-piece blanks for easy transport; comfortable EVA handles.

Price: **$9.99**

ACTION	POWER	
M=Moderate	UL=Ultra Light	H=Heavy
MF=Moderate Fast	L=Light	MH=Medium-Heavy
F=Fast	ML=Medium-Light	XH=Extra Heavy
XF=Extra Fast		

BASS PRO SHOPS CRANKIN' STICK TRIGGER

Model: CS601MLT, CS602MT, CS661MLT, CS662MT, CS663MHT, CS701MLT, CS702MT, CS703MHT, CS762MT-T, CS763MHT-T, CS762MT, CS763MHT, CS7103MHT
Length: 6'; 6'; 6'6''; 6'6''; 6'6''; 7'; 7'; 7'; 7'6''; 7'6''; 7'6''; 7'6''; 7'10''
Power: ML; M; ML; M; MH; ML; M; MH; M; MH; M; MH; MH
Action: F; F; F; F; F; F; F; F; F; F; XF; XF; XF
Pieces: 1
Line Weight: 6-14 lbs; 8-17 lbs; 6-14 lbs; 8-17 lbs; 10-20 lbs; 6-14 lbs; 8-17 lbs; 10-20 lbs; 8-17 lbs; 10-25 lbs; 8-17 lbs; 10-25 lbs; 10-25 lbs

Lure Weight: 1/16-1/2 oz; 1/4-5/8 oz; 1/16-1/2 oz; 1/4-5/8 oz; 3/8-1 oz; 1/16-1/2 oz; 1/4-5/8 oz; 3/8-1 1/2 oz; 1/4-5/8 oz; 3/8-1 1/2 oz; 1/4-5/8 oz; 3/8-1 1/2 oz; 3/8-1 1/2 oz
Features: A unique blend of IM6 graphite, fiberglass, and basalt fibers—yes, volcanic rock in its purest form, because of its ultra-high strength-to-weight ratio and incredible vibration resistance; blank is now 20 percent lighter, strong, and sensitive due to the rock-solid stability of the basalt fibers; reel seat is a more-compact version of our original XPS soft-touch graphite seat, which makes the rod even lighter and easier to handle; unidirectional, thin-wall construction to maximize feel, and fiberglass feeling tip provides distance and flexibility; contoured PowerHump premium cork handle; hard aluminum oxide guides; Pro-Guard epoxy finish.
Price: **$79.99**

ACTION	POWER	
M=Moderate	UL=Ultra Light	H=Heavy
MF=Moderate Fast	L=Light	MH=Medium-Heavy
F=Fast	ML=Medium-Light	XH=Extra Heavy
XF=Extra Fast		

BASS PRO SHOPS JOHNNY MORRIS CARBONLITE MICRO GUIDE

Model: CLM66MTF, CLM66MHTF, CLM69MHTXF, CLM70MTF, CLM70MHTF, CLM70HTXF, CLM76MHTF, CLM76HTXF
Length: 6'6''; 6'6''; 6'9''; 7'; 7'; 7'; 7'6''; 7'6"
Power: M; MH; MH; M; MH; H; MH; H
Action: F; F; XF; F; F; XF; F; F
Pieces: 1

Line Weight: 8-17 lbs; 10-20 lbs; 10-20 lbs; 8-17 lbs; 10-20 lbs; 12-30 lbs; 10-20 lbs; 12-30 lbs
Lure Weight: 1/4-5/8 oz; 3/8-1 oz; 3/8-1 oz; 1/4-5/8 oz; 3/8-1 oz; 3/8-1 1/2 oz; 3/8-1 1/2 oz; 3/8-2 oz
Features: Ultra-rich carbon fiber blank; extreme high-tech Pacific Bay micro guides; split handles; advanced P-Tec polyfoam grips; super light two-piece; soft-touch reel seat is bridgeless.
Price:. **$119.99**

ACTION	POWER	
M=Moderate	**UL=Ultra Light**	**H=Heavy**
MF=Moderate Fast	**L=Light**	**MH=Medium-Heavy**
F=Fast	**ML=Medium-Light**	**XH=Extra Heavy**
XF=Extra Fast		

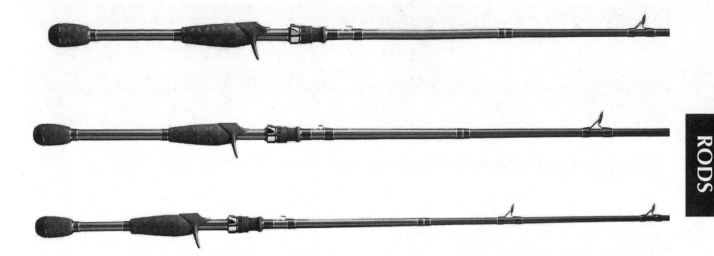

BASS PRO SHOPS JOHNNY MORRIS SIGNATURE SERIES II TRIGGER

Model: JML68MT, JML68MHT, JML72MHT, JML72MT, JML76HT
Length: 6'8''; 6'8''; 7'2''; 7'2''; 7'6''
Power: M; MH; MH; M; H
Action: XF; XF; F; F; XF
Pieces: 1
Line Weight: 8-17 lbs; 10-20 lbs; 10-20 lbs; 10-20 lbs; 12-30 lbs
Lure Weight: ¼-5/8 oz; 3/8-1 oz; 3/8-1 oz; 3/8-1 oz; 3/8-2 oz

Features: Super high-grade 85 million-modulus graphite blank; industry leading Type 1 slit carbon powerwall construction; exclusive carbon cloth butt wrap for unprecedented strength; Fuji new concept stainless steel K-guides with Alconite rings; premium molded split handles with ultra-comfortable P-Tec polyfoam grips; our super-low-profile two-piece exposed-blank reel seat with a soft-touch finish.
Price: **$139.99**

ACTION	POWER	
M=Moderate	UL=Ultra Light	H=Heavy
MF=Moderate Fast	L=Light	MH=Medium-Heavy
F=Fast	ML=Medium-Light	XH=Extra Heavy
XF=Extra Fast		

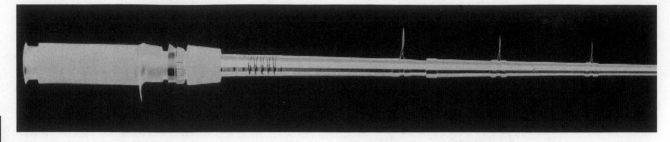

BASS PRO SHOPS POWER PLUS TROPHY CLASS TRIGGER

Model: 1051, 1052, 1053, 1054, 1055, 1056
Length: 6'6''; 6'6''; 7'; 7'; 7'6''; 7'6''
Power: MH; H; MH; H; MH; H
Pieces: 2
Line Weight: 10-25 lbs; 12-30 lbs; 10-25 lbs; 12-30 lbs; 10-25 lbs; 12-30 lbs
Lure Weight: 1/2-2 oz; 1-4 oz; 1/2-2 oz; 1-4 oz; 1/2-2 oz; 1-4 oz

Features: Unidirectional fiberglass construction eliminates the layering normally found in fiberglass rods, adding flexibility and eliminating premature breakage and stress on the wrist; features an extended EVA foam handle, for extra power and fighting leverage, that easily fits in rod holders; heavy duty double foot aluminum oxide guides; hook keeper for pre-rigging; sensitive graphite reel seat; all rods are 2 pieces; guide number includes tip.
Price: **$29.99**

ACTION	POWER	
M=Moderate	UL=Ultra Light	H=Heavy
MF=Moderate Fast	L=Light	MH=Medium-Heavy
F=Fast	ML=Medium-Light	XH=Extra Heavy
XF=Extra Fast		

BERKLEY AIR IM8
Model: A92-7-9HB, A92-8-6MH, A92-8-6H, A92-8-6XH, A92-8-6M, A92-9XH, A92-9-6M, A92-10-6XH
Length: 7'9''; 8'6''; 8'6''; 8'6''; 8'6''; 9'; 9'6''; 10'6''
Power: H; MH; H; XH; M; XH; M; XH
Pieces: 1; 2; 2; 2; 2; 2; 2; 2
Line Weight: 15-50 lbs; 10-20 lbs; 12-25 lbs; 15-50 lbs; 8-12 lbs; 20-65 lbs; 8-14 lbs; 20-80 lbs
Guide Count: 9; 10; 10; 10; 10; 10; 10; 12
Lure Weight: 1/2-4 oz; 1/2-1 1/2 oz; 1/2-1 3/4 oz; 3/4-3 oz; 3/8-3/4 oz; 3/4-3 oz; 3/8-3/4 oz; 2-8 oz

Features: Constructed of IM8 advanced-modulus graphite; air IM8 rods are lightweight and have a sensitive blank that provides the ultimate in feel with enough power to land big fish with ease; titanium-coated SS304 guides are found on all air IM8 spinning and casting models for increased durability and abrasion resistance when fishing with braided line; concept guide spacing improves sensitivity and maximizes blank strength; air IM8 gives anglers the length, power, and performance they need for demanding conditions.
Price: . . . . **$99.95–$109.95**

BERKLEY AMP
Model: AC601MH, AC661M, AC701M
Length: 6'; 6'6''; 7'
Power: MH; M; M
Pieces: 1
Line Weight: 10-25 lbs; 8-20 lbs; 8-20 lbs
Guide Count: 6
Lure Weight: 1/4-1 1/4 oz; 1/4-3/4 oz; 1/4-3/4 oz

Features: X-posed reel seats; split-grip cork handles on both spinning and casting models, allowing the hand to remain in constant contact with the rod blank, and taking sensitivity and light weight to a new level; comes with an armadillo hide finish that eliminates cut fibers and ensures the blank is free from imperfections.
Price: . . . . **$29.95–$29.99**

ACTION
M=Moderate
MF=Moderate Fast
F=Fast
XF=Extra Fast

POWER
UL=Ultra Light
L=Light
ML=Medium-Light
H=Heavy
MH=Medium-Heavy
XH=Extra Heavy

RODS: **Freshwater Baitcasting**

BERKLEY CHERRYWOOD HD
Model: CWD561MC, CWD601MHC, CWD661MHC, CWD661MC, CWD662MC, CWD701MHC, CWD701MLC, CWD701MC
Length: 5'6''; 6'; 6'6''; 6'6''; 6'6''; 7'; 7'; 7'
Power: M; MH; MH; M; M; MH; ML; M
Pieces: 1; 1; 1; 1; 2; 1; 1; 1
Line Weight: 8-17 lbs; 10-20 lbs; 10-20 lbs; 8-17 lbs; 8-17 lbs; 10-20 lbs; 6-14 lbs; 8-17 lbs

Guide Count: 6; 7; 7; 7; 7; 7; 7; 7
Lure Weight: 1/4-3/4 oz; 1/4-1 oz; 1/4-1 oz; 1/4-3/4 oz; 1/4-3/4 oz; 1/4-1 oz; 1/8-5/8 oz; 1/4-3/4 oz
Features: Balanced graphite composition blank and quality construction for excellent responsiveness and durability; chromium guide system that is 20 times tougher and up to 55 percent lighter than conventional oxide guides.
Price: **$24.99**

BERKLEY GLOWSTIK
Model: GSC702M, GSC802MH, GSC902MH, GSC1002MH
Length: 7'; 8'; 9'; 10'
Power: M; MH; MH; MH
Pieces: 2
Line Weight: 10-20 lbs; 10-25 lbs; 10-30 lbs; 10-30 lbs
Guide Count: 7; 8; 9; 10
Lure Weight: 1/2-3 oz; 1-4 oz; 1-5 oz; 1-5 oz

Features: This is the right rod for any nighttime fishing adventure; super strong, super tough E-glass technology makes this blank is nearly indestructible; exclusive lighted blank design can be activated to glow continuously for great night bite detection.
Price: . . . . **$39.95–$49.95**

ACTION		**POWER**	
M=Moderate	UL=Ultra Light	H=Heavy	
MF=Moderate Fast	L=Light	MH=Medium-Heavy	
F=Fast	ML=Medium-Light	XH=Extra Heavy	
XF=Extra Fast			

BERKLEY LIGHTNING ROD IM6

Model: LR561MC-SH, LR601MHC-SH, LR601MHC, LR601MC, LR661MHC, LR661MC, LR701MHC, LR701MC, LR761HTC
Length: 5'6''; 6'; 6'; 6'; 6'6''; 6'6''; 7'; 7'; 7'6''
Power: M; MH; MH; M; MH; M; MH; M; H
Pieces: 1
Line Weight: 8-14 lbs; 10-17 lbs; 10-17 lbs; 8-14 lbs; 10-17 lbs; 8-14 lbs; 10-20 lbs; 8-14 lbs; 12-25 lbs
Guide Count: 6; 6; 6; 6; 7; 7; 7; 7; 8

Lure Weight: 1/4-5/8 oz; 3/8-3/4 oz; 3/8-3/4 oz; 1/4-5/8 oz; 3/8-3/4 oz; 1/4-5/8 oz; 1/2-1 oz; 1/4-5/8 oz; 5/8-1 1/2 oz
Features: North America's #1 selling graphite rod; a unique combination of strength and sensitivity; the fastest, strongest, and lightest rod in its class; chrome-plated SS304 guides have made the rod lighter, stronger, and more sensitive than ever.
Price:..................................... $39.99

CABELA'S KING KAT

Model: CKKC08, CKKC09, CKKS662-M
Length: 8'; 9'; 6'6''
Power: MH; MH; M
Pieces: 2
Line Weight: 14-30 lbs; 14-30 lbs; 8-20 lbs

Features: Ultra-tough E-glass; a bright tip to help detect nighttime bites; rugged double-foot ceramic guides; stainless steel hoods on the reel seats add to the performance and durability of the King Kat rods; sure-grip EVA handles offer no-slip confidence during long fights in bad weather.
Price:..................................... $29.99

ACTION	**POWER**	
M=Moderate	UL=Ultra Light	H=Heavy
MF=Moderate Fast	L=Light	MH=Medium-Heavy
F=Fast	ML=Medium-Light	XH=Extra Heavy
XF=Extra Fast		

RODS: Freshwater Baitcasting

CABELA'S TOURNEY TRAIL

Model: PTTC564-1, TTC604-1, TTC665-1, TTC665-2, TTC705-1, TTC705-2, TTCS865-2, TTC666-1, TTC706-2, TTCS906-2, TTCM705-1, TTCM766-1, TTCM767-1, TTC706-1, TTC704-2, TTC664-2
Length: 5'6''; 6'; 6'6''; 6'6''; 7'; 7'; 8'6''; 6'6''; 7'; 9'; 7'; 7'6''; 7'6''; 7'; 7'; 6'6''
Power: M; M; MH; MH; MH; MH; MH; H; H; H; MH; H; XH; H; M; M
Action: F; F; MF; MF; MF; MF; MF; F; F; MF; F; F; F; F; F; F
Pieces: 1; 1; 1; 2; 1; 2; 2; 1; 2; 2; 1; 1; 1; 1; 2; 2
Line Weight: 8-17 lbs; 8-17 lbs; 8-17 lbs; 8-17 lbs; 10-17 lbs; 10-17 lbs; 8-17 lbs; 15-25 lbs; 10-20 lbs; 10-20 lbs; 15-30 lbs; 17-40 lbs; 20-50 lbs; 10-20 lbs; 8-14 lbs; 8-17 lbs

Lure Weight: 1/4-5/8 oz; 1/4-5/8 oz; 1/4-1 oz; 1/4-1 oz; 1/4-3/4 oz; 1/4-3/4 oz; 1/2-1 1/2 oz; 5/8-1 1/2 oz; 3/8-2 1/4 oz; 1/2-1 1/2 oz; 3/4-2 1/2 oz; 1-3 oz; 2-6 oz; 3/8-2 1/4 oz; 1/4-5/8 oz; 1/4-5/8 oz
Features: Small, yet strong, aluminum-oxide guides that are perfectly sized and wrapped to the new steel-blue blanks in a seamless bond; heavy duty graphite reel seats with cushioned hoods secure the reel; screw-down locking fore grips were added to eliminate exposed threads when the reel is snugged; higher-quality cork handles to make casting for fish more comfortable; built around IM7 100 percent graphite blanks that have fast tip-sensitive actions; limited two-year warranty.
Price: **$64.99**

CABELA'S WHUPPIN' STICK

Model: WSCM66-2, WSCH80-2, WSCMH66-2, WSCM60-2, WSCMH90-2, WSCML70-2, WSCM70-2
Length: 6'6''; 8'; 6'6''; 6'; 9'; 7'; 7'
Power: M; H; MH; M; MH; ML; M
Pieces: 2
Line Weight: 8-20 lbs; 14-50 lbs; 12-25 lbs; 12-20 lbs; 14-30 lbs; 8-20 lbs; 8-20 lbs

Features: Nearly indestructible, advanced polymer fiberglass blanks; graphite reel seats securely lock your reel in place without adding significant weight to the rod; blank through-handle construction makes it easy to feel even the light biters; stainless steel frame guides with ceramic inserts will stand up to the toughest fish; cork grips ensure all-day comfort.
Price: . . . . **$24.99–$29.99**

ACTION	**POWER**	
M=Moderate	UL=Ultra Light	H=Heavy
MF=Moderate Fast	L=Light	MH=Medium-Heavy
F=Fast	ML=Medium-Light	XH=Extra Heavy
XF=Extra Fast		

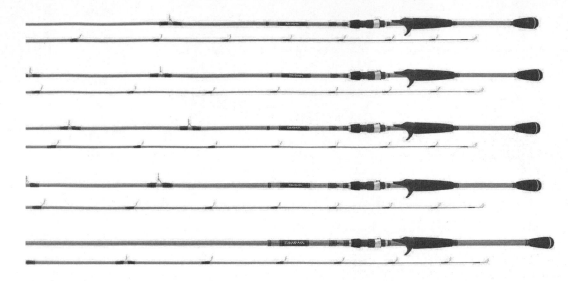

DAIWA AIRD

Model: AIRD661MXB, AIRD661MHXB, AIRD662MHXB, AIRD701MLXB, AIRD701MHXB, AIRD701HXB
Length: 6'6''; 6'6''; 6'6''; 7'; 7'; 7'
Power: M; MH; MH; ML; MH; H
Action: XF
Pieces: 1; 1; 2; 1; 1; 1
Line Weight: 8-17 lbs; 10-20 lbs; 10-20 lbs; 6-15 lbs; 10-20 lbs; 12-25 lbs
Guide Count: 10

Lure Weight: 1/4-3/4 oz; 1/4-1 oz; 1/4-1 oz; 1/8-1/2 oz; 1/4-1 oz; 3/8-1 1/2 oz
Features: IM6 graphite blank; minimized, direct contact reel seat for reduced weight and greater sensitivity with stainless hood; lightweight split-grip design with non-slip, high-density EVA foam; stainless steel guides; folding hook keeper.
Price: **$44.99**

ACTION	POWER	
M=Moderate	UL=Ultra Light	H=Heavy
MF=Moderate Fast	L=Light	MH=Medium-Heavy
F=Fast	ML=Medium-Light	XH=Extra Heavy
XF=Extra Fast		

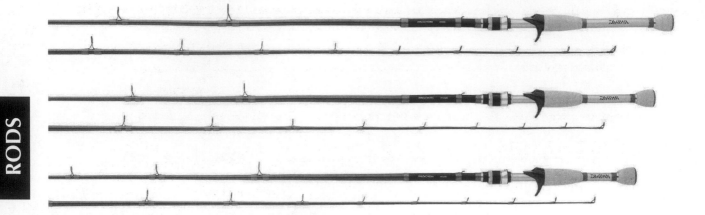

DAIWA PROCYON TRIGGER GRIP
Model: PRCN601MFB, PRCN661MXB, PRCN701MLFB, PRCN701MXB, PRCN661MHXB, PRCN701MHXB, PRCN701HFB
Length: 6'; 6'; 7'; 7'; 6'6''; 7'; 7'
Power: M; M; ML; M; MH; MH; H
Action: F; XF; F; XF; XF; XF; F
Pieces: 1
Line Weight: 8-17 lbs; 10-20 lbs; 6-14 lbs; 8-17 lbs; 10-20 lbs; 8-17 lbs; 12-25 lbs

Guide Count: 9; 9; 10; 10; 10; 10; 10
Lure Weight: 1/4-3/4 oz; 1/4-1 oz; 1/4-1/2 oz; 1/4-3/4 oz; 1/4-1 oz; 1/4-3/4 oz; 3/8-1 1/2 oz
Features: IM7 graphite construction micro pitch blank; taping Minima reel seat with machined clamp nut; woven graphite insert Minima black ring guides; lightweight split-grip cork handles; hook keeper; five-year limited warranty.
Price: **$64.95**

ACTION	POWER	
M=Moderate	UL=Ultra Light	H=Heavy
MF=Moderate Fast	L=Light	MH=Medium-Heavy
F=Fast	ML=Medium-Light	XH=Extra Heavy
XF=Extra Fast		

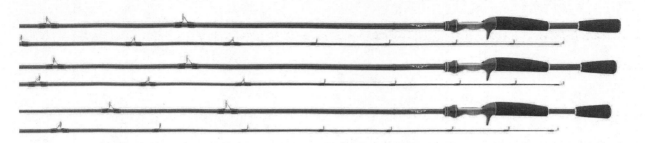

DAIWA STEEZ FLE-X-LITE

Model: STZ651MLRBA-FL, STZ701MRBA-FL, STZ721MHRBA-FL
Length: 6'5''; 7'; 7'2''
Power: ML; M; MH
Action: R
Pieces: 1
Line Weight: 6-16 lbs; 8-20 lbs; 12-25 lbs
Guide Count: 9

Lure Weight: 3/32-3/4 oz; 1/8-1 oz; 1/4-3/8 oz
Features: Exclusive SVF Fle-X-Lite graphite blank construction; Air-Beam reel seat; machined aluminum fore-screw nut; Fuji titanium-framed SiC guides; cut-proof and corrosion-free Air-Foam grips are noticeably lighter than cork or ordinary EVA foam yet offer a firm, non-slip grip; laser-engraved butt cap; limited lifetime warranty.
Price:. . . . . $479.95–$509.95

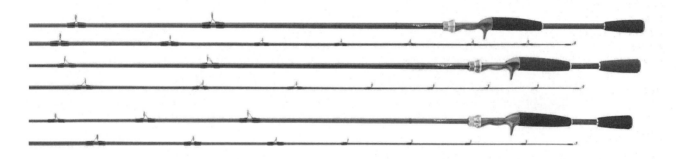

DAIWA STEEZ SVF GRAPHITE

Model: STZ601MFBA, STZ631MHFBA, STZ671MHFBA, STZ701MHFBA
Length: 6'; 6'3''; 6'7''; 7'
Power: M; MH; MH; MH
Action: F
Pieces: 1
Line Weight: 8-16 lbs; 8-20 lbs; 12-20 lbs; 12-20 lbs
Guide Count: 8; 9; 9; 9
Lure Weight: 1/8-5/8 oz; 3/16-1 oz; 1/4-1 oz; 1/4-1 oz

Features: Exclusive SVF graphite construction; bias graphite fiber construction for flexibility, strength, and virtually zero blank twist; Air-Beam reel seat; machined aluminum fore-screw nut; Fuji titanium-framed SiC guides; cut-proof and corrosion-free Air-Foam grips are noticeably lighter than cork or ordinary EVA foam yet offer a firm, non-slip grip; laser-engraved butt cap; limited lifetime warranty.
Price:. . . . . $419.95–$479.95

ACTION	**POWER**	
M=Moderate	UL=Ultra Light	H=Heavy
MF=Moderate Fast	L=Light	MH=Medium-Heavy
F=Fast	ML=Medium-Light	XH=Extra Heavy
XF=Extra Fast		

DAIWA TRIFORCE-E
Model: TFE562MFP, TFE602MFP, TFE601MFB, TFE602MFB, TFE662MFB, TFE662MHFB, TFE661MFB, TFE661MHFB, TFE701MFB, TFE701MHFB
Length: 5'6''; 6'; 6'; 6'; 6'6''; 6'6''; 6'6''; 6'6''; 7'; 7'
Power: M; M; M; M; M; MH; M; MH; M; MH
Action: F
Pieces: 2; 2; 2; 2; 2; 2; 1; 1; 1; 1
Line Weight: 8-17 lbs; 8-17 lbs; 8-17 lbs; 8-17 lbs; 8-17 lbs; 10-20 lbs; 8-17 lbs; 10-20 lbs; 8-17 lbs; 10-20 lbs

Guide Count: 7; 8; 8; 8; 8; 8; 8; 8; 8; 8
Lure Weight: 1/4-3/4 oz; 1/4-3/4 oz; 1/4-3/4 oz; 1/4-3/4 oz; 1/4-3/4 oz; 1/4-1 oz; 1/4-3/4 oz; 1/4-1 oz; 1/4-3/4; 1/4-1 oz
Features: High-quality graphite blank; strong, blank-through-handle construction; cut-proof aluminum oxide guides; custom thread wrap with durable multi-coat finish; protective foam butt cap and grip check.
Price: **$19.95**

ACTION	POWER	
M=Moderate	UL=Ultra Light	H=Heavy
MF=Moderate Fast	L=Light	MH=Medium-Heavy
F=Fast	ML=Medium-Light	XH=Extra Heavy
XF=Extra Fast		

G LOOMIS BASS SPINNERBAIT

Model: 11274-01, 11275-01, 11276-01, 11277-01, 11278-01, 11279-01

Length: 6'3''; 6'3''; 6'9''; 6'9''; 6'9''; 7'2''

Power: L; M; L; M; M; MH

Action: XF

Pieces: 1

Line Weight: 8-12 lbs; 10-17 lbs; 8-12 lbs; 10-17 lbs; 12-20 lbs; 12-25 lbs

Lure Weight: 1/4-3/8 oz; 3/8-1/2 oz; 1/4-3/8 oz; 3/8-1/2 oz; 1/2-3/4 oz; 3/4-1 1/2 oz

Features: These rods are designed specifically to fish spinnerbaits; feature extra-fast tips to help improve accuracy and lower the trajectory, so the wind has less affect on bait, loading effortlessly, allowing quick underhand snap casts to help cover a lot of water; combination of accuracy and control give an added advantage when fighting fish in heavy cover; feature fiber blend technology; Fuji guides and Fuji's ECS exposed blank trigger reel seat; SBR864C utilizes a much larger blank so it has a standard Fuji trigger real seat.

Price:..............................$225.00–$260.00

RODS

ACTION	POWER	
M=Moderate	UL=Ultra Light	H=Heavy
MF=Moderate Fast	L=Light	MH=Medium-Heavy
F=Fast	ML=Medium-Light	XH=Extra Heavy
XF=Extra Fast		

LAMIGLAS EXCEL II BASS

Model: EXL 703 C, EXL 704 C, EXL 705 C, EXL 705 Glass, EXL 733 C, EXL 734 C, EXL 735 C, EXL 736 C, EXL 765 C, EXL 766 Flip
Length: 7'; 7'; 7'; 7'; 7'3''; 7'3''; 7'3''; 7'3''; 7'6''; 7'6''
Action: F; F; F; MF; F; F; F; F; F; F
Pieces: 1
Line Weight: 8-15 lbs; 10-20 lbs; 12-25 lbs; 8-20 lbs; 10-17 lbs; 10-20 lbs; 12-25 lbs; 15-30 lbs; 12-25 lbs; 12-30 lbs

Lure Weight: 3/16-5/8 oz; 1/4-3/4 oz; 1/4-1 oz; 1/4-1 oz; 1/4-3/4 oz; 1/4-1 oz; 1/4-1 1/2 oz; 3/8-2 oz; 1/4-1 1/2 oz; 1/4-2 oz
Features: Beautiful, aqua-blue finish; feature Lamiglas IM graphite construction; split grips; Fuji SK2 reel seats; deep pressed hybrid guide system.
Price:. **$120.00**

LAMIGLAS INFINITY BASS

Model: INF 723C, INF 724C, INF 735C
Length: 7'2''; 7'2''; 7'3''
Action: F
Pieces: 1
Line Weight: 10-20 lbs; 12-25 lbs; 12-25 lbs
Lure Weight: 1/4-3/4 oz; 1/4-1 oz; 1/4-1 1/2 oz

Features: Infinity graphite composite blanks made with resins can achieve incredible strength, durability, and sensitivity, while enabling the lightest weight designs; deep pressed titanium guides; Fuji reel seats and counterbalanced woven graphite handles.
Price:. **$360.00**

ACTION	POWER	
M=Moderate	UL=Ultra Light	H=Heavy
MF=Moderate Fast	L=Light	MH=Medium-Heavy
F=Fast	ML=Medium-Light	XH=Extra Heavy
XF=Extra Fast		

LEW'S LASER LG GRAPHITE

Model: LGA60MFPC, LGA66MFC, LGAMHFC, LGA70MFC, LGA70MHFC
Length: 6'; 6'6''; 6'6''; 7'; 7'
Power: M; M; MH; M; MH
Action: F
Pieces: 1
Line Weight: 8-17 lbs; 8-17 lbs; 10-20 lbs; 8-17 lbs; 10-20 lbs
Guide Count: 9; 10; 10; 10; 10
Lure Weight: 1/4-5/8 oz; 1/4-5/8 oz; 3/8-1 oz; 1/4-5/8 oz; 3/8-1 1/2 oz

Features: Premium IM6 graphite blank; multilayer, multidirectional graphite one-piece blanks reinforced with premium resins; Lew's proprietary APT (Advanced Performance Technology) blank construction; black-coated stainless steel frame with titanium oxide guide rings; lightweight graphite reel seat with cushioned stainless steel hoods; great hand/reel stability and comfort; exposed blank for instant vibration transmission on casting models; natural cork split-grip handles offer reduced weight without compromising rod control.
Price: **$49.99**

LEW'S TOURNAMENT SL MICRO GUIDE

Model: TS66MFC, TS66MHFC, TS70MLFC, TS70MFC, TS70MHFC, TS72XHXFC
Length: 6'6''; 6'6''; 7'; 7'; 7'; 7'2''
Power: M; MH; ML; M; MH; XH
Action: F; F; F; F; F; XF
Pieces: 1
Line Weight: 8-17 lbs; 10-20 lbs; 8-14 lbs; 8-17 lbs; 10-20 lbs; 14-30 lbs
Guide Count: 12
Lure Weight: 1/4-5/8 oz; 3/8-3/4 oz; 3/16-5/8 oz; 1/4-3/4 oz; 3/8-1 oz; 1/2-2 oz
Features: Premium HM60 graphite blanks; multilayer, multidirectional 60 million-modulus graphite blank

reinforced with premium resins; Lew's proprietary APT (Advanced Performance Technology) blank construction; black-coated stainless steel frames with hard aluminum oxide micro guides, which reduce rod weight, enhance casting distance, and increase sensitivity; lightweight skeletal graphite reel seats with cushioned black stainless steel hoods; great hand/reel stability and comfort; exposed blank for instant vibration transmission; high-density EVA foam split-grip handles reduce weight without sacrificing control.
Price: **$119.99**

ACTION	POWER	
M=Moderate	UL=Ultra Light	H=Heavy
MF=Moderate Fast	L=Light	MH=Medium-Heavy
F=Fast	ML=Medium-Light	XH=Extra Heavy
XF=Extra Fast		

G. LOOMIS CLASSIC

Model: CR 721 IMX, CR 722 IMX, CR 722 GL3, CR 723 GLX, CR 723 IMX, CR 723 GL3, CR 724 IMX
Length: 6'
Power: L; M; M; MH; MH; MH; H
Action: F
Pieces: 1
Line Weight: 6-12 lbs; 8-14 lbs; 8-14 lbs; 10-17 lbs; 10-17 lbs; 10-17 lbs; 12-20 lbs
Lure Weight: 3/16-1/2 oz; 1/4-5/8 oz; 1/4-5/8 oz; 1/4-3/4 oz; 1/4-3/4 oz; 1/4-3/4 oz; 1/4-1 oz

Features: Designed for accurate, low-trajectory casting which makes them ideal for fishing in tight quarters, around low overhanging limbs and cover; Fuji's ECS (exposed blank—trigger reel seats) and 7-inch, straight cork rear-grips; anglers use them for topwater baits, spinnerbaits, small jigs, and worms where accuracy is more important than distance; these rods remain on the cutting edge of graphite technology today. The most popular models are available in three levels of graphite performance: GL3, IMX, and GLX.
Price: . . . . **$210.00–$340.00**

G. LOOMIS GL2 JIG & WORM

Model: GL2 722C JWR, GL2 723C JWR, GL2 724C JWR, GL2 802C JWR, GL2 803C JWR, GL2 804C JWR, GL2 805C JWR, GL2 852C JWR, GL2 853C JWR, GL2 854C JWR, GL2 855C JWR, GL2 893C JWR, GL2 894C JWR
Length: 6'; 6'; 6'; 6'8"; 6'8"; 6'8"; 6'8"; 7'1"; 7'1"; 7'1"; 7'1"; 7'5"; 7'5"
Power: M; MH; H; M; MH; H; XH; M; MH; H; XH; MH; H
Action: F; F; F; XF; XF; XF; XF; XF; XF; XF; XF; XF; XF
Pieces: 1

Line Weight: 10-14 lbs; 12-16 lbs; 14-20 lbs; 10-14 lbs; 12-16 lbs; 14-20 lbs; 17-25 lbs; 10-14 lbs; 12-16 lbs; 14-20 lbs; 17-25 lbs; 12-16 lbs; 14-20 lbs
Lure Weight: 1/4-5/8 oz; 1/4-3/4 oz; 1/4-1 oz; 1/8-3/8 oz; 3/16-5/8 oz; 5/16-3/4 oz; 1/4-1 oz; 1/8-3/8 oz; 3/16-5/8 oz; 5/16-3/4 oz; 1/4-1 oz; 3/16-5/8 oz; 5/16-3/4 oz
Features: GL2 Jig & Worm casting rods offer a unique blend of power, sensitivity, and fishability; handles feature split-grips, Fuji trigger reel seat, and Concept guides.
Price: . . . . **$195.00–$220.00**

ACTION	POWER	
M=Moderate	UL=Ultra Light	H=Heavy
MF=Moderate Fast	L=Light	MH=Medium-Heavy
F=Fast	ML=Medium-Light	XH=Extra Heavy
XF=Extra Fast		

G LOOMIS GLX JIG & WORM CASTING
Model: GLX 802C JWR, GLX 803C JWR, GLX 804C JWR, GLX 805C JWR, GLX 852C JWR, GLX 853C JWR, GLX 854C JWR, GLX 855C JWR, GLX 893C JWR, GLX 894C JWR, GLX 895C JWR
Length: 6'8''; 6'8''; 6'8''; 6'8''; 7'1''; 7'1''; 7'1''; 7'1''; 7'5''; 7'5''; 7'5''
Power: M; MH; H; XH; M; MH; H; XH; MH; H; H
Action: XF; XF; F; F; XF; XF; F; F; XF; F; F
Pieces: 1
Line Weight: 10-14 lbs; 12-16 lbs; 14-20 lbs; 17-25 lbs; 10-14 lbs; 12-16 lbs; 14-20 lbs; 17-25 lbs; 12-16 lbs; 14-20 lbs; 17-25 lbs

Lure Weight: 1/8-3/8 oz; 3/16-5/8 oz; 5/16-3/4 oz; 1/4-1 oz; 1/8-3/8 oz; 3/16-5/8 oz; 5/16-3/4 oz; 1/4-1 oz; 3/16-5/8 oz; 5/16-3/4 oz; 1/4-1 oz
Features: Designed specifically for fishing jigs and soft plastics; feature a split-grip handle with a mag touch trigger reel seat; Fuji titanium SIC guides and tip-tops; legendary for their sensitivity, these rods will tell you everything that's going on with that bait, no matter how deep the water or how thick the cover; they have extra-fast actions for accurate, low trajectory casts with plenty of power to handle even the biggest bass; made with a gorgeous dark green blank.
Price:............................ **$410.00–$460.00**

G LOOMIS NRX JIG & WORM
Model: NRX 802C JWR, NRX 802C JWR G, NRX 803C JWR, NRX 803C JWR G, NRX 804C JWR, NRX 804C JWR G, NRX 852C JWR, NRX 852C JWR G, NRX 854C JWR, NRX 854C JWR G, NRX 853C JWR, NRX 853C JWR G, NRX 893C JWR, NRX 893C JWR G, NRX 894C JWR, NRX 894C JWR G, NRX 895 JWR, NRX 895C JWR G
Length: 6'8''; 6'8''; 6'8''; 6'8''; 6'8''; 6'8''; 7'1''; 7'1''; 7'1''; 7'1''; 7'1''; 7'1''; 7'5''; 7'5''; 7'5''; 7'5''; 7'5''; 7'5''
Power: M; M; MH; MH; H; H; M; M; H; H; MH; MH: MH; MH; H; H; XH; XH
Action: XF; XF; XF; XF; F; F; XF; XF; F; F; XF; XF; XF; XF; XF; XF; XF; XF
Pieces: 1

Line Weight: 10-14 lbs; 10-14 lbs; 12-16 lbs; 12-16 lbs; 14-20 lbs; 14-20 lbs; 10-14 lbs; 10-14 lbs; 14-20 lbs; 14-20 lbs; 12-16 lbs; 12-16 lbs; 12-16 lbs; 12-16 lbs; 14-20 lbs; 14-20 lbs; 17-25 lbs; 17-25 lbs
Lure Weight: 1/8-3/8 oz; 1/8-3/8 oz; 3/16-3/4 oz; 3/16-3/4 oz; 5/16-3/4 oz; 5/16-3/4 oz; 1/8-3/8 oz; 1/8-3/8 oz; 5/16-3/4 oz; 5/16-3/4 oz; 3/16-5/8 oz; 3/16-5/8 oz; 3/16-5/8 oz; 3/16-5/8 oz; 5/16-3/4 oz; 5/16-3/4 oz; 1/4-1 oz; 1/4-1 oz
Features: Designed specifically for fishing jigs and soft plastics; insanely light, unbelievably sensitive, and strong; feature split-grip cork handles; Fuji titanium SIC stripper guides, with the ultra-lite, ultra-strong RECOIL guides the rest of the way.
Price:............................ **$500.00–$600.00**

ACTION	POWER	
M=Moderate	UL=Ultra Light	H=Heavy
MF=Moderate Fast	L=Light	MH=Medium-Heavy
F=Fast	ML=Medium-Light	XH=Extra Heavy
XF=Extra Fast		

RODS

OKUMA C3-40X

Model: C3x-C-6101MH, C3x-C-661M, C3x-C-661MH, C3x-C-681H, C3x-C-681MH, C3x-C-701M, C3x-C-701MH, C3x-C-701ML, C3x-C-7101M, C3x-C-7111H, C3x-C-721H, C3x-C-721XH, C3x-C-761M, C3x-C-761XXH
Length: 6'10''; 6'6''; 6'6''; 6'8''; 6'8''; 7'; 7'; 7'; 7'10''; 7'11''; 7'11''; 7'2''; 7'2''; 7'6''; 7'6''
Power: MH; M; MH; H; MH; M; MH; ML; M; H; XH; H; XH; M; XXH
Action: F
Pieces: 1
Line Weight: 12-20 lbs; 8-17 lbs; 10-20 lbs; 12-20 lbs; 10-20 lbs; 8-17 lbs; 10-20 lbs; 6-12 lbs; 8-17 lbs; 15-30 lbs; 20-40 lbs; 12-20 lbs; 15-30 lbs; 8-17 lbs; 30-60 lbs
Guide Count: 10; 9; 9; 9; 10; 10; 10; 10; 12; 11; 11; 10; 10; 12; 11

Lure Weight: 1/4-1 oz; 1/4-5/8 oz; 1/4-1 oz; 3/8-1 oz; 3/16-3/4 oz; 1/4-5/8 oz; 1/4-1 oz; 1/8-3/8 oz; 1/4-1 oz; 1-5 oz; 2-8 oz; 3/8-1 oz; 3/8-1 oz; 1/2-2 oz; 3/8-3/4 oz; 3-12 oz
Features: 40-ton carbon, ultra sensitive blank construction; custom 1K woven carbon cone grip configuration; customized ported Fuji reel seats for reduced weight; ultra hard zirconium guide inserts for braided line; titanium guide frames on all spinning models; titanium guide frames on all double foot casting guides; ALPS low-profile frames on all single foot casting guides; split-grip butt for reduced weight and improved balance; limited lifetime warranty.
Price: . . . .**$154.99–$194.99**

ACTION		POWER	
M=Moderate	UL=Ultra Light	H=Heavy	
MF=Moderate Fast	L=Light	MH=Medium-Heavy	
F=Fast	ML=Medium-Light	XH=Extra Heavy	
XF=Extra Fast			

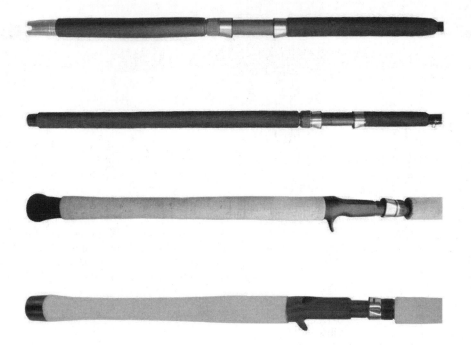

OKUMA CELILO SPECIALTY
Model: CE-C-1102Ha, CE-C-461Ha, CE-C-561Ha, CE-C-701Ha, CE-C-701XHa, CE-C-702L
Length: 11'; 4'6''; 5'6''; 7'; 7'; 7'
Power: H; H; H; H; XH; L
Action: M/MF; XF; F/XF; F; F; M
Pieces: 2; 1; 1; 1; 1; 2
Line Weight: 15-40 lbs; 40-100 lbs; 50-100 lbs; 20-50 lbs; 30-80 lbs; 2-8 lbs

Guide Count: 8; 5; 6; 10; 10; 8
Features: Sensitive graphite composite blanks; aluminum oxide guide inserts; Fuji guides on 701H and 701XH; stainless steel hooded reel seats; aluminum gimbal on halibut and sturgeon rods; rugged graphite butt section on halibut rod; one-year warranty.
Price:.............................**$44.99–$79.99**

ACTION	POWER	
M=Moderate	UL=Ultra Light	H=Heavy
MF=Moderate Fast	L=Light	MH=Medium-Heavy
F=Fast	ML=Medium-Light	XH=Extra Heavy
XF=Extra Fast		

RODS: Freshwater Baitcasting

OKUMA EVX

Model: EVx-C-601Ma, EVx-C-661Ha, EVx-C-661Ma, EVx-C-661MHa, EVx-C-661MLa, EVx-C-681MHa, EVx-C-691MHa, EVx-C-701Ma, EVx-C-701MHa, EVx-C-701MLa, EVx-C-751Ha, EVx-C-751MHa, EVx-C-761H-Ta
Length: 6'; 6'6''; 6'6''; 6'6''; 6'6''; 6'8''; 6'9''; 7'; 7'; 7'; 7'5''; 7'5''; 7'6''
Power: M; H; M; MH; ML; MH; MH; M; MH; ML; H; MH; H
Action: MF; MF; MF; F; MF; MF; MF; F; F; MF; F; MF; MF
Pieces: 1
Line Weight: 8-17 lbs; 12-25 lbs; 8-17 lbs; 10-20 lbs; 6-12 lbs; 10-20 lbs; 12-25 lbs; 8-17 lbs; 10-20 lbs; 6-12 lbs; 12-25 lbs; 10-20 lbs; 12-25 lbs

Guide Count: 10; 11; 11; 11; 11; 11; 11; 11; 11; 11; 10; 10; 11
Lure Weight: 1/4-5/8 oz; 3/8-1 1/4 oz; 1/4-5/8 oz; 1/4-1 oz; 1/8-3/8 oz; 1/4-1 oz; 3/8-1 1/2 oz; 1/4-5/8 oz; 1/4-1 oz; 1/8-3/8 oz; 3/8-1 1/4 oz; 1/4-1 oz; 3/8-1 1/4 oz
Features: IM8 graphite blank construction; crank bait rods are glass blank construction; ALPS stainless steel guide frames; zirconium guide inserts for braided line; Fuji ACS trigger reel seat on casting models; Fuji DPS carbon reel seat on spinning models; premium cork full or split grips; casting rods with rear split grip and no foregrip; spinning rods with rear split grip and no foregrip; crank bait rods with full rear cork butt; no foregrip; integrated compressed cork butt cap; limited lifetime warranty.
Price:............................. $99.99–$119.99

OKUMA REFLEXIONS

Model: Rx-C-661M, Rx-C-661MH, Rx-C662M, Rx-C-701M, Rx-C-701MH, Rx-C-701ML, Rx-C-7101M-T
Length: 6'6''; 6'6''; 6'6''; 7'; 7'; 7'; 7'10''
Power: M; MH; M; M; MH; ML; M
Action: MF; MF; MF; F; MF; MF; MF
Pieces: 1; 1; 2; 1; 1; 1; 1
Line Weight: 8-17 lbs; 10-20 lbs; 8-17 lbs; 8-17 lbs; 12-25 lbs; 6-15 lbs; 10-20 lbs

Guide Count: 9; 9; 8; 9; 9; 9; 9
Lure Weight: 1/4-5/8 oz; 1/4-1 oz; 1/4-5/8 oz; 1/4-5/8 oz; 3/8-1 1/4 oz; 1/8-5/8 oz; 1/4-1 oz
Features: IM6 rod blanks and low-profile stainless steel guide frames with braid-ready zirconium inserts; spiit-grip cork handles; stainless steel hooded reel seat; thru-blank reel seats on casting models to reduce weight and increase sensitivity; limited lifetime warranty.
Price:................................. $64.99

ACTION	POWER	
M=Moderate	UL=Ultra Light	H=Heavy
MF=Moderate Fast	L=Light	MH=Medium-Heavy
F=Fast	ML=Medium-Light	XH=Extra Heavy
XF=Extra Fast		

OKUMA TARVOS

Model: TV-C-661M, TV-C-661MH, TV-C-701M, TV-C-701MH
Length: 6'6''; 6'6''; 7'; 7'
Power: M; MH; M; MH
Action: M/MF
Pieces: 1
Line Weight: 6-15 lbs; 8-17 lbs; 6-15 lbs; 6-15 lbs

Guide Count: 9; 9; 10; 10
Lure Weight: 1/4-3/4 oz; 1/4-1 oz; 1/4-3/4 oz; 1/4-3/4 oz
Features: Graphite composite rod blank construction; stainless steel guide frames; titanium oxide guide inserts; stainless steel hooded reel seat; split-grip butt design; comfortable EVA fore and rear grips; stainless steel hook keeper; one-year limited warranty.
Price:. **$42.99**

SHIMANO COMPRE BASS CASTING WORM & JIG

Model: CPC68MC, CPCX68MC, CPC68MHC, CPCX68MHC, CPC72MC, CPCX72MC, CPC72MHC, CPCX72MHC, CPC72HC
Length: 6'8''; 6'8''; 6'8''; 6'8''; 7'2''; 7'2''; 7'2''; 7'2''; 7'2''
Power: M; M; MH; MH; M; M; MH; MH; H
Action: F; XF; F; XF; F; XF; F; XF; F

Line Weight: 6-12 lbs; 8-14 lbs; 10-17 lbs; 12-20 lbs; 6-12 lbs; 8-14 lbs; 10-17 lbs; 12-20 lbs; 12-25 lbs
Lure Weight: 1/8-1/4 oz; 1/4-3/8 oz; 1/4-3/4 oz; 1/4-1 oz; 1/8-1/4 oz; 1/4-3/8 oz; 1/4-3/4 oz; 1/4-1 oz; 1/2-1 1/2 oz
Features: IM9 graphite construction; Fuji aluminum oxide guides; custom Shimano reel seats.
Price:. **$99.99**

ACTION	POWER	
M=Moderate	UL=Ultra Light	H=Heavy
MF=Moderate Fast	L=Light	MH=Medium-Heavy
F=Fast	ML=Medium-Light	XH=Extra Heavy
XF=Extra Fast		

Freshwater Baitcasting

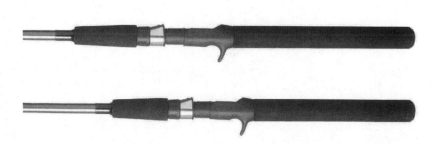

SHIMANO CUMARA

Model: CUC68MA, CUCX68MA, CUC68MHA, CUCX68MHA, CUC72MA, CUCX72MA, CUC72MHA, CUCX72MHA, CUCX711HA, CUC711XHA, CUCSB610MHA, CUCSBX610MHA, CUCSBX72MHA, CUCC70MA, CUCC70MHA, CUCC76MA, CUCC76MHA, CUCC711MA, CUCC711MHA, CUCU79HA
Length: 6'8''; 6'8''; 6'8''; 6'8''; 7'2''; 7'2''; 7'2''; 7'2''; 7'11''; 7'11''; 6'10''; 6'10''; 7'2''; 7'; 7'; 7'6''; 7'6''; 7'11''; 7'11''; 7'9''
Power: M; M; MH; MH; M; M; MH; MH; H; XH; MH; MH; MH; M; MH; M; MH; M; MH; H
Action: F; XF; F; XF; F; XF; F; XF; XF; F; F; XF; XF; MF; MF; MF; MF; MF; F; F

Line Weight: 6-12 lbs; 8-14 lbs; 10-17 lbs; 12-20 lbs; 6-12 lbs; 8-14 lbs; 10-17 lbs; 12-20 lbs; 15-30 lbs; 15-30 lbs; 8-17 lbs; 10-20 lbs; 12-25 lbs; 8-14 lbs; 10-20 lbs; 8-17 lbs; 10-20 lbs; 10-20 lbs; 12-25 lbs; 15-30 lbs
Lure Weight: 1/8-1/4 oz; 1/4-3/8 oz; 1/4-3/4 oz; 1/4-1 oz; 1/8-1/4 oz; 1/4-3/8 oz; 1/4-3/4 oz; 1/4-1 oz; 3/8-1 oz; 1-3 oz; 3/8-1/2 oz; 1/2-1 oz; 3/4-1 1/4 oz; 1/4-5/8 oz; 3/8-1 oz; 1/4-3/4 oz; 3/8-1 oz; 3/8-3/4 oz; 3/8-1 oz; 1-3 oz
Features: Convenient hook keeper; Fuji KR-concept Alconite guides; custom Shimano reel seat; shaped EVA foam grips; micro guides technique-specific actions; laser-etched badge.
Price: $259.99

SHIMANO FX

Model: FXC60MB-2, FXC66MHB2, FXC70MB-2
Length: 6'; 6'6''; 7'
Power: M; MH; M
Action: F
Pieces: 2
Line Weight: 6-15 lbs; 10-20 lbs; 8-17 lbs

Lure Weight: 1/4-3/4 oz; 1/4-1 oz; 1/4-5/8 oz
Features: Durable aeroglass blank construction features; reinforced aluminum oxide guides; solid locking graphite reel seat; comfortable EVA handles.
Price: $19.99

ACTION		POWER	
M=Moderate	UL=Ultra Light		H=Heavy
MF=Moderate Fast	L=Light		MH=Medium-Heavy
F=Fast	ML=Medium-Light		XH=Extra Heavy
XF=Extra Fast			

SHIMANO SELLUS

Model: SUC68MH, SUCX68MH, SUC72MH, SUCX72MH, SUCSB610M, SUCSB610MH, SUCT68M, SUCCB68M, SUCC870M, SUCC870MH, SUCX76MH
Length: 6'8''; 6'8''; 7'2''; 7'2''; 6'10''; 6'10''; 6'8''; 6'8''; 7'; 7'; 7'6''
Power: MH; MH; MH; MH; M; MH; M; M; M; MH; MH
Action: F; XF; F; XF; F; F; F; F; F; F; XF
Line Weight: 10-17 lbs; 12-20 lbs; 10-17 lbs; 12-20 lbs; 8-15 lbs; 10-20 lbs; 10-20 lbs; 8-14 lbs; 8-17 lbs; 10-20 lbs; 15-30 lbs

Lure Weight: 1/4-3/4 oz; 1/4-1 oz; 1/4-3/4 oz; 1/4-1 oz; 1/4-1/2 oz; 1/2-1 oz; 3/8-1 oz; 1/4-5/8 oz; 1/4-3/4 oz; 3/8-1 oz; 3/8-1 oz
Features: 24-ton graphite blank technique specific actions; low-profile aluminum oxide guides; custom Shimano reel seat; custom-shaped EVA split-grip handle; laser-etched technique badge; multipurpose hook keeper.
Price: **$59.99**

SHIMANO SOJOURN

Model: SJC66MA, SJC66M2A, SJC66MHA, SJC70MA
Length: 6'6''; 6'6''; 6'6''; 7'
Power: M; M; MH; M
Action: F
Pieces: 1; 2; 1; 1

Line Weight: 10-20 lbs; 10-20 lbs; 15-30 lbs; 10-20 lbs
Lure Weight: 1/4-3/4 oz; 1/4-3/4 oz; 1/4-1 oz; 1/4-3/4 oz
Features: Graphite composite blank; low-profile aluminum oxide guides; custom Shimano reel seat; custom-shaped cork handle; EVA butt cap; multipurpose hook keeper.
Price: **$29.99**

ACTION	POWER	
M=Moderate	UL=Ultra Light	H=Heavy
MF=Moderate Fast	L=Light	MH=Medium-Heavy
F=Fast	ML=Medium-Light	XH=Extra Heavy
XF=Extra Fast		

ST. CROIX LEGEND ELITE

Model: LEC60MF, LEC66MF, LEC66MHF, LEC68MXF, LEC70MF, LEC70MHF, LEC70HF
Length: 6'; 6'6''; 6'6''; 6'8''; 7'; 7'; 7'
Power: M; M; MH; M; M; MH; H
Action: F; F; F; XF; F; F; F
Pieces: 1
Line Weight: 10-17 lbs; 10-17 lbs; 12-20 lbs; 8-14 lbs; 10-17 lbs; 12-20 lbs; 14-25 lbs
Lure Weight: 1/4-5/8 oz; 1/4-5/8 oz; 3/8-1 oz; 1/4-5/8 oz; 1/4-5/8 oz; 3/8-1 oz; 3/8-1 1/2 oz
Features: Integrated Poly Curve tooling technology; Advanced Reinforcing Technology; super high-modulus SCVI graphite with FRS in lower section for maximum power and strength with reduced weight; high-modulus/high-strain SCV graphite with FRS and carbon-matte scrim for unparalleled strength and durability; slim-profile ferrules; phenomenally sensitive, light, and smooth casting; Fuji SiC Concept Guide System with titanium-finished frames; Fuji VSS reel seat/frosted silver hood on spinning models; Fuji ACS reel seat/frosted silver hood on casting models; machined-aluminum wind check; super-grade cork handle; two coats of Flex Coat slow-cure finish; includes deluxe rod sack; lifetime limited warranty.
Price: . . . . **$320.00–$370.00**

ACTION	POWER	
M=Moderate	UL=Ultra Light	H=Heavy
MF=Moderate Fast	L=Light	MH=Medium-Heavy
F=Fast	ML=Medium-Light	XH=Extra Heavy
XF=Extra Fast		

ST. CROIX LEGEND TOURNAMENT BASS

Model: TBC68MF, TBC68MXF, TBC68MHF, TBC610MLXF, TBC610MXF, TBC71MF, TBC71MHF, TBC71MHXF, TBC72MM, TBC73MHF, TBC73XHF, TBC74HF, TBC76MHMF, TBC78MHM, TBC79HMF, TBC710HF, TBC710HM, TBC711HMF

Length: 6'8''; 6'8''; 6'8''; 6'10''; 6'10''; 7'1''; 7'1''; 7'1''; 7'2''; 7'3''; 7'3''; 7'4''; 7'6''; 7'8''; 7'9''; 7'10''; 7'10''; 7'11''

Power: M; M; MH; ML; M; M; MH; MH; M; MH; XH; H; MH; MH; H; H; H; H

Action: F; XF; F; XF; XF; F; F; XF; M; F; F; F; MF; M; MF; F; M; MF

Pieces: 1

Line Weight: 10-17 lbs; 8-14 lbs; 12-20 lbs; 6-10 lbs; 10-14 lbs; 10-17 lbs; 12-20 lbs; 12-17 lbs; 8-14 lbs; 12-25 lbs; 17-30 lbs; 14-25 lbs; 12-25 lbs; 10-20 lbs; 14-30 lbs; 14-30 lbs; 12-25 lbs; 14-30 lbs

Lure Weight: 1/4-5/8 oz; 1/4-5/8 oz; 3/8-1 oz; 1/8-1/2 oz; 1/8-5/16 oz; 1/4-5/8 oz; 3/8-1 oz; 5/16-3/4 oz; 1/4-5/8 oz; 5/8-1 1/4 oz; 1-2 1/2 oz; 3/8-1 1/2 oz; 3/8-1 1/4 oz; 3/8-1 oz; 1/2-2 oz; 1-4 oz; 1/2-1 3/8 oz; 1/2-2 oz

Features: Integrated Poly Curve tooling technology; Advanced Reinforcing Technology; high-modulus/high-strain SCIV graphite with FRS for unparalleled strength and durability; technique-specific bass series features unrivaled technology and performance; Fuji K-Series Concept Tangle Free guides with Alconite rings and polished frames; ideal for super braid, mono, and fluorocarbon lines, the sloped frame and ring shed tangles before they become a problem; Fuji SK2 split reel seat for the ultimate in light weight and sensitivity; machined-aluminum wind check and trim pieces; split-grip/super-grade cork handle; two coats of Flex Coat slow-cure finish; lifetime limited warranty.

Price:. . . . . **$250.00–$280.00**

ACTION	POWER	
M=Moderate	**UL=Ultra Light**	**H=Heavy**
MF=Moderate Fast	**L=Light**	**MH=Medium-Heavy**
F=Fast	**ML=Medium-Light**	**XH=Extra Heavy**
XF=Extra Fast		

ST. CROIX LEGENDXTREME

Model: LXC68MF, LXC68MXF, LXC68MHF, LXC610MXF, LXC70MF, LXC70MHF, LXC71MHXF, LXC72MM, LXC74HF, LXC76MHMF, LXC78MHM, LXC711HMF

Length: 6'8''; 6'8''; 6'8''; 6'10''; 7'; 7'; 7'1''; 7'2''; 7'4''; 7'6''; 7'8''; 7'11''

Power: M; M; MH; M; M; MH; MH; M; H; MH; MH; H

Action: F; XF; F; XF; F; F; XF; M; F; MF; M; MF

Pieces: 1

Line Weight: 10-17 lbs; 8-14 lbs; 12-20 lbs; 10-14 lbs; 10-17 lbs; 12-20 lbs; 12-20 lbs; 8-14 lbs; 14-25 lbs; 12-25 lbs; 10-20 lbs; 14-30 lbs

Lure Weight: 1/4-5/8 oz; 1/4-5/8 oz; 3/8-1 oz; 1/8-5/16 oz; 1/4-5/8 oz; 3/8-1 oz; 1/4-3/4 oz; 1/4-5/8 oz; 3/8-1 1/2 oz; 3/8-1 1/4 oz; 3/8-1 oz; 1/2-2 oz

Features: Integrated Poly Curve tooling technology; Taper Enhancement Technology blank design provides curved patterns for improved action with increased sensitivity; Advanced Reinforcing Technology; super high-modulus SCVI graphite with FRS in lower section for maximum power and strength with reduced weight; high-modulus/ high-strain SCV graphite with FRS and carbon-matte scrim for unparalleled strength, durability, and sensitivity; slim-profile ferrules; Fuji K-R Concept Tangle Free guides with SiC rings and exclusive E-color finish frames; ideal for super braid, mono, and fluorocarbon lines, the sloped frame and ring shed tangles before they become a problem; Fuji SK2 split reel seat for the ultimate in light weight and sensitivity; Xtreme-Skin handle repels water, dirt, and fish slime and cleans up easily; manufactured by St. Croix to provide outstanding angler comfort, casting efficiency, and sensitivity; machined-aluminum wind check, handle trim pieces and butt cap with logo badge; two coats of Flex Coat slow-cure finish; includes protective rod sack; lifetime limited warranty.

Price: . . . . **$390.00–$430.00**

ACTION	POWER	
M=Moderate	UL=Ultra Light	H=Heavy
MF=Moderate Fast	L=Light	MH=Medium-Heavy
F=Fast	ML=Medium-Light	XH=Extra Heavy
XF=Extra Fast		

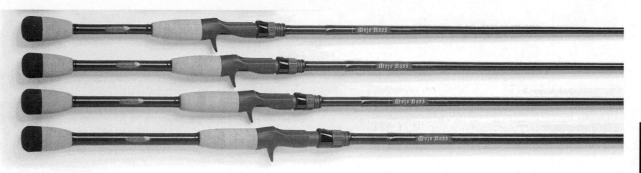

ST. CROIX MOJO BASS

Model: MBC66MF, MBC66MHF, MBC68MXF, MBC70MF, MBC70MHF, MBC70MHM, MBC70HF, MBC76MHMF, MBC79HF, MBC711HMF
Length: 6'6''; 6'6''; 6'8''; 7'; 7'; 7'; 7'; 7'6''; 7'9''; 7'11''
Power: M; MH; M; M; MH; MH; H; MH; H; H
Action: F; F; XF; F; F; M; F; MF; F; MF
Pieces: 1
Line Weight: 10-17 lbs; 12-20 lbs; 8-14 lbs; 10-17 lbs; 12-20 lbs; 10-20 lbs; 14-25 lbs; 12-25 lbs; 14-30 lbs; 14-30 lbs
Lure Weight: 1/4-5/8 oz; 3/8-1 oz; 1/4-5/8 oz; 1/4-5/8 oz; 3/8-1 oz; 3/8-1 oz; 3/8-1 1/2 oz; 3/8-1 1/4 oz; 1-4 oz; 1/2-2 oz

Features: Premium-quality SCII graphite; super premium, 100 percent linear S-glass on Mojo Bass Glass models; technique-specific bass series designed and built for superior performance; Kigan Master Hand 3D guides featuring slim, strong aluminum-oxide rings with black frames; Fuji ECS reel seat/black hood on casting models; Fuji DPS reel seat/black hoods on spinning models; split-grip/premium-grade cork handle; two coats of Flex Coat slow-cure finish; five-year warranty.
Price:..........................**$110.00–$130.00**

ACTION	**POWER**	
M=Moderate	**UL**=Ultra Light	**H**=Heavy
MF=Moderate Fast	**L**=Light	**MH**=Medium-Heavy
F=Fast	**ML**=Medium-Light	**XH**=Extra Heavy
XF=Extra Fast		

ST. CROIX RAGE

Model: RC68MF, RC68MXF, RC68MHF, RC610MXF, RC71MF, RC71MHF, RC71MHXF, RC72MM, RC74HF, RC76MHMF, RC78MHM, RC11HMF
Length: 6'8"; 6'8"; 6'8"; 6'10"; 7'1"; 7'1"; 7'1"; 7'2"; 7'4"; 7'6"; 7'8"; 7'11"
Power: M; M; MH; M; M; MH; MH; M; H; MH; MH; H
Action: F; XF; F; XF; F; F; XF; M; F; MF; M; MF
Pieces: 1
Line Weight: 10-17 lbs; 8-14 lbs; 12-20 lbs; 10-14 lbs; 10-17 lbs; 12-20 lbs; 12-17 lbs; 8-14 lbs; 14-25 lbs; 12-25 lbs; 10-20 lbs; 14-30 lbs
Lure Weight: 1/4-5/8 oz; 1/4-5/8 oz; 3/8-1 oz; 1/8-5/16 oz; 1/4-5/8 oz; 3/8-1 oz; 5/16-3/4 oz; 1/4-5/8 oz; 3/8-1 1/2 oz; 3/8-1 1/4 oz; 3/8-1 oz
Features: Integrated Poly Curve tooling technology; premium, high-modulus SCIII graphite; incredibly lightweight and sensitive with superb balance and extreme strength; Pacific Bay Minima micro guide configuration for high performance and improved durability by eliminating insert failure, plus 20 percent to 30 percent weight savings compared to ceramic guides; Pacific Bay Minima casting reel seat/black hood provides maximum rod blank exposure and is 30 percent lighter than conventional trigger reel seats; Pacific Bay Minima spinning reel seat/black hood provides maximum rod blank exposure and is 10 percent to 20 percent lighter than conventional spinning reel seats; contoured handle provides split-grip performance; featuring a precision-shaped core wrapped with a neoprene skin for maximum comfort and sensitivity; EVA trim pieces provide additional refinement; two coats of Flex Coat slow-cure finish; five-year warranty.
Price: . . . . $150.00–$170.00

ACTION		POWER	
M=Moderate	UL=Ultra Light	H=Heavy	
MF=Moderate Fast	L=Light	MH=Medium-Heavy	
F=Fast	ML=Medium-Light	XH=Extra Heavy	
XF=Extra Fast			

DAIWA DXI INSHORE

Model: DXI661MLFB, DXI661MFB, DXI701MLFB, DXI701MFB, DXI761MLFB, DXI761MFB
Length: 6'6''; 6'6''; 7'; 7'; 7'6''; 7'6''
Power: ML; M; ML; M; ML; M
Action: F
Pieces: 1
Line Weight: 8-17 lbs; 8-20 lbs; 8-17 lbs; 8-20 lbs; 8-17 lbs; 8-20 lbs

Guide Count: 9; 9; 10; 10; 10; 10
Lure Weight: 1/8-3/4 oz; 1/4-1 oz; 1/8-3/4 oz; 1/4-1 oz; 1/8-3/4 oz; 1/4-1 oz
Features: IM6 graphite blank construction; Minima zirconia ring guides; Fuji (ACS casting & VSS spinning) reel seat; split-design natural cork grip; woven carbon and stainless steel reel clamp; hook keeper; five-year limited warranty.
Price: . . . .**$89.95–$99.95**

ACTION	POWER	
M=Moderate	UL=Ultra Light	H=Heavy
MF=Moderate Fast	L=Light	MH=Medium-Heavy
F=Fast	ML=Medium-Light	XH=Extra Heavy
XF=Extra Fast		

RODS: **Saltwater Baitcasting**

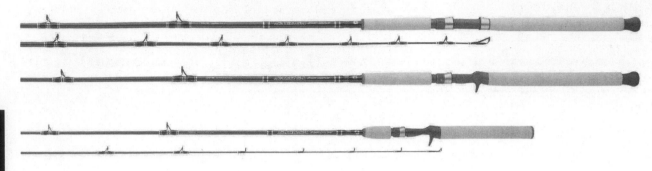

DAIWA SALTIGA INSHORE COAST-TO-COAST

Model: CC701HFB, CC701XHFB, CC761HFB, CC761XHFB, CC801HFB, CC801XHFB
Length: 7'; 7'; 7'6''; 7'6''; 8'; 8'
Power: H; XH; H; XH; H; XH
Action: F
Pieces: 1
Line Weight: 15-25 lbs; 17-30 lbs; 15-25 lbs; 17-30 lbs; 15-25 lbs; 17-30 lbs

Guide Count: 9
Lure Weight: 1/2-1 1/2 oz; 1/2-2 oz; 1/2-1 1/2 oz; 1/2-2 oz; 1/2-1 1/2 oz; 1/2-2 oz
Features: Bias construction high-modulus graphite blank; tough Fuji Alconite guides; Fuji SiC tip-top (Northeast models only); genuine Fuji reel seat; high-quality cork grip; convenient hook keeper; protective rubber butt cap; limited lifetime warranty.
Price:.................................... **$94.95**

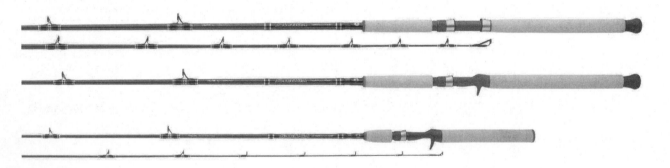

DAIWA SALTIGA INSHORE GULF COAST

Model: GC661MLFB, GC701MLXB, GC701MXB, GC761MXB
Length: 6'6''; 7'; 7'; 7'6''
Power: ML; ML; M; M
Action: F; XF; XF; XF
Pieces: 1
Line Weight: 6-14 lbs; 6-14 lbs; 8-20 lbs; 8-20 lbs

Guide Count: 9; 10; 10; 10
Lure Weight: 1/8-1/2 oz; 1/8-1/2 oz; 1/4-1 oz; 1/4-1 oz
Features: Bias construction high-modulus graphite blank; tough Fuji Alconite guides; Fuji SiC tip-top (Northeast models only); genuine Fuji reel seat; high-quality cork grip; convenient hook keeper, protective rubber butt cap; limited lifetime warranty.
Price:....................................$149.95

ACTION	POWER	
M=Moderate	UL=Ultra Light	H=Heavy
MF=Moderate Fast	L=Light	MH=Medium-Heavy
F=Fast	ML=Medium-Light	XH=Extra Heavy
XF=Extra Fast		

LAMIGLAS BIG FISH
Model: BFC 5610, BFC 5610 RT, BFC 70 H
Length: 5'6''; 5'6''; 7'
Power: XH; XH; H
Action: F
Pieces: 1
Line Weight: 50-100 lbs; 50-100 lbs; 20-50 lbs

Features: Smooth, balanced designs are focused on 20- to 100-pound pound line classes, placing them in the heart of halibut, tuna, shark, large striper, and wreck fisheries; features aluminum reel seats; slick butts; roller tip; wireline rod with silicon nitrate guides; premiere cod rod.
Price:. . . . .**$180.00–$220.00**

LAMIGLAS TRI-FLEX GRAPHITE INSHORE
Model: TFX 6015 C, TFX 7020 CT, TFX 7030 C, TFX 7030 CT, TFX 7040 CT, TFX 7650 CT
Length: 6'; 7'; 7'; 7'; 7'; 7'6''
Action: F
Pieces: 1
Line Weight: 8-17 lbs; 8-20 lbs; 15-30 lbs; 15-30 lbs; 20-40 lbs; 20-50 lbs
Lure Weight: 1/4-1 oz; 1-4 oz; 3/4-3 oz; 3-6 oz; 4-10 oz; 6-16 oz

Features: Cork handles immediately categorize these rods as inshore, but don't overlook these nine highly capable models wherever the need for refined power of tri-flex graphite exists (specifically, the new TFX 6015 C, TFX 6015 S, and TRX 6615 S); latest editions are precision-balanced rods for throwing bucktails for striped bass, fluke, and bluefish; others are equally at home casting swim baits to tuna as they are throwing eels to stripers or crabs to tarpon; easy handling and can-do nature.
Price:. . . . .**$220.00–$300.00**

ACTION	POWER	
M=Moderate	UL=Ultra Light	H=Heavy
MF=Moderate Fast	L=Light	MH=Medium-Heavy
F=Fast	ML=Medium-Light	XH=Extra Heavy
XF=Extra Fast		

LAMIGLAS TRI-FLEX GRAPHITE SALTWATER

Model: BL 5630 C, BL 7020 C, BL 7030 C, BL 7040 C, BL 7050 LB, BL 7640 C
Length: 5'6''; 7'; 7'; 7'; 7'; 7'6''
Action: F; MF: MF; M; MF; M
Pieces: 1
Line Weight: 20-40 lbs; 10-20 lbs; 15-30 lbs; 20-40 lbs; 20-50 lbs; 20-50 lbs

Lure Weight: 1-6 oz; 1-3 oz; 1-6 oz; 2-8 oz; 2-10 oz; 6-12 oz
Features: A combination of lightweight power, durability, sensitivity, and structural integrity that will provide years, and perhaps decades, of exciting battles.
Price:............................. **$260.00–$320.00**

G LOOMIS ESCAPE GLX

Model: ETR 84-3 MLS-10 GLX, ETR 84-3 MS-12 GLX
Length: 7'
Power: ML; M
Action: F
Pieces: 3
Line Weight: 6-12 lbs
Lure Weight: 1/4-1/2 oz; 1/4-5/8 oz

Features: Three-piece, high-performance, technical fishing tools; has specific line and lure ratings as well as the optimum line recommended; guides on the GLX models are nickel-titanium RECOIL, making it virtually impossible to experience any issues with rings popping out or frames fracturing; handles feature cork grips with fixed reel seats; comes in a handsome, protective rod sock and travel case.
Price:........................... **$655.00–$665.00**

ACTION	POWER	
M=Moderate	UL=Ultra Light	H=Heavy
MF=Moderate Fast	L=Light	MH=Medium-Heavy
F=Fast	ML=Medium-Light	XH=Extra Heavy
XF=Extra Fast		

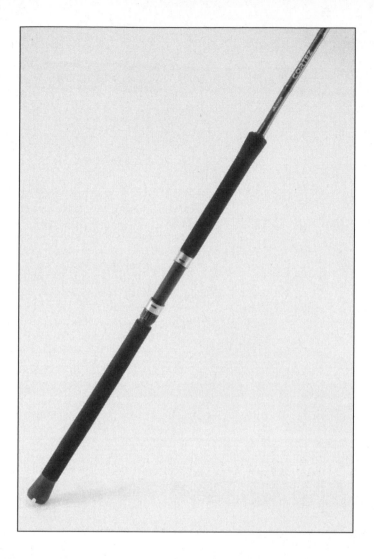

OKUMA CORTEZ

Model: CZ-C-661M, CZ-C-661MH, CZ-C-701M, CZ-C-701MH
Length: 6'6''; 6'6''; 7'; 7'
Power: M; MH; M; MH
Action: MF
Pieces: 1
Line Weight: 20-30 lbs; 30-50 lbs; 20-30 lbs; 30-50 lbs
Guide Count: 9; 9; 10; 10

Features: Extremely durable carbon and glass blank mixture for ultimate strength; EVA fore and rear grips for comfort and durability; double-footed stainless steel guide frames; polished titanium oxide guide inserts; cushioned stainless steel hooded reel seat; graphite gimbals on all models; durable non-skid, rubber gimbals on all models; all Cortez rods are one-piece blank construction; one-year warranty.
Price: **$64.99**

ACTION	POWER	
M=Moderate	UL=Ultra Light	H=Heavy
MF=Moderate Fast	L=Light	MH=Medium-Heavy
F=Fast	ML=Medium-Light	XH=Extra Heavy
XF=Extra Fast		

OKUMA PEZ VELA

Model: PV-C-661M, PV-C-661MH, PV-C-701M, PV-C-701MH
Length: 6'6''; 6'6''; 7'; 7'
Power: M; MH; M; MH
Action: MF
Pieces: 1
Line Weight: 12-25 lbs; 15-30 lbs; 12-25 lbs; 15-30 lbs
Guide Count: 7

Features: Extremely durable carbon and glass rod blank mixture; EVA fore and rear grips on spinning models; casting models feature EVA fore grip and a graphite butt; double-footed stainless steel guide frames; polished titanium oxide guide inserts; cushioned stainless steel hooded reel seat; durable non-skid, rubber gimbals on all models; all Pez Vela rods are one-piece blank construction; one-year warranty.
Price:.............................$69.99–$74.99

OKUMA SARASOTA

Model: Sr-C-661M, Sr-C-661MH, Sr-C-661ML, Sr-C-701M, Sr-C-701ML
Length: 6'6''; 6'6''; 6'6''; 7'; 7'
Power: M; MH; ML; M; ML
Action: MF
Pieces: 1
Line Weight: 20-40 lbs; 30-50 lbs; 15-30 lbs; 20-40 lbs; 15-30 lbs
Guide Count: 9; 9; 9; 10; 10
Features: Durable E-glass blank construction; glass fiber outer wrap increases hoop strength; double-footed stainless steel guide frames HD model uses heavy duty-style guide frames; use Pacific Bay roller stripper and tip guides; polished titanium oxide guide inserts; stainless steel hooded reel seats; heavy duty aluminum hooded reel seat on HD/T models; graphite gimbals on all models; custom epoxy wrapped foregrip transition cone; one-year warranty.
Price:...................................$49.99

ACTION	**POWER**	
M=Moderate	UL=Ultra Light	H=Heavy
MF=Moderate Fast	L=Light	MH=Medium-Heavy
F=Fast	ML=Medium-Light	XH=Extra Heavy
XF=Extra Fast		

SHIMANO SAGUARO

Model: SGC66M, SGC66MH, SGC70ML, SGC70M, SGC70MH
Length: 6'6''; 6'6''; 7'; 7'; 7'
Power: M; MH; ML; M; MH
Action: F
Pieces: 1
Line Weight: 15-30 lbs; 20-50 lbs; 10-20 lbs; 15-30 lbs; 20-50 lbs

Guide Count: 7; 7; 8; 8; 8
Features: Composite rod blank; aluminum O ring; T-glass; graphite reel seat with stainless steel hoods; comfortable EVA handles; one-year warranty.
Price: **$54.99**

SHIMANO TALAVERA

Model: TEC60H, TEC60XH, TEC66M, TEC70ML, TEC70M, TEC70MH
Length: 6'; 6'; 6'6''; 7'; 7'; 7'
Power: H; XH; M; ML; M; MH
Action: F
Pieces: 1
Line Weight: 20-50 lbs; 30-80 lbs; 15-30 lbs; 10-20 lbs; 15-30 lbs; 20-50 lbs

Features: Shimano aeroglass or graphite composite (on selected models); graphite reel seat; Fuji heavy duty aluminum oxide boat guides (on selected models); Fuji aluminum oxide guides; EVA grip; AFTCO roller stripper and tip with Fuji heavy duty aluminum oxide boat guides (trolling models only); graphite gimbal with cap (on selected models); black aluminum reel seat (trolling models only).
Price: . . . . **$79.99–$89.99**

ACTION	POWER	
M=Moderate	UL=Ultra Light	H=Heavy
MF=Moderate Fast	L=Light	MH=Medium-Heavy
F=Fast	ML=Medium-Light	XH=Extra Heavy
XF=Extra Fast		

ST. CROIX LEGEND INSHORE GULF COAST

Model: LGCC66XLM, LGCC66LM, LGCC66MLM, LGCC70MLM

Length: 6'6''; 6'6''; 6'6''; 7'

Power: XL; L; ML; ML

Action: M

Pieces: 1

Line Weight: 6-10 lbs; 8-12 lbs; 8-14 lbs; 8-14 lbs

Lure Weight: 1/32-1/8 oz; 1/16-1/4 oz; 1/8-3/8 oz; 1/8-3/8 oz

Features: Integrated Poly Curve tooling technology; Advanced Reinforcing Technology; high-modulus/high-strain SCIV graphite with FRS for unparalleled strength and durability; designed specifically for inshore saltwater angling; Kigan Master Hand Zero Tangle guides with zirconia rings and titanium frames for the ultimate protection against saltwater corrosion; the sloped, wide-leg design prevents line tangles with mono, fluorocarbon, and super braid lines; Fuji SK2 split reel seat for the ultimate in light weight and sensitivity; super-grade cork handle on spinning models; split-grip/super-grade cork handle on casting models; corrosion-proof wind check and reel seat trim pieces; two coats of Flex Coat slow-cure finish; lifetime limited warranty.

Price:.............................$290.00–$300.00

ACTION	POWER	
M=Moderate	UL=Ultra Light	H=Heavy
MF=Moderate Fast	L=Light	MH=Medium-Heavy
F=Fast	ML=Medium-Light	XH=Extra Heavy
XF=Extra Fast		

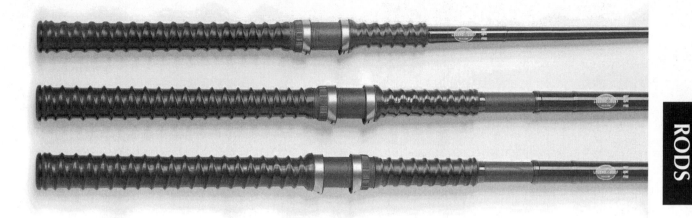

ST. CROIX LEGEND SURF

Model: LSC100MMF2, LSC106MHMF2, LSC110MHMF2
Length: 10'; 10'6''; 11'
Power: M; MH; MH
Action: MF
Pieces: 2
Line Weight: 10-20 lbs; 12-25 lbs; 15-40 lbs
Lure Weight: 1-4 oz; 2-6 oz; 3-8 oz
Features: Integrated Poly Curve tooling technology; Advanced Reinforcing Technology; high-modulus/high-strain SCIV graphite with FRS for unparalleled strength and durability; off-set, slim-profile ferrules on two-piece models provide one-piece performance; designed for extreme surf fishing performance; Fuji LC surf guides with Alconite ring for greater casting distance and accuracy; sloped frame reduces line tangling; Fuji DPS reel seat/frosted silver hoods; custom X-grip neoprene handle provides comfort and durability while reducing weight; positive grip improves when wet; two coats of Flex Coat slow-cure finish; lifetime limited warranty.
Price: . . . . **$420.00–$460.00**

ACTION	POWER	
M=Moderate	UL=Ultra Light	H=Heavy
MF=Moderate Fast	L=Light	MH=Medium-Heavy
F=Fast	ML=Medium-Light	XH=Extra Heavy
XF=Extra Fast		

RODS: Saltwater Baitcasting

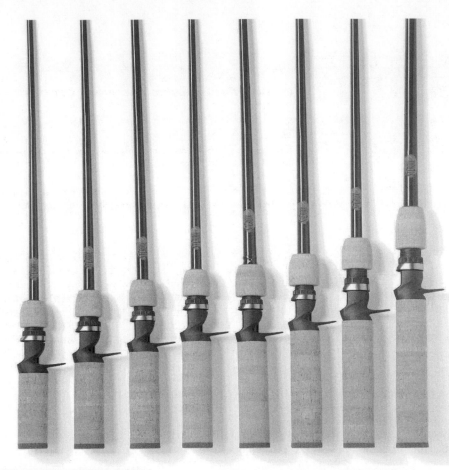

ST. CROIX TIDEMASTER INSHORE

Model: TIC66MHF, TIC66HF, TIC70LM, TIC70MLF, TIC70MF, TIC70MM, TIC70MHF, TIC70HF, TIC76MF, TIC76MHF, TIC76HF, TIC80MHF, TIC80HF
Length: 6'6''; 6'6''; 7'; 7'; 7'; 7'; 7'; 7'; 7'6''; 7'6''; 7'6''; 8'; 8'
Power: MH; H; L; ML; M; M; MH; H; M; MH; H; MH; H
Action: F; F; M; F; F; M; F; F; F; F; F; F; F
Pieces: 1
Line Weight: 10-20 lbs; 12-25 lbs; 6-12 lbs; 8-14 lbs; 8-17 lbs; 8-17 lbs; 10-20 lbs; 12-25 lbs; 8-17 lbs; 10-20 lbs; 12-25 lbs; 14-30 lbs; 17-40 lbs
Lure Weight: 1/2-1 1/4 oz; 3/4-2 oz; 1/8-3/8 oz; 1/8-1/2 oz; 3/8-3/4 oz; 1/4-5/8 oz; 1/2-1 1/4 oz; 3/4-2 oz; 3/8-3/4 oz; 1/2-1 1/4 oz; 3/4-2 oz; 1/2-2 oz; 3/4 -3 oz

Features: Premium-quality SCII graphite; outstanding strength, sensitivity, and hook-setting power; designed specifically for inshore saltwater angling; Batson Forecast hard aluminum-oxide guides with 316 stainless-steel frames for dramatically improved corrosion resistance compared to 304 stainless-steel frames; Fuji DPS reel seat/frosted silver hoods on spinning models; Fuji ECS or TCS reel seat/frosted silver hood on casting models; premium-grade cork handle; two coats of Flex Coat slow-cure finish; five-year warranty.
Price: . . . . **$140.00–$200.00**

ACTION	POWER	
M=Moderate	UL=Ultra Light	H=Heavy
MF=Moderate Fast	L=Light	MH=Medium-Heavy
F=Fast	ML=Medium-Light	XH=Extra Heavy
XF=Extra Fast		

BEAVERKILL FULL FLEX—LEGACY

Model: F703-3-3, F763-3-3, F804-3-3, F864-3-3, F904-3-3, F905-3-3
Length: 7'; 7'6''; 8'; 8'6''; 9'; 9'
Pieces: 3
Line Weight: 3W–5W
Features: Super-grade Portuguese cork grips; stripping guides are high-frame, three-leg, one-piece stainless steel with a silicon carbide molded ring; snake guides, the sidemounted hook keeper, and tip-tops are stainless-steel-coated with groove-resistant titanium carbide; lustrous emerald green proprietary blanks using a slip ferrule system are hand-crafted in the USA; forest green Beaverkill nylon-covered carrying case with integral dual-pocket rod pouch.
Price: **$395.00**

BEAVERKILL MID FLEX—LEGACY

Model: F703-2-3, F763-2-3, F804-2-3, F864-2-4-3, F904-2-3, F905-2-3, F906-2-3, F907-2-3, F908-2-3, F1008-2-3, F909-2-3
Length: 7'; 7'6''; 8'; 8'6''; 9'; 9'; 9'; 9'; 9'; 10'; 9'
Pieces: 3
Line Weight: 3W–9W
Features: Super-grade Portuguese cork grips; stripping guides are high-frame, three-leg, one-piece stainless steel with a silicon carbide molded ring; snake guides, the sidemounted hook keeper, and tip-tops are stainless-steel-coated with groove-resistant titanium carbide; lustrous emerald green proprietary blanks using a slip ferrule system are hand-crafted in the USA; forest green Beaverkill nylon-covered carrying case with integral dual-pocket rod pouch.
Price: **$395.00**

ACTION	POWER	
M=Moderate	UL=Ultra Light	H=Heavy
MF=Moderate Fast	L=Light	MH=Medium-Heavy
F=Fast	ML=Medium-Light	XH=Extra Heavy
XF=Extra Fast		

RODS: Freshwater Fly Fishing

BEAVERKILL TIP FLEX—LEGACY

Model: F904-1-3, F905-1-3, F906-1-3, F907-1-3, F908-1-3, F909-1-3, F9010-1-3, F9012-1-3
Length: 9'
Pieces: 3
Line Weight: 4W–12W
Features: Super-grade Portuguese cork grips; stripping guides are high-frame, three-leg, one-piece stainless steel with a silicon carbide molded ring; snake guides, the sidemounted hook keeper, and tip-tops are stainless-steel-coated with groove-resistant titanium carbide; lustrous emerald green proprietary blanks using a slip ferrule system are hand-crafted in the USA; forest green Beaverkill nylon-covered carrying case with integral dual-pocket rod pouch.
Price: **$395.00**

DAIWA ALGONQUIN

Model: AQF905A, AQF906A, AQF907A, AQF908EBA, AQF969EBA
Length: 9'; 9'; 9'; 9'; 9'6"
Pieces: 2
Line Weight: 4W–9W
Guide Count: 11
Features: High-quality graphite blank; aluminum oxide stripper and quality-plated snake guides; machined aluminum reel seat; removable extension butt on eight and nine weight models; natural cork grips.
Price: **$29.99**

ACTION	POWER	
M=Moderate	UL=Ultra Light	H=Heavy
MF=Moderate Fast	L=Light	MH=Medium-Heavy
F=Fast	ML=Medium-Light	XH=Extra Heavy
XF=Extra Fast		

EAGLE CLAW Featherlight
Model: FL300-6'6, FL300-7, FL300-8
Length: 6'6''; 7'; 8'
Action: L
Pieces: 2
Line Weight: 3W–6W
Guide Count: 9
Features: Classic featherlight action has been updated for a slightly quicker response; traditional fiberglass construction for the ultimate in feel, durability, and forgiveness; beautiful cork handles fit comfortably in your hand and provide a sure grip every time; perfectly matched components such as reel seats and guides complement every rod; one-year warranty.
Price: **$22.99**

EAGLE CLAW POWERLIGHT
Model: PLF8644, PLF954
Length: 8'6''; 9'
Action: MF
Pieces: 4
Line Weight: 4W–5W
Guide Count: 9; 10
Features: Powerful IM7 graphite is the backbone of this entirely new series of performance rods; ultra-light to medium-heavy actions are available for just about any species you are targeting; custom cork handles provide exceptional performance while maintaining their beautiful appearance and incredible durability; gun smoke finished guides and reel seats; fly rods feature four-piece construction for easy travel and storage; one-year warranty.
Price: **$39.99**

ACTION	POWER	
M=Moderate	UL=Ultra Light	H=Heavy
MF=Moderate Fast	L=Light	MH=Medium-Heavy
F=Fast	ML=Medium-Light	XH=Extra Heavy
XF=Extra Fast		

L.L.BEAN QUEST II FOUR-PIECE

Model: 9', 5 wt; 9', 6 wt; 9', 8 wt; 9', 9 wt
Length: 9'
Pieces: 4
Line Weight: 5W–9W

Features: Fine-tuned for beginner to intermediate casters; just tie on a fly and you're ready to fish; includes a rod, a reel loaded with backing, fly line, and a leader.
Price:. . . . .**$129.00–$149.00**

L.L.BEAN QUEST II TWO-PIECE

Model: 6'6", 3 wt; 7'6", 4 wt; 8'6", 5 wt; 9', 5 wt; 8'6", 6 wt
Length: 6'6"; 7'6"; 8'6"; 9'; 8'6"
Pieces: 2

Line Weight: 3W–6W
Features: Fine-tuned for beginner to intermediate casters; fish effectively on streams, lakes, and rivers; will grow with you, providing years of angling performance.
Price:. **$69.00**

ACTION	**POWER**	
M=Moderate	UL=Ultra Light	H=Heavy
MF=Moderate Fast	L=Light	MH=Medium-Heavy
F=Fast	ML=Medium-Light	XH=Extra Heavy
XF=Extra Fast		

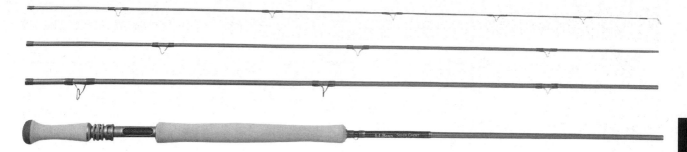

L.L.BEAN SILVER GHOST

Model: 10', 4 wt; 10', 5 wt; 10', 6 wt; 10', 7 wt; 10', 8 wt
Length: 10'
Pieces: 4
Line Weight: 4W–8W

Features: Lightweight design is durable and delivers outstanding performance; effectively handles heavier nymph rigs; great choice for big streamers in fast-moving water.
Price: . . . .$315.00–$365.00

L.L.BEAN STREAMLIGHT ULTRA TWO-PIECE

Model: 5'9", 3 wt; 6'11", 4 wt; 6'6", 3 wt; 8', 5 wt; 8'6", 5 wt; 9', 5 wt; 8'6", 6 wt; 9', 6 wt; 9'7", 7 wt; 9', 8 wt; 9', 9 wt
Length: 5'9"; 6'11"; 6'6"; 8'; 8'6"; 9'; 8'6"; 9'; 9'7"; 9'; 9'

Pieces: 2
Line Weight: 3W–9W
Features: Redesigned to be lighter with an improved taper; a rod you won't outgrow as your casting improves; reel-on-rod case included.
Price: . . . . $99.00–$125.00

ACTION	POWER	
M=Moderate	UL=Ultra Light	H=Heavy
MF=Moderate Fast	L=Light	MH=Medium-Heavy
F=Fast	ML=Medium-Light	XH=Extra Heavy
XF=Extra Fast		

G. LOOMIS GLX CLASSICS

Model: FR 1084-2 GLX, FR 1085-2 GLX, FR 1086-2 GLX, FR 1088-2 GLX
Length: 9'
Power: MS
Action: F
Pieces: 2
Line Weight: 4W–8W

Features: Lighter and more efficient than ever; made for the fanatical angler that specializes and has exacting expectations for his or her style of fishing; very accurate in linesize, but their biggest attribute may be their versatility; they load as well at 15 feet as they do at 60 feet, and they are extremely powerful given their extreme light weight.
Price: . . . . **$600.00–$620.00**

G. LOOMIS NRX LITE PRESENTATION

Model: NRX 903-4 LP G, NRX 1043-4 LP G, NRX 1084-4 LP G, NRX 1085-4 LP G, NRX 903-4 LP, NRX 1043-4 LP, NRX 1084-4 LP, NRX 1085-4 LP
Length: 7'6''; 8'8''; 9'; 9'; 7'6''; 8'8''; 9'; 9'
Power: M
Action: M
Pieces: 4
Line Weight: 3W–5W
Features: For when conditions call for long, delicate casts using extremely light leaders; they are smooth casting, soft tapers for managing long, whisper-thin leaders and small- to medium-sized dry flies; they track true for exceptional accuracy and control, plus they are light as a feather with beautiful lines; featuring select species cork and your choice of our original, stealthy look in matte black with bright blue wraps or a more traditional evergreen with subtle green wraps and silver trim.
Price: . . . . **$720.00–$755.00**

ACTION	POWER	
M=Moderate	UL=Ultra Light	H=Heavy
MF=Moderate Fast	L=Light	MH=Medium-Heavy
F=Fast	ML=Medium-Light	XH=Extra Heavy
XF=Extra Fast		

G. LOOMIS NRX NYMPH

Model: NRX 1203-4 Nymp G, NRX 1204-4 Nymph G,
NRX 1203-4 Nymph, NRX 1204-4 Nymph
Length: 10'
Power: XS
Action: XF
Pieces: 4
Line Weight: 3W–4W

Features: Extremely fast, 10-foot, four-piece rods with light, sensitive tips to help anglers make short, accurate casts for drifting nymphs; long, light leaders, guide the flies along the bottom, almost pulling the rig downstream; extra length and extra fast action helps improve casting accuracy and line mending while giving you quick hooksets and positive fish-fighting control.
Price:. . . . .**$775.00–$785.00**

G. LOOMIS NRX TROUT

Model: NRX 1083-4 G, NRX 1084-4 G, NRX 1085-4 G,
NRX 1086-4 G, NRX 1083-4, NRX 1084-4, NRX 1085-4,
NRX 1086-4
Length: 9'
Power: MS
Action: MF; F; F; F; MF; F; F; F
Pieces: 4

Line Weight: 3W–6W
Features: Black ion-coated REC recoil guides; each rods custom reel seat has no exposed threads so as to make it easy to lock the reel to the reel seat; grips feature HD cork design, where the cork transitions to provide more sensitivity where needed, and more durability in where needed.
Price:. . . . .**$730.00–$745.00**

ACTION	POWER	
M=Moderate	UL=Ultra Light	H=Heavy
MF=Moderate Fast	L=Light	MH=Medium-Heavy
F=Fast	ML=Medium-Light	XH=Extra Heavy
XF=Extra Fast		

RODS: **Freshwater Fly Fishing**

RODS

OKUMA CRISIUM

Model: CRF-34-70-2, CRF-45-86-2, CRF-56-90-2, CRF-67-86-2, CRF-67-96-2, CRF-78-90-2
Length: 7'; 8'6''; 9'; 8'6''; 9'6''; 9'
Action: MF
Pieces: 2
Line Weight: 3W–8W

Guide Count: 7; 10; 10; 10; 10; 10
Features: Lightweight graphite construction; two-piece rod design; titanium oxide stripper guide; stainless steel snake guides; rosewood reel seat; Okuma rod bag; one-year warranty.
Price: . . . .$59.99–$64.99

OKUMA SLV

Model: SLV-10-90-4, SLV-3-80-4, SLV-4-86-4, SLV-5-90-4, SLV-6-90-4, SLV-7-90-4, SLV-8-90-4, SLV-8-96-4
Length: 8'; 8'; 8'; 9'; 9'; 9'; 9'6''; 9'6''
Action: MF
Pieces: 4
Line Weight: 3W–10W

Guide Count: 10; 9; 10; 10; 10; 10; 10; 11
Features: Lightweight graphite construction; four-piece rod design; titanium oxide stripper guide; stainless steel snake guides; aluminum pipe reel seat with aluminum hoods; Okuma rod bag; one-year warranty.
Price: . . . .$74.99–$89.99

ACTION	POWER	
M=Moderate	UL=Ultra Light	H=Heavy
MF=Moderate Fast	L=Light	MH=Medium-Heavy
F=Fast	ML=Medium-Light	XH=Extra Heavy
XF=Extra Fast		

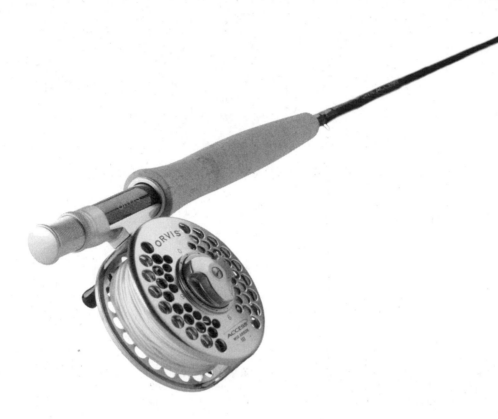

ORVIS ACCESS

Model: 3-weight 8'4" Fly Rod—Mid Flex, 4-weight 7' Fly Rod—Mid Flex, 4-weight 8' Fly Rod—Mid Flex, 4-weight 8'6" Fly Rod—Mid Flex, 4-weight 9' Fly Rod—Mid Flex, 4-weight 9' Fly Rod—Tip Flex, 4-weight 10' Fly Rod—Tip Flex, 5-weight 8'6" Fly Rod—Mid Flex, 5-weight 8'6" Fly Rod—Mid Flex, 2-piece, 5-weight 9' Fly Rod—Mid Flex, 5-weight 9' Fly Rod—Tip Flex, 5-weight 9' Fly Rod—Mid Flex (2-piece), 5-weight 10' Fly Rod—Tip Flex, Switch 5-weight 11' Fly Rod—Tip Flex, 6-weight 9' Fly Rod—Tip Flex, 6-weight 9' Fly Rod—Tip Flex, 2-piece, Switch

6-weight 11' Fly Rod—Tip Flex
Length: 8'4"; 7'; 8'; 8'6"; 9'; 9'; 10'; 8'6"; 8'6"; 9'; 9'; 9'; 10'; 11'; 9'; 9'; 11'
Action: M; M; M; M; M; F; F; M; M; M; F; M; F; F; F; F; F
Pieces: 4
Line Weight: 3W–6W
Features: Incredibly lightweight and offer remarkably smooth, precise, and balanced casting performance.
Price: . . . . **$425.00–$475.00**

ACTION	**POWER**	
M=Moderate	UL=Ultra Light	H=Heavy
MF=Moderate Fast	L=Light	MH=Medium-Heavy
F=Fast	ML=Medium-Light	XH=Extra Heavy
XF=Extra Fast		

RODS

ORVIS HELIOS 2

Model: 2-weight 6' Fly Rod—Mid Flex, 2-weight 8'4" Fly Rod—Mid Flex, 3-weight 7'6" Fly Rod—Mid Flex, 3-weight 8'4" Fly Rod—Mid Flex, 3-weight 10' Fly Rod—Tip Flex, 4-weight 7' Fly Rod—Mid Flex, 4-weight 8'6" Fly Rod—Mid Flex, 4-weight 9' Fly Rod—Mid Flex, 4-weight 9' Fly Rod—Tip Flex, 4-weight 10' Fly Rod—Tip Flex, 5-weight 7'9" Fly Rod—Mid Flex, 5-weight 8'6" Fly Rod—Mid Flex, 5-weight 8'6" Fly Rod—Tip Flex, 5-weight 9' Fly Rod—Mid Flex, 5-weight 9' Fly Rod—Tip Flex, 5-weight 10' Fly Rod—Tip Flex, 6-weight 9' Fly Rod—Mid Flex, 6-weight 9' Fly Rod—Tip Flex

Length: 6'; 8'4"; 7'6"; 8'4"; 10'; 7'; 8'6"; 9'; 9'; 10'; 7'9"; 8'6"; 8'6"; 9'; 9'; 10'; 9'; 9'
Action: M; M; M; M; F; M; M; M; F; F; M; M; F; M; F; F; M; F
Pieces: 3; 4; 4; 4; 4; 4; 4; 4; 4; 4; 4; 4; 4; 4; 4; 4; 4; 4
Line Weight: 2W–6W
Features: Lightweight, sensitive, and extremely powerful; 20 percent stronger than the original Helios; 20 percent lighter in hand; 100 percent increase in tip-impact strength; fine-tuned tapers for unrivaled tracking, accuracy, and lifting power.
Price: **$795.00**

ACTION		POWER	
M=Moderate	UL=Ultra Light	H=Heavy
MF=Moderate Fast	L=Light	MH=Medium-Heavy
F=Fast	ML=Medium-Light	XH=Extra Heavy
XF=Extra Fast		

REDINGTON CLASSIC TROUT

Model: 276-4, 376-4, 386-4, 480-4, 486-4, 490-4, 586-4, 590-4, 690-4, 380-6, 590-6
Length: 7'6''; 7'6''; 8'6''; 8'; 8'6''; 9'; 8'6''; 9'; 9'; 8'; 9'
Action: M
Pieces: 4; 6
Line Weight: 2W–6W
Features: Medium action. Offered in 4-piece and 6-piece configurations. Six-piece offers extreme packability for the backpacking and traveling angler. Titanium oxide stripping guides. Dark clay brown blank with matching Rosewood reel seat insert. Custom machined reel seat components. Alignment dots for easy rod set up. Divided brown ballistic Nylon rod tube.
Price: . . . . **$149.95–$169.95**

ACTION	POWER	
M=Moderate	**UL=Ultra Light**	**H=Heavy**
MF=Moderate Fast	**L=Light**	**MH=Medium-Heavy**
F=Fast	**ML=Medium-Light**	**XH=Extra Heavy**
XF=Extra Fast		

RODS: Freshwater Fly Fishing

REDINGTON CROSSWATER

Model: 476-2, 580-2, 586-2, 590-2, 690-2, 890-2, 990-2, 590-4, 890-4
Length: 7'6"; 8'; 8'6"; 9'; 9'; 9'; 9'; 9'; 9'
Action: MF
Pieces: 2; 4
Line Weight: 4W–9W

Features: Medium-fast action. Attractive trim details and cosmetics. Alignment dots for easy rod set-up. Weights available from 4-weight to 9-weight for multiple fishing needs. Durable anodized aluminum reel seat, ideal for all fresh and saltwater applications. Rod comes with black cloth rod sock.
Price: . . . . **$149.95–$169.95**

ACTION	POWER	
M=Moderate	UL=Ultra Light	H=Heavy
MF=Moderate Fast	L=Light	MH=Medium-Heavy
F=Fast	ML=Medium-Light	XH=Extra Heavy
XF=Extra Fast		

REDINGTON VOYANT

Model: 376-4, 486-4, 490-4, 586-4, 590-4, 596-4, 5100-4, 690-4, 696-4, 6100-4, 790-4, 7100-4, 890-4, 990-4, 1090-4

Length: 7'6"; 8'6"; 9'; 8'6"; 9'; 9'6"; 10'; 9'; 9'6"; 10'; 9'; 10'; 9'; 9'; 9'

Action: F

Pieces: 4

Line Weight: 3W–10W

Features: Fast action. Smooth casting, high-performing, and versatile enough for the beginner to the more advanced anglers. Alignment dots for easy rod set-up. Half-wells grip (3wt–6wt). Full-wells grip (7wt–10wt). Durable anodized aluminum and wood reel seat. Comes in a cloth tube with zippered closure and a black cloth rod bag. Lifetime warranty.

Price: . . . . **$149.95–$169.95**

RODS

ACTION	**POWER**	
M=Moderate	UL=Ultra Light	H=Heavy
MF=Moderate Fast	L=Light	MH=Medium-Heavy
F=Fast	ML=Medium-Light	XH=Extra Heavy
XF=Extra Fast		

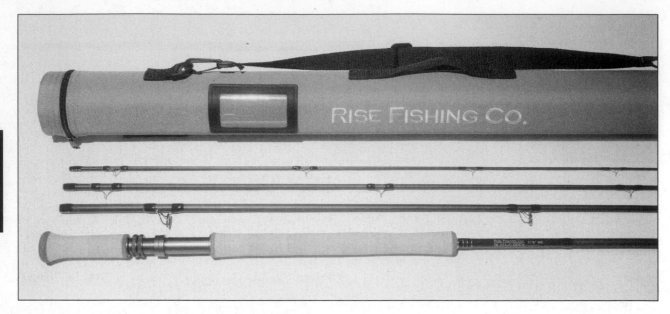

RISE BLACKWATER SPEY AND SWITCH

Model: 11-6/7wt, 11-7/8wt, 119-8wt, 126-8wt, 133-8wt, 14-9wt
Length: 11'; 11'; 11'9''; 12'6''; 13'3''; 14'

Action: MF
Pieces: 4
Line Weight: 6W–9W
Price: . . . . **$450.00–$580.00**

ACTION	POWER	
M=Moderate	UL=Ultra Light	H=Heavy
MF=Moderate Fast	L=Light	MH=Medium-Heavy
F=Fast	ML=Medium-Light	XH=Extra Heavy
XF=Extra Fast		

RODS

RISE IN-STREAM SERIES

Model: 80-4wt, 86-4wt, 90-4wt, 86-5wt, 90-5wt
Length: 8'; 8'6''; 9'; 8'6''; 9'
Action: M; M; M; MF; MF
Pieces: 4
Line Weight: 4W–5W
Features: Made from IM7 and IM8 graphite makes these lightweight, crisp-feeling rods; the reel seat is a nickel silver uplocking seat with burled rosewood glossy finish; all guides are lightweight titanium carbide; the In-Stream series is a beautiful dark red finish with black wraps; all In-Stream series fly rods come with a case and a lifetime warranty.
Price: . . . . **$189.99–$199.99**

ACTION	POWER	
M=Moderate	UL=Ultra Light	H=Heavy
MF=Moderate Fast	L=Light	MH=Medium-Heavy
F=Fast	ML=Medium-Light	XH=Extra Heavy
XF=Extra Fast		

RODS: **Freshwater Fly Fishing**

SAGE BASS II

Model: Bluegill, Smallmouth, Largemouth, Peacock
Length: 7'11''
Action: F
Pieces: 4
Line Weight: 230 gr; 290 gr; 330 gr; 390 gr
Features: Fast-action graphite III construction; built within tournament specifications; Fuji ceramic stripping guides; hard chromed snake guides; saltwater safe, red anodized aluminum reel seat; custom, pre-shaped cork handle 6½" full-wells grip; fighting butt; olive ballistic cloth rod/reel case; Sage BASS II taper line included.
Price:....................................**$550.00**

SAGE CIRCA

Model: 7'9'', 3 wt; 8'9'', 3 wt; 7'9'', 4 wt; 8'9'', 4 wt; 8'9'', 5 wt
Length: 7'9''; 8'9''; 7'9''; 8'9''; 8'9''
Line Weight: 3W–5W
Features: A soft-action premium fly rod featuring Sage's groundbreaking Konnetic technology; designed for intermediate to advanced casters; built for delicate, accurate presentations.
Price:....................................**$775.00**

ACTION		**POWER**	
M=Moderate	UL=Ultra Light	H=Heavy
MF=Moderate Fast	L=Light	MH=Medium-Heavy
F=Fast	ML=Medium-Light	XH=Extra Heavy
XF=Extra Fast		

SAGE ONE ELITE 590-4
Model: One Elite 590-4
Length: 9'
Action: F
Pieces: 4
Line Weight: 5W
Features: All-water rod; fast-action Konnetic technology construction; black ice shaft color; black primary thread

wraps with gray titanium trim wraps; elite, Flor-grade, snubnose, half-wells cork handle; titanium reel seat with laser-etched logo on end cap; titanium winding check; titanium stripper guides with ceramic insert; black hook keeper; extra (spare) tip section.
Price:.....................................**$1295.00**

SAGE ONE SERIES
Model: 376-4, 390-4, 486-4, 490-4, 496-4, 4100-4, 586-4, 590-4, 596-4, 5100-4, 690-4, 691-4, 696-4, 697-4, 6100-4, 6101-4, 790-4, 796-4, 7100-4, 890-4, 896-4, 8100-4, 990-4, 1090-4, 1190-4, 1290-4
Length: 7'6''; 9'; 8'6''; 9'; 9'6''; 10'; 8'6''; 9'; 9'6''; 10'; 9'; 9'; 9'6''; 9'6''; 10'; 10'; 9'; 9'6''; 10'; 9'; 9'6''; 10'; 9'; 9'; 9'; 9'
Action: F
Pieces: 4

Line Weight: 3W–12W
Features: Fast-action Konnetic technology construction; Fuji ceramic stripping guides; hard chromed snake guides; high-grade, custom-tapered, shaped cork handles; walnut wood and golden bronze-colored aluminum anodized freshwater reel seat; weights 6 through 10 have an all golden bronze-colored aluminum anodized reel seat; black powder-coated aluminum rod tube with Sage medallion.
Price:...........................**$775.00–$795.00**

ACTION	POWER	
M=Moderate	UL=Ultra Light	H=Heavy
MF=Moderate Fast	L=Light	MH=Medium-Heavy
F=Fast	ML=Medium-Light	XH=Extra Heavy
XF=Extra Fast		

SAGE TXL-F
Model: 000710-4, 00710-4, 0710-4, 1710-4, 2710-4, 3610-4, 3710-4, 4610-4, 4710-4
Length: 7'10''; 7'10''; 7'10''; 7'10''; 7'10''; 6'10''; 7'10''; 6'10''; 7'10''
Action: MF
Pieces: 4
Line Weight: 0W–4W
Features: Moderate-fast action G5 technology exclusive; Sage TXL-F ultra-light guide package; greater sensitivity using micro ferrule technology; smooth, more efficient power transfer between sections; increased feel and control with an ergonomic handle; snub nose, half-wells grip; bronze anodized reel seat with natural walnut insert; 1 5/8" antique bronze powder-coated aluminum tube with black cloth bag.
Price:. **$625.00**

ACTION		**POWER**	
M=Moderate	**UL=Ultra Light**	**H=Heavy**	
MF=Moderate Fast	**L=Light**	**MH=Medium-Heavy**	
F=Fast	**ML=Medium-Light**	**XH=Extra Heavy**	
XF=Extra Fast			

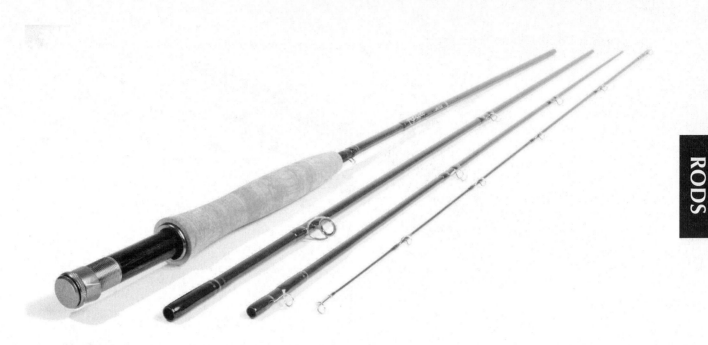

SCOTT A4

Model: 753/4, 803/4, 804/4, 854/4, 904/4, 1004/4, 855/4, 905/4, 905/4W, 1005/4, 906/4, 956/4, 1006/4, 907/4, 957/4, 1007/4, 908/4, 958/4, 1008/4, 909/4, 9010/4, 9012/4
Length: 7'6''; 8'; 8'; 8'6''; 9'; 10'; 8'6''; 9'; 9'; 10'; 9'; 9'6''; 10'; 9'; 9'6''; 10'; 9'; 9'6''; 10'; 9'; 9'; 9'

Pieces: 4
Line Weight: 3W–12W
Features: Multi-modulus design for fine-tuned flex and recovery; natural finish—naturally stronger, naturally lighter; handcrafted in the USA—built from beginning to end in Montrose, Colorado.
Price: **$395.00**

ACTION	**POWER**	
M=Moderate	UL=Ultra Light	H=Heavy
MF=Moderate Fast	L=Light	MH=Medium-Heavy
F=Fast	ML=Medium-Light	XH=Extra Heavy
XF=Extra Fast		

SCOTT F2
Model: 602/3, 653/3; 703/3; 774/3
Length: 6'; 6'6''; 7'; 7'7''
Pieces: 3
Line Weight: 2W–4W

Features: A continuous taper and smooth progressive action; proprietary S2 high-performance fiberglass epoxy composite; faster recovery and greater feel; handcrafted in the USA—built from beginning to end in Montrose, Colorado.
Price:. **$645.00**

ACTION	POWER	
M=Moderate	UL=Ultra Light	H=Heavy
MF=Moderate Fast	L=Light	MH=Medium-Heavy
F=Fast	ML=Medium-Light	XH=Extra Heavy
XF=Extra Fast		

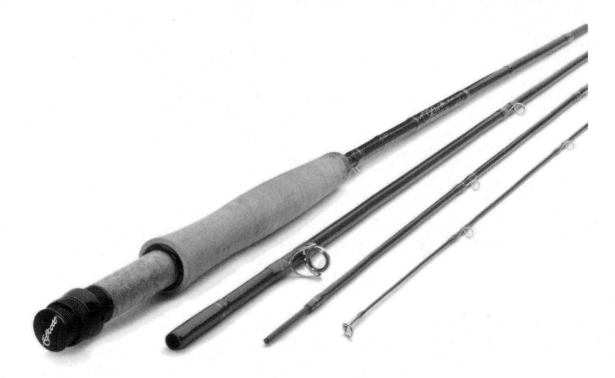

SCOTT G2

Model: 772/4, 842/4, 773/4, 843/4, 883/4, 774/4, 844/4, 884/4, 904/4, 845/4, 885/4, 905/4, 906/4
Length: 7'7''; 8'4''; 7'7''; 8'4''; 8'8''; 7'7''; 8'4''; 8'8''; 9'; 8'4''; 8'8''; 9'; 9'
Pieces: 4
Line Weight: 2W–6W

Features: X-core technology offers enhanced feel with unequalled stability; multi-modulus design for fine-tuned flex and recovery; natural finish—naturally stronger, naturally lighter; Scott hollow internal ferrule allows for continuous taper and smooth progressive action; Advanced Reinforced Carbon reduces torque and increases strength; handcrafted in the USA—built from beginning to end in Montrose, Colorado.
Price: $745.00

ACTION	POWER	
M=Moderate	UL=Ultra Light	H=Heavy
MF=Moderate Fast	L=Light	MH=Medium-Heavy
F=Fast	ML=Medium-Light	XH=Extra Heavy
XF=Extra Fast		

SCOTT L2H

Model: 1105/4, 1106/4, 1256/4, 1157/4, 1257/4, 1158/4, 1308/4, 1409/4, 1510/4
Length: 11'; 11'; 12'6''; 11'6''; 12'6''; 11'6''; 13'; 14'; 15'
Pieces: 4
Line Weight: 5W–10W

Features: Multi-modulus design for fine-tuned flex and recovery; natural finish—naturally stronger, naturally lighter; Advanced Reinforced Carbon reduces torque and increases strength; handcrafted in the USA—built from beginning to end in Montrose, Colorado.
Price:. . . . .$545.00–$645.00

ACTION	POWER	
M=Moderate	UL=Ultra Light	H=Heavy
MF=Moderate Fast	L=Light	MH=Medium-Heavy
F=Fast	ML=Medium-Light	XH=Extra Heavy
XF=Extra Fast		

SCOTT M

Model: 803/4, 884/4, 904/4, 885/4, 905/4, 906/4
Length: 8'; 8'8''; 9'; 8'8''; 9'; 9'
Pieces: 4
Line Weight: 3W–6W
Features: X-Core technology enhances feel, incredible stability, and unequalled performance; the finest cork, components and craftsmanship; natural finish—naturally stronger, naturally lighter; Advanced Reinforced Carbon reduces torque and increases strength; handcrafted in the USA—built from beginning to end in Montrose, Colorado.
Price: **$995.00**

ACTION	**POWER**	
M=Moderate	UL=Ultra Light	H=Heavy
MF=Moderate Fast	L=Light	MH=Medium-Heavy
F=Fast	ML=Medium-Light	XH=Extra Heavy
XF=Extra Fast		

SCOTT SC

Model: 653, 6114, 754, 7105
Length: 6'5''; 6'11''; 7'5''; 7'10''
Pieces: 2
Line Weight: 3W–5W

Features: Hollow blanks with butt swells; Hariki handmade nickel silver ferrules; agate guides in handmade nickel silver frames; handcrafted in the USA—built from beginning to end in Montrose, Colorado.
Price: **$2950.00**

ACTION	POWER	
M=Moderate	UL=Ultra Light	H=Heavy
MF=Moderate Fast	L=Light	MH=Medium-Heavy
F=Fast	ML=Medium-Light	XH=Extra Heavy
XF=Extra Fast		

SCOTT T3H
Model: 1064/4, 1106/4, 1286/4, 1287/4, 1357/4, 1108/4, 1288/4, 1358/4, 1409/4, 1509/4, 1510/4, 1610/4
Length: 10'6''; 11'; 12'8''; 12'8''; 13'6''; 11'; 12'8''; 13'6''; 14'; 15'; 15'; 16'
Pieces: 4
Line Weight: 4W–10W
Features: X-Core technology enhances feel, incredible stability, and unequalled performance; Advanced Reinforced Carbon for reducing torque and increasing strength; multi-modulus design for fine-tuned flex and recovery; natural finish—naturally stronger, naturally lighter; Mil-Spec III anodized reel seats and titanium guides offer the highest levels of corrosion resistance; handcrafted in the USA—built from beginning to end in Montrose, Colorado.
Price:. . . . . **$925.00–$995.00**

ACTION	POWER	
M=Moderate	UL=Ultra Light	H=Heavy
MF=Moderate Fast	L=Light	MH=Medium-Heavy
F=Fast	ML=Medium-Light	XH=Extra Heavy
XF=Extra Fast		

SHAKESPEARE UGLY STIK BIGWATER

Model: BWF11009089, BWF11009010
Length: 9'
Pieces: 2
Line Weight: 8W–10W
Guide Count: 9
Features: Howald process and Ugly Stik Clear Tip design for guaranteed strength and sensitivity; double-footed Fuji stainless steel guides with aluminum oxide inserts; durable EVA grips and graphite Fuji reel seats with corrosion-resistant stainless steel hoods; epoxy-coated blanks for protection from UV rays; exclusive ugly back; 60-day/five-year warranty.
Price: **$59.95**

ACTION		**POWER**	
M=Moderate	UL=Ultra Light	H=Heavy	
MF=Moderate Fast	L=Light	MH=Medium-Heavy	
F=Fast	ML=Medium-Light	XH=Extra Heavy	
XF=Extra Fast			

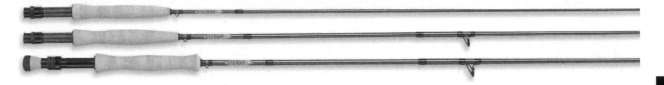

ST. CROIX AVID SERIES FLY

Model: A762.4, A603.2, A663.4, A703.2, A793.4, A664.4, A704.2, A794.4, A864.4, A904.2, A904.4, A805.4, A865.4, A905.2, A905.4, A906.2, A906.4, A907.4
Length: 7'6''; 6'; 6'6''; 7'; 7'9''; 6'6''; 7'; 7'9''; 8'6''; 9'; 9'; 8'; 8'6''; 9'; 9'; 9'; 9'; 9'
Pieces: 4; 2; 4; 2; 4; 4; 2; 4; 4; 2; 4; 4; 2; 4; 2; 4; 4
Line Weight: 2W–7W
Features: Integrated Poly Curve tooling technology; premium, high-modulus SCIII graphite; slim-profile ferrules; Fuji Alconite stripper guides with black frames; hard chrome, single-foot fly guides on 2, 3, 4, 5, 6 wt models; hard chrome snake guides on 7 wt model; uplocking, anodized aluminum reel seat with an ebony wood insert on 2, 3, 4, 5, 6 wt models; uplocking, anodized aluminum reel seat on 7 wt model; select-grade cork handle; two coats of Flex Coat slow-cure finish; rugged rod case with handle and divided polypropylene liner; lifetime limited warranty.
Price:............................ **$240.00–$300.00**

ACTION	POWER	
M=Moderate	**UL**=Ultra Light	**H**=Heavy
MF=Moderate Fast	**L**=Light	**MH**=Medium-Heavy
F=Fast	**ML**=Medium-Light	**XH**=Extra Heavy
XF=Extra Fast		

ST. CROIX BANK ROBBER

Model: BR905.4, BR906.4, BR907.4
Length: 9'
Action: F
Pieces: 4
Line Weight: 5W–7W
Features: Integrated Poly Curve tooling technology; Advanced Reinforcing Technology; super high-modulus SCVI graphite with FRS in lower section for maximum power and strength with reduced weight; high-modulus/ high-strain SCV graphite with FRS and carbon-matte scrim for unparalleled strength, durability, and sensitivity; designed with Kelly Galloup especially for streamer fishing; slim-profile ferrules; one-piece performance in four-piece designs; Fuji K Series Tangle-Free stripper guides with Alconite rings; REC Recoil snake guides; anodized, machined-aluminum reel seat with built-in hook-keeper; Flora-grade cork handle; two coats of Flex Coat slow-cure finish; alignment dots; rugged rod case with handle and divided polypropylene liner; lifetime limited warranty.
Price: **$450.00**

ACTION	POWER	
M=Moderate	UL=Ultra Light	H=Heavy
MF=Moderate Fast	L=Light	MH=Medium-Heavy
F=Fast	ML=Medium-Light	XH=Extra Heavy
XF=Extra Fast		

ST. CROIX HIGH STICK DRIFTER
Model: HSD964.4, HSD1004.4, HSD1005.4
Length: 9'6''; 10'; 10'
Action: F
Pieces: 4
Line Weight: 4W–5W
Features: Integrated Poly Curve tooling technology; Advanced Reinforcing Technology; super high-modulus SCVI graphite with FRS in lower section for maximum power and strength with reduced weight; high-modulus/high-strain SCV graphite with FRS and carbon-matte scrim for unparalleled strength, durability, and sensitivity; designed with Kelly Galloup especially for nymph fishing; slim-profile ferrules; one-piece performance in four-piece designs; Fuji K series tangle-free stripper guides with Alconite rings; REC Recoil snake guides; anodized, machined-aluminum reel seat with built-in hook-keeper; Flora-grade cork handle; two coats of Flex Coat slow-cure finish; alignment dots; rugged rod case with handle and divided polypropylene liner; lifetime limited warranty.
Price: **$450.00**

ACTION	POWER	
M=Moderate	UL=Ultra Light	H=Heavy
MF=Moderate Fast	L=Light	MH=Medium-Heavy
F=Fast	ML=Medium-Light	XH=Extra Heavy
XF=Extra Fast		

RODS

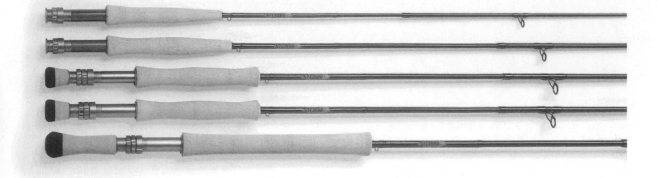

ST. CROIX IMPERIAL

Model: 1602.2, 1663.2, 1703.4, 1863.4, 1764.2, 1764.4, 1804.2, 1804.4, 1864.4, 1904.2, 1904.4, 1805.2, 1805.4, 1865.2, 1865.4, 1905.2, 1905.4, 1906.2, 1906.4, 11006.4, 1907.4, 11007.4, 1908.2, 1908.4, 1968.4, 11008.4, 1909.2, 1909.4, 19010.2, 19010.4
Length: 6'; 6'6''; 7'; 8'6''; 7'6''; 7'6''; 8'; 8'; 8'6''; 9'; 9'; 8'; 8'; 8'6''; 8'6''; 9'; 9'; 9'; 9'; 10'; 9'; 10'; 9'; 9'; 9'6''; 10'; 9'; 9'; 9'; 9'
Action: F
Pieces: 2; 2; 4; 4; 2; 4; 2; 4; 4; 2; 4; 2; 4; 2; 4; 2; 4; 2; 4; 4; 4; 4; 2; 4; 4; 4; 2; 4; 2; 4

Line Weight: 2W–10W
Features: Dynamic blend of high-modulus/high-strain SCIV graphite and premium-quality SCII graphite; lightweight, fast-action fly rods designed for maximum performance and value; aluminum-oxide stripper guides with black frames; hard chrome snake guides; uplocking, machined-aluminum reel seat with a rosewood insert on 2, 3, 4, 5 & 6 wt models; uplocking, machined-aluminum reel seat on 7, 8, 9 & 10 wt models; premium-grade cork handle; two coats of Flex Coat slow-cure finish; rugged rod case with handle and divided polypropylene liner; lifetime limited warranty.
Price: . . . . **$200.00–$270.00**

ACTION		POWER	
M=Moderate	UL=Ultra Light		H=Heavy
MF=Moderate Fast	L=Light		MH=Medium-Heavy
F=Fast	ML=Medium-Light		XH=Extra Heavy
XF=Extra Fast			

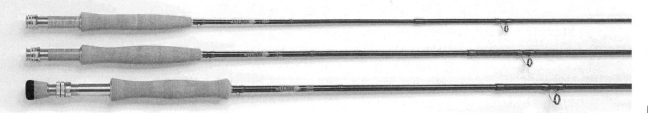

ST. CROIX LEGEND ELITE

Model: EFW793.4, EFW864.4, EFW904.4, EFW865.4, EFW905.4, EFW906.4, EFW907.4, EFW967.4, EFW908.4, EFW968.4, EFW909.4, EFW9010.4
Length: 7'9''; 8'6''; 9'; 8'6''; 9'; 9'; 9'; 9'6''; 9'; 9'6''; 9'; 9'
Action: F
Pieces: 4
Line Weight: 3W–10W
Features: Integrated Poly Curve tooling technology; Advanced Reinforcing Technology; super high-modulus SCVI graphite with FRS in lower section for maximum power and strength with reduced weight; high-modulus/high-strain SCV graphite with FRS and carbon-matte scrim for unparalleled strength and durability; slim-profile ferrules; phenomenally sensitive, light, and smooth casting; Fuji SiC Concept Guide System with titanium-finished frames; Fuji VSS reel seat/frosted silver hood on spinning models; Fuji ACS reel seat/frosted silver hood on casting models; machined-aluminum wind check; super-grade cork handle; two coats of Flex Coat slow-cure finish; includes deluxe rod sack; lifetime limited warranty.
Price: . . . . **$420.00–$490.00**

ACTION	POWER	
M=Moderate	UL=Ultra Light	H=Heavy
MF=Moderate Fast	L=Light	MH=Medium-Heavy
F=Fast	ML=Medium-Light	XH=Extra Heavy
XF=Extra Fast		

ST. CROIX RIO SANTO

Model: RS804.2, RS804.4, RS765.2, RS865.2, RS865.4, RS905.2, RS905.4, RS906.2, RS906.4, RS908.2, RS908.4
Length: 8'; 8'; 7'6''; 8'6''; 8'6''; 9'; 9'; 9'; 9'; 9'; 9'
Action: MF
Pieces: 2; 4; 2; 2; 4; 2; 4; 2; 4; 2; 4
Line Weight: 4W–8W

Features: Premium-quality SCII graphite; smooth, versatile, moderate-fast actions; aluminum-oxide stripper guides with black frames; stainless steel snake guides; uplocking, aluminum reel seat; premium-grade cork handle; two coats of Flex Coat slow-cure finish; includes cloth rod sack; five-year warranty.
Price: . . . . **$110.00–$140.00**

ACTION	POWER	
M=Moderate	UL=Ultra Light	H=Heavy
MF=Moderate Fast	L=Light	MH=Medium-Heavy
F=Fast	ML=Medium-Light	XH=Extra Heavy
XF=Extra Fast		

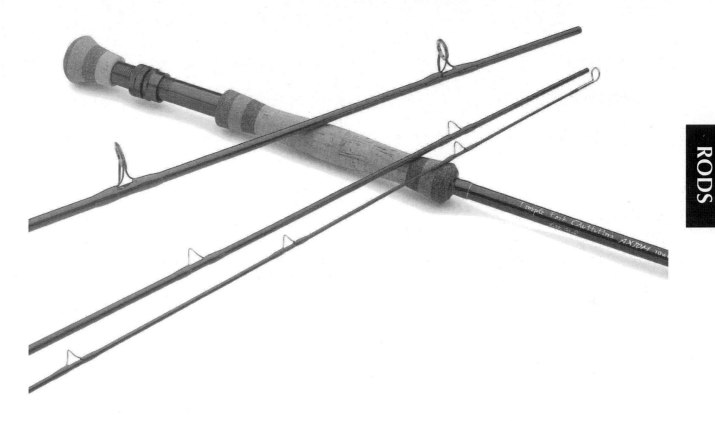

TEMPLE FORK AXIOM

Model: TF 05 90 4 A, TF 06 90 4 A, TF 07 90 4 A , TF 08 90 4 A, TF 09 90 4 A, TF 10 90 4 A
Length: 9'
Action: F
Pieces: 4
Line Weight: 5W–10W
Features: Kevlar is sandwiched between two layers of carbon fiber to reduce the ovaling effect a rod blank experiences under load, creating an exceptionally smooth, powerful rod with remarkable damping (tip bounce) qualities; ultra-high line speed with crisp, clean, accurate loops; feature a rich translucent blue blank accentuated with gold script and accents; Flor-grade cork (reverse half wells on the 4 and 5, full wells with decorative burl rings on the 6–10); gun metal blue uplocking reel seat; large stripping guides with gold titanium oxide inserts.
Price: . . . . **$275.00–$300.00**

ACTION	POWER	
M=Moderate	UL=Ultra Light	H=Heavy
MF=Moderate Fast	L=Light	MH=Medium-Heavy
F=Fast	ML=Medium-Light	XH=Extra Heavy
XF=Extra Fast		

RODS

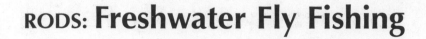

TEMPLE FORK BUG LAUNCHERS
Model: TF BL 4/5, TF BL 5/6
Length: 7'; 8'
Action: F
Pieces: 2
Line Weight: 4W–6W

Features: Thinner diameter compressed cork grips for a better fit in smaller hands; made from general graphite; extended reel seat allows smaller anglers to use two hands for more control.
Price: **$90.00**

ACTION		POWER	
M=Moderate	UL=Ultra Light		H=Heavy
MF=Moderate Fast	L=Light		MH=Medium-Heavy
F=Fast	ML=Medium-Light		XH=Extra Heavy
XF=Extra Fast			

TEMPLE FORK LEFTY KREH FINESSE

Model: TF .5 50 3 F, TF 01 69 4 F, TF 02 73 4 F, TF 03 79 4 F, TF 03 89 4 F, TF 04 79 4 F, TF 04 89 4 F, TF 05 79 4 F, TF 05 89 4 F

Length: 5'; 6'9''; 7'3''; 7'9''; 8'9''; 7'9''; 8'9''; 7'9''; 8'9''

Action: M

Pieces: 3; 4; 4; 4; 4; 4; 4; 4; 4

Line Weight: 0.5W–5W

Features: Ideal rods for meadow streams, limestone creeks, and spring creeks; at short to medium distances, these rods cast effortlessly, turning over long leaders easily; shorter lengths are perfect for tight quarters, while the longer length rods will keep a back cast well above tall grasses; handsomely appointed with rosewood inserts on an uplocking reel seat, which nicely accentuates the deep olive finish.

Price: . . . . **$170.00–$190.00**

ACTION	POWER	
M=Moderate	**UL=Ultra Light**	**H=Heavy**
MF=Moderate Fast	**L=Light**	**MH=Medium-Heavy**
F=Fast	**ML=Medium-Light**	**XH=Extra Heavy**
XF=Extra Fast		

RODS

TEMPLE FORK LEFTY KREH PROFESSIONAL SERIES II

Model: TFO 02 80 3 P2, TFO 03 76 4 P2, TFO 03 76 4 P2, TFO 04 80 4 P2, TFO 04 86 4 P2, TFO 04 90 4 P2, TFO 05 76 4 P2, TFO 05 86 4 P2, TFO 05 90 4 P2, TFO 05 10 4 P2, TFO 06 90 4 P2, TFO 06 10 4 P2
Length: 8'; 7'6''; 8'6''; 8'; 8'6''; 9'; 7'6''; 8'6''; 9'; 10'; 9'; 10'
Action: MF
Pieces: 3; 4; 4; 4; 4; 4; 4; 4; 4; 4; 4; 4
Line Weight: 2W–6W

Features: Smooth casting and powerful, yet forgiving; perfect rods for all anglers and skill levels; include matte black finished blanks and subtle gold logos; feature alignment dots color coded by line weight, premium grade cork with burled accents, and oversized stripper guides; new anodized reel seats with braided carbon fiber inserts make these rods as forgiving on the eyes as they are in the hand; each rod comes with an attractive rod sock with the logo.
Price: . . . . **$150.00–$200.00**

ACTION		POWER	
M=Moderate	UL=Ultra Light		H=Heavy
MF=Moderate Fast	L=Light		MH=Medium-Heavy
F=Fast	ML=Medium-Light		XH=Extra Heavy
XF=Extra Fast			

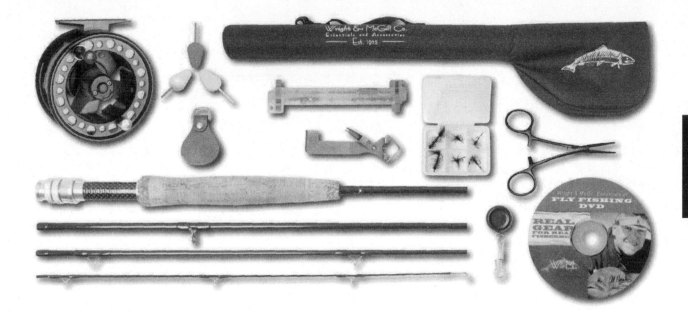

WRIGHT & MCGILL PLUNGE

Model: WMEPC8644, WMEPC954, WMEPC984
Length: 8'6''; 9'; 9'
Power: S
Action: MF
Pieces: 4
Line Weight: 4W–8W

Features: High-modulus graphite, four-piece fly rod in one of two lengths and actions; floating fly line, fly line backing, tapered leader; W & M Power L Nipper, Qwik Drop Shot Dispenser; 5" black forceps; tool retractor; leader straightener; fly box; high float strike indicators; Umpqua fly assortment; travel case; Wright & McGill Essentials of Fly Fishing DVD included.
Price: . . . . **$159.99–$169.99**

ACTION	POWER	
M=Moderate	UL=Ultra Light	H=Heavy
MF=Moderate Fast	L=Light	MH=Medium-Heavy
F=Fast	ML=Medium-Light	XH=Extra Heavy
XF=Extra Fast		

G. LOOMIS NRX SALTWATER

Model: NRX 1087-4 G, NRX 1088-4 G, NRX 1089-4 G, NRX 10810-4 G, NRX 10811-4 G, NRX 10812-4 G, NRX 1087-4, NRX 1088-4, NRX 1089-4, NRX 10810-4, NRX 10811-4, NRX 10812-4
Length: 9'
Power: S
Action: F
Pieces: 4
Line Weight: 7W–12W

Features: Utilize a stiffer, lighter, and higher-density carbon married with Nano Silica resin systems, to create a material that makes the rods lighter, yet more durable, extremely sensitive, and yet stiffer; feature black ion-coated REC recoil guides; custom reel seat has no exposed threads, to make it easy to lock the reel to the reel seat; grips feature HD cork design, where the cork transitions to provide more sensitivity where needed, and more durability in where needed.
Price:.............................$795.00–$900.00

ACTION	POWER	
M=Moderate	UL=Ultra Light	H=Heavy
MF=Moderate Fast	L=Light	MH=Medium-Heavy
F=Fast	ML=Medium-Light	XH=Extra Heavy
XF=Extra Fast		

ORVIS ACCESS SALTWATER

Model: 6-weight 9' Fly Rod—Tip Flex, 6-weight 9'6" Fly Rod—Tip Flex, 7-weight 9' Fly Rod—Tip Flex, 7-weight 10' Fly Rod—Tip Flex, Switch 7-weight 11' Fly Rod—Tip Flex, 8-weight 9' Fly Rod—Mid Flex, 8-weight 9' Fly Rod—Tip Flex, 8-weight 10' Fly Rod—Tip Flex, Switch 8-weight 11' Fly Rod—Tip Flex, 9-weight 9' Fly Rod—Tip Flex, 2-piece, 9-weight 9' Fly Rod—Tip Flex, 10-weight 9' Fly Rod—Tip Flex, 12-weight 9' Fly Rod—Tip Flex

Length: 9' 9'6''; 9'; 10'; 11'; 9'; 9'; 10'; 11'; 9'; 9'; 9'; 9'

Action: F; F; F; F; F; M; F; F; F; F; F; F; F

Pieces: 4; 4; 4; 4; 4; 4; 4; 4; 4; 2; 4; 4; 4

Line Weight: 6W–12W

Features: Contain proprietary carbon-based composite graphite and use a brand-new epoxy-based plasticized resin system, making the rods very light and very strong; the blank uses tapers that were previously perfected with the Helios; graphite modulus is higher than almost every premium rod on the market; glossy, rootbeer, graphite blank is complimented by the woven graphite reel seat; milled aluminum hardware on the reel seat is anodized in champagne; the reel seat is lightweight, simple, and attractive; sunburst rod wrapping with gold tipping; gold alignment ticks by the rod maker; snake guides are all-chrome, and the stripping guides are black anodized steel; two oversized black anodized stripping guides for distance casting; low-profile cork/rubber fighting butt; super-grade cork handle-half wells shape.

Price: . . . . **$450.00–$475.00**

ACTION	POWER	
M=Moderate	UL=Ultra Light	H=Heavy
MF=Moderate Fast	L=Light	MH=Medium-Heavy
F=Fast	ML=Medium-Light	XH=Extra Heavy
XF=Extra Fast		

ORVIS HELIOS 2 SALTWATER

Model: 6-weight 9' Fly Rod—Tip Flex, 6-weight 9'6" Fly Rod—Tip Flex, 6-weight 10' Fly Rod—Tip Flex, 7-weight 9' Fly Rod—Tip Flex, 7-weight 10' Fly Rod—Tip Flex, 8-weight 9' Fly Rod—Mid Flex, 8-weight 9' Fly Rod—Tip Flex, 8-weight 10' Fly Rod—Tip Flex, 9-weight 9' Fly Rod—Tip Flex, 10-weight 9' Fly Rod—Tip Flex, 11-weight 9' Fly Rod—Tip Flex, 12-weight 9' Fly Rod—Tip Flex, 14-weight 8'6" Fly Rod—Tip Flex

Length: 9'; 9'6''; 10'; 9'; 10'; 9'; 9'; 10'; 9'; 9'; 9'; 9'; 8'6''
Action: F; F; F; F; F; M; F; F; F; F; F; F; F
Pieces: 4
Line Weight: 6W–14W
Features: Winner of six industry awards; 20 percent lighter in hand; 20 percent stronger; 100 percent increase in tip impact; fine-tuned tapers for unrivaled tracking, accuracy, and lifting power.
Price: **$850.00**

ACTION		POWER	
M=Moderate	UL=Ultra Light		H=Heavy
MF=Moderate Fast	L=Light		MH=Medium-Heavy
F=Fast	ML=Medium-Light		XH=Extra Heavy
XF=Extra Fast			

REDINGTON PREDATOR
Model: 6710-4, 690-4, 790-4, 8710-4, 890-4, 983-4, 990-4, 1083-4, 1090-4, 1190-4, 1290-4, 1480-4
Length: 7'10''; 9'; 9'; 7'10''; 9'; 8'3''; 9'; 8'3''; 9'; 9'; 9'; 9'
Action: F
Pieces: 4
Line Weight: 6W–14W
Features: Fast-action power for picking up line and fighting large fish; carbon fiber weave in butt section and at ferrules for improved strength and durability; 54 and 42 million modulus, red core blank; anodized machined aluminum reel seat, ideal for all saltwater applications; durable oversized guides, titanium oxide ring, robust for saltwater and for shooting line for extra distance; gun smoke frame snake and stripping guides, titanium oxide ring; comes with fabric rod tube with dividers.
Price:. $249.95

RODS

ACTION	POWER	
M=Moderate	UL=Ultra Light	H=Heavy
MF=Moderate Fast	L=Light	MH=Medium-Heavy
F=Fast	ML=Medium-Light	XH=Extra Heavy
XF=Extra Fast		

Saltwater Fly Fishing

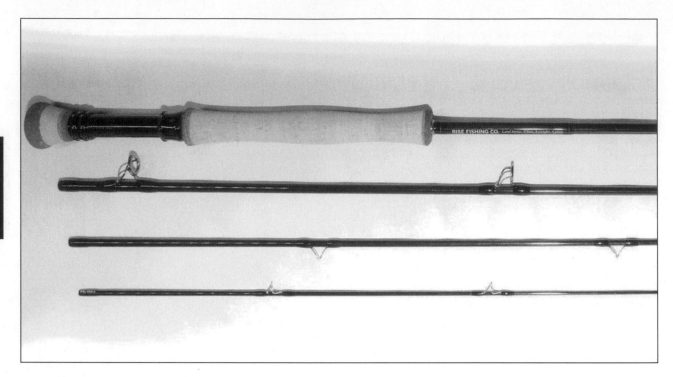

RISE LEVEL SERIES

Model: 90-5wt, 90-6wt, 90-7wt, 90-8wt, 90-9wt, 90-10wt, 90-12wt, 90-14wt
Length: 9'
Action: F
Pieces: 4
Line Weight: 5W–14W
Features: Made from IM8 and IM10 graphite; black anodized saltwater-safe seat with oversized lightweight chrome guides; fighting butt and cork handle are made from super-grade cork with composite cork accents; rich blue with black wraps; four-piece and come with a case and lifetime warranty.
Price: . . . . **$199.99–$299.99**

ACTION	POWER	
M=Moderate	UL=Ultra Light	H=Heavy
MF=Moderate Fast	L=Light	MH=Medium-Heavy
F=Fast	ML=Medium-Light	XH=Extra Heavy
XF=Extra Fast		

SAGE BASS II

Model: Bluegill, Smallmouth, Largemouth, Peacock
Length: 7'11''
Action: F
Pieces: 4
Line Weight: 230 gr; 290 gr; 330 gr; 390 gr
Features: Fast-action graphite III construction, built within tournament specifications; Fuji ceramic stripping guides; hard chromed snake guides; saltwater safe; red anodized aluminum reel seat; custom, pre-shaped cork handle 6½" full-wells grip; fighting butt; olive ballistic cloth rod/reel case; Sage BASS II taper line included.
Price: **$550.00**

SAGE ONE ELITE 590-4

Model: One Elite 590-4
Length: 9'
Action: F
Pieces: 4
Line Weight: 5W
Features: All-water rod; fast-action Konnetic technology construction; black ice shaft color; black primary thread wraps with gray titanium trim wraps; elite, Flor-grade, snubnose, half-wells cork handle; titanium reel seat with laser-etched logoed end cap; titanium winding check, titanium stripper guides with ceramic insert black hook keeper; extra (spare) tip section.
Price: **$1,295.00**

ACTION	POWER	
M=Moderate	UL=Ultra Light	H=Heavy
MF=Moderate Fast	L=Light	MH=Medium-Heavy
F=Fast	ML=Medium-Light	XH=Extra Heavy
XF=Extra Fast		

SAGE ONE SERIES

Model: 376-4, 390-4, 486-4, 490-4, 496-4, 4100-4, 586-4, 590-4, 596-4, 5100-4, 690-4, 691-4, 696-4, 697-4, 6100-4, 6101-4, 790-4, 796-4, 7100-4, 890-4, 896-4, 8100-4, 990-4, 1090-4, 1190-4, 1290-4
Length: 7'6''; 9'; 8'6''; 9'; 9'6''; 10'; 8'6''; 9'; 9'6''; 10'; 9'; 9'; 9'6''; 9'6''; 10'; 10'; 9'; 9'6''; 10'; 9'; 9'6''; 10'; 9'; 9'; 9'; 9'
Action: F
Pieces: 4

Line Weight: 3W–12W
Features: Fast-action Konnetic Technology construction; Fuji ceramic stripping guides; hard chromed snake guides; high-grade, custom-tapered, shaped cork handles; walnut wood and golden bronze-colored aluminum anodized freshwater reel seat; weights 6 through 10 have an all golden bronze colored aluminum anodized reel seat; black powder coated aluminum rod tube with Sage medallion.
Price:. . . . .$775.00–$795.00

SAGE X13

Model: 589-4, 690-4, 790-4, 890-4, 990-4, 1090-4, 1190-4, 1191-4, 1290-4, 1291-4, 1390-4, 1480-4, 1680-4
Length: 8'9''; 9'; 9'; 9'; 9'; 9'; 9'; 9'; 9'; 9'; 9'; 8'; 9'
Action: XF
Pieces: 4
Line Weight: 5W–16W
Features: Aggressive fast-action; proprietary taper design

utilizing SaltH20 technology; Fuji hard chrome-plated; stripping guides feature Alconite ceramic inserts, which offer the utmost durability and line wear resistance; tip-tops and snake guides are oversized on all models for ease of line movement; black anodized reel seat; cork and EVA fighting butt; heavy-knurled lock rings; aluminum tube; and black fabric rod bag.
Price:. . . . .$785.00–$795.00

ACTION	POWER	
M=Moderate	**UL=Ultra Light**	**H=Heavy**
MF=Moderate Fast	**L=Light**	**MH=Medium-Heavy**
F=Fast	**ML=Medium-Light**	**XH=Extra Heavy**
XF=Extra Fast		

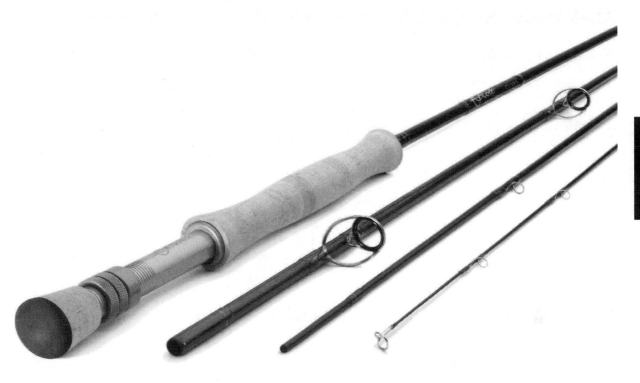

SCOTT S4S

Model: 908/2, 909/2; 9010/2; 9011/2; 9012/2; 905/4;
806/4; 906/4; 907/4; 808/4; 908/4; 909/4; 8010/4; 9010/4;
9011/4; 9012/4; 8813/4
Length: 9'; 9'; 9'; 9'; 9'; 9'; 8'; 9'; 9'; 8'; 9'; 9'; 8'; 9'; 9';
9'; 8'8''
Pieces: 2; 2; 2; 2; 2; 4; 4; 4; 4; 4; 4; 4; 4; 4; 4; 4; 4
Line Weight: 8W–13W

Features: X-core technology; enhanced feel, incredible stability, and unequalled performance; Mil-Spec III anodized reel seats and titanium; titanium guides offer the highest levels of corrosion resistance; Advanced Reinforced Carbo reduces torque and increases strength; handcrafted in the USA—built from beginning to end in Montrose, Colorado.
Price: **$775.00**

ACTION	POWER	
M=Moderate	UL=Ultra Light	H=Heavy
MF=Moderate Fast	L=Light	MH=Medium-Heavy
F=Fast	ML=Medium-Light	XH=Extra Heavy
XF=Extra Fast		

RODS

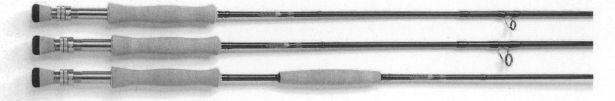

ST. CROIX LEGEND ELITE SALTWATER

Model: ESW906.4, ESW907.4, ESW908.4, ESW909.4, ESW9010.4, ESW9012.4, ESW9012.4.FG
Length: 9'
Action: F
Pieces: 4
Line Weight: 6W–12W
Features: Integrated Poly Curve tooling technology; Advanced Reinforcing Technology; super high-modulus SCVI graphite with NSi resin in lower section for added power with reduced weight; featuring 3M Powerlux resin for unparalleled strength and durability; high-modulus/high-strain SCV graphite with NSi resin and carbon-matte scrim; slim-profile ferrules; one-piece performance in four-piece designs; max-power butt sections for handling powerful fish and stiff winds; Fuji MN Saltwater Alconite stripper guides with chrome frames; hard chrome snake guides; REC hard-anodized aluminum reel seat; Flora-grade cork handle; two coats of Flex Coat slow-cure finish; alignment dots; rugged rod case with handle and divided polypropylene liner; lifetime limited warranty.
Price: . . . . **$460.00–$530.00**

ACTION	POWER	
M=Moderate	UL=Ultra Light	H=Heavy
MF=Moderate Fast	L=Light	MH=Medium-Heavy
F=Fast	ML=Medium-Light	XH=Extra Heavy
XF=Extra Fast		

REELS: Freshwater Spinning

ABU-GARCIA CARDINAL S
Model: 5, 10, 20, 30, 40, 60
Gear Ratio: 5.2:1; 5.2:1; 5.1:1; 5.1:1; 5.1:1; 4.8:1
Inches/Turn: 20.5; 21; 27; 29; 29; 30
Retrieve Speed: Std
Spool Cap. (M): 4 lbs/100 yds; 6 lbs/110 yds; 8 lbs/130 yds; 8 lbs/175 yds; 12 lbs/180 yds; 14 lbs/205 yds
Spool Cap. (B): 4 lbs/160 yds; 6 lbs/150 yds; 8 lbs/190 yds; 10 lbs/180 yds; 14 lbs/210 yds; 20 lbs/200 yds
Weight: 6.3 oz; 6.8 oz; 8.68 oz; 9.1 oz; 9.6 oz; 13.1 oz

Hand Retrieve: R or L
Max Drag: 6 lbs; 6 lbs; 14 lbs; 14 lbs; 14 lbs; 20 lbs
Features: Three ball bearings plus one roller bearing provides smooth operation; lightweight graphite body and rotor; machined aluminum spool provides strength without adding excess weight; Everlast bail system for improved durability; slow oscillation provides even line lay with all types of line.
Price: . . . .$29.00–$39.00

ABU-GARCIA CARDINAL STX
Model: 5, 10, 20, 30, 40
Gear Ratio: 5.2:1; 5.2:1; 5.1:1; 5.1:1; 5.1:1
Inches/Turn: 20.5; 21; 27; 29; 29
Retrieve Speed: Std
Spool Cap. (M): 4 lbs/100 yds; 6 lbs/110 yds; 8 lbs/130 yds; 8 lbs/175 yds; 12 lbs/180 yds
Spool Cap. (B): 4 lbs/160 yds; 6 lbs/150 yds; 8 lbs/190 yds; 10 lbs/180 yds; 14 lbs/210 yds

Weight: 6.4 oz; 6.9 oz; 8.9 oz; 9.2 oz; 9.7 oz
Hand Retrieve: R or L
Max Drag: 6 lbs; 6 lbs; 14 lbs; 14 lbs; 14 lbs
Features: Six ball bearings plus one roller bearing provides smooth operation; lightweight graphite body and rotor; machined aluminum spool provides strength without adding excess weight; Everlast bail system for improved durability; slow oscillation provides even line lay with all types of line.
Price: **$49.99**

ABU-GARCIA CARDINAL SX

Model: 5, 10, 20, 30, 40
Gear Ratio: 5.2:1; 5.2:1; 5.1:1; 5.1:1; 5.1:1
Inches/Turn: 20.5; 21; 27; 29; 29
Retrieve Speed: Std
Spool Cap. (M): 4 lbs/100 yds; 6 lbs/110 yds; 8 lbs/130 yds; 8 lbs/175 yds; 12 lbs/180 yds
Spool Cap. (B): 4 lbs/160 yds; 6 lbs/150 yds; 8 lbs/190 yds; 10 lbs/180 yds; 14 lbs/210 yds

Weight: 6.4 oz; 6.9 oz; 8.8 oz; 9.2 oz; 9.7 oz
Hand Retrieve: R or L
Max Drag: 6 lbs; 6 lbs; 14 lbs; 14 lbs; 14 lbs
Features: Five ball bearings plus one roller bearing provides smooth operation; lightweight graphite body and rotor; machined aluminum spool provides strength without adding excess weight; Everlast bail system for improved durability; slow oscillation provides even line lay with all types of line.
Price: **$39.99**

ABU-GARCIA ORRA S

Model: 10, 20, 30, 40
Gear Ratio: 5.2:1; 5.8:1; 5.8:1; 5.8:1
Inches/Turn: 24.5; 31; 33; 33
Retrieve Speed: Std
Spool Cap. (B): 6 lbs/150 yds; 8 lbs/130 yds; 8 lbs/175 yds; 10 lbs/210 yds
Weight: 7.8 oz; 8.7 oz; 9.2 oz; 10.2 oz
Hand Retrieve: R or L
Max Drag: 10 lbs; 12 lbs; 12 lbs; 18 lbs
Features: Six stainless steel HPCR bearings plus one roller bearing provides increased corrosion protection; one-piece gear box design allows for more precise gear alignment for smoother operation; machined aluminum braid ready spool allows braid to be tied directly to the spool without any slip; Hybrid Carbon Matrix drag system for super smooth reliable drag performance; slow oscillation provides even line lay with all types of line; X-Cräftic alloy frame for increased corrosion resistance; Duragear brass gear for extended gear life; Everlast bail system for improved durability; stainless steel main shaft and components for improved corrosion resistance.
Price: **$69.95**

ABU-GARCIA ORRA SX

Model: 10, 20, 30, 40, 60
Gear Ratio: 5.2:1; 5.8:1; 5.8:1; 5.8:1; 4.8:1
Retrieve Speed: Std
Spool Cap. (M): 4 lbs/110 yds; 4 lbs/135 yds; 6 lbs/125 yds; 8 lbs/125 yds; 17 lbs/250 yds
Spool Cap. (B): 6 lbs/125 yds; 8 lbs/125 yds; 10 lbs/125 yds; 14 lbs/125 yds; 20 lbs/200 yds
Weight: 8.1 oz; 9.1 ozs; 9.5 oz; 10.8 oz; 13.6 oz
Hand Retrieve: R or L

Max Drag: 10 lbs; 12 lbs; 12 lbs; 18 lbs; 20 lbs
Features: Seven stainless steel ball bearings plus one roller bearing provides smooth operation; X-Cräftic alloy frame for increased corrosion resistance; graphite sideplates; Power Disk drag system gives smooth drag performance; MagTrax brake system gives consistent brake pressure throughout the cast; compact bent handle and star provide a more ergonomic design; Duragear brass gear for extended gear life.
Price:. . . . . **$99.95–$119.95**

ABU-GARCIA REVO PREMIER

Model: 10, 20, 30, 40
Gear Ratio: 5.2:1; 5.1:1; 5.8:1; 5:8.1
Inches/Turn: 25; 27; 33; 33
Retrieve Speed: Std
Spool Cap. (M): 6 lbs/110 yds; 8 lbs/130 yds; 10 lbs/140 yds; 12 lbs/180 yds
Spool Cap. (B): 6 lbs/150 yds; 8 lbs/190 yds; 10 lbs/180 yds; 14 lbs/210 yds
Weight: 6.9 oz; 8.2 oz; 8.5 oz; 9.0 oz
Hand Retrieve: R or L
Max Drag: 9 lbs; 12 lbs; 12 lbs; 18 lbs
Features: Ten stainless steel high-performance corrosion-resistant bearings plus one roller bearing provides increased corrosion protection; X2-Cräftic alloy frame for increased corrosion resistance; C6 carbon sideplates provide significant weight reduction without sacrificing strength and durability; Carbon Matrix drag system provides smooth, consistent drag pressure across the entire drag range; D2 Gear Design provides a more efficient gear system while improving gear durability; Infinitely Variable Centrifugal Brake gives very precise brake adjustments allowing anglers to easily cast a wide variety of baits; Infini II spool design for extended castability and extreme loads; compact bent carbon handle provides a more ergonomic design that is extremely lightweight; flat EVA knob provide greater comfort and durability; titanium-coated line guide reduces friction and improves durability; right- or left-hand models available.
Price: **$249.95**

ABU-GARCIA REVO S

Model: 20, 40, 10, 30
Gear Ratio: 5.1:1; 5.8:1; 5.2:1; 5.8:2
Inches/Turn: 27; 33; 25; 33
Retrieve Speed: Std
Spool Cap. (M): 8 lbs/130 yds; 12 lbs/180 yds; 6 lbs/110 yds; 10 lbs/140 yds
Spool Cap. (B): 8 lbs/190 yds; 14 lbs/210 yds; 6 lbs/150 yds; 10 lbs/180 yds
Weight: 8.2 oz; 10.1 oz; 7.44 oz; 9.0 oz
Hand Retrieve: R or L

Max Drag: 12 lbs; 18 lbs; 9 lbs; 12 lbs
Features: Seven stainless steel ball bearings plus one roller bearing provides smooth operation; X2-Cräftic alloy frame for increased corrosion resistance; lightweight graphite sideplates; Carbon Matrix drag system provides smooth, consistent drag pressure across the entire drag range; D2 Gear Design provides a more efficient gear system while improving gear durability; pitch centrifugal brake system; compact bent handle and star provide a more ergonomic design.
Price: **$129.95**

ABU-GARCIA REVO SX

Model: 10, 20, 30, 40
Gear Ratio: 5.2:1; 5.1:1; 5.8:1; 5.8:1
Inches/Turn: 25; 27; 33; 33
Retrieve Speed: Std
Spool Cap. (M): 4 lbs/110 yds; 4 lbs/135 yds; 6 lbs/125 yds; 8 lbs/125 yds
Spool Cap. (B): 6 lbs/125 yds; 8 lbs/125 yds; 10 lbs/125 yds; 14 lbs/125 yds
Weight: 7.44 oz; 8.2 oz; 8.9 oz; 10.2 oz
Hand Retrieve: R or L
Max Drag: 9 lbs; 12 lbs; 12 lbs
Features: Nine stainless steel ball bearings plus one roller bearing provides smooth operation; X2-Cräftic alloy frame for increased corrosion resistance; C6 carbon handle sideplate provides significant weight reduction without sacrificing strength and durability; Carbon Matrix drag system provides smooth, consistent drag pressure across the entire drag range; D2 Gear Design provides a more efficient gear system while improving gear durability; MagTrax brake system gives consistent brake pressure throughout the cast; Infini II spool design for extended castability and extreme loads; compact bent handle and star provide a more ergonomic design; titanium-coated line guide reduces friction and improves durability.
Price:. $159.95

BASS PRO SHOPS CATMAXX

Model: 70, 80
Gear Ratio: 4.5:1
Inches/Turn: 22
Spool Cap. (M): 25 lbs/190 yds; 25 lbs/290 yds
Weight: 25.2 oz; 26.3 oz
Hand Retrieve: R or L
Max Drag: 37.4 lbs; 39.6 lbs

Reel Bearings: 3+1
Features: Built on abuse-absorbing graphite bodies; 100 percent aluminum spools; feature a quality four-bearing system including PowerLock instant anti-reverse; easy handling, great drag system, big line capacity, and oversized machined-aluminum handle.
Price:. **$44.99**

BASS PRO SHOPS CRAPPIE MAX

Model: 750, 1000
Gear Ratio: 5.6:1
Inches/Turn: 24
Spool Cap. (M): 4 lbs/160 yds; 6 lbs; 160 yds
Weight: 5.1 oz; 6.9 oz
Hand Retrieve: R or L
Reel Bearings: 3

Features: Full graphite frame and sidecover; gold-anodized aluminum spool; stainless steel bail wire; hard chrome-plated line roller; ultra-smooth with three chrome-plated steel ball bearings, plus 18-point multi-stop anti-reverse for lightning-fast response time; die-cast handle, soft rubber paddle, and free graphite spare spool.
Price: **$19.99**

REELS

BASS PRO SHOPS EXTREME
Model: 10B, 20B, 40B, 50B
Gear Ratio: 5.6:1; 5.1:1; 5.1:1; 5.1:1
Inches/Turn: 31; 33; 36; 40
Spool Cap. (M): 6 lbs/90 yds; 8 lbs/80 yds; 12 lbs/115 yds; 12 lbs/200 yds
Weight: 7.5 oz; 10.4 oz; 11 oz; 11 oz
Hand Retrieve: R or L

Max Drag: 19.5 lbs; 19.5 lbs; 22 lbs; 22 lbs
Reel Bearings: 5+1
Features: Standard features include: one-piece aluminum frame with sealed sideplates; ported, forged aluminum spool; super-light graphite rotor; left- or right-hand retrieve; stainless steel shaft and bail wire; titanium nitride-coated roller; machined-aluminum handle with soft-touch knob.
Price:..................................**$59.99**

BASS PRO SHOPS PRO QUALIFIER

Model: 10, 20, 20H, 40, 40H, 50
Gear Ratio: 5.6:1; 5.1:1; 6.1:1; 5.1:1; 6.1:1; 5.1:1
Inches/Turn: 31; 33; 39; 36; 43; 40
Spool Cap. (M): 6 lbs/90 yds; 8 lbs/80 yds; 8 lbs/80 yds; 12 lbs/115 yds; 12 lbs/115 yds; 14 lbs/160 yds
Weight: 7.5 oz; 10.4 oz; 10.4 oz; 11 oz; 11 oz; 11 oz
Hand Retrieve: R or L
Max Drag: 19.5 lbs; 19.5 lbs; 19.5 lbs; 22 lbs; 22 lbs; 22 lbs

Reel Bearings: 7+1
Features: Ultra-slim body design, popular Mag Spool Technology and premium eight-bearing system with double-shielded stainless steel ball bearings and Powerlock instant anti-reverse; carbon fiber sealed drag, a major upgrade for long-term smoothness, power, and consistency; lightweight anodized-aluminum body/sidecovers; forged-aluminum spool; stainless steel bail wire and mainshaft; strong machined-aluminum handle.
Price: **$69.99**

CABELA'S FISH EAGLE CLASSIC

Model: 2000A, 2500A, 3000A
Gear Ratio: 5.2:1
Spool Cap. (M): 6 lbs/115 yds; 8 lbs/145 yds; 10 lbs/195 yds
Weight: 8.3 oz; 10.6 oz; 11.6 oz
Hand Retrieve: R or L
Reel Bearings: 3+1

Features: Four-bearing system with three ball bearings for smooth casts and retrieves; one-way, instant anti-reverse clutch gives solid hooksets every time; on/off-selectable; main spool is machined and anodized aluminum, while the included spare spool is graphite; lightweight body is made of graphite with metal side covers for precise gear alignment; machine-cut brass pinion gear is extremely durable for years of use; smooth multi-disc drag system; anti-twist, titanium-coated line roller; convertible fold-down handle.
Price: **$29.99**

CABELA'S FISH EAGLE TOURNAMENT II
Model: 1000A, 2000A, 25000A, 3000A
Gear Ratio: 5.2:1
Spool Cap. (M): 4 lbs/115 yds; 6 lbs/115 yds; 8 lbs/145 yds; 10 lbs/195 yds
Weight: 8.4 oz; 9.9 oz; 11.7 oz; 12.4 oz
Hand Retrieve: R or L
Reel Bearings: 5+1

Features: The aluminum spool with its titanium-coated spool lip combines power with the anti-twist titanium line roller for superior winding and even line lay that translates into longer casts with less kinks; the five-bearing system and one-way clutch bearing offer amazingly smooth retrieves; lightweight, sturdy graphite body and rotor; aluminum fold-down handle.
Price: **$39.99**

CABELA'S PRO GUIDE

Model: 3000
Gear Ratio: 6.2:1
Spool Cap. (M): 10 lbs/195 yds
Weight: 11 oz
Hand Retrieve: R or L
Max Drag: 14 lbs

Reel Bearings: 9+1
Features: Ten-bearing system for smooth casts and a one-way instant anti-reverse clutch for solid hooksets; the main spool is aluminum, while the body is a hybrid of metal and graphite for lightweight strength; anti-twist, titanium-coated line roller; convertible aluminum fold-down handle.
Price: **$49.99**

DAIWA LEXA

Model: 1500SH, 2500SH, 3500SH
Gear Ratio: 6.0:1; 6.0:1; 6.2:1
Inches/Turn: 29.9; 35; 41.3
Spool Cap. (M): 4 lbs/155 yds; 6 lbs/210 yds
Weight: 8.1 oz; 8.9 oz; 12.2 oz
Hand Retrieve: R or L
Max Drag: 8.8 lbs; 8.8 lbs; 17.6 lbs
Reel Bearings: 4+1

Features: A hollow air bail is super strong yet light in weight, with no protrusions to snag line; air rotor weighs up to 15 percent less than ordinary rotors; features aluminum construction, a felt-sealed body, and digital gear design; advanced locomotive levelwind promotes precise, even line winding; smooth performance and feel from a five-bearing system; infinite anti-reverse; an ABS aluminum spool, for long casts with fewer snarls; Twist Buster II line twist reduction; and a lifetime bail spring.
Price: **$119.99**

DAIWA SS TOURNAMENT
Model: 700, 1300, 1600, 2600
Gear Ratio: 4.9:1; 5.1:1; 4.9:1; 4.6:1
Inches/Turn: 26; 32; 28.7; 29.9
Spool Cap. (M): 4 lbs/145 yds; 6 lbs/240 yds; 10 lbs/210 yds; 10 lbs/210 yds
Weight: 7 oz; 8.5 oz; 11.5 oz; 13.7 oz
Hand Retrieve: R or L
Max Drag: 8.8 lbs; 15.4 lbs; 15.4 lbs; 17.6 lbs

Reel Bearings: 3
Features: Long-cast technology; exclusive worm gear for perfect line winding; three stainless steel bearings; aluminum spool; super-smooth drag with oversized felt/stainless discs and precision click adjustment; SiC line roller; lifetime bail spring; right- or left-hand retrieve.
Price:............................$104.99–$119.99

DAIWA STEEZ

Model: 2500, 2508
Gear Ratio: 4.8:1
Inches/Turn: 27.9
Spool Cap. (M): 8 lbs/110 yds; 8 lbs/170 yds
Weight: 6.9 oz; 7 oz
Hand Retrieve: R or L
Max Drag: 15.4 lbs
Reel Bearings: 11+1
Features: The lightest reels of their kind; air metal magnesium body, side-cover, and rotor; air spool (ultra-lightweight composite) with reverse-taper (ABS) design; Digigear digital gear design; eleven CRBB; super corrosion-resistant ball bearings plus roller bearing; tubular Sstainless air bail; infinite anti-reverse; advanced locomotive levelwind; washable design with sealed, waterproof drag system; precision, super micro-pitch drag adjustment; pillar-type tight oscillation system; ultra-quiet and smooth precision; stainless main shaft.
Price: . . . . **$749.99–$799.99**

DAIWA STEEZ EX
Model: 2508H, 3012H
Gear Ratio: 5.6:1
Inches/Turn: 33
Spool Cap. (M): 8 lbs/110 yds; 8 lbs/170 yds
Weight: 6.8 oz; 8.5 oz
Hand Retrieve: R or L
Max Drag: 15.4 lbs
Reel Bearings: 12+1

Features: Built for fresh or salt water with a corrosion-proof Zaion body; ultra-lightweight, corrosion-proof Zaion body and air rotor; mag-sealed construction (body and line roller); max drag 15.4 pounds; 13 bearing system (7 CRBB/5BB+1RB); Digigear digital gear design for speed, power and durability; lightweight, hollow, stainless steel air bail; machined aluminum handle with cork knob; silent oscillation; ABS air spool with cut-proof, titanium nitride spool lip; infinite anti-reverse; and neoprene reel bag.
Price:. **$799.99**

DAIWA TOURNAMENT BASIA QD

Model: 45QDA
Gear Ratio: 4.1:1
Inches/Turn: 34.7
Spool Cap. (M): 12 lbs/260 yds
Weight: 18.5 oz
Hand Retrieve: R or L
Max Drag: 22 lbs
Features: Large diameter aluminum ABS long-cast spool has been combined with immaculate line lay to deliver a casting experience that seems more like a dream than reality; features include a machined alloy handle and a magnesium alloy body and rotor; superb quick drag offers the perfect crossover from front drag to free spool, without the need for conversions; drilled holes on the spool skirt allow light in for identifying the running reel much more quickly; extreme durability with superior performance.
Price: $599.99

DAIWA WINDCAST Z CARP

Model: 5000, 5500
Gear Ratio: 4.9:1
Inches/Turn: 40
Spool Cap. (M): 17 lbs/310 yds; 25 lbs/230 yds
Weight: 20.5 oz
Hand Retrieve: R or L
Max Drag: 20.5 lbs
Reel Bearings: 8+1
Features: Designed primarily for carp fishing, these rods are fast, distance-casting reels that are well matched to a variety of fishing styles; a tapered spool delivers high-speed line release for distance casting—a feature that's also enhanced by a traveling line guard; a quick drag allows big fish anglers to crossover between the free spool mode and the drag engaged, with less than one turn of the drag knob; eight corrosion-resistant ball bearings and long-cast spool make it ideal for the surf as well; other features include an aluminum wishbone handle, a high-impact HIP clip, and a built-in cushion on the pin for forgiving but secure line location.
Price: $229.99

LEW'S LASER LITE SPEED SPIN

Model: 50, 75, 100
Gear Ratio: 5.2:1
Inches/Turn: 22; 23; 24
Spool Cap. (M): 4 lbs/80 yds; 6 lbs/80 yds; 6 lbs/90 yds
Weight: 6.0 oz; 6.4 oz; 6.7 oz
Hand Retrieve: R or L
Reel Bearings: 6+1

Features: Rugged graphite body and rotor; double-anodized aluminum spool with holes and gold accent lines; larger diameter spool for longer casts and faster line retrieve; strong and balanced thick aluminum bail; thin compact gear box; seven-bearing system, zero-reverse one-way clutch bearing; machined aluminum handle with soft-touch knob; adjustable for right- or left-hand retrieve; speed lube for exceptional smoothness and uninterrupted performance in all weather conditions; oversized multiple disc drag system for smooth performance.
Price:. **$29.99**

OKUMA DEAD EYE

Model: 25, 30
Gear Ratio: 5.0:1
Inches/Turn: 25
Spool Cap. (M): 4 lbs/310 yds; 4 lbs/355 yds
Weight: 8 oz; 7.8 oz
Hand Retrieve: R or L
Max Drag: 8 lbs; 13 lbs
Reel Bearings: 5+1
Features: Multi-disc, Japanese-oiled felt drag system; rigid, forged aluminum handle design with EVA handle knob;

5BB+1RB ball bearings for ultimate smoothness; quick-set anti-reverse roller bearing; precision machine-cut brass pinion gear; lightweight, corrosion-resistant frame & sideplates; machined aluminum, two-tone anodized spool; precision elliptical gearing system; Hydro Block watertight drag seal; RESII: computer-balanced rotor equalizing system; corrosion-resistant, stainless steel bail wire; one-year limited warranty.
Price: **$49.99**

OKUMA EPIXOR

Model: 20b, 25b, 30b, 40b, 55b
Gear Ratio: 5.0:1; 5.0:1; 5.0:1; 5.0:1; 4.9:1
Inches/Turn: 22; 24.5; 25; 28; 30
Spool Cap. (M): 4 lbs/190 yds; 6 lbs/180 yds; 6 lbs/200 yds; 8 lbs/270 yds; 10 lbs/380 yds
Weight: 8 oz; 8.7 oz; 10.1 oz; 10.6 oz; 14.8 oz
Hand Retrieve: R or L
Max Drag: 8 lbs; 8 lbs; 13 lbs; 13 lbs; 18 lbs
Reel Bearings: 9+1

Features: Multi-disc, Japanese-oiled felt drag system; rigid, forged aluminum handle design with EVA handle knob; 5BB+1RB ball bearings for ultimate smoothness; quick-set anti-reverse roller bearing; precision machine-cut brass pinion gear; lightweight, corrosion-resistant frame and sideplates; machined aluminum, two-tone anodized spool; precision elliptical gearing system; Hydro Block watertight drag seal; RESII: computer balanced rotor equalizing system; corrosion-resistant, stainless steel bail wire; one-year limited warranty.
Price: . . . .**$64.99–$74.99**

OKUMA EPIXOR BAITFEEDER

Model: 30, 50, 65, 80
Gear Ratio: 5.0:1; 4.5:1; 4.5:1; 4.5:1
Inches/Turn: 27; 31; 36; 40
Spool Cap. (M): 6 lbs/330 yds; 10 lbs/440 yds ; 12 lbs/540 yds; 15 lbs/510 yds
Weight: 12.2 oz; 17.4 oz; 26.7 oz; 28.1 oz
Hand Retrieve: R or L
Max Drag: 12 lbs; 17 lbs; 22 lbs; 22 lbs
Reel Bearings: 9+1

Features: On/off auto-trip bait feeding system; multi-disc, Japanese-oiled felt drag system; nine stainless steel ball bearings; one quick-set anti-reverse roller bearing; precision machine-cut brass pinion gear; corrosion-resistant graphite body; machined aluminum, two-tone anodized and ported spool; rigid, forged aluminum handle design; S-curve oscillation system; Hydro Block water tight drag seal; corrosion-resistant, stainless steel bail wire; RESII: computer balanced rotor equalizing system; one-year warranty.
Price: . . . .**$99.99–$109.99**

OKUMA RTX HIGH SPEED

Model: 25S, 30S, 35S, 40S
Gear Ratio: 6.0:1
Inches/Turn: 29.5; 30; 33.5; 34
Spool Cap. (M): 4 lbs/310 yds; 4 lbs/355 yds; 6 lbs/325 yds; 8 lbs/325 yds
Weight: 6.6 oz; 6.6 oz; 8.6 oz; 8.2 oz
Hand Retrieve: R or L
Max Drag: 8 lbs; 13 lbs; 13 lbs; 13 lbs
Reel Bearings: 7+1

Features: Extremely lightweight C-40X carbon frame, sideplate and rotor; multi-disc, Japanese-oiled felt drag system; 7BB+1RB stainless steel ball bearings; quick-set anti-reverse roller bearing; precision Alumilite alloy main gear and oscillating gears; machined aluminum, two-tone anodized spool; precision elliptical gearing system; rigid, forged aluminum handle design with EVA handle knob; Hydro Block watertight drag seal; durable one-piece solid aluminum, gun smoke anodized bail wire; RESII: computer balanced rotor equalizing system; one-year limited warranty.
Price:. **$99.99**

OKUMA TRIO HIGH SPEED
Model: 30S, 40S, 55S
Gear Ratio: 6.0:1
Inches/Turn: 30; 34; 40
Spool Cap. (M): 6 lbs/200 yds; 8 lbs/270 yds; 10 lbs/380 yds
Weight: 10.4 oz; 10.8 oz; 14.7 oz
Hand Retrieve: R or L
Max Drag: 18 lbs; 20 lbs; 24 lbs
Reel Bearings: 9+1
Features: An intelligently designed, agile, and rugged performer for all freshwater and inshore salt water fishing applications; available in both standard gearing and high-speed models; multi-disc, Japanese-oiled felt drag washers; dual force drag system; 9BB+1RB stainless steel bearings; quick-set anti-reverse roller bearing; precision machine-cut brass pinion gear; corrosion-resistant coating process; corrosion-resistant, high-density gearing; crossover aluminum and graphite hybrid body design; crossover aluminum and graphite hybrid rotor design; patented elliptical oscillation system; hybrid spool design with graphite arbor and aluminum lip; aluminum drag chamber precision spool system; rigid, forged aluminum handle design; Hydro Block watertight drag seal; heavy-duty, solid aluminum, anodized bail wire; RESII: computer balanced rotor equalizing system; one-year warranty.
Price: . . . .$74.99–$89.99

PENN BATTLE

Model: 1000; 2000; 3000; 4000; 5000; 6000; 7000; 8000
Gear Ratio: 5.2:1; 6.2:1; 6.2:1; 6.2:1; 5.6:1; 5.6:1; 5.3:1; 5.3:1
Inches/Turn: 20; 29; 31; 34; 37; 39; 39; 41
Spool Cap. (M): 4 lbs/115 yds; 6 lbs/210 yds; 8 lbs/170 yds; 10 lbs/230 yds; 15 lbs/220 yds; 17 lbs/280 yds; 20 lbs/310 yds; 25 lbs/350 yds
Spool Cap. (B): 8 lbs/130 yds; 10 lbs,/225 yds; 15 lbs/205 yds; 20 lbs/275 yds; 30 lbs/305 yds; 40 lbs/365 yds; 50 lbs/430 yds; 65 lbs/450 yds

Weight: 7.9 oz; 9.6 oz; 11.6 oz; 12.6 oz; 20.3 oz; 21.8 oz; 27.8 oz; 29.2 oz
Hand Retrieve: R or L
Max Drag: 7 lbs; 7 lbs; 10 lbs; 13 lbs; 20 lbs; 20 lbs; 25 lbs; 25 lbs
Reel Bearings: 6+1
Features: Machined and anodized aluminum spool; infinite anti-reverse; Techno-balanced rotor gives smooth retrieves; stainless steel main shaft six-shielded stainless steel ball bearings; machined and anodized aluminum handle with soft-touch knob.
Price:. . . . . **$99.99–$119.99**

PFLUEGER ARBOR

Model: 7430X; 7435X; 7440X; 7450X
Gear Ratio: 4.3:1
Inches/Turn: 25; 26.6; 29.7; 32.4
Spool Cap. (M): 6 lbs/120 yds; 8 lbs/155 yds; 10 lbs/150 yds; 12 lbs/225 yds
Spool Cap. (B): 8 lbs/160 yds; 10 lbs/195 yds; 15 lbs/250 yds; 15 lbs/330 yds
Hand Retrieve: R or L
Max Drag: 10 lbs; 10 lbs; 18 lbs; 25 lbs
Reel Bearings: 7+1

Features: Seven stainless steel ball bearings; on/off instant anti-reverse bearing; lightweight hybrid construction provides the strength of an aluminum body without the weight; lightweight graphite rotor; large arbor spool design for maximum line control; machined, ported, and double anodized braid ready aluminum spool; smoothed sealed carbon fiber drag system; solid aluminum bail wire; sure-click bail provides an audible signal when bail is fully opened and ready to cast; spare aluminum spool; convertible right- or left-hand retrieve.
Price: . . . .$79.95–$89.95

PFLUEGER PATRIARCH

Model: 9525X; 9530X; 9535X; 9540X
Gear Ratio: 05:02.1
Inches/Turn: 24.5; 27; 28.8; 32.7
Spool Cap. (M): 4 lbs/110 yds; 6 lbs/120 yds; 8 lbs/140 yds; 10 lbs/170 yds
Spool Cap. (B): 6 lbs/110 yds; 8 lbs/115 yds; 10 lbs/150 yds; 14 lbs/160 yds
Hand Retrieve: R or L
Max Drag: 8 lbs; 8 lbs; 16 lbs; 16 lbs
Reel Bearings: 9+1

Features: The ultra lightweight, magnesium body, rotor, and sideplate are protected with proprietary three-step coating to provide premium corrosion resistance and durability; its solid titanium main shaft is 30 percent stronger and 43 percent lighter than comparable stainless steel shafts; carbon handle with EVA knob is 20 percent lighter than comparable aluminum handles; sealed carbon drag system and durable titanium-coated line roller.
Price: **$199.99**

PFLUEGER PRESIDENT

Model: 6920X; 6925X; 6930X; 6935X; 6940X
Gear Ratio: 5.2:1
Inches/Turn: 20.7; 22.4; 25.2; 27.4; 30.2
Spool Cap. (M): 4 lbs/100 yds; 4 lbs/110 yds; 6 lbs/145 yds; 8 lbs/185 yds; 10 lbs/230 yds
Spool Cap. (B): 6 lbs/125 yds; 6 lbs/140 yds; 8 lbs/190 yds; 10 lbs/220 yds; 14 lbs/280 yds
Weight: 5.9 oz; 7.2 oz; 8.3 oz; 9.9 oz; 10.9 oz
Hand Retrieve: R or L
Max Drag: 6 lbs; 6 lbs; 9 lbs; 10 lbs; 12 lbs;

Reel Bearings: 7+1; 9+1; 9+1; 9+1; 9+1
Features: Lightweight graphite body; corrosion-resistant; stainless steel main shaft and components; nine stainless steel ball bearings (model 6920 has seven); one instant anti-reverse bearing; machined, ported, double-anodized aluminum spool; braid-ready spool; titanium-coated spool lip and line roller; smooth multi-disc drag; solid aluminum bail wire; Sure-Click Bail with audible signal; soft-touch knob; on/off anti-reverse; converts to left- or right-hand retrieve.
Price:. . . . .**$49.99–$59.99**

PFLUEGER SUPREME MG
Model: 8225MGX; 8230MGX; 8235MGX; 8240MGX
Gear Ratio: 5.2:1; 6.2:1; 6.2:1; 6.2:1
Inches/Turn: 22.4; 30; 32.7; 35.1
Spool Cap. (M): 4 lbs/110 yds; 6 lbs/145 yds; 8 lbs/185 yds; 10 lbs/230 yds
Spool Cap. (B): 6 lbs/140 yds; 8 lbs/190 yds; 10 lbs/220 yds; 14 lbs/280 yds
Weight: 6.6 oz; 7.5 oz; 8.9 oz; 9.7 oz
Hand Retrieve: R or L
Max Drag: 6 lbs; 9 lbs; 10 lbs; 12 lbs
Reel Bearings: 9+1

Features: Nine stainless steel ball bearings; on/off instant anti-reverse bearing; ultra lightweight magnesium body, rotor, and sideplate; machined, ported, and double-anodized braid-ready aluminum spool; smooth multi-disc drag system with stainless steel and oiled felt washer; solid aluminum bail wire; sure-click bail provides an audible signal when bail is fully opened and ready to cast; anti-twist titanium line roller; machined aluminum handle with soft-touch knob; spare aluminum spool; convertible left- and right-hand retrieve.
Price: **$99.99**

QUANTUM ENERGY PTI
Model: 15, 25, 30
Gear Ratio: 5.3:1; 5.2:1; 5.2:1
Inches/Turn: 26; 28; 31
Spool Cap. (M): 6 lbs/140 yds; 8 lbs/150 yds; 10 lbs/150 yds
Weight: 7.0 oz; 8.3 oz; 8.6 oz
Hand Retrieve: R or L
Max Drag: 8 lbs; 19 lbs; 19 lbs

Reel Bearings: 11
Features: Polymer-stainless hybrid PT bearings; LMS line management system; continuous anti-reverse; machined aluminum handle; double-anodized aluminum spool; new SCR aluminum frame and side cover.
Price: **$139.99**

QUANTUM EXO PTI

Model: 15, 25, 30, 40, 50
Gear Ratio: 5.3:1; 5.2:1; 5.2:1; 5.2:1; 5.2:1
Inches/Turn: 26; 28; 31; 33; 36
Spool Cap. (M): 8 lbs/100 yds; 8 lb./150 yds; 10 lbs/150 yds; 10 lbs/230 yds; 12 lbs/225yds
Weight: 6.0 oz; 6.9 oz; 7.4 oz; 9.4 oz; 9.7 oz
Hand Retrieve: R or L
Max Drag: 6 lbs; 16 lbs; 20 lbs; 20 lbs; 20 lbs

Reel Bearings: 10+1
Features: Stacked ceramic front-adjustable drag system; polymer-stainless hybrid PT bearings; line management system; extra-hard PT gears; lightweight, machined aluminum crank handle; continuous anti-reverse.
Price:. . . . . $199.95–$209.95

QUANTUM HELLCAT
Model: 20, 30, 40
Gear Ratio: 5.1:1
Inches/Turn: 27; 28; 30
Spool Cap. (M): 6 lbs/130 yds; 8 lbs/190 yds; 10 lbs/170 yds
Weight: 10.0 oz; 11.1 oz; 11.8 oz

Hand Retrieve: R or L
Reel Bearings: 11
Features: Line management system; continuous anti-reverse; aluminum long stroke spool design; smooth front-adjustable drag system; corrosion-resistant stainless steel bail wire.
Price: **$79.99**

QUANTUM SMOKE

Model: 10, 15, 25, 30, 40, 50
Gear Ratio: 5.3:1; 5.3:1; 5.2:1; 5.2:1; 5.2:1; 5.2:1;
Inches/Turn: 24; 26; 28; 31; 33; 36
Spool Cap. (M): 4 lbs/125 yds; 6 lbs/140 yds; 8 lbs/150 yds; 10 lbs/150 yds; 10 lbs/230 yds; 12 lbs/ 225 yds
Weight: 6.2 oz; 6.3 oz; 7.5 oz; 7.8 oz; 9.7 oz; 10.0 oz
Hand Retrieve: R or L

Max Drag: 6 lbs; 6 lbs; 16 lbs; 16 lbs; 20 lbs; 20 lbs
Reel Bearings: 9+1
Features: ThinLine aluminum body and side cover; stacked ceramic front-adjustable drag system; polymer stainless hybrid; PT bearings; line management system; extra-hard PT gears; continuous anti-reverse; aluminum long stroke spool design.
Price: . . . . $159.95–$169.95

QUANTUM SNAPSHOT
Model: 10FC; 20FC; 30FC; 40FC
Gear Ratio: 5.2:1; 5.2:1; 5.2:1; 4.7:1
Spool Cap. (M): 4 lbs/125 yds; 6 lbs/140 yds; 8 lbs/160 yds; 10 lbs/230 yds
Weight: 6.7 oz; 8.6 oz; 9.1 oz; 11.7 oz
Hand Retrieve: R or L

Max Drag: 4 lbs; 8 lbs; 8 lbs
Reel Bearings: 1
Features: Aluminum long stroke spool design; smooth front-adjustable drag system; corrosion-resistant stainless steel bail wire; multi-stop anti-reverse.
Price: **$24.99**

QUANTUM TOUR KVD
Model: 25, 30, 40, 50
Gear Ratio: 5.2:1
Inches/Turn: 28; 31; 33; 36
Spool Cap. (M): 8 lbs/150 yds; 10 lbs/150 yds; 10 lbs/230 yds; 12 lbs/225 yds
Weight: 7.3 oz; 7.6 oz; 9.5 oz; 9.8 oz
Hand Retrieve: R or L
Max Drag: 16 lbs; 20 lbs; 20 lbs; 20 lbs
Reel Bearings: 10

Features: Dual PT continuous anti-reverse; super free spool pinion design; titanium-coated line guide reduces friction on casts and retrieves; MaxCast skeletal spool; one-piece aluminum frame and side cover; quick-release side cover; drag with ceramic, stainless, and carbon fiber discs for smooth, fish-fighting power; high-performance polymer-stainless hybrid PT bearings; adjustable infinite cast control; all metal frame and side covers keep components in perfect alignment; soft-touch laser-etched EVA handle grips; fully machined aluminum handle.
Price: . . . . **$179.99–$189.99**

SHIMANO SAHARA

Model: 500, 1000, 2500, 3000, 4000
Gear Ratio: 4.7:1; 6.0:1; 6.2:1; 6.2:1; 5.8:1
Inches/Turn: 21; 29; 35; 35; 36
Spool Cap. (M): 4 lbs/100 yds; 4 lbs/140 yds; 8 lbs/140 yds; 10 lbs/140 yds; 12 lbs/160 yds
Spool Cap. (B): 8 lbs/105 yds; 10 lbs/95 yds; 15 lbs/145 yds; 20 lbs/145 yds; 30 lbs/175 yds
Weight: 6.2 oz; 7.4 oz; 9.2 oz; 9.2 oz; 12.5 oz
Hand Retrieve: R or L

Max Drag: 6 lbs; 7 lbs; 11 lbs; 15 lbs; 15 lbs
Reel Bearings: 4+1; 3+1; 3+1; 3+1; 3+1
Features: New XGT7 graphite frame and sideplate; three SS ball, one roller; front drag; Super Stopper II; cold-forged aluminum spool; new M compact body; stamping bail; floating shaft; oversized power roller line roller; approved for use in salt water.
Price: . . . .**$79.99–$89.99**

SHIMANO SAROS

Model: 1000, 2500, 3000, 4000
Gear Ratio: 6.0:1; 6.0:1; 6.0:1; 5.8:1
Inches/Turn: 29; 34; 34; 37
Spool Cap. (M): 4 lbs/140 yds; 10 lbs/120 yds; 10 lbs/140 yds; 12 lbs/160 yds
Spool Cap. (B): 10 lbs/95 yds; 15 lbs/145 yds; 20 lbs/145 yds; 30 lbs/175 yds

Weight: 7.1 oz; 9.3 oz; 9.5 oz; 11.5 oz
Hand Retrieve: R or L
Max Drag: 7 lbs; 11 lbs; 15 lbs; 15 lbs
Reel Bearings: 5+1
Features: X-ship technology for increased cranking efficiency and more power; lightweight XT-7 frame/rotor/sideplate; rapid fire drag adjustment; six-bearing system.
Price: . . . . **$139.99–$149.99**

SHIMANO SEDONA FD
Model: 500; 1000; 2500; 4000
Gear Ratio: 4.7:1; 6.2:1; 6.2:1; 5.7:1
Inches/Turn: 21; 28; 32; 33
Spool Cap. (M): 2 lbs/ 190 yds; 2 lbs/270 yds; 10 lbs/120 yds; 10 lbs/200 yds
Weight: 6.2 oz; 7.7 oz; 9.5 oz; 12.5 oz
Hand Retrieve: R or L

Max Drag: 4 lbs; 7 lbs; 15 lbs; 20 lbs
Reel Bearings: 4+1
Features: Exclusive S-concept technology propulsion line management system lightweight graphite frame, sideplate and rotor; propulsion line management system; four-shielded ball bearings plus one roller bearing; cold-forged aluminum spool; Power Roller III; Dyna-Balance system.
Price: **$59.99**

SHIMANO SPIREX FG
Model: 1000, 2500, 4000
Gear Ratio: 6.2:1; 6.2:1; 5.7:1
Inches/Turn: 28; 32; 33
Spool Cap. (M): 2 lbs/270 yds; 10 lbs/120 yds; 10 lbs/200 yds
Weight: 8.8 oz; 10.6 oz; 13.9 oz
Hand Retrieve: R or L

Max Drag: 7 lbs; 15 lbs; 20 lbs
Reel Bearings: 5
Features: Rock-solid reliability meets advanced technology; hands-down favorite for walleye and smallmouth anglers; S-concept; graphite frame, sideplate, and rotor; cold-forged aluminum spool; propulsion line management system; Dyna-Balance; Fluidrive.
Price:. **$59.99**

SHIMANO SPIREX RG
Model: 1000, 2500, 4000
Gear Ratio: 6.2:1; 6.2:1; 5.7:1
Inches/Turn: 28; 33; 33
Spool Cap. (M): 6 lbs/110 yds; 8 lbs/140 yds; 12 lbs/160 yds
Weight: 9.9 oz; 11.3 oz; 14.5 oz
Hand Retrieve: R or L

Max Drag: 6 lbs; 7 lbs; 9 lbs
Reel Bearings: 5
Features: Rock-solid reliability meets advanced technology; hands-down favorite for walleye and smallmouth anglers; S-concept; graphite frame, sideplate, and rotor; cold-forged aluminum spool; propulsion line management system; Dyna-Balance; Fluidrive.
Price: **$59.99**

SHIMANO STRADIC CI4+

Model: 1000, 2500, 3000, 4000
Gear Ratio: 6.0:1; 6.0:1; 6.0:1; 5.8:1
Inches/Turn: 34; 34; 35; 37
Spool Cap. (M): 4 lbs/140 yds; 8 lbs/140 yds; 8 lbs/170 yds; 10 lbs/200 yds
Spool Cap. (B): 15 lbs/85 yds; 15 lbs/145 yds; 20 lbs/145 yds; 30 lbs/175 yds
Weight: 6.0 oz; 7.0 oz; 7.0 oz; 9.0 oz
Hand Retrieve: R or L
Max Drag: 7 lbs; 15 lbs; 15 lbs; 20 lbs
Reel Bearings: 6+1

Features: Ultra-lightweight CI4+ frame, sideplate, and rotor construction; X-ship; Paladin gear durability enhancement; propulsion line management system: propulsion spool lip, Power Roller III, redesigned bail trip; Aero Wrap II oscillation; SR-concept: SR 3D gear, SR handle, SR one-piece bail wire; S A-RB ball bearings; aluminum spool; S-concept: S-rotor, S-guard, S-arm cam; machined aluminum handle; direct drive mechanism (thread in handle attachment); round EVA handle grip; waterproof drag; Magnumlite rotor; maintenance port; Fluidrive II; floating shaft; Dyna-Balance; Super Stopper II; repairable clicker; approved for use in salt water; rated for use with mono, fluorocarbon, and PowerPro lines.
Price: . . . . $219.99–$239.99

SHIMANO STRADIC FJ

Model: 1000, 2500, 3000, 4000, 5000, 6000, 8000
Gear Ratio: 6.0:1; 6.0:1; 6.0:1; 6.2:1; 6.2:1; 4.8:1; 4.8:1
Inches/Turn: 30; 34; 35; 39; 41; 35; 35
Spool Cap. (M): 4 lbs/140 yds; 8 lbs/140 yds; 8 lbs/170 yds; 10 lbs/200 yds; 12 lbs/195 yds; 16 lbs/170 yds; 16 lbs/250 yds
Spool Cap. (B): 15 lbs/85 yds; 15 lbs/145 yds; 20 lbs/145 yds; 30 lbs/175 yds; 30 lbs/200 yds; 50 lbs/240 yds; 50 lbs/265 yds
Weight: 7.5 oz; 9.2 oz; 9.3 oz; 10.8 oz; 10.8 oz; 20.8 oz; 20.5 oz
Hand Retrieve: R or L

Max Drag: 7 lbs; 15 lbs; 15 lbs; 20 lbs; 20 lbs; 29 lbs; 29 lbs
Reel Bearings: 5+1
Features: X-ship for easier turning handle under load; propulsion line management system; SA-RB bearings; aluminum frame (graphite on 1000); lightweight graphite sideplate and rotor; cold-forged aluminum spool; S-concept rotor, guard, and arm cam; machined-aluminum handle; Fluidrive II floating shaft; Dyna-Balance; Super Stopper II; salt water approved; rated for use with mono, fluorocarbon, or braid.
Price:..........................**$179.99–$239.99**

SHIMANO SUSTAIN FG

Model: 1000, 2500, 3000, 4000, 5000, 6000, 10000
Gear Ratio: 6.0:1; 6.0:1; 6.0:1; 6.2:1; 6.2:1; 4.8:1; 4.8:1
Inches/Turn: 30; 34; 35; 39; 41; 35; 37
Spool Cap. (M): 4 lbs/140 yds; 8 lbs/140 yds; 10 lbs/140 yds; 12 lbs/160 yds; 12 lbs/195 yds; 16 lbs/170 yds; 16 lbs/340 yds
Spool Cap. (B): 15 lbs/145 yds; 15 lbs/145 yds; 20 lbs/145 yds; 15 lbs/265 yds; 20 lbs/220 yds; 30 lbs/290 yds; 65 lbs/260 yds
Weight: 6.5 oz; 8.3 oz; 8.3 oz; 9.9 oz; 10.6 oz; 19.6 oz; 19.0 oz

Hand Retrieve: R or L
Max Drag: 7 lbs; 20 lbs; 15 lbs; 24 lbs; 20 lbs; 28 lbs; 28 lbs
Reel Bearings: 7+1; 8+1; 8+1; 8+1; 8+1; 8+1; 8+1;
Features: X-ship design; Magnumlite CI4 rotor; aluminum sideplate; rapid fire drag; Paladin gear durability enhancement; propulsion line management system; Aero Wrap II oscillation; aluminum spool; machined aluminum handle; direct drive mechanism (thread-in attachment); EVA handle knob; maintenance port; Fluidrive II; floating shaft; Dyna-Balance; Super Stopper II.
Price: . . . . **$329.99–$399.99**

SHIMANO SYMETRE FL

Model: 500, 1000, 2500, 3000, 4000
Gear Ratio: 4.7:1; 6.0:1; 6.2:1; 6.2:1; 5.8:1
Inches/Turn: 21; 29; 35; 35; 36
Spool Cap. (M): 4 lbs/100 yds; 6 lbs/110 yds; 8 lbs/140 yds; 10 lbs/140 yds; 12 lbs/160 yds;
Spool Cap. (B): 8 lbs/105 yds; 10 lbs/95 yds; 15 lbs/145 yds; 20 lbs/145 yds; 30 lbs/175 yds
Weight: 6.1 oz; 6.5 oz; 9 oz; 9 oz; 11.8 oz
Hand Retrieve: R or L

Max Drag: 6 lbs; 7 lbs; 11 lbs; 15 lbs; 15 lbs
Reel Bearings: 4+1
Features: Four A-RB plus one A-RB stainless steel bearings; X-ship technology; XGT7 stronger and lighter frame technology; aluminum cold-forged spool; Super Stopper II; Dyna-Balance; propulsion line management system; Varispeed II oscillation system.
Price: . . . . **$99.99–$109.99**

SHIMANO SYNCOPATE FG

Model: 1000, 2500, 4000
Gear Ratio: 5.2:1; 5.2:1; 5.1:1
Inches/Turn: 25; 29; 32
Spool Cap. (M): 4 lbs/140 yds; 8 lbs/140 yds; 10 lbs/200 yds
Spool Cap. (B): 15 lbs/85 yds; 15 lbs/145 yds; 30 lbs/175 yds
Weight: 7.6 oz; 9.2 oz; 12.7 oz
Hand Retrieve: R or L

Max Drag: 7 lbs; 7 lbs; 13 lbs
Reel Bearings: 4
Features: Propulsion spool lip; graphite frame; graphite sideplate; graphite rotor; aluminum spool; Varispeed oscillation ported handle shank; Quick Fire II; Dyna-Balance; Power Roller II; fresh water or salt water; use with mono, fluoro, and braid.
Price:. **$29.99**

ABU GARCIA ORRA S
Model: 10, 20, 30, 40
Gear Ratio: 5.2:1; 5.8:1; 5.8:1; 5.8:1
Inches/Turn: 24.5; 31; 33; 33
Retrieve Speed: Std
Spool Cap. (B): 6 lbs/150 yds; 8 lbs/130 yds; 8 lbs/175 yds; 10 lbs/210 yds
Weight: 7.8 oz; 8.7 oz; 9.2 oz; 10.2 oz
Hand Retrieve: R or L
Max Drag: 10 lbs; 12 lbs; 12 lbs; 18 lbs

Features: Stunning design and a sleek look highlight the advancement in spinning reel technology; smooth performing sealed Hybrid Carbon Matrix drag system and includes a durable braid-ready aluminum spool that eliminates the need for a mono backing; unique corkscrew design of the spool allows braid to be tied directly to the spool without the line slipping.
Price:. **$69.95**

CABELA'S SALT STRIKER BAITFEEDER

Model: 40B, 65B, 80B
Gear Ratio: 5.0:1; 4.8:1; 4.8:1
Spool Cap. (M): 10 lbs/190 yds; 15 lbs/310 yds; 20 lbs/350 yds
Weight: 12.1 oz; 24.4 oz; 25.6 oz
Hand Retrieve: R or L

Reel Bearings: 9+1
Features: Nine ball bearing drive provides an unbeatably smooth retrieve; quick-set instant anti-reverse; lightweight graphite body and sideplate; anodized-aluminum spool with holes minimizes weight and dissipates heat; striking blue highlights.
Price: **$69.99**

REELS: Saltwater Spinning

DAIWA STEEZ

Model: 2500, 2508
Gear Ratio: 4.8:1
Inches/Turn: 27.9
Spool Cap. (M): 8 lbs/110 yds; 8 lbs/170 yds
Weight: 6.9 oz; 7 oz
Hand Retrieve: R or L
Max Drag: 15.4 lbs
Reel Bearings: 11+1
Features: Weighs 5.5 ounces; magnesium frame and handle-side sideplate; swept handle for less wobble, better feel and maximum winding leverage; tough, A7075 tempered aluminum drive gear and phosphor bronze pinion; eleven precision ball bearings, plus roller bearing; free-floating A7075 aluminum alloy spool starts faster, spins longer; fast spool change; Magforce-V automatic magnetic spool brake; eight-disc wet drag with precision click adjustment; precision click-free spool adjustment; infinite anti-reverse; Digigear digital gear design; eleven super corrosion-resistant ball bearings plus roller bearing; tubular stainless air Bail; infinite anti-reverse; advanced locomotive levelwind washable design with sealed, waterproof drag system; precision, super micro-pitch drag adjustment; pillartype tight oscillation system, ultra-quiet, and smooth; precision, stainless main shaft.
Price: . . . . $749.99–$799.99

DAIWA STEEZ EX
Model: 2508H, 3012H
Gear Ratio: 5.6:1
Inches/Turn: 33
Spool Cap. (M): 8 lbs/110 yds; 8 lbs/170 yds
Weight: 6.8 oz; 8.5 oz
Hand Retrieve: R or L
Max Drag: 15.4 lbs
Reel Bearings: 12+1

Features: Built for the fresh or salt water with a corrosion-proof Zaion body; ultra lightweight, corrosion-proof Zaion body and air rotor; mag-sealed construction (body and line roller); max drag 15.4 pounds; thirteen bearing system (7 CRBB/5BB+1RB); Digigear digital gear design for speed, power, and durability; lightweight, hollow, stainless steel air bail; machined aluminum handle with cork knob; silent oscillation; ABS air spool with cut-proof, titanium nitride spool lip; infinite anti-reverse; and neoprene reel bag.
Price: **$799.99**

OKUMA CEDROS

Model: 30S, 40S, 45S, 55S, 65S, 80S
Gear Ratio: 6.2:1; 6.2:1; 6.2:1; 6.2:1; 5.7:1; 5.7:1
Inches/Turn: 30; 34; 35; 40; 42; 46
Spool Cap. (M): 6 lbs/200 yds; 8 lbs/270 yds; 10 lbs/240 yds; 10 lbs/380 yds; 12 lbs/430 yds; 15 lbs/420 yds
Weight: 11.1 oz; 12.1 oz; 16.5 oz; 16.9 oz; 22.8 oz; 23 oz
Hand Retrieve: R or L
Max Drag: 18 lbs; 20 lbs; 24 lbs; 24 lbs; 31 lbs; 33 lbs
Reel Bearings: 4+1
Features: Precision dual force drag system; multi-disc, Japanese-oiled felt drag system; 4HPB+1RB corrosion-resistant stainless steel ball bearings; quick-set anti-reverse roller bearing; precision machine-cut brass pinion gear; corrosion-resistant coating process; corrosion-resistant, high-density gearing; rigid die-cast aluminum frame and sideplate; precision elliptical gearing system; machined aluminum, two-tone anodized and ported spool; custom blue anodized machined aluminum handle knob; EVA handle knob on 30-size; Hydro Block water tight drag seal; heavy-duty, solid aluminum, gold anodized bail wire; RESII: Computer balanced rotor equalizing system; narrow blade body design for reduced fatigue; one-year warranty.
Price:. . . . . **$109.99–$149.99**

OKUMA CEDROS BAITFEEDER

Model: 55, 65
Gear Ratio: 4.5:1; 4.8:1
Inches/Turn: 30; 34
Spool Cap. (M): 10 lbs/380 yds; 12 lbs/430 yds
Weight: 19.1 oz; 26.6 oz
Hand Retrieve: R or L
Max Drag: 24 lbs; 31 lbs
Reel Bearings: 4+1
Features: On/off auto-trip bait feeding system; precision dual force drag system; multi-disc, Japanese-oiled felt drag system; 4HPB+1RB corrosion-resistant stainless steel ball bearings; quick-set anti-reverse roller bearing; precision machine-cut brass pinion gear; corrosion-resistant coating process; corrosion-resistant, high-density gearing; rigid die-cast aluminum frame and sideplate; precision elliptical gearing system; machined aluminum, two-tone anodized and ported spool; custom blue anodized machined aluminum handle knob; Hydro Block water tight drag seal; heavy-duty, solid aluminum, gold anodized bail wire; RESII: computer balanced rotor equalizing system; narrow blade body design for reduced fatigue; one-year warranty.
Price: . . . . **$159.99–$164.99**

OKUMA CORONADO BAITFEEDER
Model: 40a, 55a, 65a, 80a
Gear Ratio: 4.5:1; 4.5:1; 4.8:1; 4.8:1
Inches/Turn: 28; 30; 34; 34
Spool Cap. (M): 8 lbs/410 yds; 10 lbs/380 yds; 12 lbs/540 yds; 15 lbs/420 yds
Weight: 12 oz; 16.7 oz; 23.6 oz; 24.7 oz
Hand Retrieve: R or L
Max Drag: 20 lbs; 24 lbs; 31 lbs; 33 lbs
Reel Bearings: 4+1
Features: On/off auto-trip bait feeding system; precision dual force drag system; multi-disc, Japanese-oiled felt drag system; 4BB+1RB corrosion-resistant stainless steel ball bearings; quick-set anti-reverse roller bearing; precision machine-cut brass pinion gear; corrosion-resistant coating process; corrosion-resistant, high-density gearing; lightweight, corrosion-resistant graphite body and rotor; precision elliptical gearing system; machined aluminum, two-tone anodized spool; Hydro Block water tight drag seal; heavy-duty, solid aluminum, anodized bail wire; RESII: computer balanced rotor equalizing system; narrow blade body design for reduced fatigue; one-year warranty.
Price: . . . .**$89.99–$99.99**

OKUMA RAW II
Model: 30, 40, 55, 65, 80
Gear Ratio: 5.0:1; 5.0:1; 4.5:1; 4.8:1; 4.8:1
Inches/Turn: 25; 28; 30; 34; 38
Spool Cap. (M): 6 lbs/200 yds; 8 lbs/270 yds; 10 lbs/380 yds; 12 lbs/430 yds; 15 lbs/420 yds
Weight: 10.5 oz; 11 oz; 17 oz; 23.4 oz; 24.2 oz
Hand Retrieve: R or L
Max Drag: 25 lbs; 30 lbs; 35 lbs; 50 lbs; 50 lbs
Reel Bearings: 7+1
Features: Precision dual force drag system; multi-disc, carbonite drag washers; 7 HPB+1RB corrosion-resistant stainless steel ball bearings; quick-set anti-reverse roller bearing; precision machine-cut brass pinion gear; corrosion-resistant coating process; corrosion-resistant, high-density gearing; rigid die-cast aluminum frame, sideplate, and rotor; precision elliptical gearing system; machined aluminum, two-tone anodized spool; carbon fiber handle system on the 30/40 sizes; standard EVA handle knob on 30/40 sizes; heavy-duty aluminum handle on 55/65/80 sizes; oversized round EVA handle grip on 55/65/80 size; Hydro Block water tight drag seal; heavy-duty, solid aluminum bail wire; one-year warranty.
Price: . . . . **$149.99–$174.99**

PENN BATTLE

Model: 1000; 2000; 3000; 4000; 5000; 6000; 7000; 8000
Gear Ratio: 5.2:1; 6.2:1; 6.2:1; 6.2:1; 5.6:1; 5.6:1; 5.3:1; 5.3:1
Inches/Turn: 20; 29; 31; 34; 37; 39; 39; 41
Spool Cap. (M): 4 lbs/115 yds; 6 lbs/210 yds; 8 lbs/170 yds; 10 lbs/230 yds; 15 lbs/220 yds; 17 lbs/280 yds; 20 lbs/310 yds; 25 lbs/350 yds
Spool Cap. (B): 8 lbs/130 yds; 10 lbs,/225 yds; 15 lbs/205 yds; 20 lbs/275 yds; 30 lbs/305 yds; 40 lbs/365 yds; 50 lbs/430 yds; 65 lbs/450 yds

Weight: 7.9 oz; 9.6 oz; 11.6 oz; 12.6 oz; 20.3 oz; 21.8 oz; 27.8 oz; 29.2 oz
Hand Retrieve: R or L
Max Drag: 7 lbs; 7 lbs; 10 lbs; 13 lbs; 20 lbs; 20 lbs; 25 lbs; 25 lbs
Reel Bearings: 6+1
Features: Machined and anodized aluminum spool; infinite anti-reverse; Techno-balanced rotor gives smooth retrieves; stainless steel main shaft six-shielded stainless steel ball bearings; machined and anodized aluminum handle with soft-touch knob.
Price:.............................$99.99–$119.99

PENN CONQUER

Model: 2000; 4000; 5000; 7000; 8000
Gear Ratio: 5.1:1; 5.8:1; 4.8:1; 4.8:1; 4.7:1
Inches/Turn: 28; 32; 31; 37; 40
Spool Cap. (M): 6 lbs/185 yds; 10 lbs/200 yds; 15 lbs/190 yds; 17 lbs/210 yds; 20 lbs/310 yds
Spool Cap. (B): 10 lbs/210 yds; 15 lbs/280 yds; 20 lbs/250 yds; 30 lbs/325 yds; 50 lbs/420 yds
Weight: 9.9 oz; 11.1 oz; 14.6 oz; 18.1 oz; 23.4 oz

Hand Retrieve: R or L
Max Drag: 12 lbs; 19 lbs; 22 lbs; 32 lbs; 32 lbs
Reel Bearings: 10+1
Features: One-piece machined aluminum gear box; forged, machined, and anodized aluminum spool; ten-shielded stainless steel ball bearings; infinite anti-reverse; braid-ready to handle the strain that superlines puts on a reel; friction trip ramp prevents premature bait trip when casting.
Price: . . . . **$199.99–$219.95**

PENN FIERCE

Model: 1000; 2000; 3000; 4000; 5000; 6000; 7000; 8000
Gear Ratio: 5.2:1; 6.2:1; 6.2:1; 6.2:1; 5.6:1; 5.6:1; 5.3:1; 5.3:1
Inches/Turn: 20; 29; 31; 34; 37; 39; 39; 41
Spool Cap. (M): 4 lbs/115 yds; 6 lbs/210 yds; 8 lbs/170 yds; 10 lbs/230 yds; 15 lbs/220 yds; 17 lbs/280 yds; 20 lbs/310 yds; 25 lbs/350 yds
Spool Cap. (B): 8 lbs/130 yds; 10 lbs,/225 yds; 15 lbs/205 yds; 20 lbs/275 yds; 30 lbs/305 yds; 40 lbs/365 yds; 50 lbs/430 yds; 65 lbs/450 yds
Weight: 7.7 oz; 8.8 oz; 11.7 oz; 12.5 oz; 19 oz; 20.6 oz; 26.4 oz; 27.4 oz;

Hand Retrieve: R or L
Max Drag: 7 lbs; 7 lbs; 10 lbs; 13 lbs; 20 lbs; 20 lbs; 25 lbs; 25 lbs
Reel Bearings: 4+1
Features: Machined and anodized aluminum spool; infinite anti-reverse; stainless steel main shaft; four stainless steel ball bearings; infinite anti-reverse; Techno-balanced rotor gives smooth retrieves; machined and anodized handle with soft-touch knob.
Price: . . . .**$59.99–$79.99**

PENN TORQUE

Model: S5; S7; S9
Gear Ratio: 5.9:1; 5.1:1; 5.1:1
Inches/Turn: 38; 40; 50
Spool Cap. (M): 15 lbs/300 yds; 20 lbs/340 yds; 25 lbs/440 yds
Spool Cap. (B): 30 lbs/400 yds; 65 lbs/390 yds; 80 lbs/490 yds
Weight: 21.3 oz; 28.6 oz; 30.8 oz
Hand Retrieve: R or L

Max Drag: 38 lbs; 41 lbs; 50 lbs
Reel Bearings: 7+1
Features: One-piece aluminum frame; forged and machined aluminum spool, sideplates, and one-piece handle arm; integral clutch sleeve eliminates any back play during hook set; seven sealed stainless steel ball bearings; machine-cut marine grade bronze main gear; hardened stainless steel pinion gear; innovative bail trip switch allows the angler to choose between manual and auto mode.
Price:..........................$659.99–$699.99

QUANTUM CABO PTS

Model: 40, 50, 60, 80
Gear Ratio: 5.3:1; 5.3:1; 4.9:1; 4.9:1
Inches/Turn: 33; 36; 37; 41
Spool Cap. (M): 10 lbs/230 yds; 12 lbs/225 yds; 14 lbs/300 yds; 20 lbs/330 yds
Weight: 13.9 oz; 14.1 oz; 24 oz; 25 oz
Hand Retrieve: R or L
Max Drag: 30 lbs; 35 lbs; 40 lbs; 50 lbs
Reel Bearings: 7+1

Features: Eight PT bearings; hybrid ceramic bearings in high-load areas; sealed Magnum CSC drag; sealed Magnum clutch; TiMag titanium fail-proof bail system with magnetic trip; line management system with ball-bearing line roller; SaltGuard 2.0 multi-layer corrosion protection; SCR alloy body and side cover; SCR alloy rotor on 60 and 80 models; carbon fiber composite rotor on 40 and 50 models; super-hard PT gears.
Price: . . . . **$189.95–$229.95**

QUANTUM SMOKE PTS INSHORE
Model: 25, 30, 40, 50
Gear Ratio: 5.2:1; 5.2:1; 5.3:1; 5.3:1
Inches/Turn: 28; 31; 33; 36
Spool Cap. (M): 8 lbs/150 yds; 10 lbs/150 yds; 10 lbs/250 yds; 12 lbs/225 yds
Weight: 7.6 oz; 7.9 oz; 9.7 oz; 10.0 oz
Hand Retrieve: R or L
Max Drag: 16 lbs; 18 lbs; 20 lbs; 25 lbs

Reel Bearings: 9+1
Features: Sealed CSC drag system SCR base; alloy aluminum body and sidecovers; rigid and lightweight; C4LF carbon fiber rotor; MaxCast II spool; sealed clutch; fail-proof titanium bail wire; SaltGuard 2.0 multi-layer corrosion protection.
Price: . . . . **$179.99–$189.99**

SHIMANO SAHARA
Model • 500, 1000, 2500, 3000, 4000
Gear Ratio: 4.7:1; 6.0:1; 6.2:1; 6.2:1; 5.8:1
Inches/Turn: 21; 29; 35; 35; 36
Spool Cap. (M): 4 lbs/100 yds; 4 lbs/140 yds; 8 lbs/140 yds; 10 lbs/140 yds; 12 lbs/160 yds
Spool Cap. (B): 8 lbs/105 yds; 10 lbs/95 yds; 15 lbs/145 yds; 20 lbs/145 yds; 30 lbs/175 yds
Weight: 6.2 oz; 7.4 oz; 9.2 oz; 9.2 oz; 12.5 oz

Hand Retrieve: R or L
Max Drag: 6 lbs; 7 lbs; 11 lbs; 15 lbs; 15 lbs
Reel Bearings: 4+1; 3+1; 3+1; 3+1; 3+1
Features: New XGT7 graphite frame and sideplate; three SS ball, one roller; front drag; Super Stopper II; cold-forged aluminum spool; new M compact body; stamping bail; floating shaft; oversized power roller line roller; approved for use in salt water.
Price: . . . .$79.99–$89.99

SHIMANO SAROS

Model: 1000, 2500, 3000, 4000
Gear Ratio: 6.0:1; 6.0:1; 6.0:1; 5.8:1
Inches/Turn: 29; 34; 34; 37
Spool Cap. (M): 4 lbs/140 yds; 10 lbs/120 yds; 10 lbs/140 yds; 12 lbs/160 yds
Spool Cap. (B): 10 lbs/95 yds; 15 lbs/145 yds; 20 lbs/145 yds; 30 lbs/175 yds
Weight: 7.1 oz; 9.3 oz; 9.5 oz; 11.5 oz

Hand Retrieve: R or L
Max Drag: 7 lbs; 11 lbs; 15 lbs; 15 lbs
Reel Bearings: 5+1
Features: X-ship technology for increased cranking efficiency and more power; lightweight XT-7 frame/rotor/sideplate; rapid fire drag adjustment; six-bearing system.
Price:............................**$139.99–$149.99**

SHIMANO SEDONA FD
Model: 500; 1000; 2500; 4000
Gear Ratio: 4.7:1; 6.2:1; 6.2:1; 5.7:1
Inches/Turn: 21; 28; 32; 33
Spool Cap. (M): 2 lbs/ 190 yds; 2 lbs/270 yds; 10 lbs/120 yds; 10 lbs/200 yds
Weight: 6.2 oz; 7.7 oz; 9.5 oz; 12.5 oz
Hand Retrieve: R or L
Max Drag: 4 lbs; 7 lbs; 15 lbs; 20 lbs

Reel Bearings: 4+1
Features: Enjoy high-end performance for affordable price; exclusive S-concept technology; propulsion line management system; lightweight graphite frame, sideplate, and rotor; four-shielded ball bearings plus one roller bearing; cold-forged aluminum spool; Power Roller III; Dyna-Balance system.
Price:. **$59.99**

SHIMANO SPHEROS

Model: 3000, 4000, 5000, 6000, 8000, 14000, 18000
Gear Ratio: 5.1:1; 5.1:1; 4.7:1; 4.7:1; 4.7:1; 4.7:1; 4.6:1; 4.6:1
Inches/Turn: 27; 29; 31; 33; 33; 38; 38
Spool Cap. (M): 10 lbs/140 yds; 10 lbs/200 yds; 12 lbs/195 yds; 12 lbs/265 yds; 14 lbs/270 yds; 20 lbs/350 yds; 20 lbs/380 yds
Spool Cap. (B): 10 lbs/240 yds; 15 lbs/270 yds; 20 lbs/255 yds; 30 lbs/245 yds; 40 lbs/300 yds; 50 lbs/600 yds; 50 lbs/655 yds
Weight: 12.5 oz; 12.3 oz; 19.6 oz; 20.1 oz; 19.6 oz; 27.7 oz; 26.8 oz
Hand Retrieve: R or L

Max Drag: 22 lbs; 22 lbs; 22 lbs; 27 lbs; 27 lbs; 44 lbs; 44 lbs
Reel Bearings: 3+1
Features: Aluminum frame graphite sideplate; graphite rotor (aluminum on 14000 & 18000 sizes); Power Roller III line roller; S-arm cam; Aero Wave oscillation (3000 and 8000 sizes only); Aero Wrap oscillation (14000 and 18000 sizes only); 3+1 bearings (4+1 on 14000 and 18000 sizes only); Super Stopper II anti-reverse; direct drive mechanism; Dyna-Balance; Fluidrive II; cold-forged aluminum Spool; waterproof drag; easy access drag washers; Dartainium drag (6000 to 18000 sizes only); rubber handle grips; repairable clicker.
Price: . . . . **$109.99–$179.99**

SHIMANO SPIREX FG
Model: 1000, 2500, 4000
Gear Ratio: 6.2:1; 6.2:1; 5.7:1
Inches/Turn: 28; 32; 33
Spool Cap. (M): 2 lbs/270 yds; 10 lbs/120 yds; 10 lbs/200 yds
Weight: 8.8 oz; 10.6 oz; 13.9 oz
Hand Retrieve: R or L

Max Drag: 7 lbs; 15 lbs; 20 lbs
Reel Bearings: 5
Features: Rock-solid reliability meets advanced technology; hands-down favorite for walleye and smallmouth anglers; S-concept; graphite frame, sideplate, and rotor; cold-forged aluminum spool; propulsion line management system; Dyna-Balance; Fluidrive.
Price:..................................... **$59.99**

SHIMANO SPIREX RG
Model: 1000, 2500, 4000
Gear Ratio: 6.2:1; 6.2:1; 5.7:1
Inches/Turn: 28; 33; 33
Spool Cap. (M): 6 lbs/110 yds; 8 lbs/140 yds; 12 lbs/160 yds
Weight: 9.9 oz; 11.3 oz; 14.5 oz
Hand Retrieve: R or L

Max Drag: 6 lbs; 7 lbs; 9 lbs
Reel Bearings: 5
Features: Rock-solid reliability meets advanced technology; hands-down favorite for walleye and smallmouth anglers; S-concept; graphite frame, sideplate, and rotor; cold-forged aluminum spool; propulsion line management system; Dyna-Balance; Fluidrive.
Price: **$59.99**

SHIMANO STRADIC CI4+

Model: 1000, 2500, 3000, 4000
Gear Ratio: 6.0:1; 6.0:1; 6.0:1; 5.8:1
Inches/Turn: 34; 34; 35; 37
Spool Cap. (M): 4 lbs/140 yds; 8 lbs/140 yds; 8 lbs/170 yds; 10 lbs/200 yds
Spool Cap. (B): 15 lbs/85 yds; 15 lbs/145 yds; 20 lbs/145 yds; 30 lbs/175 yds
Weight: 6.0 oz; 7.0 oz; 7.0 oz; 9.0 oz
Hand Retrieve: R or L
Max Drag: 7 lbs; 15 lbs; 15 lbs; 20 lbs
Reel Bearings: 6+1
Features: Ultra-lightweight CI4+ frame, sideplate, and rotor construction; X-ship; Paladin gear durability enhancement; propulsion line management system: propulsion spool lip, Power Roller III, redesigned bail trip; Aero Wrap II Oscillation; SR-concept: SR 3D gear, SR handle, SR one-piece bail wire; S A-RB ball bearings; aluminum spool; S-concept: S-rotor, S-guard, S-arm cam; machined aluminum handle; direct drive mechanism (thread in handle attachment); round EVA handle grip; waterproof drag; Magnumlite rotor; maintenance port; Fluidrive II; floating shaft; Dyna-Balance; Super Stopper II; repairable clicker; approved for use in salt water; rated for use with mono, fluorocarbon, and PowerPro lines.
Price: . . . . **$219.99–$239.99**

SHIMANO STRADIC FJ

Model: 1000, 2500, 3000, 4000, 5000, 6000, 8000
Gear Ratio: 6.0:1; 6.0:1; 6.0:1; 6.2:1; 6.2:1; 4.8:1; 4.8:1
Inches/Turn: 30; 34; 35; 39; 41; 35; 35
Spool Cap. (M): 4 lbs/140 yds; 8 lbs/140 yds; 8 lbs/170 yds; 10 lbs/200 yds; 12 lbs/195 yds; 16 lbs/170 yds; 16 lbs/250 yds
Spool Cap. (B): 15 lbs/85 yds; 15 lbs/145 yds; 20 lbs/145 yds; 30 lbs/175 yds; 30 lbs/200 yds; 50 lbs/240 yds; 50 lbs/265 yds
Weight: 7.5 oz; 9.2 oz; 9.3 oz; 10.8 oz; 10.8 oz; 20.8 oz; 20.5 oz
Hand Retrieve: R or L

Max Drag: 7 lbs; 15 lbs; 15 lbs; 20 lbs; 20 lbs; 29 lbs; 29 lbs
Reel Bearings: 5+1
Features: X-ship for easier turning handle under load; propulsion line management system; SA-RB bearings; aluminum frame (graphite on 1000); lightweight graphite sideplate and rotor; cold-forged aluminum spool; S-concept rotor, guard, and arm cam; machined-aluminum handle; Fluidrive II floating shaft; Dyna-Balance; Super Stopper II; salt water approved; rated for use with mono, fluorocarbon, or braid.
Price: . . . . **$179.99–$239.99**

SHIMANO SUSTAIN FG

Model: 1000, 2500, 3000, 4000, 5000, 6000, 10000
Gear Ratio: 6.0:1; 6.0:1; 6.0:1; 6.2:1; 6.2:1; 4.8:1; 4.8:1
Inches/Turn: 30; 34; 35; 39; 41; 35; 37
Spool Cap. (M): 4 lbs/140 yds; 8 lbs/140 yds; 10 lbs/140 yds; 12 lbs/160 yds; 12 lbs/195 yds; 16 lbs/170 yds; 16 lbs/340 yds
Spool Cap. (B): 15 lbs/145 yds; 15 lbs/145 yds; 20 lbs/145 yds; 15 lbs/265 yds; 20 lbs/220 yds; 30 lbs/290 yds; 65 lbs/260 yds
Weight: 6.5 oz; 8.3 oz; 8.3 oz; 9.9 oz; 10.6 oz; 19.6 oz; 19.0 oz
Hand Retrieve: R or L
Max Drag: 7 lbs; 20 lbs; 15 lbs; 24 lbs; 20 lbs; 28 lbs; 28 lbs
Reel Bearings: 7+1; 8+1; 8+1; 8+1; 8+1; 8+1; 8+1;

Features: X-ship; new Magnumlite CI4 rotor (1000-4000); aluminum sideplate; rapid fire drag; new reel stand on 1000-5000 only; Paladin gear durability enhancement; propulsion line management system: propulsion spool lip, power roller III; redesigned bail trip; aero wrap II oscillation; SR-concept: SR 3D gear, SR one-piece bail wire; shielded A-RB ball bearings; aluminum spool; S-concept: S rotor, S guard, S arm cam; new machined aluminum handle; direct drive mechanism (thread in handle attachment); EVA handle knob; waterproof drag; maintenance port; Fluidrive II; floating shaft; Dyna-Balance Super Stopper II; repairable clicker; approved for use in salt water; rated for use with mono, fluorocarbon, and PowerPro lines.
Price: . . . .$329.99–$399.99

SHIMANO SYMETRE FL

Model: 500, 1000, 2500, 3000, 4000
Gear Ratio: 4.7:1; 6.0:1; 6.2:1; 6.2:1; 5.8:1
Inches/Turn: 21; 29; 35; 35; 36
Spool Cap. (M): 4 lbs/100 yds; 6 lbs/110 yds; 8 lbs/140 yds; 10 lbs/140 yds; 12 lbs/160 yds;
Spool Cap. (B): 8 lbs/105 yds; 10 lbs/95 yds; 15 lbs/145 yds; 20 lbs/145 yds; 30 lbs/175 yds
Weight: 6.1 oz; 6.5 oz; 9 oz; 9 oz; 11.8 oz

Hand Retrieve: R or L
Max Drag: 6 lbs; 7 lbs; 11 lbs; 15 lbs; 15 lbs
Reel Bearings: 4+1
Features: New XGT7 graphite frame and sideplate; four bearings, one roller bearing; front drag; Super Stopper anti-reverse; cold-forged aluminum spool; approved for use in salt water.
Price: . . . . **$99.99–$109.99**

SHIMANO SYNCOPATE FG

Model: 1000, 2500, 4000
Gear Ratio: 5.2:1; 5.2:1; 5.1:1
Inches/Turn: 25; 29; 32
Spool Cap. (M): 4 lbs/140 yds; 8 lbs/140 yds; 10 lbs/200 yds
Spool Cap. (B): 15 lbs/85 yds; 15 lbs/145 yds; 30 lbs/175 yds
Weight: 7.6 oz; 9.2 oz; 12.7 oz

Hand Retrieve: R or L
Max Drag: 7 lbs; 7 lbs; 13 lbs
Reel Bearings: 4
Features: Propulsion spool lip; graphite frame; graphite sideplate; graphite rotor; aluminum spool; Varispeed oscillation; ported handle shank; Quick Fire II; Dyna-Balance; Power Roller II; P3; approved for use in salt water; rated for use with mono, fluorocarbon, and PowerPro lines.
Price: **$29.99**

SHIMANO THUNNUS

Model: 4000, 6000, 8000, 12000
Gear Ratio: 4.8:1; 4.8:1; 4.8:1; 4.4:1
Inches/Turn: 30; 35; 36; 37
Spool Cap. (M): 12 lbs/160 yds; 20 lbs/120 yds; 20 lbs/195 yds; 20 lbs/265 lbs
Spool Cap. (B): 40 lbs/145 yds; 65 lbs/130 yds; 65 lbs/180 yds; 80 lbs/230 yds
Weight: 12.7 oz; 18 oz; 19.4 oz; 27.7 oz
Hand Retrieve: R or L
Max Drag: 15 lbs; 20 lbs; 20 lbs; 25 lbs
Reel Bearings: 6+1
Features: Lightweight CI4 frame and rotor (AL on 12000); aluminum sideplate; Paladin gear durability enhancement; propulsion line management system: propulsion spool lip, SR one-piece bail wire, Power Roller III; redesigned bail trip; Varispeed oscillation; S-concept, S-rotor, S-arm cam, direct drive mechanism (thread-in handle attachment); oversized Septon grips for power and comfort; waterproof drag; machined aluminum handle; Dartainium II drag washers (cross carbon); repairable clicker; shielded A-RB ball bearings; Super Stopper II anti-reverse; Dyna-Balance; floating shaft; Fluidrive II gearing; approved for use in salt water; rated for use with mono, fluorocarbon, and PowerPro lines.
Price:............................$259.99–$299.99

ABU-GARCIA ABUMATIC 276I

Model: Abumatic 276i
Gear Ratio: 3.6:1
Inches/Turn: 19
Spool Cap. (M): 8 lbs/110 yds
Weight: 9.2 oz
Hand Retrieve: R or L

Max Drag: 8 lbs
Reel Bearings: 1+1
Features: Duragear drive; instant anti-reverse; ultra-smooth spool drag system; titanium nitride line guide; dual rotating swing-arm pick-up pins.
Price: **$29.95**

ABU-GARCIA ABUMATIC 276UI
Model: Abumatic 276Ui
Gear Ratio: 3.6:1
Inches/Turn: 19
Spool Cap. (M): 8 lbs/110 yds
Weight: 10.1 oz
Hand Retrieve: R or L

Max Drag: 8 lbs
Reel Bearings: 1+1
Features: Dual bearing Duragear drive; instant anti-reverse; ultra-smooth spool drag system; titanium nitride line guide; dual rotating swing-arm pick-up pins.
Price: **$34.95**

ABU-GARCIA ABUMATIC 476I

Model: Abumatic 476i
Gear Ratio: 3.6:1
Inches/Turn: 19
Spool Cap. (M): 12 lbs/100 yds
Weight: 10.1 oz
Hand Retrieve: R or L
Max Drag: 10 lbs

Reel Bearings: 1+1
Features: Duragear drive; instant anti-reverse; ultra-smooth spool drag system; titanium nitride line guide; dual rotating swing-arm pick-up pins.
Price: **$34.95**

ABU-GARCIA ABUMATIC 576I

Model: Abumatic 576i
Gear Ratio: 3.6:1
Inches/Turn: 19
Spool Cap. (M): 8 lbs/110 yds
Weight: 9.4 oz
Hand Retrieve: R or L

Max Drag: 8 lbs
Reel Bearings: 3+1
Features: Duragea drive; instant anti-reverse; ultra-smooth spool drag system; titanium nitride line guide; dual rotating swing-arm pick-up pins; fresh and salt water ready.
Price: **$44.95**

ABU-GARCIA ABUMATIC 1276SLI
Model: Abumatic 1276SLI
Gear Ratio: 3.6:1
Inches/Turn: 22
Spool Cap. (M): 14 lbs/100 yds
Weight: 10.2 oz
Hand Retrieve: R or L

Max Drag: 10 lbs
Reel Bearings: 4+1
Features: Four-bearing Duragear drive; instant anti-reverse bearing; ultra-smooth spool drag system; titanium nitride front cone, rotor, and line guide; dual rotating swing-arm titanium nitride pick-up pin; fresh and salt water ready.
Price:. **$64.95**

ABU-GARCIA ABUMATIC CLASSIC 170I

Model: Abumatic Classic 170i
Gear Ratio: 3.9:1
Inches/Turn: 25
Spool Cap. (M): 12 lbs/140 yds
Weight: 11.8 oz
Hand Retrieve: R
Max Drag: 10 lbs

Reel Bearings: 3+1
Features: Three-bearing Duragear drive; instant anti-reverse; ultra-smooth carbon matrix SYNCRO drag system; aluminum die-cast and machined body and front cone; dual rotating swing-arm pick-up pins; oscillating far-cast spool with no-twist line system; easy one-touch casting; fresh and salt water ready.
Price: **$54.95**

BASS PRO SHOPS EXTREME: SC10

Model: Extreme: SC10
Gear Ratio: 4.6:1
Inches/Turn: 27
Spool Cap. (M): 10 lbs/135 yds
Weight: 10 oz
Hand Retrieve: R or L

Max Drag: 9 lbs
Reel Bearings: 3+1
Features: Powerlock instant anti-reverse; aluminum frame, cover and oscillating spool; all-metal gears; free flow line guide; no-twist line pick-up system; aluminum handle; star drag; thumbar with silicone grid; line pickup roller.
Price:. **$29.99**

BASS PRO SHOPS TINYLITE MCB
Model: TinyLite MCB
Gear Ratio: 4.1:1
Inches/Turn: 16
Spool Cap. (M): 4 lbs/70 yds
Weight: 5.2 oz
Hand Retrieve: R or L

Reel Bearings: 1
Features: Trouble-free handling and loads of fun; polished stainless steel front and rear cones; smooth ball bearing drive system; multi-stop anti-reverse allows quick on/off adjustment; pre-spooled with 70 yards of 4-pound mono.
Price: **$15.99**

BASS PRO SHOPS TINYLITE TRIGGER SB

Model: TinyLite Trigger SB
Gear Ratio: 4.1:1
Inches/Turn: 16
Spool Cap. (M): 4 lbs/70 yds
Weight: 5.5 oz
Hand Retrieve: R or L

Reel Bearings: 1
Features: Trouble-free handling and loads of fun; polished stainless steel front and rear cones; smooth ball bearing drive system; multi-stop anti-reverse allows quick on/off adjustment; pre-spooled with 70 yards of 4-pound mono.
Price: **$15.99**

DAIWA GOLDCAST
Model: 80, 100, 120
Gear Ratio: 4.1:1
Inches/Turn: 18.3, 20.8, 21.3
Spool Cap. (M): 8 lbs/75 yds; 10 lbs/80 yds; 12 lbs/100 lbs
Weight: 9.2 oz; 9.9 oz; 12 oz
Hand Retrieve: R or L
Reel Bearings: 1

Features: Ball bearing drive; rotating tungsten carbide line pickup; rugged metal body, gearing and nose cone Fast 4.1: 1 right/left retrieve; oscillating spool levelwind; optimized line aperture for maximum casting; pre-wound with premium line; ultra-smooth, multi-disc drag.
Price: . . . .**$56.99–$58.99**

DAIWA MINICAST MC40

Model: Minicast MC40
Gear Ratio: 4.1:1
Inches/Turn: 16.1
Spool Cap. (M): 4 lbs/85 yds
Weight: 5.5 oz

Hand Retrieve: R or L
Reel Bearings: Bushings
Features: Aluminum alloy body and nose cone; smooth disc drag; easy push-button casting; pre-wound with 4-pound test line.
Price: **$29.95**

DAIWA SILVERCAST -A
Model: 80A, 100A, 120A, 170A
Gear Ratio: 4.3:1
Inches/Turn: 21.8; 24.9; 25.9; 29.4
Spool Cap. (M): 8 lbs/75 yds; 10 lbs/80 yds; 12 lbs/100 yds; 17 lbs/80 yds
Weight: 8.8 oz; 9.2 oz; 10.1 oz; 14.1 oz
Hand Retrieve: R or L
Reel Bearings: 3

Features: Hardbodyz rigid aluminum alloy construction; three ball bearings; rotating, titanium nitrided line pickup turns with the line for less wear, easier casting; oversized line aperture for optimum performance; smooth disc drag with dial adjustment; soft-touch handle knob; pre-wound with premium line.
Price: **$29.99**

DAIWA UNDERSPIN
Model: US40XD-CP, US80XD-CP, US120XD-CP
Gear Ratio: 4.1:1; 4.3:1; 4.3:1
Inches/Turn: 16.1; 21.8; 25.9
Spool Cap. (M): 8 lbs/75 yds; 10 lbs/80 yds; 12 lbs/100 lbs
Weight: 5.5 oz; 9.2 oz; 10.8 oz
Hand Retrieve: R or L
Reel Bearings: 1

Features: Smooth ball bearing drive; Hardbodyz rigid aluminum alloy construction; rugged metal gearing; rotating, titanium nitrided line pickup turns with the line for less wear, easier casting; oversized line aperture for casting performance; smooth drag with easy rear adjustment (front drag on 40 size); soft-touch handle knob; converts quickly to right- or left-hand retrieve; pre-wound with premium line.
Price: . . . .**$17.99–$21.99**

EAGLE CLAW TITAN
Model: SC100, SC200, SC400
Gear Ratio: 3.3:1
Spool Cap. (M): 8 lbs/100 yds; 10 lbs/100 yds; 20 lbs/205 yds
Weight: 8 oz; 9 oz; 14 oz

Hand Retrieve: R or L
Reel Bearings: 1+1
Features: SC100 & SC200 have star drag system; two ball bearings with one-way clutch; stainless steel front and rear cover; one-year warranty.
Price: **$21.99**

PFLUEGER CETINA
Model: SC10X, SC4UX, SC4X, SC6UX, SC6X
Gear Ratio: 3.8:1; 4.1:1; 3.6:1; 3.4:1; 3.4:1
Inches/Turn: 18.5; 14; 14; 15; 14.5
Spool Cap. (M): 10 lbs/75 yds; 4 lbs/70 yds; 4 lbs/70 yds; 4lbs/90 yds; 4 lbs/90 yds
Hand Retrieve: R or L
Reel Bearings: 4+1

Features: Four ball bearings; instant anti-reverse bearing; aluminum frame with machined aluminum front cone; titanium coated line guide and dual pick-up pins (only on PFLCETINASC6, PFLCETINASC10, and PFLCETINASC6U); smooth carbon fiber drag system.
Price: **$49.95**

PFLUEGER PRESIDENT
Model: MSSCX, MCSCX, 6USCX, 6SCX, 10SCX
Gear Ratio: 4.1:1; 4.1:1; 3.4:1; 3.4:1; 3.8:1
Inches/Turn: 14; 14; 14.5; 14.5; 18.5
Spool Cap. (M): 2 lbs/90 yds; 2 lbs/90 yds; 4 lbs/110 yds; 4 lbs/110 yds; 8 lbs/90 yds
Hand Retrieve: R or L
Reel Bearings: 5

Features: Four ball bearings; instant anti-reverse bearing; rigid aluminum frame; ported machined aluminum front cone; aluminum handle with soft-touch knob; titanium-coated line guide and dual pick-up pins; spool applied, adjustable disc-drag system; heavy-duty metal gears; convertible left- and right-hand retrieve; pre-spooled with line.
Price:.................................... **$39.99**

ZEBCO DELTA
Model: ZD3, ZD2
Gear Ratio: 2.9:1; 3.4:1
Inches/Turn: 14; 16
Spool Cap. (M): 6 lbs/85 yds; 10 lbs/85 yds
Weight: 9.5 oz; 13 oz
Hand Retrieve: R or L
Reel Bearings: 5

Features: Ideal for light to medium fishing situations; double-anodized aircraft-grade aluminum covers; 5 bearing system; triple-cam multi-disc drag; multi-point positive pickup system; ceramic line guide; positive worm-gear drive train; Continuous Anti-Reverse.
Price: **$47.99**

ZEBCO GOLD
Model: 11, 11T, 22
Gear Ratio: 4.3:1; 4.3:1; 3.4:1
Spool Cap. (M): 4 lbs/75 yds; 4 lbs/75 yds; 8 lbs/125 yds
Hand Retrieve: R or L
Reel Bearings: 3

Features: Ball-bearing drive; dual ceramic pickup pins for instant line recovery; classic design with updated components.
Price:. **$26.99**

REELS

REELS

ZEBCO HAWG SEEKER

Model: Hawg Seeker
Gear Ratio: 2.58:1
Inches/Turn: 19
Hand Retrieve: R or L
Reel Bearings: 2

Features: The revolutionary BiteAlert technology used in the Hawg Seeker series is the fisherman's best friend. It allows the fisherman to hear and see a bite, even on the darkest of nights. These ultra-tough reels have the added technoloogy to give you that extra advantage on the water.
Price: **$54.99**

ZEBCO MAGNUM 808

Model: Magnum 808
Gear Ratio: 2.6:1
Spool Cap. (M): 25 lbs/125 yds
Weight: 20

Hand Retrieve: R or L
Features: Classic reel upgraded with modern components; metal gears ensure smooth retrieves; Auto Bait Alert and dial-adjustable drag.
Price:. **$25.99**

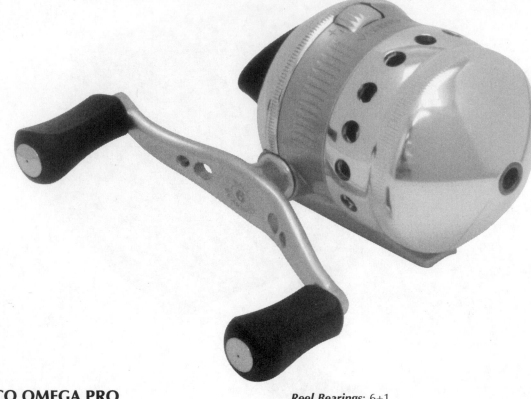

ZEBCO OMEGA PRO
Model: Z02PRO, Z03PRO
Gear Ratio: 3.4:1
Spool Cap. (M): 6 lbs/85 yds; 10 lbs/85 yds
Weight: 10.5 oz
Hand Retrieve: R or L

Reel Bearings: 6+1
Features: The pinnacle of spincast performance; all-metal gears; aircraft aluminum covers; triple-cam multi-disc drag system; 3X positive line pickup; oscillating spool.
Price: . . . .**$79.99–$74.99**

ZEBCO OMEGA Z03

Model: Omega Z03
Gear Ratio: 2.9:1
Spool Cap. (M): 10 lbs/90 yds
Hand Retrieve: R or L

Reel Bearings: 7
Features: Pro-level spincast performance; all-metal gears; aircraft aluminum covers; 3X positive line pickup (ZO3); oscillating spool.
Price: **$49.95**

ZEBCO PLATINUM 733

Model: Platinum 733
Gear Ratio: 2.6:1
Inches/Turn: 14
Spool Cap. (M): 20 lbs/90 yds
Weight: 14

Hand Retrieve: R or L
Reel Bearings: 1
Features: Ideal for catfish and other large species; powerful ball bearing drive and selective anti-reverse; dual ceramic pickup pins.
Price: **$26.99**

ZEBCO PRO STAFF
Model: PS2010B, PS2020B
Gear Ratio: 3.9:1; 3.6:1
Inches/Turn: 16; 17
Spool Cap. (M): 6 lbs/90 yds; 8 lbs/90 yds
Weight: 5.6 oz; 8 oz
Hand Retrieve: R or L

Reel Bearings: 4
Features: Some of the most popular reels of all time; built to last with corrosion-resistant brass and stainless steel components; 3-bearing ball bearing drive system; positive pickup design; selective multi-stop anti-reverse with premium mono line.
Price:. **$19.99**

ABU-GARCIA ABUMATIC 276I

Model: Abumatic 276i
Gear Ratio: 3.6:1
Inches/Turn: 19
Spool Cap. (M): 8 lbs/110 yds
Weight: 9.2 oz
Hand Retrieve: R or L

Max Drag: 8 lbs
Reel Bearings: 1+1
Features: Duragear drive; instant anti-reverse; ultra-smooth spool drag system; titanium nitride line guide; dual rotating swing-arm pick-up pins.
Price: **$29.95**

ABU-GARCIA ABUMATIC 276UI

Model: Abumatic 276Ui
Gear Ratio: 3.6:1
Inches/Turn: 19
Spool Cap. (M): 8 lbs/110 yds
Weight: 10.1 oz
Hand Retrieve: R or L
Max Drag: 8 lbs

Reel Bearings: 1+1
Features: Dual-bearing Duragear drive; instant anti-reverse; ultra-smooth spool drag system; titanium nitride line guide; dual rotating swing-arm pick-up pins.
Price: **$34.95**

ABU-GARCIA ABUMATIC 476I

Model: Abumatic 476i
Gear Ratio: 3.6:1
Inches/Turn: 19
Spool Cap. (M): 12 lbs/100 yds
Weight: 10.1 oz
Hand Retrieve: R or L
Max Drag: 10 lbs

Reel Bearings: 1+1
Features: Duragear drive; instant anti-reverse; ultra-smooth spool drag system; titanium nitride line guide; dual rotating swing-arm pick-up pins.
Price: **$34.95**

ABU-GARCIA ABUMATIC 576I

Model: Abumatic 576i
Gear Ratio: 3.6:1
Inches/Turn: 19
Spool Cap. (M): 8 lbs/110 yds
Weight: 9.4 oz
Hand Retrieve: R or L

Max Drag: 8 lbs
Reel Bearings: 3+1
Features: Duragear drive; instant anti-reverse; ultra-smooth spool drag system; titanium nitride line guide; dual rotating swing-arm pick-up pins; fresh and salt water ready.
Price: **$44.95**

ABU-GARCIA ABUMATIC 1276SLI

Model: Abumatic 1276SLI
Gear Ratio: 3.6:1
Inches/Turn: 22
Spool Cap. (M): 14 lbs/100 yds
Weight: 10.2 oz
Hand Retrieve: R or L

Max Drag: 10 lbs
Reel Bearings: 4+1
Features: Four-bearing Duragear drive; instant anti-reverse bearing; ultra-smooth spool drag system; titanium nitride front cone, rotor, and line guide; dual rotating swing-arm; titanium nitride pick-up pin; fresh and salt water ready.
Price: **$64.95**

ABU-GARCIA ABUMATIC CLASSIC 170I

Model: Abumatic Classic 170i
Gear Ratio: 3.9:1
Inches/Turn: 25
Spool Cap. (M): 12 lbs/140 yds
Weight: 11.8 oz
Hand Retrieve: R
Max Drag: 10 lbs
Reel Bearings: 3+1

Features: Three-bearing Duragear drive; instant anti-reverse; ultra-smooth carbon Matrix SYNCRO drag system; aluminum die-cast and machined body and front cone; dual rotating swing-arm pick-up pins; oscillating far-cast spool with no-twist line system; easy one-touch casting; fresh and salt water ready.
Price:. **$54.95**

ZEBCO SALTFISHER 808
Gear Ratio: 2.58:1
Spool Cap. (M): 20 lbs/150 yds
Weight: 22
Hand Retrieve: R

Reel Bearings: 1
Features: Salt water grade spincast products; large-sized combos and reels; true salt water protection.
Price: **$29.99**

ABU GARCIA PRO MAX

Model: 2, 2-L
Gear Ratio: 7.1:1
Inches/Turn: 31
Retrieve Speed: High
Spool Cap. (M): 12 lbs/145 yds
Spool Cap. (B): 30 lbs/130 yds
Weight: 7.9 oz
Hand Retrieve: R; L
Max Drag: 15 lbs
Reel Bearings: 8

Features: Seven stainless steel ball bearings plus one roller bearing provides smooth operation; machined double anodized aluminum spool provides strength without adding excess weight; Power Disk drag system gives smooth drag performance; Duragear brass gear for extended gear life; MagTrax brake system gives consistent brake pressure throughout the cast; recessed reel foot plus a compact bent handle and star provide a more ergonomic design; lightweight one-piece graphite frame and graphite sideplates.
Price: **$79.95**

ABU GARCIA REVO MGX
Model: MGX, MGX-L, MGX-SHS, MGX-SHS-L
Gear Ratio: 7.1:1; 7.1:1; 7.9:1; 7.9:1
Inches/Turn: 28; 28; 31; 31
Retrieve Speed: Std; std; high; super high
Spool Cap. (M): 12 lbs/115 yds
Spool Cap. (B): 30 lbs/110 yds
Weight: 5.4 oz
Hand Retrieve: R; L; R; L
Max Drag: 12 lbs
Reel Bearings: 10
Features: Nine stainless steel high-performance corrosion-resistant bearings plus one roller bearing provides increased corrosion protection; one-piece X-mag alloy frame provides a super light yet extremely strong frame; Infini II spool design for extended castability and extreme loads; C6 carbon sideplates provide significant weight reduction without sacrificing strength and durability; carbon matrix drag system provides smooth, consistent drag pressure across the entire drag range; aircraft-grade aluminum main gear provides weight reduction without sacrificing durability; IVCB-IV infinitely variable centrifugal brake gives very precise brake adjustments allowing anglers to easily cast a wide variety of baits; compact bent carbon handle provides a more ergonomic design that is extremely lightweight; flat EVA knobs provide greater comfort and durability; titanium coated line guide reduces friction and improves durability; recessed reel foot allows for a more ergonomic reel design.
Price: **$349.99**

ABU GARCIA REVO PREMIER
Model: PRM, PRM-HS, PRM-L
Gear Ratio: 6.4:1; 7.1:1; 6.4:1
Inches/Turn: 26; 29; 26
Retrieve Speed: Std; High; Std
Spool Cap. (M): 12 lbs/145 yds
Spool Cap. (B): 30 lbs/140 yds
Weight: 5.87 oz
Hand Retrieve: R; R; L
Max Drag: 20 lbs
Reel Bearings: 11
Features: Ten stainless steel high-performance corrosion-resistant bearings plus one roller bearing provides increased corrosion protection; X2- Cräftic alloy frame for increased corrosion resistance; C6 carbon sideplates provide significant weight reduction without sacrificing strength and durability; carbon matrix drag system provides smooth, consistent drag pressure across the entire drag range; D2 Gear Design provides a more efficient gear system while improving gear durability; Infinitely Variable Centrifugal Brake gives very precise brake adjustments allowing anglers to easily cast a wide variety of baits; Infini II spool design for extended castability and extreme loads; compact bent carbon handle provides a more ergonomic design that is extremely lightweight; flat EVA knob provides greater comfort and durability; titanium-coated line guide reduces friction and improves durability; right- or left-hand models available.
Price: **$299.99**

ABU GARCIA REVO S
Model: S, S-L
Gear Ratio: 6.4:1
Inches/Turn: 26
Retrieve Speed: Std
Spool Cap. (M): 12 lbs/145 yds
Spool Cap. (B): 30 lbs/140 yds
Weight: 7.44 oz
Hand Retrieve: R; L
Max Drag: 20 lbs
Reel Bearings: 7+1

Features: Seven stainless steel ball bearings plus one roller bearing provides smooth operation; X2-Cräftic alloy frame for increased corrosion resistance; lightweight graphite sideplates; carbon matrix drag system provides smooth, consistent drag pressure across the entire drag range; D2 Gear Design provides a more efficient gear system while improving gear durability; pitch centrifugal brake system; compact bent handle and star provide a more ergonomic design.
Price:. **$129.95**

ABU GARCIA REVO SX

Model: SX, SX-HS, SX-HS-L, SX-L
Gear Ratio: 6.4:1; 7.1:1; 7.1:1; 6.4:1
Inches/Turn: 26; 29; 29; 26
Retrieve Speed: Std; High; High; Std
Spool Cap. (M): 12 lbs/145 yds
Spool Cap. (B): 30 lbs/140 yds
Weight: 6.66 oz
Hand Retrieve: R; R; L; L
Max Drag: 20 lbs
Reel Bearings: 10
Features: Nine stainless steel ball bearings plus one roller bearing provides smooth operation; X2- Cräftic alloy frame for increased corrosion resistance; C6 carbon handle sideplate provides significant weight reduction without sacrificing strength and durability; carbon matrix drag system provides smooth, consistent drag pressure across the entire drag range; D2 Gear Design provides a more efficient gear system while improving gear durability; MagTrax brake system gives consistent brake pressure throughout the cast; Infini II spool design for extended castability and extreme loads; compact bent handle and star provide a more ergonomic design; titanium-coated line guide reduces friction and improves durability.
Price:....................................**$349.99**

BASS PRO SHOPS BIONIC PLUS
Model: 10HE, 10HLE, 10SE, 10SHE, 10SHLE
Gear Ratio: 6.3:1; 6.3:1; 5.3:1; 7.0:1; 7.0:1
Inches/Turn: 25; 25; 20; 27; 27
Spool Cap. (M): 12 lbs/130 yds
Spool Cap. (B): 30 lbs/190 yds
Weight: 8.1 oz
Hand Retrieve: R; L; R; R; L
Max Drag: 12 lbs
Reel Bearings: 5+1

Features: All-aluminum frame; striking white finish; smart cast anti-backlash system; six-bearing system including Powerlock instant anti-reverse; forged double-anodized aluminum V-grooved spool; aluminum recurve handle and drag star.
Price: **$79.99**

BASS PRO SHOPS EXTREME
Model: 10SHA, 10HA, 10SA, 10SHLA, 10HLA,
Gear Ratio: 7.1:1; 6.3:1; 5.3:1; 7.1:1; 6.3:1
Inches/Turn: 27; 24; 20; 27; 24
Spool Cap. (M): 12 lbs/120 yds
Weight: 7.2 oz
Hand Retrieve: R; R; R; L; L
Max Drag: 12 lbs
Reel Bearings: 6+1

Features: Tournament-proven dual braking system; double-anodized V-grooved spool is free-floating; 4-disc aramid fiber/stainless steel washer drag system; one-piece cast, then CNC-machined aluminum frame; easy-access sideplate with push-button release; titanium nitride-coated line guide seven-bearing system; recurve handle; click drag star.
Price: **$89.99**

BASS PRO SHOPS JOHNNY MORRIS CARBONLITE

Model: 10SHA, 10HA, 10HLA, 10SA
Gear Ratio: 7.1:1; 6.4:1; 6.4:1; 5.4:1
Inches/Turn: 29; 26; 26; 22
Spool Cap. (M): 12 lbs/120 yds
Weight: 5.6 oz
Hand Retrieve: R; R; L; R
Max Drag: 14 lbs
Reel Bearings: 9+1

Features: Weighs just 5.9 ounces; one-piece machined aircraft-grade frame; Duralumin gears and shaft V-grooved, ported, machined; Duralumin spool; nine stainless steel, double-shielded ball bearings; a powerlock anti reverse bearing dual braking system; titanium nitride-coated line guide; carbon fiber recurve handle; drag system with six alternating carbon fiber and stainless washers.
Price: **$129.99**

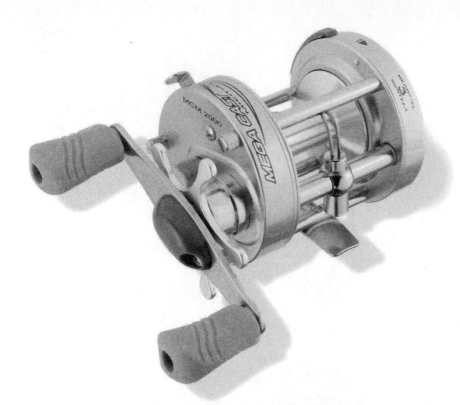

BASS PRO SHOPS MEGACAST

Model: 1000, 2000
Gear Ratio: 5.2:1
Inches/Turn: 23
Spool Cap. (M): 12 lbs/200 yds
Weight: 9.7 oz

Hand Retrieve: R; L
Max Drag: 8.8 lbs
Reel Bearings: 2+1
Features: Versatile, dependable, and strong; unyielding all-metal frame; three-bearing system includes PowerLock instant anti-reverse; on/off bait clicker switch; easy-adjusting star drag.
Price: **$39.99**

BASS PRO SHOPS PRO QUALIFER
Model: 10SD, 10SLD, 10SSD, 10SHLA, 10SHD, 10HD, 10HLA
Gear Ratio: 5.2:1; 5.2:1; 4.7:1; 7.1:1; 7.1:1; 6.4:1; 6.4:1
Inches/Turn: 21; 21; 19; 29; 29; 26; 26
Spool Cap. (M): 12 lbs/150 yds; 12 lbs/150 yds; 12 lbs/150 yds; 12 lbs/120 yds; 12 lbs/120 yds; 12 lbs/120 yds; 12 lbs/120 yds;
Weight: 8.8 oz
Hand Retrieve: R; L; R; L; R; R; L

Max Drag: 10 lbs
Reel Bearings: 6+1
Features: Built to put you at the top of your game; one-piece machined-aluminum frame; double-anodized, machined-aluminum drilled spool; seven-bearing system with Powerlock instant anti-reverse dual braking system; pin-release sideplate for quick brake adjustments; built-in lube port.
Price: **$99.99**

BASS PRO SHOPS TOURNEY SPECIAL
Model: 10HC, 10SC, 10SHC
Gear Ratio: 6.3:1; 5.3:1; 7.0:1
Inches/Turn: 26; 21; 28
Spool Cap. (M): 12 lbs/130 yds
Spool Cap. (B): 30 lbs/185 yds
Weight: 7.6 oz
Hand Retrieve: R

Max Drag: 12 lbs
Reel Bearings: 4+1
Features: Smart cast dual centrifugal brake; five bearing system includes instant anti reverse; available in right- or left-hand retrieve; striking new black and silver finish.
Price:. **$49.99**

CABELA'S TOURNAMENT ZX
Model: BCR-1, BCL-1, BCRHS-1, BCLHS-1
Gear Ratio: 6.5:1; 6.5:1; 7.2:1; 7.2:1
Inches/Turn: 25.7; 25.7; 28.5; 28.5
Spool Cap. (M): 10 lbs/110 yds
Weight: 6.1 oz
Hand Retrieve: R; L; R; L
Max Drag: 8 lbs
Reel Bearings: 8+1

Features: Eight stainless steel ball bearings for smooth performance; externally controlled magnetic braking system; high-strength, one-piece aluminum frame; aircraft-grade graphite side covers; ported aluminum spool; aluminum handle with EVA handle knobs; carbon-fiber drag washer.
Price: **$79.99**

DAIWA AIRD

Model: 100P, 100H, 100HL, 100HS
Gear Ratio: 4.9:1; 6.3:1; 6.3:1; 7.1:1
Inches/Turn: 20.6; 25.7; 25.7; 30
Spool Cap. (M): 12 lbs/120 yds
Spool Cap. (B): 40 lbs/140 yds; 40 lbs/135 yds; 40 lbs/140 yds; 40 lbs/135 yds
Weight: 7.7 oz
Hand Retrieve: L; R; L; R
Max Drag: 8.8 lbs
Reel Bearings: 8+1

Features: Open access, low-profile design for easy thumbing and line maintenance; weighs just 7.7 ounces; ultimate tournament carbon drag with 8.8-pound drag max nine bearing system (8BB+1RB); Magforce cast control swept handle for less wobble, better feel, and winding power; machined aluminum perforated spool; oversized soft-touch grips.
Price: **$89.99**

REELS

DAIWA LAGUNA

Model: 100H, 100HL, 100HS
Gear Ratio: 6.3:1; 6.3:1; 7.1:1
Inches/Turn: 25.7; 25.7; 30
Spool Cap. (M): 12 lbs/120 yds
Weight: 7.4 oz
Hand Retrieve: R; L; R
Max Drag: 8.8
Reel Bearings: 5+1

Features: Open access, low-profile frame for easy thumbing and line maintenance; lightweight composite frame and sideplates; swept handle for less wobble, better feel and winding power; five ball bearings plus roller bearing; Magforce magnetic anti-backlash control; lightweight, drilled aluminum spool; dual-system infinite; anti-reverse.
Price: **$59.95**

DAIWA MEGAFORCE THS (WITH TWITCHIN' BAR)

Model: 100THS, 100THSL
Gear Ratio: 7.3:1
Inches/Turn: 31.5
Spool Cap. (M): 12 lbs/150 yds
Weight: 8.8 oz
Hand Retrieve: R; L

Max Drag: 8.8 lbs
Reel Bearings: 6
Features: Twitchin' Bar six ball bearings; hyper speed 7.3: 1 gear ratio; swept handle Magforce-Z automatic antibacklash control; precision click drag adjustment.
Price:. **$89.95**

DAIWA PX TYPE-R
Model: PX-R, PXL-R
Gear Ratio: 6.8:1
Inches/Turn: 26
Spool Cap. (M): 6 lbs/95 yds
Weight: 5.8 oz
Hand Retrieve: R; L

Max Drag: 13 lbs
Reel Bearings: 10
Features: Weighs just 5.8 ounces; magnesium body; ten ball bearings; carbon swept handle; cork handle knobs; hyper speed 6.8:1 gear ratio; UT drag with a drag max of 13 pounds.; Magforce-Z cast control.
Price: **$499.95**

DAIWA STEEZ EX
Model: 100XS, 100HS, 100H, 100HSL, 100HL
Gear Ratio: 7.9:1; 7.1:1; 6.3:1; 7.1:1; 6.3:1
Inches/Turn: 33.2; 29.8; 26; 29.8; 26
Spool Cap. (M): 14 lbs/120 yds
Weight: 5.8 oz; 5.8 oz; 5.4 oz; 5.8 oz; 5.4 oz
Hand Retrieve: R; R; R; L; L
Max Drag: 13.2 lbs
Reel Bearings: 11+1

Features: Super lightweight magnesium frame and sideplate; swept handle with cutouts for reduced weight; oversized, lightweight 100 MM Handle on 7.1 and 7.9 models; ultimate tournament cfarbon drag with 13.2-pound drag max; free-floating A7075 aluminum alloy spool starts faster, spins longer; fast spool change; eleven precision ball bearings plus roller bearing; tough Dura-Loc pinion; Magforce-Z cast control; precision, micro-click adjustment on star drag and free-spool cap; infinite anti-reverse; free neoprene reel cover included.
Price: **$599.95**

REELS: **Freshwater Baitcasting**

DAIWA T3
Model: 1016HS, 1016H, 1016HSL, 1016HL
Gear Ratio: 7.1:1; 6.3:1; 7.1:1; 6.3:1
Inches/Turn: 29.5; 26.3; 29.5; 26.3
Spool Cap. (M): 14 lbs/120 yds
Weight: 6.5 oz
Hand Retrieve: R; R; L; L
Max Drag: 13.2 lbs
Reel Bearings: 8+1
Features: T-wing system; Magforce 3D cast control system; weighs just 6.5 ounces; ultra-low profile; Zaion frame, clutch cover and sideplate; ultimate tournament drag with micro-click adjustment; available with 6.3:1 or 7.1:1 gear ratios; eight ball bearings (including 4 CRBB) plus roller bearing; aluminum swept handle arm with urethane-covered cork grips; free-floating, lightweight aluminum spool; infinite anti-reverse; fast, one-touch spool change.
Price: **$429.95**

DAIWA T3 BALLISTIC
Model: S100XS, S100HS, S100H, S100XSL, S100HSL, S100HL
Gear Ratio: 8.1:1; 7.1:1; 6.3:1; 8.1:1; 7.1:1; 6.3:1
Inches/Turn: 34; 29.5; 26.3; 34; 29.5; 26.3
Spool Cap. (M): 14 lbs/120 yds
Weight: 7.9 oz; 7.8 oz; 7.8 oz; 7.9 oz; 7.8 oz; 7.8 oz
Hand Retrieve: R; R; R; L; L; L
Max Drag: 11 lbs; 13.2 lbs; 13.2 lbs; 11 lbs; 13.2 lbs; 13.2 lbs
Reel Bearings: 5+1

Features: T-wing system; Magforce 3D cast control system; ultra-low profile Zaion frame, clutch cover, and sideplate; natural black marble Zaion finish; ultimate tournament drag with micro-click adjustment; available with 6.3:1 or 7.1:1 gear ratios; five ball bearings plus roller bearing; aluminum swept handle; free-floating, lightweight aluminum spool; infinite anti-reverse; fast, one-touch spool change.
Price:. $249.95

DAIWA TD LUNA

Model: 253, 300, 253L, 300L
Gear Ratio: 5.1:1
Inches/Turn: 23.6
Spool Cap. (M): 12 lbs/235 yds; 14 lbs/320 yds; 12 lbs/235 yds; 14 lbs/320 yds
Weight: 11.1 oz; 12.9 oz; 11.1 oz; 12.9 oz
Hand Retrieve: R; R; L; L
Max Drag: 11 lbs; 15.3 lbs; 11 lbs; 15.3 lbs
Reel Bearings: 5+1
Features: Frame and sideplates machined from solid bar stock aluminum; five CRBB super corrosion-resistant ball bearings, plus roller bearing; free-floating spool for maximum casting performance; Magforce-Z automatic magnetic anti-backlash control (Centriflex automatic centrifugal system on 300 size); ultra-smooth, multi-disc drag with Daiwa's exclusive fiber composite and stainless washers; infinite anti-reverse Dura-Loc pinion for solid gear engagement; rugged, six-point drive train support; machined aircraft aluminum spool; cut proof titanium nitrided stainless steel line guide; spool click on 300 size; hard anodized to resist corrosion.
Price: **$279.99**

DAIWA TD ZILLION HIGH POWER
Model: 100PA, 100PLA
Gear Ratio: 4.9:1
Inches/Turn: 22
Spool Cap. (M): 14 lbs/120 yds
Weight: 8.8 oz
Hand Retrieve: R; L
Max Drag: 8.8 lbs
Reel Bearings: 6+1
Features: High-torque 4.9:1 gear ratio—ideal for crankbait applications; six ball bearings, including four anti-corrosion

CRBB ball bearings, plus roller bearing; six ball bearings, including four anti-corrosion CRBB ball bearings, plus roller bearing; swept handle for less wobble, better feel and maximum winding leverage; fast spool change; Magforce-Z automatic anti-backlash system; eight-disc wet drag with precision click adjustment; rigid aluminum frame and handle-side sideplate firmly support the drive train; aluminum guard plate protects finish on top of reel; soft-touch grips.
Price: **$319.99**

DAIWA TD ZILLION HIGH SPEED
Model: 100HA, 100SHLA, 100HLA, 100SHA
Gear Ratio: 6.3:1; 7.1:1; 6.3:1; 7.1:1
Inches/Turn: 28; 31.6; 28; 31.6
Spool Cap. (M): 12 lbs/150 yds
Weight: 8.6 oz; 8.8 oz; 8.6 oz; 8.8 oz
Hand Retrieve: R; R; L; R
Max Drag: 8.8 lbs
Reel Bearings: 6+1
Features: Choice of ultra-fast 7.1:1 retrieve or all-purpose 6.3:1; six ball bearings (including CRBB), plus roller bearing; swept handle for less wobble, better feel, and maximum winding leverage; free-floating perforated aluminum spool starts faster, spins longer; fast spool change Magforce-Z automatic anti-backlash system; eight-disc wet drag with precision click adjustment; aluminum guard plate protects finish on top of reel; rigid aluminum frame and handle-side sideplate firmly support the drive train; soft-touch grips.
Price: **$319.99**

DAIWA TD ZILLION TYPE R
Model: 100HSHR, 100HSHLR
Gear Ratio: 7.3:1
Inches/Turn: 32
Spool Cap. (M): 14 lbs/120 yds
Weight: 8.5 oz
Hand Retrieve: R; L
Max Drag: 8.5 lbs
Reel Bearings: 11

Features: Hyper Speed 7.3:1 retrieve; eleven hyper speed ball bearings; carbon swept handle; ultimate tournament carbon drag; super rigid aluminum frame and sideplate; Magforce-Z anti-backlash control; free-floating perforated aluminum spool; infinite anti-reverse.
Price: **$439.99**

DAIWA Z SERIES

Model: HS, H, HL
Gear Ratio: 7.2:1; 6.4:1; 6.4:1
Inches/Turn: 33.5; 29.5; 29.5
Spool Cap. (M): 14 lbs/155 yds
Weight: 9.9 oz
Hand Retrieve: R; R; L
Max Drag: 16.5 lbs
Reel Bearings: 8+1
Features: Magforce-3D; hyper speed 7.2:1 or all-around 6.4:1 gear ratio models; seven-disc carbon UT drag with a drag max of 16.5 pounds–click adjustment; eight CRBB corrosion-resistant ball bearings plus roller bearing; rugged, dual system anti-reverse combines infinite anti-reverse with a multi-stop system; low-friction, titanium-nitrided line guide; aluminum swept handle with large, ball bearing grips; tough aluminum frame; precision high brass drive gear and ultratough aluminum bronze alloy pinion; high-leverage, aluminum star drag with precise click adjustment; super lightweight perforated aluminum alloy spool.
Price: **$649.95**

LEW'S BB1 SPEED SPOOL
Model: 1, 1H, 1L, 1HZ, 1HZL, 1SHZ, 1SHZL
Gear Ratio: 5.1:1; 7.1:1; 5.1:1; 6.4:1; 6.4:1; 7.1:1; 7.1:1
Inches/Turn: 21; 28; 21; 28; 28; 31; 31
Spool Cap. (M): 12 lbs/160 yds
Weight: 7.1 oz; 7.1 oz; 7.1 oz; 7.2 oz; 7.2 oz; 7.2 oz; 7.2 oz
Hand Retrieve: R; R; L; R; L; R; L
Max Drag: 14 lbs
Reel Bearings: 10
Features: One-piece die-cast aluminum frame; machined forged aluminum, double anodized, U-shaped large capacity spool; premium ten-bearing system with double-shielded ball bearings and multi-stop anti-reverse (BB1 and BB1L models); premium ten-bearing system with double-shielded ball bearings and zero-reverse anti-reverse (BB1HZ, BB1SHZ, BB1HZL, BB1SHZL); positive on/off SmartPlus; six-pin centrifugal braking system; learn more about the SmartPlus system; aluminum spool tension knob with audible clicker; carbon composite metal star drag system with 14 pounds of drag power; bowed 95mm aluminum cranking handle with Lew's custom soft-touch contoured paddle handle knob; oversized titanium line guide positioned further away from the spool to minimize line friction and maximize casting performance; quick release sideplate mechanism provides easy access to centrifugal brake system.
Price:....................................**$159.99**

LEW'S SPEED SPOOL TOURNAMENT

Model: 1H, 1HL, 1SH
Gear Ratio: 6.4:1; 6.4:1; 7.1:1
Inches/Turn: 28; 28; 31
Spool Cap. (M): 12 lbs/120 yds
Weight: 7.9 oz
Hand Retrieve: R; L; R
Max Drag: 14 lbs
Reel Bearings: 9+1
Features: One-piece die-cast aluminum frame; ten double-shielded premium stainless steel bearings; drilled and forged, double anodized aluminum U-style spool; high-strength solid brass gearing; external-adjust multi-setting brake dual magnetic/centrifugal cast control; zero-reverse one-way clutch bearing; easily removable palming graphite sideplate; metal spool tension adjustment with audible click metal star drag delivers up to 14 pounds of drag power; lightweight graphite sideplate; rugged carbon composite drag system with audible click; lightweight aluminum bowed handle with Lew's custom paddle knobs; external lube port; titanium-coated zirconia line guide.
Price: **$149.99**

LEW'S SUPERDUTY SPEED SPOOL

Model: 1S, 1H, 1SH, 1HL, 1SHL
Gear Ratio: 5.4:1; 6.4:1; 7.1:1; 6.4:1; 7.1:1
Inches/Turn: 23; 28; 31; 28; 31
Spool Cap. (M): 12 lbs/150 yds
Weight: 7.8 oz
Hand Retrieve: R; R; R; L; L
Max Drag: 14 lbs
Reel Bearings: 10+1
Features: Sturdy, lightweight one-piece all aluminum frame and aluminum handle sideplate; eleven double-shielded premium stainless steel bearing system with zero-reverse anti-reverse; lightweight machined, anodized, deep-capacity aluminum spool with braid line connection; high-strength brass gearing for increased strength and durability; external-adjust magnetic control system; zero-reverse one-way clutch bearing; easily removable palming graphite side plate with soft-touch armor finish; external handle side metal spool tension adjustment with audible click; rugged carbon composite metal star drag system that provides up to 14 pounds of drag power; bent anodized aluminum power crank 95 mm reel handle with Lew's custom paddle handle knobs; titanium-coated line guide.
Price: **$179.99**

LEW'S TEAM LEW'S GOLD SPEED SPOOL

Model: 1H, 1SH
Gear Ratio: 6.4:1; 7.1:1
Inches/Turn: 28; 31
Spool Cap. (M): 12 lbs/120 yds
Weight: 7 oz
Hand Retrieve: R; R
Max Drag: 14 lbs
Reel Bearings: 10+1
Features: One-piece die-cast aluminum frame and sideplates; titanium deposition finish on metal sideplates; double anodized gold detail finishing; premium double-shielded eleven-bearing system with zero-reverse anti-reverse; aircraft-grade Duralumin drilled U-shaped spool, drive gear, crank shaft and worm shaft; external-adjust multi-setting brake dual cast control system, using both an external click-dial for setting the magnetic brake, plus four individually, disc-mounted adjustable internal brake shoes that operate on centrifugal force; metal spool tension adjustment with audible click; rugged carbon composite drag system; provides up to 14 pounds of drag power; audible click metal star drag system; bowed, lightweight carbon handle with Lew's custom soft-touch contoured handle knobs; titanium-coated zirconia line guide.
Price: **$249.99**

LEW'S TOURNAMENT MG
Model: 1SMG, 1SLMG, 1HMB, 1SHMG, 1SHLMG
Gear Ratio: 5.4:1; 5.4:1; 6.4:1; 7.1:1; 7.1:1
Inches/Turn: 23; 23; 28; 31; 31
Spool Cap. (M): 12 lbs/150 yds
Weight: 7.9 oz
Hand Retrieve: R; L; R; R; L
Max Drag: 14 lbs
Reel Bearings: 9+1
Features: One-piece die-cast aluminum frame; sturdy graphite side covers; easily removable palming sideplate; deep, machine forged and anodized aluminum spools; anodized aluminum power crank 95MM reel handle; high-strength solid brass gearing; premium 10 double-shielded stainless steel bearing system with zero-reverse; anti-reverse zero-reverse one-way clutch bearing; externally adjustable magnetic brake system; external handle side aluminum spool tension adjustment knob; rugged carbon composite metal star drag system (14 pounds of drag power); zirconia line guide.
Price: **$129.99**

REELS

LEW'S TOURNAMENT PRO SPEED SPOOL

Model: 1H, 1HL, 1SH, 1SHL
Gear Ratio: 6.4:1; 6.4:1; 7.1:1; 7.1:1
Inches/Turn: 28; 28; 31; 31
Spool Cap. (M): 12 lbs/120 yds
Weight: 6.7 oz
Hand Retrieve: R; L; R; L
Max Drag: 14 lbs
Reel Bearings: 10+1
Features: One-piece die-cast aluminum frame; eleven double-shielded premium stainless steel bearing system with zero-reverse anti-reverse; aircraft-grade machine-forged Duralumin drilled and anodized U-shaped spool and gear system; external-adjust multi-setting brake dual cast control system, using both an external click-dial for setting the magnetic brake, plus four individually, disc-mounted adjustable internal brake shoes that operate on centrifugal force; zero-reverse one-way clutch bearing; easily removable palming graphite sideplate metal spool tension adjustment with audible click; rugged carbon composite metal drag system with audible click metal star; bowed lightweight carbon reel handle with Lew's custom paddle handle knob; external lube port; titanium-coated zirconia line guide.
Price: **$199.99**

OKUMA AKENA

Model: 400
Gear Ratio: 5.1:1
Inches/Turn: 23
Spool Cap. (M): 14 lbs/270 yds
Weight: 12.7 oz
Hand Retrieve: R or L
Max Drag: 10 lbs
Reel Bearings: 5+1
Features: Aluminum left and right sideplates; machined aluminum, gold anodized spool; multi-disc carbonite drag system; 5BB+1RB Stainless steel bearing drive system; quick-set anti-reverse roller bearing; precision machine-cut brass main and pinion gear; adjustable 6-pin velocity control system; non-disengaging levelwind system 400 size; disengaging levelwind on the 250 size; aluminum twin paddle handle with oversized knobs; on/off bait clicker function on 400-size reels; one-year warranty program.
Price:....................................**$109.99**

OKUMA CALERA

Model: 266W, 266WLX
Gear Ratio: 6.6:1
Inches/Turn: 28.5
Spool Cap. (M): 10 lbs/160 yds
Weight: 8.2 oz
Hand Retrieve: R; L
Max Drag: 11 lbs
Reel Bearings: 4+1
Features: Corrosion-resistant graphite frame and sideplates; A6061-T6 machined aluminum, anodized V-shaped spool; multi-disc composite drag system; 4BB+1RB bearing drive system; micro-click drag star for precise drag settings; external adjustable magnetic cast control system; internal eight-position velocity control system; quick-set anti-reverse roller bearing; easy change palm sideplates access port; ergonomic handle design allows cranking closer to body; zirconium line guide inserts for use with braided line; available gear ratio: 6.6:1; available in both right- and left-hand retrieve; one-year warranty.
Price: **$89.99**

OKUMA CITRIX

Model: 254a, 273a, 273LXa
Gear Ratio: 5.4; 7.3:1; 5.4:1
Inches/Turn: 23.4; 31.6; 31.6
Spool Cap. (M): 10 lbs/160 yds
Weight: 8.4 oz
Hand Retrieve: R; R; L
Max Drag: 11 lbs
Reel Bearings: 9+1
Features: Rigid die-cast aluminum frame; A6061-T6 machined aluminum, anodized spool; multi-disc carbonite drag system; 9BB+1RB bearing drive system; micro-click drag star for precise drag settings; external adjustable centrifugal cast control system; quick-Sset anti-reverse roller bearing; graphite left and right sideplates; easy change palm sideplates access port; ergonomic handle design allows cranking closer to·body; available gear ratios 7.3:1 and 5.4:1; 7.1:1 gear ratio available in left-hand retrieve; one-year warranty.
Price: **$119.99**

OKUMA CITRIX 350

Model: 364a, 364LXa, 364Pa, 364PLXa
Gear Ratio: 6.4:1
Inches/Turn: 31
Spool Cap. (M): 12 lbs/250 yds
Weight: 11 oz
Hand Retrieve: R; L; R; L
Max Drag: 25 lbs
Reel Bearings: 7+1
Features: Rigid die-cast aluminum frame and sideplates; corrosion-resistant coating process; durable brass main and pinion gear system; A6061-T6 machined aluminum, anodized spool; multi-disc carbonite drag system with 25-pounds max drag; micro-click drag star for precise drag settings; 7BB+1RB stainless steel bearing drive system; precision Japanese ABEC-5 spool bearings; dual anti-reverse system for maximum reliability; synchronized levelwind optimized for braided line; seven-position velocity control system under palm cover; zirconium line guide inserts for use with braided line; on/off bait clicker for trolling, chunking, or bait fishing; available in both right- and left-hand retrieve; one-year warranty program.
Price: . . . . **$169.99–$184.99**

OKUMA HELIOS AIR

Model: 273, 273LX
Gear Ratio: 7.3:1
Inches/Turn: 31.6
Spool Cap. (M): 10 lbs/160 yds
Weight: 5.7 oz
Hand Retrieve: R; L
Max Drag: 14 lbs
Reel Bearings: 8+1
Features: Extremely light magnesium frame and sideplates; this tournament reel was designed for freshwater use; A6061-T6 machined aluminum, anodized spool; heavy duty, aluminum gears and shafts; multi-disc carbonite drag system; micro-click carbon fiber drag star for precise drag settings; 8BB+1RB stainless steel bearing drive system; precision Japanese ABEC-5 spool bearings; quick-set anti-reverse roller bearing; seven-position velocity control system under palm cover; ergonomic swept carbon fiber handle design; easy change palm sideplate access port; lightweight at only 5.7 ounces; zirconium line guide inserts for use with braided line; available in both right- and left-hand retrieve; three-year limited warranty.
Price: **$269.99**

OKUMA ISIS

Model: 250, 400, 400LX
Gear Ratio: 5.1:1
Inches/Turn: 23
Spool Cap. (M): 8 lbs/380 yds; 14 lbs/270 yds; 14 lbs/270 yds
Weight: 11.4 oz; 12.6 oz; 12.6 oz
Hand Retrieve: R; R; L
Max Drag: 10 lbs
Reel Bearings: 4+1
Features: A6061-T6 extruded aluminum, anodized frame; ported frame design for reduced weight; forged aluminum, gun smoke anodized sideplates; machined aluminum, gold anodized spool; multi-disc carbonite drag system; ratcheting drag star for precise drag settings; 4BB+1RB stainless steel bearing drive system; quick-set anti-reverse roller bearing; dual anti-reverse; silent ratcheting and quick-set roller bearing; precision machine-cut brass main and pinion gear; adjustable six-pin velocity control system; engaged levelwind on all models; forged aluminum twin paddle handle on all models; on/off bait clicker function on 400 models; titanium-coated line guide insert; one-year warranty program.
Price:.....................................**$209.99**

OKUMA TORMENTA

Model: 266WLX
Gear Ratio: 6.6:1
Inches/Turn: 28.5
Spool Cap. (M): 10 lbs/160 yds
Weight: 8 oz
Hand Retrieve: R or L
Max Drag: 11 lbs
Reel Bearings: 2+1
Features: Corrosion-resistant graphite frame and sideplate; A6061-T6 machined aluminum, anodized U-shaped spool; multi-disc composite drag system; 2BB+1RB bearing drive system; micro-click drag star for precise drag settings; external adjustable magnetic cast control system; quick-set anti-reverse roller bearing; easy change palm sideplate access port; ergonomic handle design allows cranking closer to body; zirconium line guide inserts for use with braided line; available gear ratio: 6.6:1; available in both right- and left-hand retrieve; one-year warranty.
Price:. **$64.99**

PFLUEGER PATRIARCH LOW PROFILE
Model: 71LPX, 71LHLPX, 79LPX
Gear Ratio: 7.1:1; 7.1:1; 7.9:1
Inches/Turn: 29; 29; 32
Spool Cap. (M): 10 lbs/175 yds
Spool Cap. (B): 20 lbs/190 yds
Weight: 6.28 oz
Hand Retrieve: R; L; R
Max Drag: 20 lbs
Reel Bearings: 11
Features: Ten double-shielded stainless steel ball bearings; instant anti-reverse bearing; C45 carbon-infused sideplates, lightweight with unmatched strength; bent carbon fiber handle with EVA handle knobs; rigid aluminum frame; non-detachable cam locking sideplate allows quick break adjustments without loosing the sideplate; double anodized, ported, machined aircraft aluminum spool; ultimate brake system combines centrifugal and magnetic brakes for limitless range of cast control; smooth carbon fiber drag system; titanium line guide; aircraft aluminum main gear and main shaft.
Price: **$199.95**

PFLUEGER SUPREME LOW PROFILE
Model: 54LPX, 64LPX, 64LHLPX, 71LPX
Gear Ratio: 5.4:1; 6.4:1; 6.4:1; 7.1:1
Inches/Turn: 22; 26; 26; 29
Spool Cap. (M): 10 lbs/175 yds
Spool Cap. (B): 20 lbs/190 yds
Weight: 7.83 oz
Hand Retrieve: R; R; L; R
Max Drag: 20 lbs

Reel Bearings: 9
Features: Eight double-shielded stainless steel ball bearings; instant anti-reverse bearing; hybrid gaphite sideplates, lightweight and incredibly durable; rigid aluminum frame; non-detachable cam locking sideplate allows quick break adjustments without loosing the sideplate.
Price: **$99.95**

PFLUEGER SUPREME XT
Model: 64LPX, 71LPX, 71HLPX
Gear Ratio: 6.4:1; 7.1:1; 7.1:1
Inches/Turn: 26; 29; 29
Spool Cap. (M): 10 lbs/175 yds
Spool Cap. (B): 20 lbs/190 yds
Weight: 6.53 oz
Hand Retrieve: R; R; L
Max Drag: 20 lbs
Reel Bearings: 10
Features: Nine double-shielded stainless steel ball bearings; instant anti-reverse bearing; C45 carbon-infused sideplates, lightweight with unmatched strength; double anodized aluminum handle with EVA knobs; rigid aluminum frame; non-detachable cam locking sideplate allows quick break adjustments without loosing the sideplate; double anodized, ported, machined aircraft aluminum spool; CBS six-pin adjustable centrifugal brake system; smooth carbon fiber drag system; titanium line guide; aircraft aluminum main gear and main shaft.
Price: **$149.99**

QUANTUM ANTIX
Model: 100H, 100S, 101S
Gear Ratio: 7.0:1; 6.3:1; 6.3:1
Inches/Turn: 30; 27; 27
Spool Cap. (M): 12 lbs/125 yds
Weight: 8.3 oz
Hand Retrieve: R; R; L
Reel Bearings: 9+1

Features: Ultralight skeletal V spool; ACS external adjustable centrifugal braking; continuous anti-reverse; one-piece aluminum frame; MaxCast skeletal spool; flippin' switch; DynaMag magnetic cast control; quick-release side cover.
Price:. **$99.95**

QUANTUM AURA
Model: 360CX
Gear Ratio: 6.2:1
Inches/Turn: 28
Spool Cap. (M): 12 lbs/125 yds
Weight: 7.6 oz
Hand Retrieve: R
Max Drag: 12 lbs
Reel Bearings: 3

Features: Durable multi-coated finish; lightweight aluminum crank handle; continuous anti-reverse; titanium-coated line guide reduces friction on casts and retrieves; DynaMag magnetic cast control; forged aluminum spool; quick-release side cover.
Price: **$49.99**

QUANTUM CODE
Model: 860CXB, 870CXB
Gear Ratio: 6.3:1; 7.0:1
Inches/Turn: 29; 32
Spool Cap. (M): 12 lbs/110 yds
Weight: 9 oz; 9.1 oz
Hand Retrieve: R
Reel Bearings: 7+1

Features: Right- and left-hand models; lightweight aluminum crank handle; ACS external adjustable centrifugal braking; continuous anti-reverse; titanium-coated line guide reduces friction on casts and retrieves; one-piece aluminum frame; MaxCast skeletal spool; flippin' switch; quick-release side cover.
Price: **$89.95**

QUANTUM EXO PT 100/200

Model: 100HPT, 100PPT, 100SPT, 200HPT, 200PPT, 200SPT, 201HPT, 201SPT, 101HPT, 101SPT
Gear Ratio: 7.3:1; 5.3:1; 6.6:1; 7.3:1; 5.3:1; 6.6:1; 7.3:1; 6.6:1; 7.3:1; 6.6:1
Inches/Turn: 31; 24; 28; 35; 25; 32; 35; 32; 31; 28
Spool Cap. (M): 12 lbs/145 yds; 12 lbs/145 yds; 12 lbs/145 yds; 14 lbs/175 yds; 14 lbs/175 yds; 14 lbs/175 yds; 14 lbs/175 yds; 14 lbs/175 yds; 12 lbs/145 yds; 12 lbs/145 yds

Weight: 5.9 oz; 5.9 oz; 5.9 oz; 6.8 oz; 6.8 oz; 6.8 oz; 6.8 oz; 6.8 oz; 5.9 oz; 5.9 oz
Hand Retrieve: R; R; R; R; R; R; L; L; L; L
Reel Bearings: 10+1
Features: Ceramic drag system; polymer-stainless hybrid PT bearings; lightweight aluminum crank handle; continuous anti-reverse; one-piece aluminum frame; MaxCast skeletal spool; quick-release side cover; adjustable centrifugal cast control.
Price: . . . . **$249.95–$269.95**

QUANTUM EXO PT 300
Model: 300HPT, 300PPT, 300SPT, 301HPT, 301SPT
Gear Ratio: 7.3:1; 5.3:1; 6.6:1; 7.3:1; 6.6:1
Inches/Turn: 35; 25; 32; 35; 32
Spool Cap. (M): 20 lbs/200 yds
Weight: 7.5 oz
Hand Retrieve: R; R; R; L; L
Reel Bearings: 6+1

Features: Ceramic drag system; polymer-stainless hybrid PT bearings; lightweight aluminum crank handle; MaxCast skeletal spool; quick-release side cover; adjustable centrifugal cast control.
Price: **$299.95**

QUANTUM KINETIC PT
Model: 100HPTA, 100SPTA, 101HPTA, 101SPTA
Gear Ratio: 7.0:1; 6.3:1; 7.0:1; 6.3:1
Inches/Turn: 28; 26; 28; 26
Spool Cap. (M): 12 lbs/145 yds
Weight: 7.5 oz
Hand Retrieve: R; R; L; L
Max Drag: 16 lbs; 18 lbs; 16 lbs; 18 lbs
Reel Bearings: 7+1

Features: Ceramic drag system; polymer-stainless hybrid PT bearings; easy access lubrication port; right- and left-hand models; durable multi-coated finish; lightweight aluminum crank handle; ACS external adjustable centrifugal braking; continuous anti-reverse; titanium-coated line guide reduces friction on casts and retrieves; one-piece aluminum frame; MaxCast skeletal spool; quick-release side cover.
Price: **$119.95**

QUANTUM SMOKE PT

Model: 100HPT, 100SPT, 101HPT, 101SPT, 150HPT, 150PPT, 150SPT, 151HPT
Gear Ratio: 7.0:1; 6.3:1; 7.0:1; 6.3:1; 7.3:1; 5.3:1; 6.6:1; 7.3:1
Inches/Turn: 28; 26; 28; 26; 34; 23; 28; 34
Spool Cap. (M): 12 lbs/105 yds; 12 lbs/135 yds; 12 lbs/105 yds; 12 lbs/135 yds; 12 lbs/165 yds; 12 lbs/165 yds; 12 lbs/165 yds; 12 lbs/165 yds
Weight: 6.2 oz; 6.2 oz; 6.2 oz; 6.2 oz; 6.8 oz; 6.8 oz; 6.8 oz; 6.8 oz
Hand Retrieve: R; R; L; L; R; R; R; L

Max Drag: 15 lbs; 17 lbs; 15 lbs; 17 lbs; 15 lbs; 19 lbs; 17 lbs; 15 lbs
Reel Bearings: 7+1; 7+1; 7+1; 7+1; 8+1; 8+1; 8+1; 8+1
Features: Ceramic drag system; polymer-stainless hybrid PT bearings; super free spool pinion design; right- and left-hand models; ultralight skeletal V spool; durable multi-coated finish; ACS external adjustable centrifugal braking; continuous anti-reverse; titanium-coated line guide reduces friction on casts and retrieves; one-piece aluminum frame and side cover; quick-release side cover.
Price: . . . . **$199.95–$219.95**

QUANTUM ULTREX
Model: 100S
Gear Ratio: 6.3:1
Inches/Turn: 26
Spool Cap. (M): 12 lbs/100 yds
Weight: 7.7 oz
Hand Retrieve: R
Reel Bearings: 1+1

Features: Right- and left-hand models; continuous anti-reverse; DynaMag magnetic cast control; ultra-smooth stainless steel bearings.
Price: **$39.99**

SHIMANO CAENAN
Model: 100, 101
Gear Ratio: 6.5:1
Inches/Turn: 27
Spool Cap. (M): 8 lbs/180 yds
Weight: 7.2 oz
Hand Retrieve: R; L
Max Drag: 10 lbs
Reel Bearings: 6+1

Features: Aluminum lo-mass spool system; super stopper; assist stopper; high-speed 6.5:1 retrieve; high-density EVA power grips; six-shielded stainless steel ball bearings; variable brake system with reduced mass hub; disengaging levelwind system; Quickfire II clutch bar; 1/8 turn easy access attached sideplate; drilled handle shank; ceramic line guide; recessed reel foot; metal cast control knob; rated for use with mono, fluorocarbon, and PowerPro lines; approved for use in salt water.
Price:................................... **$89.99**

SHIMANO CAIUS

Model: 200, 201
Gear Ratio: 6.5:1
Inches/Turn: 27
Spool Cap. (M): 8 lbs/180 yds
Weight: 7.9 oz; 7.2 oz
Hand Retrieve: R; L
Max Drag: 11 lbs
Reel Bearings: 3+1

Features: Aluminum lo-mass spool system; super stopper; high-speed 6.5:1 retrieve; three-shielded stainless steel ball bearings; new easy MAG II brake system; disengaging levelwind system; Quickfire II clutch bar; drilled handle shank; ceramic line guide; recessed reel foot; rated for use with mono, fluorocarbon, and PowerPro lines; approved for use in salt water.
Price: **$69.99**

SHIMANO CALAIS DC

Model: 200DC, 201DC
Gear Ratio: 7.0:1
Inches/Turn: 31
Spool Cap. (M): 30 lbs/150 yds
Weight: 9.5 oz
Hand Retrieve: R; L
Max Drag: 12 lbs
Reel Bearings: 10+1
Features: 4x8 digital control; S A-RB bearings; magnumlite spool; septon handle material; super free; high-efficiency gearing; tapered titanium levelwind insert; greaseless spool support bearings; super stopper; assist stopper; escape hatch; septon handle material; PV power handles; cold-forged handle shank; drilled, cold-forged drag star; dartainium drag; recessed reel foot; clicking drag adjustment; metal plated finish; asymmetrical spool window; aluminum frame and sideplates; platinum premiere service plan; metal series; approved for use in salt water; rated for use with mono, fluorocarbon, and PowerPro lines.
Price: **$649.99**

SHIMANO CALCUTTA TE DC

Model: 100DC, 200DC, 201DC, 250DC
Gear Ratio: 5.8:1; 5.0:1; 5.0:1; 5.0:1
Inches/Turn: 23
Spool Cap. (M): 30 lbs/115 yds; 40 lbs/95 yds; 40 lbs/95 yds; 40 lbs/115 yds
Weight: 8.6 oz; 9.9 oz; 9.9 oz; 10.2 oz
Hand Retrieve: R; R; L; R
Max Drag: 8.5 lbs; 10 lbs; 10 lbs; 10 lbs
Reel Bearings: 10+1
Features: Anti-rust bearings; lo-mass drilled spool system; A7075 aluminum spool; super free; digital control; high-efficiency gearing; super stopper with assist stopper; dartainium drag; clicking drag adjustment; clicking cast control adjustment; recessed reel foot; drilled crossbar; cold-forged handle shank; adjustable handle shank; rubber handle grip (except 250); septon handle grip (250 only); paddle-style grip (except 250); PV power paddles (250 only); machined aluminum frame; stamped aluminum handle side sideplate; titanium levelwind insert; metal series; platinum service plan; approved for use in salt water; rated for use with mono, fluorocarbon, and PowerPro lines.
Price: **$529.99**

SHIMANO CARDIFF

Model: 200A, 201A, 300A, 301A, 400A, 401A
Gear Ratio: 5.8:1; 5.8:1; 5.8:1; 5.8:1; 5.2:1; 5.2:1
Inches/Turn: 24; 24; 24; 24; 22; 22
Spool Cap. (M): 8 lbs/230 yds; 8 lbs/230 yds; 12 lbs/230 yds; 12 lbs/230 yds; 12 lbs/330 yds; 12 lbs/330 yds
Weight: 8.6 oz; 8.6 oz; 8.9 oz; 8.9 oz; 11.9 oz; 11.9 oz
Hand Retrieve: R; L; R; L; R; L
Max Drag: 10 lbs; 10 lbs; 10 lbs; 10 lbs; 11 lbs; 11 lbs
Reel Bearings: 4+1

Features: Anti-rust bearings; one-piece die-cast aluminum frame; handle side variable brake system; super stopper with assist stopper; non-disengaging levelwind system (400 and 401 only); recessed reel foot (except on models 400A and 401A); three post quick take down (except on 2-post models, CDF100A); rubber handle grip; aluminum sideplates and spool; clicker (400A and 401A only); metal series; approved for use in salt water; rated for use with mono, fluorocarbon, and PowerPro lines.
Price: . . . .**$109.99–$119.99**

SHIMANO CHRONARCH CI4+
Model: 150CI4, 150CI4HG, 151CI4, 151CI4HG
Gear Ratio: 6.2:1; 7.6:1; 6.2:1; 7.6:1
Inches/Turn: 26; 31; 26; 32
Spool Cap. (M): 10 lbs/145 yds
Weight: 6.5 oz
Hand Retrieve: R; R; L; L
Max Drag: 11 lbs
Reel Bearings: 7+1

Features: CI4+ frame; CI4+ sideplates; recessed reel foot; high-efficiency gearing; super free bearing supported pinion gear system; X-ship; Dartanium II (cross carbon) drag washers; seven bearings; 6 S A-RB BB; 1 A-RB roller clutch bearing; SVS infinity braking system; magnumlite spool; septon PV grips; disengaging levelwind system; Quickfire II clutch bar; made in Japan; approved for use in salt water.
Price: **$269.99**

SHIMANO CITICA

Model: 200G7, 200G6, 201G6, 200G5
Gear Ratio: 7.1:1; 6.5:1; 6.5:1; 5.5:1
Inches/Turn: 30; 27; 27; 23
Spool Cap. (M): 8 lbs/180 yds
Weight: 7.5 oz
Hand Retrieve: R; R; L; R
Max Drag: 11 lbs
Reel Bearings: 3+1

Features: Aluminum frame; lightweight graphite sideplates; recessed reel foot; high-efficiency gearing; super free bearing supported pinion gear system; variable brake system with reduced mass hub; super stopper; assist stopper; 1/8 turn easy access attached sideplate; metal cast control knob; anodized spool and handle; disengaging levelwind system; Quickfire II clutch bar; lo-mass drilled spool system; dartainium drag; four bearings; three-shielded stainless steel BB; approved for use in salt water.
Price: **$129.99**

SHIMANO CORE

Model: 50MG7, 51MG7, 100MG, 101MG, 100MG7
Gear Ratio: 7.0:1; 7.0:1; 6.2:1; 6.2:1; 7.0:1
Inches/Turn: 28; 28; 26; 26; 30
Spool Cap. (M): 20 lbs/115 yds
Weight: 5.5 oz; 5.5 oz; 6.1 oz; 6.1 oz; 6.7 oz
Hand Retrieve: R; L; R; L; R
Max Drag: 10 lbs; 10 lbs; 11 lbs; 11 lbs; 11 lbs
Reel Bearings: 8+1; 8+1; 4+1; 4+1; 4+1
Features: Ultra-lightweight magnesium frame and sideplate (CORE50 and 51MG7) has graphite sideplates); ultra-lightweight A7075 aluminum spool construction; magnumlite spool design; S A-RB ball bearings; A-RB roller bearing; high-efficiency gearing; super stopper; super free; variable brake system; reduced mass VBS hub; escape hatch; dartainium drag; cold-forged aluminum drag star; clicking drag adjustment; aluminum cast control knob; rubber-shielded cast control knob; tapered titanium levelwind insert; cold-forged aluminum handle shank; drilled handle shank; septon handle grips; recessed reel foot; high-speed 6.2:1 gear ratio (CORE100MG only); lightweight aluminum drive gear; paddle grips (CORE100MG only); super high-speed 7.0:1 gear ratio (CORE100MG7 and CORE50/51MG7); heavy duty brass drive gear (CORE100MG7 only); PV power grips (CORE100MG7 only); 1/8 turn easy access attached sideplate (CORE50/51MG only); approved for use in salt water; rated for use with mono, fluorocarbon, and PowerPro lines.
Price: . . . . **$349.99–$399.99**

ABU GARCIA ORRA 2 WINCH
Model: Winch, Winch-L
Gear Ratio: 5.4:1
Inches/Turn: 22
Retrieve Speed: Low
Spool Cap. (M): 12 lbs/180 yds
Spool Cap. (B): 30 lbs/180 yds
Weight: 7.6 oz
Hand Retrieve: R; L
Max Drag: 15 lbs

Reel Bearings: 8
Features: Seven stainless steel ball bearings plus one roller bearing provides smooth operation; X-Cräftic alloy frame for increased corrosion resistance; graphite sideplates; Power Disk drag system gives smooth drag performance; MagTrax brake system gives consistent brake pressure throughout the cast; Duragear brass gear for extended gear life; extended bent handle for increased cranking power; large PVC knobs provide greater grip.
Price: **$99.95**

ABU GARCIA REVO TORO NACL

Model: 50, 50-HS, 51, 60, 60-HS, 61
Gear Ratio: 5.4:1; 6.4:1; 5.4:1; 5.4:1; 6.4:1; 5.4:1
Inches/Turn: 26; 30.9; 26; 26; 30.9; 26
Retrieve Speed: Std; High; Std; Std; High; Std
Spool Cap. (M): 14 lbs/200 yds; 14 lbs/200 yds; 14 lbs/200 yds; 14 lbs/250 yds; 14 lbs/250 yds; 14 lbs/250 yds
Spool Cap. (B): 30 lbs/250 yds; 30 lbs/250 yds; 30 lbs/250 yds; 30 lbs/330 yds; 30 lbs/330 yds; 30 lbs/330 yds
Weight: 10.9 oz; 10.9 oz; 10.9 oz; 11 oz; 11 oz; 11 oz
Hand Retrieve: R; R; L; R; R; L
Max Drag: 22 lbs
Reel Bearings: 6+1
Features: Six stainless steel high-performance corrosion-resistant bearings plus one roller bearing provides increased corrosion protection; X2-Cräftic alloy frame and sideplate for increased corrosion resistance; carbon matrix drag system provides smooth, consistent drag pressure across the entire drag range; aircraft-grade aluminum spool allows for a high-strength spool that is extremely lightweight for greater casting performance; pitch centrifugal brake system; Duragear brass gear for extended gear life; lube port for easy access maintenance; synchronized level wind system improves line lay and castability; titanium-coated line guide reduces friction and improves durability; extended bent handle with power knobs for increased cranking power; dual anti-reverse provides additional backup for high-pressure situations.
Price: **$299.95**

BASS PRO SHOPS JOHNNY MORRIS SIGNATURE SERIES

Model: 10 HD, 10HLD, 10SHD, 20HD
Gear Ratio: 6.4:1; 6.4:1; 7.1:1; 6.4:1
Inches/Turn: 28; 28; 31; 28
Spool Cap. (M): 12 lbs/120 yds
Weight: 8.6 oz
Hand Retrieve: R; L; R; R
Max Drag: 14 lbs
Reel Bearings: 10+1

Features: Die-cast aluminum frame and sideplates; black carbon-titanium deposition finish; double-anodized-aluminum spool; premium Japanese stainless steel ball bearings; 100 percent double-shielded ten-bearing system; Powerlock instant anti-reverse; Duralumin drive gear; dual braking system; beefed-up, super-smooth carbon drag system; lightweight carbon-fiber recurve handle with ribbed silicon knob; padded clutch bar; titanium-nitride guide.
Price: **$159.99**

BASS PRO SHOPS SNAGGING SPECIAL LEVELWIND
Model: SS-30
Gear Ratio: 4.4:1
Inches/Turn: 31.7
Spool Cap. (M): 30 lbs/380 yds
Weight: 24.8 oz
Hand Retrieve: R

Max Drag: 22 lbs
Reel Bearings: 2
Features: Rugged, lightweight graphite frame; deep anodized, machined aluminum spool; two stainless steel ball bearings; audible bait clicker; stainless steel levelwind; smooth, multi-disc drag system; metal line guide; cast control knob; powerful gear ratio of 4.4:1.
Price: **$49.99**

DAIWA AIRD
Model: 100P, 100H, 100HL, 100HS
Gear Ratio: 4.9:1; 6.3:1; 6.3:1; 7.1:1
Inches/Turn: 20.6; 25.7; 25.7; 30
Spool Cap. (M): 12 lbs/120 yds
Spool Cap. (B): 40 lbs/140 yds; 40 lbs/135 yds; 40 lbs/140 yds; 40 lbs/135 yds
Weight: 7.7 oz
Hand Retrieve: L; R; L; R
Max Drag: 8.8 lbs

Reel Bearings: 8+1
Features: Open access, low-profile design for easy thumbing and line maintenance; weighs just 7.7 ounces; ultimate tournament carbon drag with 8.8-pound drag max; nine bearing system (8BB+1RB); Magforce cast control; swept handle for less wobble, better feel and winding power; machined aluminum perforated spool; oversized soft-touch grips.
Price:.................................. **$89.99**

DAIWA LAGUNA
Model: 100H, 100HL, 100HS
Gear Ratio: 6.3:1; 6.3:1; 7.1:1
Inches/Turn: 25.7; 25.7; 30
Spool Cap. (M): 12 lbs/120 yds
Weight: 7.4 oz
Hand Retrieve: R; L; R
Max Drag: 8.8
Reel Bearings: 5+1

Features: Open-access, low-profile frame for easy thumbing and line maintenance; lightweight composite frame and sideplates; swept handle for less wobble, better feel, and winding power; five ball bearings plus roller bearing; Magforce magnetic anti-backlash control; lightweight, drilled aluminum spool; dual-system infinite anti-reverse.
Price: **$59.95**

DAIWA LEXA 400
Model: HS-P, HSL-P, WR-P
Gear Ratio: 7.1:1; 7.1:1; 5.1:1
Inches/Turn: 37.7; 37.7; 27.1
Spool Cap. (M): 17 lbs/245 yds
Spool Cap. (B): 55 lbs/300 yds
Weight: 16 oz
Hand Retrieve: R; L; R
Max Drag: 25 lbs
Reel Bearings: 4+3

Features: Aluminum frame and sideplate (gear side); seven bearing system (2CRBB, 4BB+1RB); Magforce cast control; infinite anti-reverse; swept handle with weight-reducing cutouts; counter-balanced power handle on P models; super-leverage 120mm handle on 400 size models; A7075 aluminum spool—super lightweight and extra strong (100 size); extra line capacity for strong lines, powerful fish; ultimate tournament carbon drag.
Price: **$249.99**

DAIWA MEGAFORCE THS (WITH TWITCHIN' BAR)

Model: 100THS, 100THSL
Gear Ratio: 7.3:1
Inches/Turn: 31.5
Spool Cap. (M): 12 lbs/150 yds
Weight: 8.8 oz
Hand Retrieve: R; L

Max Drag: 8.8 lbs
Reel Bearings: 6
Features: Twitchin' bar; six ball bearings; hyper speed 7.3:1 gear ratio; swept handle; Magforce-Z automatic anti-backlash control; precision click drag adjustment.
Price:................................... **$89.95**

DAIWA MILLIONAIRE M7HTMAG

Model: Millionaire M7HTMAG
Gear Ratio: 5.8:1
Inches/Turn: 28
Spool Cap. (M): 15 lbs/330 yds
Weight: 12.2 oz
Hand Retrieve: R
Max Drag: 11 lbs
Reel Bearings: 5+1

Features: Six ball bearings (5 CRBB) plus roller bearing; lightweight aluminum spool; counter-balanced power handle; fast 5.8:1 retrieve picks up 28" per crank; high-grade brass drive gear and stainless steel pinion; infinite anti-reverse; rigid, one-piece frame; smooth star-adjust drag; Magforce-Z.
Price:. **$299.95**

DAIWA MILLIONAIRE M7HTMAGST

Model: Millionaire M7HTMAGST
Gear Ratio: 5.8:1
Inches/Turn: 28
Spool Cap. (M): 15 lbs/330 yds
Weight: 11.5 oz
Hand Retrieve: R
Max Drag: 11 lbs
Reel Bearings: 8+1

Features: Factory super tuned for optimum performance; super tuned machine-cut spool made of super-balanced, super-lightweight aluminum alloy; carbon swept handle for reduced weight, maximum leverage and control; EVA double handle knob; fast 5.8:1 retrieve picks up 28" per crank; high-grade brass drive gear and stainless steel pinion; nine ball bearings (8 CRBB) plus roller bearing; rigid, one-piece aluminum frame; smooth star-adjust drag; advanced design, super tuned, Magforce-Z.
Price:....................................**$499.95**

DAIWA PX TYPE-R
Model: PX-R, PXL-R
Gear Ratio: 6.8:1
Inches/Turn: 26
Spool Cap. (M): 6 lbs/95 yds
Weight: 5.8 oz
Hand Retrieve: R; L
Max Drag: 13 lbs

Reel Bearings: 10
Features: Weighs just 5.8 ounces; magnesium body; ten ball bearings; carbon swept handle; cork handle knobs; hyper speed 6.8:1 gear ratio; UT drag with a drag max of 13 pounds; Magforce-Z cast control.
Price: **$499.95**

DAIWA STEEZ EX

Model: 100XS, 100HS, 100H, 100HSL, 100HL
Gear Ratio: 7.9:1; 7.1:1; 6.3:1; 7.1:1; 6.3:1
Inches/Turn: 33.2; 29.8; 26; 29.8; 26
Spool Cap. (M): 14 lbs/120 yds
Weight: 5.8 oz; 5.8 oz; 5.4 oz; 5.8 oz; 5.4 oz
Hand Retrieve: R; R; R; L; L
Max Drag: 13.2 lbs
Reel Bearings: 11+1

Features: Super lightweight magnesium frame and sideplate; swept handle with cutouts for reduced weight; oversized, lightweight 100 MM Handle on 7.1 and 7.9 models; ultimate tournament carbon drag with 13.2-pound drag max; free-floating A7075 aluminum alloy spool starts faster, spins longer; fast spool change; eleven precision ball bearings plus roller bearing; tough Dura-Loc pinion; Magforce-Z cast control; precision, micro-click adjustment on star drag and free-spool cap; infinite anti- reverse; free neoprene reel cover included.
Price: **$599.95**

DAIWA T3
Model: 1016HS, 1016H, 1016HSL, 1016HL
Gear Ratio: 7.1:1; 6.3:1; 7.1:1; 6.3:1
Inches/Turn: 29.5; 26.3; 29.5; 26.3
Spool Cap. (M): 14 lbs/120 yds
Weight: 6.5 oz
Hand Retrieve: R; R; L; L
Max Drag: 13.2 lbs
Reel Bearings: 8+1

Features: T-wing system; Magforce 3D cast control system; weighs just 6.5 ounces; ultra-low profile; Zaion frame, clutch cover, and sideplate; ultimate tournament drag with micro-click adjustment; available with 6.3:1 or 7.1:1 gear ratios; eight ball bearings (including 4 CRBB) plus roller bearing; aluminum swept handle arm with urethane-covered cork grips; free-floating, lightweight aluminum spool; infinite anti-reverse; fast, one-touch spool change.
Price: **$429.95**

REELS

DAIWA T3 BALLISTIC
Model: S100XS, S100HS, S100H, S100XSL, S100HSL, S100HL
Gear Ratio: 8.1:1; 7.1:1; 6.3:1; 8.1:1; 7.1:1; 6.3:1
Inches/Turn: 34; 29.5; 26.3; 34; 29.5; 26.3
Spool Cap. (M): 14 lbs/120 yds
Weight: 7.9 oz; 7.8 oz; 7.8 oz; 7.9 oz; 7.8 oz; 7.8 oz
Hand Retrieve: R; R; R; L; L; L
Max Drag: 11 lbs; 13.2 lbs; 13.2 lbs
Reel Bearings: 5+1

Features: T-wing system; Magforce 3D cast control system; ultra-low profile; Zaion frame, clutch cover, and sideplate; natural black marble Zaion finish; ultimate tournament drag with micro-click adjustment; available with 6.3:1 or 7.1:1 gear ratios; five ball bearings plus roller bearing; aluminum swept handle; free-floating, lightweight aluminum spool; infinite anti-reverse; fast, one-touch spool change.
Price:.................................**$249.95**

DAIWA TD LUNA

Model: 253, 300, 253L, 300L
Gear Ratio: 5.1:1
Inches/Turn: 23.6
Spool Cap. (M): 12 lbs/235 yds; 14 lbs/320 yds; 12 lbs/235 yds; 14 lbs/320 yds
Weight: 11.1 oz; 12.9 oz; 11.1 oz; 12.9 oz
Hand Retrieve: R; R; L; L
Max Drag: 11 lbs; 15.3 lbs; 11 lbs; 15.3 lbs
Reel Bearings: 5+1
Features: Frame and sideplates machined from solid bar stock aluminum; five CRBB super corrosion-resistant ball bearings, plus roller bearing; free-floating spool for maximum casting performance; Magforce-Z automatic magnetic anti-backlash control (Centriflex automatic centrifugal system on 300 size); ultra-smooth, multi-disc drag with Daiwa's exclusive fiber composite and stainless washers; infinite anti-reverse; Dura-Loc pinion for solid gear engagement; rugged, six-point drive train support; machined aircraft aluminum spool; cut-proof titanium nitrided stainless steel line guide; spool click on 300 size; hard anodized to resist corrosion.
Price: **$279.99**

DAIWA TD ZILLION HIGH POWER

Model: 100PA, 100PLA
Gear Ratio: 4.9:1
Inches/Turn: 22
Spool Cap. (M): 14 lbs/120 yds
Weight: 8.8 oz
Hand Retrieve: R; L
Max Drag: 8.8 lbs
Reel Bearings: 6+1
Features: Choice of ultra-fast 7.1:1 retrieve or all-purpose 6.3:1; six ball bearings (including CRBB), plus roller

bearing; swept handle for less wobble, better feel, and maximum winding leverage; free-floating perforated aluminum spool starts faster, spins longer; fast spool change; Magforce-Z automatic anti-backlash system; eight-disc wet drag with precision click adjustment; aluminum guard plate protects finish on top of reel; rigid aluminum frame and handle-side sideplate firmly support the drive train; soft-touch grips.
Price: **$319.99**

DAIWA TD ZILLION HIGH SPEED

Model: 100HA, 100SHLA, 100HLA, 100SHA
Gear Ratio: 6.3:1; 7.1:1; 6.3:1; 7.1:1
Inches/Turn: 28; 31.6; 28; 31.6
Spool Cap. (M): 12 lbs/150 yds
Weight: 8.6 oz; 8.8 oz; 8.6 oz; 8.8 oz
Hand Retrieve: R; R; L; R
Max Drag: 8.8 lbs
Reel Bearings: 6+1
Features: Choice of ultra-fast 7.1:1 retrieve or all-purpose 6.3:1; six ball bearings (including CRBB), plus roller bearing; swept handle for less wobble, better feel, and maximum winding leverage; free-floating perforated aluminum spool starts faster, spins longer; fast spool change; Magforce-Z automatic anti-backlash system; eight-disc wet drag with precision click adjustment; aluminum guard plate protects finish on top of reel; rigid aluminum frame and handle-side sideplate firmly support the drive train; soft-touch grips.
Price: **$319.99**

DAIWA TD ZILLION TYPE R

Model: 100HSHR, 100HSHLR
Gear Ratio: 7.3:1
Inches/Turn: 32
Spool Cap. (M): 14 lbs/120 yds
Weight: 8.5 oz
Hand Retrieve: R; L
Max Drag: 8.5 lbs

Reel Bearings: 11
Features: Hyper speed 7.3:1 retrieve; eleven hyper speed ball bearings; carbon swept handle; ultimate tournament carbon drag; super rigid aluminum frame and sideplate; Magforce-Z anti-backlash control; free-floating perforated aluminum spool; infinite anti-reverse.
Price: **$439.99**

DAIWA Z SERIES

Model: HS, H, HL
Gear Ratio: 7.2:1; 6.4:1; 6.4:1
Inches/Turn: 33.5; 29.5; 29.5
Spool Cap. (M): 14 lbs/155 yds
Weight: 9.9 oz
Hand Retrieve: R; R; L
Max Drag: 16.5 lbs
Reel Bearings: 8+1
Features: Magforce-3D; hyper speed 7.2:1 or all-around 6.4:1 gear ratio models; seven-disc carbon UT drag with a drag max of 16.5 pound–click adjustment; eight CRBB corrosion-resistant ball bearings plus roller bearing; rugged, dual system anti-reverse combines infinite anti-reverse with a multi-stop system; low-friction, titanium-nitrided line guide; aluminum swept handle with large, ball bearing grips; tough aluminum frame; precision high brass drive gear and ultra-tough aluminum bronze alloy pinion; high-leverage, aluminum star drag with precise click adjustment; super lightweight perforated aluminum alloy spool.
Price: **$649.95**

OKUMA CALERA
Model: 266W, 266WLX
Gear Ratio: 6.6:1
Inches/Turn: 28.5
Spool Cap. (M): 10 lbs/160 yds
Weight: 8.2 oz
Hand Retrieve: R; L
Max Drag: 11 lbs
Reel Bearings: 4+1
Features: Corrosion-resistant graphite frame and sideplates; A6061-T6 machined aluminum, anodized V-shaped spool; multi-disc composite drag system; 4BB+1RB bearing drive system; micro-click drag star for precise drag settings; external adjustable magnetic cast control system; internal eight-position velocity control system; quick-set anti-reverse roller bearing; easy change palm sideplate access port; ergonomic handle design allows cranking closer to body; zirconium line guide inserts for use with braided line; available gear ratio is 6.6:1; available in both right- and left-hand retrieve; one-year warranty.
Price: **$89.99**

OKUMA AKENA

Model: 400
Gear Ratio: 5.1:1
Inches/Turn: 23
Spool Cap. (M): 14 lbs/270 yds
Weight: 12.7 oz
Hand Retrieve: R or L
Max Drag: 10 lbs
Reel Bearings: 5+1
Features: Rigid one-piece anodized aluminum frame; aluminum left and right sideplates; machined aluminum, gold anodized spool; multi-disc carbonite drag system; 5BB+1RB stainless steel bearing drive system; quick-set anti-reverse roller bearing; precision machine-cut brass main and pinion gear; adjustable six-pin velocity control system; non-disengaging levelwind system 400 size; disengaging levelwind on the 250 size; aluminum twin paddle handle with oversized knobs; on/off bait clicker function on 400-size reels; one-year warranty.
Price: **$109.99**

OKUMA CEDROS SALT WATER

Model: 273
Gear Ratio: 7.3:1
Inches/Turn: 31.5
Spool Cap. (M): 10 lbs/205 yds
Weight: 8.4 oz
Hand Retrieve: R or L
Max Drag: 14 lbs
Reel Bearings: 6+1
Features: Rigid die-cast aluminum frame and sideplates constructed with T-480 aluminum alloy; titanium coating process on sideplates; corrosion-resistant coating process; heavy duty, aluminum gearing and shafts; A6061-T6 machined aluminum, anodized spool; unique stainless steel clutch slider; multi-disc carbonite drag system; micro-click drag star for precise drag settings; 6BB+1RB stainless steel bearing drive system; precision Japanese ABEC-5 spool bearings; quick-set anti-reverse roller bearing; seven-position velocity control system; heavy duty custom aluminum handle design; durable EVA handle knobs for comfort; easy change left sideplate access port; zirconium line guide inserts for use with braided line; designed specifically for salt water use; available in right- and left-hand retrieve; three-year limited warranty.
Price:. **$249.99**

OKUMA CITRIX

Model: 254a, 273a, 273LXa
Gear Ratio: 5.4; 7.3:1; 5.4:1
Inches/Turn: 23.4; 31.6; 31.6
Spool Cap. (M): 10 lbs/160 yds
Weight: 8.4 oz
Hand Retrieve: R; R; L
Max Drag: 11 lbs
Reel Bearings: 9+1
Features: Rigid die-cast aluminum frame; A6061-T6 machined aluminum, anodized spool; multi-disc carbonite drag system; 9BB+1RB bearing drive system; micro-click drag star for precise drag settings; external adjustable centrifugal cast control system; quick-set anti-reverse roller bearing; graphite left and right sideplates; easy change palm sideplate access port; ergonomic handle design allows cranking closer to body; available gear ratios of 7.3:1 and 5.4:1; 7.3:1 gear ratio available in left-hand retrieve; one-year warranty.
Price: **$119.99**

OKUMA CITRIX 350

Model: 364a, 364LXa, 364Pa, 364PLXa
Gear Ratio: 6.4:1
Inches/Turn: 31
Spool Cap. (M): 12 lbs/250 yds
Weight: 11 oz
Hand Retrieve: R; L; R; L
Max Drag: 25 lbs
Reel Bearings: 7+1
Features: Rigid die-cast aluminum frame and sideplates; corrosion-resistant coating process; durable brass main and pinion gear system; A6061-T6 machined aluminum, anodized spool; multi-disc carbonite drag system with 25-pounds max drag; micro-click drag star for precise drag settings; 7BB+1RB stainless steel bearing drive system; precision Japanese ABEC-5 spool bearings; dual anti-reverse system for maximum reliability; synchronized levelwind optimized for braided line; seven-position velocity control system under palm cover; zirconium line guide inserts for use with braided line; on/off bait clicker for trolling, chunking or bait fishing; available in both right- and left-hand retrieve; one-year warranty.
Price:.............................$16.99–$184.99

OKUMA ISIS

Model: 250, 400, 400LX
Gear Ratio: 5.1:1
Inches/Turn: 23
Spool Cap. (M): 8 lbs/380 yds; 14 lbs/270 yds; 14 lbs/270 yds
Weight: 11.4 oz; 12.6 oz; 12.6 oz
Hand Retrieve: R; R; L
Max Drag: 10 lbs
Reel Bearings: 4+1
Features: A6061-T6 extruded aluminum, anodized frame; ported frame design for reduced weight; forged aluminum, gun smoke anodized sideplates; machined aluminum, gold anodized spool; multi-disc carbonite drag system; ratcheting drag star for precise drag settings; 4BB+1RB stainless steel bearing drive system; quick-set anti-reverse roller bearing; dual anti-reverse with silent ratcheting and quick-set roller bearing; precision machine-cut brass main and pinion gear; adjustable six-pin velocity control system; engaged levelwind on all models; forged aluminum twin paddle handle on all models; on/off bait clicker function on 400 models; titanium-coated line guide insert; one-year warranty.
Price:. **$209.99**

OKUMA SERRANO

Model: 200, 200W
Gear Ratio: 6.2:1
Inches/Turn: 26
Spool Cap. (M): 10 lbs/205 yds; 10 lbs/160 yds
Weight: 7.2 oz
Hand Retrieve: R; L
Max Drag: 11 lbs
Reel Bearings: 10+1
Features: Rigid die-cast aluminum frame; corrosion-resistant coating process; aluminum sidesplate holds gears in perfect alignment; A6061-T6 machined aluminum, anodized spool; lightweight inertia-free hi-rise spool on SR-200W; heavy duty, machine-cut, Dura brass gearing; multi-disc carbonite drag system; micro-click drag star for precise drag settings; 10BB+1RB stainless steel bearing drive system; precision Japanese ABEC-5 spool bearings; quick-set anti-reverse roller bearing; seven-position velocity control system; ergonomic handle design allows cranking closer to body; easy change left sideplate access port; zirconium line guide inserts for use with braided line; three-year warranty.
Price: **$174.99**

PFLUEGER PATRIARCH LOW PROFILE
Model: 71LPX, 71LHLPX, 79LPX
Gear Ratio: 7.1:1; 7.1:1; 7.9:1
Inches/Turn: 29; 29; 32
Spool Cap. (M): 10 lbs/175 yds
Spool Cap. (B): 20 lbs/190 yds
Weight: 6.28 oz
Hand Retrieve: R; L; R
Max Drag: 20 lbs
Reel Bearings: 11

Features: Ten double-shielded stainless steel ball bearings; instant anti-reverse bearing; C45 carbon infused sideplates, lightweight with unmatched strength; bent carbon fiber handle with EVA handle knobs; rigid aluminum frame; non-detachable cam locking side plate allows quick break adjustments without loosing the sideplate; double anodized, ported, machined aircraft aluminum spool; ultimate brake system combines centrifugal and magnetic brakes for limitless range of cast control; smooth carbon fiber drag system; titanium line guide; aircraft aluminum main gear and main shaft.
Price: **$199.95**

PFLUEGER SUPREME LOW PROFILE
Model: 54LPX, 64LPX, 64LHLPX, 71LPX
Gear Ratio: 5.4:1; 6.4:1; 6.4:1; 7.1:1
Inches/Turn: 22; 26; 26; 29
Spool Cap. (M): 10 lbs/175 yds
Spool Cap. (B): 20 lbs/190 yds
Weight: 7.83 oz
Hand Retrieve: R; R; L; R

Max Drag: 20 lbs
Reel Bearings: 9
Features: Eight double-shielded stainless steel ball bearings; instant anti-reverse bearing hybrid graphite sideplates that are lightweight and incredibly durable; rigid aluminum frame; non-detachable cam locking sideplate allows quick break adjustments without loosing the sideplate.
Price: **$99.95**

PFLUEGER SUPREME XT
Model: 64LPX, 71LPX, 71HLPX
Gear Ratio: 6.4:1; 7.1:1; 7.1:1
Inches/Turn: 26; 29; 29
Spool Cap. (M): 10 lbs/175 yds
Spool Cap. (B): 20 lbs/190 yds
Weight: 6.53 oz
Hand Retrieve: R; R; L
Max Drag: 20 lbs
Reel Bearings: 10

Features: Nine double-shielded stainless steel ball bearings; instant anti-reverse bearing; C45 carbon infused sideplates that are lightweight with unmatched strength; double-anodized aluminum handle with EVA knobs; rigid aluminum frame; non-detachable cam locking sideplate allows quick break adjustments without loosing the sideplate; double-anodized, ported, machined aircraft aluminum spool; six-pin adjustable centrifugal brake system; smooth carbon fiber drag system; titanium line guide; aircraft aluminum main gear and main shaft.
Price: **$149.99**

REELS

SHIMANO CAENAN
Model: 100, 101
Gear Ratio: 6.5:1
Inches/Turn: 27
Spool Cap. (M): 8 lbs/180 yds
Weight: 7.2 oz
Hand Retrieve: R; L
Max Drag: 10 lbs
Reel Bearings: 6+1

Features: Aluminum lo-mass spool system; super stopper; assist stopper; high-speed 6.5:1 retrieve; high-density EVA power grips; six-shielded stainless steel ball bearings; variable brake system with reduced mass hub; disengaging levelwind system; Quickfire II clutch bar; 1/8 turn easy access attached sideplate; drilled handle shank; ceramic line guide; recessed reel foot; metal cast control knob; rated for use with mono, fluorocarbon, and PowerPro lines; approved for use in salt water.
Price: **$89.99**

SHIMANO CAIUS

Model: 200, 201
Gear Ratio: 6.5:1
Inches/Turn: 27
Spool Cap. (M): 8 lbs/180 yds
Weight: 7.9 oz; 7.2 oz
Hand Retrieve: R; L
Max Drag: 11 lbs
Reel Bearings: 3+1

Features: Aluminum lo-mass spool system; super stopper; high-speed 6.5:1 retrieve; three-shielded stainless steel ball bearings; new easy MAG II brake system; disengaging levelwind system; Quickfire II clutch bar; drilled handle shank; ceramic line guide; recessed reel foot; rated for use with mono, fluorocarbon, and PowerPro lines; approved for use in salt water.
Price: **$69.99**

REELS

SHIMANO CALAIS DC

Model: 200DC, 201DC
Gear Ratio: 7.0:1
Inches/Turn: 31
Spool Cap. (M): 30 lbs/150 yds
Weight: 9.5 oz
Hand Retrieve: R; L
Max Drag: 12 lbs
Reel Bearings: 10+1
Features: 4x8 digital control; S A-RB bearings; magnumlite spool; septon handle material; super free; high-efficiency gearing; tapered titanium levelwind insert; greaseless spool support bearings; super stopper; assist stopper; escape hatch; septon handle material; PV power handles; cold-forged handle shank; drilled, cold-forged drag star; dartainium drag; recessed reel foot; clicking drag adjustment; metal plated finish; asymmetrical spool window; aluminum frame and sideplates; platinum premiere service plan; metal series; approved for use in salt water; rated for use with mono, fluorocarbon, and PowerPro lines.
Price:. **$649.99**

SHIMANO CALCUTTA TE DC

Model: 100DC, 200DC, 201DC, 250DC
Gear Ratio: 5.8:1; 5.0:1; 5.0:1; 5.0:1
Inches/Turn: 23
Spool Cap. (M): 30 lbs/115 yds; 40 lbs/95 yds; 40 lbs/95 yds; 40 lbs/115 yds
Weight: 8.6 oz; 9.9 oz; 9.9 oz; 10.2 oz
Hand Retrieve: R; R; L; R
Max Drag: 8.5 lbs; 10 lbs; 10 lbs; 10 lbs
Reel Bearings: 10+1
Features: Anti-rust bearings; lo-mass drilled spool system; A7075 aluminum spool; super free; digital control; high-efficiency gearing; super stopper with assist stopper; dartainium drag; clicking drag adjustment; clicking cast control adjustment; recessed reel foot; drilled crossbar; cold-forged handle shank; adjustable handle shank; rubber handle grip (except 250); septon handle grip (250 only); paddle-style grip (except 250); PV power paddles (250 only); machined aluminum frame; stamped aluminum handle side sideplate; titanium levelwind insert; metal series; platinum service plan; approved for use in salt water; rated for use with mono, fluorocarbon, and PowerPro lines.
Price: **$529.99**

SHIMANO CARDIFF

Model: 200A, 201A, 300A, 301A, 400A, 401A
Gear Ratio: 5.8:1; 5.8:1; 5.8:1; 5.8:1; 5.2:1; 5.2:1
Inches/Turn: 24; 24; 24; 24; 22; 22
Spool Cap. (M): 8 lbs/230 yds; 8 lbs/230 yds; 12 lbs/230 yds; 12 lbs/230 yds; 12 lbs/330 yds; 12 lbs/330 yds
Weight: 8.6 oz; 8.6 oz; 8.9 oz; 8.9 oz; 11.9 oz; 11.9 oz
Hand Retrieve: R; L; R; L; R; L
Max Drag: 10 lbs; 10 lbs; 10 lbs; 10 lbs; 11 lbs; 11 lbs
Reel Bearings: 4+1

Features: Anti-rust bearings; one-piece die-cast aluminum frame; handle side variable brake system; super stopper with assist stopper; non-disengaging levelwind system (400 and 401 only); recessed reel foot (except on models 400A and 401A); three post quick take down (except on 2-post models, CDF100A); rubber handle grip; aluminum sideplates and spool; clicker (400A and 401A only); metal series; approved for use in salt water; rated for use with mono, fluorocarbon, and PowerPro lines.
Price: . . . . $109.99–$119.99

SHIMANO CHRONARCH CI4+

Model: 150CI4, 150CI4HG, 151CI4, 151CI4HG
Gear Ratio: 6.2:1; 7.6:1; 6.2:1; 7.6:1
Inches/Turn: 26; 31; 26; 32
Spool Cap. (M): 10 lbs/145 yds
Weight: 6.5 oz
Hand Retrieve: R; R; L; L
Max Drag: 11 lbs
Reel Bearings: 7+1

Features: CI4+ frame; CI4+ sideplates; recessed reel foot; high-efficiency gearing; super free bearing supported pinion gear system; X-ship; Dartanium II (cross carbon) drag washers; seven bearings; 6 S A-RB BB; 1 A-RB roller clutch bearing; SVS infinity braking system; magnumlite spool; septon PV grips; disengaging levelwind system; Quickfire II clutch bar; made in Japan; approved for use in salt water.
Price: **$269.99**

SHIMANO CITICA

Model: 200G7, 200G6, 201G6, 200G5
Gear Ratio: 7.1:1; 6.5:1; 6.5:1; 5.5:1
Inches/Turn: 30; 27; 27; 23
Spool Cap. (M): 8 lbs/180 yds
Weight: 7.5 oz
Hand Retrieve: R; R; L; R
Max Drag: 11 lbs
Reel Bearings: 3+1

Features: Aluminum frame; lightweight graphite sideplates; recessed reel foot; high-efficiency gearing; super free bearing supported pinion gear system; variable brake system with reduced mass hub; super stopper; assist stopper; 1/8 turn easy access attached sideplate; metal cast control knob; anodized spool and handle; disengaging levelwind system; Quickfire II clutch bar; lo-mass drilled spool system; dartainium drag; four bearings; three-shielded stainless steel BB; approved for use in salt water.
Price: $129.99

SHIMANO CORE
Model: 50MG7, 51MG7, 100MG, 101MG, 100MG7
Gear Ratio: 7.0:1; 7.0:1; 6.2:1; 6.2:1; 7.0:1
Inches/Turn: 28; 28; 26; 26; 30
Spool Cap. (M): 20 lbs/115 yds
Weight: 5.5 oz; 5.5 oz; 6.1 oz; 6.1 oz; 6.7 oz
Hand Retrieve: R; L; R; L; R
Max Drag: 10 lbs; 10 lbs; 11 lbs; 11 lbs; 11 lbs
Reel Bearings: 8+1; 8+1; 4+1; 4+1; 4+1
Features: Ultra-lightweight magnesium frame and sideplates; (CORE50 and 51MG7) has graphite sideplates; ultralightweight A7075 aluminum spool construction; magnumlite spool design; S A-RB ball bearings; A-RB roller bearing; high-efficiency gearing; super stopper; super free; variable brake system; reduced mass VBS hub; escape hatch; dartainium drag; cold-forged aluminum drag star; clicking drag adjustment; aluminum cast control knob; rubber-shielded cast control knob; tapered titanium levelwind insert; cold-forged aluminum handle shank; drilled handle shank; septon handle grips; recessed reel foot; high-speed 6.2:1 gear ratio (CORE100MG only); lightweight aluminum drive gear; paddle grips (CORE100MG only); super high-speed 7.0:1 gear ratio (CORE100MG7 and CORE50/51MG7); heavy duty brass drive gear (CORE100MG7 only); PV power grips (CORE100MG7 only); 1/8 turn easy access attached sideplate (CORE50/51MG only); approved for use in salt water; rated for use with mono, fluorocarbon, and PowerPro lines.
Price:. . . . .**$349.99–$399.99**

CABELA'S PRESTIGE

Model: 1, 2, 3
Gear Ratio: 3; 3.38; 3.75
Weight: 5.4 oz; 6.4 oz; 6.1 oz
Spool Cap. (M): 20 lbs/70 yds WF4; 20 lbs/100 yds WF6; 30 lbs/200 yds WF8

Hand Retrieve: L or R
Line Weight: 3-4; 5-6; 7-8
Features: Mid-arbor design for plenty of backing capacity; molded, paddle-style handle; three sizes available.
Price: **$49.99**

CABELA'S PRESTIGE PREMIER
Model: 1, 2, 3, 4
Gear Ratio: 2.99; 3.38; 3.81; 4.34
Weight: 4.23 oz; 4.58 oz; 5.64 oz; 8.28 oz
Spool Cap. (M): 20 lbs/80 yds WF4; 20 lbs/100 yds WF6;
20 lbs/200 yds WF8; 30 lbs/270 yds WF10

Hand Retrieve: L or R
Line Weight: 1-4; 5-6; 7-8; 9-10
Features: Mid-arbor design for plenty of backing capacity;
molded, paddle-style handle; four sizes available.
Price:. **$89.99**

CABELA'S RLS+

Model: 1, 2, 3, 4
Gear Ratio: 3.23; 3.46; 3.7; 4.13
Weight: 4.9 oz; 5.22 oz; 5.54 oz; 6.31 oz
Spool Cap. (M): 20 lbs/70 yds WF4; 20 lbs/100 yds WF6; 20 lbs/150 yds WF8; 20 lbs/250 yds WF10

Hand Retrieve: L or R
Line weight: 3-4; 5-6; 7-8; 8-10
Features: New lighter weight design; Rulon drag system; large-arbor for a quicker retrieve; easily converts from right- to left-hand.
Price: . . . .**$124.99–$139.99**

CABELA'S TLR

Model: 4, 5
Gear Ratio: 4.49
Weight: 7.76; 7.87
Spool Cap. (M): 30 lbs/200 yds WF10; 30 lbs/200 yds WF12

Hand Retrieve: L or R
Line Weight: 9-10; 11-12
Features: Changeable weight system; durable anodized finish; sealed Rulon disc drag.
Price: **$159.99**

CABELA'S WIND RIVER

Model: 1, 3, 5
Gear Ratio: 3; 3.38; 3.75;
Weight: 5.4 oz; 6.4 oz; 6.1 oz
Spool Cap. (M): 20 lbs/70 yds WF4; 20 lbs/100 yds WF6; 30 lbs/200 yds WF8

Hand Retrieve: L or R
Line Weight: 3-4; 5-6; 7-8
Features: Die-cast/machined-aluminum frame and spool; V-cut arbor spool; smooth Rulon drag.
Price:................................... **$29.99**

CABELA'S WLX
Model: 2.3, 4.5, 5.6, 7.8, 9.10, 11.12
Gear Ratio: 3; 3.15; 3.3; 3.63; 3.95; 4.25
Weight: 3.9 oz; 4.5 oz; 5 oz; 5.75 oz; 6.25 oz; 7.5 oz
Spool Cap. (M): 20 lbs/40 yds; 20 lbs/100 yds; 20 lbs/100 yds; 20 lbs/150 yds; 30 lbs/220 yds; 30 lbs/300 yds
Hand Retrieve: L or R

Line Weight: 2-3; 4-5; 5-6; 7-8; 9-10; 11-12
Features: Engineered exclusively for Cabela's by Waterworks-Lamson; lightweight 6061-T6 aircraft-grade aluminum; sealed drag with smooth-braking Rulon discs; rugged, non-glare anodized finish.
Price: . . . . **$189.99–$229.99**

HARDY FORTUNA X
Model: 1, 2, 3, 4
Gear Ratio: 4.01; 4.25; 4.57; 5.24
Weight: 7.8 oz; 8.4 oz; 12 oz; 13.9 oz
Spool Cap. (M): 20 lbs/200 yds WF8; 30 lbs/200 yds WF10; 30 lbs/275 yds WF12; 30 lbs/550 yds WF14
Hand Retrieve: L or R

Features: Low start-up inertia; largest sizes generate up to 32 pounds of top-end drag; large backing capacities; multi carbon disk brake system; top grade 6061 anodized bar stock aluminium; simple left- to right-hand wind change with tool supplied; secure, quick release, interchangeable spools; seven-point sealed drag system; salt water safe; supplied with neoprene pouch.
Price:. . . . . **$695.00–$845.00**

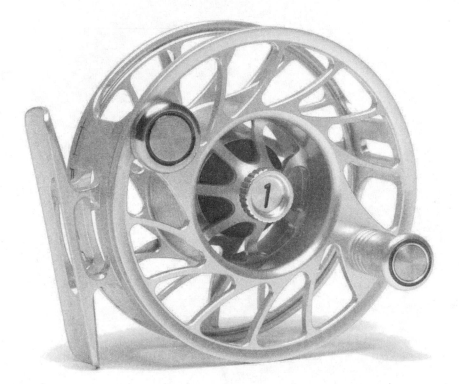

HATCH 1 PLUS FINATIC
Diameter: 2.9 in.
Weight: 2.8 oz
Hand Retrieve: L or R
Line Weight: 0W–2W

Features: We're talking small. You might even use one of these as a key chain. We had never considered a reel of this size since we very rarely fish with 0–2 weight rods. However, our minds changed when we had so many requests. How could we refuse?
Price: **$350.00**

HATCH 3 PLUS FINATIC
Diameter: 3.25 in.
Weight: 4.8 oz
Hand Retrieve: L or R
Line Weight: 3W–5W

Features: The 3 Plus is capable of running 3–5 weight lines with ample backing capacity for the occasional whopper that might come along. At first glance you'll notice this ain't no dainty trout reel. This little wonder means business.
Price: **$400.00**

HATCH 4 PLUS FINATIC
Diameter: 3.425 in.
Weight: 5.2 oz
Hand Retrieve: L or R
Line Weight: 4W–6W

Features: The 4 Plus bridges the gap in size and weight between the 3 and 5 plus models. If you're looking for the perfect reel for your 9' 5-weight rod then look no further.
Price: **$450.00**

REELS

HATCH 7 PLUS FINATIC
Diameter: 4 in.
Weight: 8.6 oz
Hand Retrieve: L or R
Line Weight: 7W–9W

Features: If I was stranded on a desert island and had only one reel to bring, it would be the 7 Plus. We have sold more of these bad boys than any other size in the Hatch line up. From bonefish to permit, steelhead to carp, this reel has you covered.
Price: **$600.00**

HATCH 9 PLUS FINATIC
Diameter: 4.25 in.
Weight: 10.6 oz
Hand Retrieve: L or R
Line Weight: 9W–12W

Features: Where the rubber meets the road my friends! If you've been dreaming of a reel that has the look, feel, and performance of a Ferrari, then look no further. Capable of running 9–12 weight lines, and your choice of mid or large arbor spools, this reel is one versatile hombre.
Price: **$750.00**

L.L.BEAN DOUBLE L MID-ARBOR

Model: #1, #2, #3, #4
Spool Cap. (M): 20 lbs/95 yds WF-3; 20 lbs/115 yds WF-5; 30 lbs/160 yds WF-7; 30 lbs/230 yds WF-9
Hand Retrieve: L or R

Features: Heritage design with added benefits of a larger diameter arbor; retrieves line faster than traditional arbor reels; Aerospace-grade machined aluminum; quick change spool.
Price:. . . . .**$119.00–$149.00**

L.L.BEAN QUEST LARGE ARBOR

Model: #1, #2, #3
Weight: 6.1 oz; 7 oz; 8.6 oz
Spool Cap. (M): 20 lbs/130 yds WF-3; 20 lbs/140 yds WF-5; 30 lbs/240 yds WF-7
Hand Retrieve: L or R

Features: Our most popular reel for beginners; now even better; housing and spool are made from durable die-cast aluminum; smooth in-line disc-drag system protects finer tippets while stopping hard fighting fish.
Price: . . . . **$45.00–$55.00**

L.L.BEAN STREAMLIGHT ULTRA LARGE
Model: #1, #2, #3
Weight: 4.9 oz; 5.3 oz; 6.3 oz
Spool Cap. (M): 20 lbs/105 yds WF-3; 20 lbs/115 lbs WF-5; 30 lbs/170 yds WF-8
Hand Retrieve: L or R

Features: Packed with features you'd find on reels that cost twice as much; machined from bar-stock aluminum that's deeply anodized for corrosion resistance; in-line rulon disc drag is smooth and strong; please note: the flaw noted in customer reviews has been identified and corrected in all inventory.
Price: . . . . **$85.00–$105.00**

OKUMA CASCADE

Model: 4/6, 7/9
Gear Ratio: 2.9; 3.3
Weight: 4 oz; 6 oz
Spool Cap. (M): 20 lbs/125 yds WF4; 20 lbs/135 yds WF7
Hand Retrieve: L or R
Line Weight: 4-5-6; 7-8-9

Features: Fully adjustable multi-disc drag system; roller bearing allows the drag to engage in one direction only; precision machined brass bushing drive system; precision machined stainless steel spool shaft; super lightweight graphite frame construction; corrosio-resistant super large arbor spool design; easy to change left- to right-hand retrieval conversion.
Price: **$34.99**

OKUMA HELIOS

Model: 34, 45, 56, 78a, 89a
Gear Ratio: 2.7; 3; 3.2; 3.5; 3.7
Weight: 4.5 oz; 5 oz; 5.3 oz; 5.9 oz; 6.2 oz
Spool Cap. (M): 12 lbs/105 yds WF3; 20 lbs/110 yds WF4; 20 lbs/130 yds WF5; 20 lbs/150 yds WF7; 20 lbs/250 yds WF8
Hand Retrieve: L or R
Line Weight: 3-4; 4-5; 5-6; 7-8; 8-9

Features: Maintenance-free waterproof drag system; multi-disc cork and stainless steel drag washers; roller bearing allows the drag to engage in one direction only; 2BB+1RB stainless steel drive system; precision machine stainless steel spool shaft; anodized aluminum machined rigid frame; machined aluminum large arbor spool design; non-slip positive grip rubberized handle knobs; easy to change left- to right-hand retrieval conversion.
Price: . . . . $194.99–$209.99

<u>OKUMA INTEGRITY</u>

Model: 5/6b, 7/8b, 8/9b, 10/11b
Gear Ratio: 3; 3; 3.4; 3.9
Weight: 7 oz; 7.5 oz; 8 oz; 8.5 oz
Spool Cap. (M): 12 lbs/70 yds WF5; 20 lbs/50 yds WF7; 20 lbs/100 yds WF8; 30 lbs/170 yds WF10
Hand Retrieve: L or R
Line Weight: 5-6; 7-8; 8-9; 10-11

Features: 5/6 and 7/8 with multi-disc Rulidium drag washers; 8/9 and 10/11 with multi-disc cork drag washers; roller bearing engages drag system in one direction; precision machined stainless steel spool shaft; Alumilite die-cast aluminum frame design; rigid die-cast aluminum, large arbor spool design; precision machined, brass bushing drive; easy to change left- to right-hand retrieval conversion.
Price: . . . .**$69.99–$74.99**

OKUMA SIERRA

Model: 4/5, 5/6, 7/8, 8/9, 10/11
Gear Ratio: 2.6; 2.9; 2.6; 2.9; 3.5
Weight: 5.3 oz; 5.3 oz; 5.3 oz; 5.7 oz; 6 oz
Spool Cap. (M): 12 lbs/105 yds WF4; 20 lbs/160 yds WF5; 20 lbs/75 yds WF7; 20 lbs/150 yds WF8; 30 lbs/285 yds WF10
Hand Retrieve: L or R
Line Weight: 4-5; 5-6; 7-8; 8-9; 10-11

Features: Fully adjustable Teflon and stainless drag system; roller bearing allows the drag to engage in one direction only; precision machined brass bushing drive system; precision machined stainless steel spool shaft; Alumilite die-cast aluminum frame; die-cast standard arbor spool design; easy to change left- to right-hand retrieval conversion.
Price: . . . .**$44.99–$59.99**

OKUMA SLV

Model: 2/3, 4/5, 5/6, 7/8, 8/9, 10/11
Gear Ratio: 2.6; 3; 3.2; 3.5; 3.7; 4.5
Weight: 4.5 oz; 4.8 oz; 5.3 oz; 5.5 oz; 6.1 oz; 9.7 oz
Spool Cap. (M): 12 lbs/50 yds WF2; 12 lbs/95 yds WF4; 20 lbs/140 yds WF5; 20 lbs/145 yds WF7; 30 lbs/150 yds WF8; 30 lbs/220 yds WF10
Hand Retrieve: L or R
Line Weight: 2-3; 4-5; 5-6; 7-8; 8-9; 10-11

Features: Multi-disc cork and stainless steel drag washers; roller bearing allows the drag to engage in one direction only; precision machined brass bushing drive system; precision machined stainless steel spool shaft; Alumilite die-cast; aluminum frame die-cast super large arbor spool design; non-slip positive grip rubberized handle knobs; easy to change left- to right-hand retrieval conversion.
Price: **$64.99**

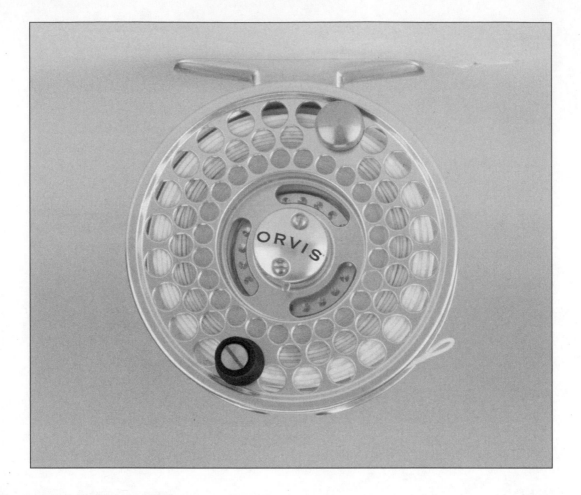

ORVIS ACCESS MID-ARBOR
Model: I, II, III, IV, V
Gear Ratio: 2.75; 3; 3.25; 3.5; 4
Weight: 4.29 oz; 4.45 oz; 4.62 oz; 5.28 oz; 5.88 oz
Spool Cap. (M): 12 lbs/150 yds WF1; 20 lbs/150 yds WF3; 20 lbs/150 yds WF5; 20 lbs/225 yds WF7; 30 lbs/250 yds WF9
Hand Retrieve: L or R
Line Weight: 1-3; 3-5; 5-7; 7-9; 9-11

Features: New Mirage gold anodizing; new larger Mirage-style handle; totally sealed drag surfacel carbon fiber/stainless steel washer drag system; 6061 aircraft bar stock; available in sizes I-V; all models have a two carbon fiber, stainless steel washer drag system; positive drag click system; available in new gold, black, titanium.
Price:.........................$145.00–$185.00

ORVIS CFO DISC DRAG

Model: I, II, III
Gear Ratio: 2.75; 2.875; 3
Weight: 3.6 oz; 3.9 oz; 4 oz
Spool Cap. (M): 12 lbs/125 yds WF1; 20 lbs/75 yds WF3; 20 lbs/75 yds WF5
Hand Retrieve: L or R
Line Weight: 1-3; 3-5; 5-7
Features: The CFO fly-fishing reel has been the choice of technical fly fisherman since 1971. Reengineered to be lighter, smoother, and tougher. Although this fly fishing reel is machined using the most modern of materials and state-of-the-art machining technology, the CFO disc drag fly reel is a reverent nod to fly-fishing tradition. The reel's signature look and sound are synonymous for thousands of fly fisherman with great moments on the water. It matches as perfectly in spirit, looks, and performance with Orvis Superfine or bamboo fly rods as it does with our high-tech Helios fly rods.
Price:. . . . . $225.00–$255.00

REELS: Freshwater Fly Fishing

ORVIS CLEARWATER LARGE ARBOR

Model: II, IV
Gear Ratio: 3.375; 3.875
Weight: 5.5 oz; 6.3 oz
Hand Retrieve: L or R
Line Weight: 4-6; 7-9
Features: Finally a cast aluminum large arbor fly-fishing reel that's lightweight enough to balance properly with your favorite fly rod and truly the best value fly reel around. Two years in design and development and with a powerful inline, Rulon to stainless, stacked disc drag that can hold its own with high-performance machined reels, the all new Clearwater Large Arbor costs significantly less than its machined cousins, but has not only the looks, but the guts of a higher-priced version. Easily converted to either left- or right-hand retrieve, the Clearwater fly reel has a positive click drag knob for consistent settings every time. Whether you're looking for your first large arbor, fishing on a budget, or want a spare or two in the bag, the new Clearwater Large Arbor can handle anything a machined reel can and completely changes the game in die-cast reels.
Price: $79.00

REELS

ORVIS CLEARWATER LARGE ARBOR CASSETTE

Model: Clearwater Large Arbor Cassette
Gear Ratio: 3.875
Weight: 6.9 oz
Hand Retrieve: L or R
Line Weight: 6-8
Features: Finally a cast aluminium large arbor that's lightweight enough to balance properly with your favourite rod. Two years in design and development and with a powerful inline, Rulon to stainless, stacked disc drag that can hold its own with high-performance machined reels,

the all new Clearwater Large Arbor cassette fly reel costs significantly less than its machined cousins, but has not only the looks, but the guts of a higher-priced version. Easily converted to either left or right hand retrieve, the Clearwater has a positive click drag knob for consistent settings every time. The innovative cassette offers extreme versatility and allows the angler to switch to the correct rig quickly and easily. Great performance, excellent versatility, and an incredibly low price. Cassette fly reel comes with two spare spools and a Cordura reel case.
Price:. **$125.00**

ORVIS MIRAGE

Model: I, II, III, IV, V, VI, VII Shallow, VII Deep
Gear Ratio: 3; 3.25; 3.5; 4; 4.25; 4.5; 5; 5
Weight: 3.8 oz; 4.3 oz; 4.8 oz; 7.2 oz; 7.7 oz; 10 oz; 11.7 oz; 11.5 oz
Spool Cap. (M): 12 lbs/150 yds WF1; 20 lbs/150 yds WF3; 20 lbs/150 yds WF5; 20 lbs/225 yds WF7; 30 lbs/250 yds WF9; 30 lbs/350 yds WF11; 30 lbs/350 yds WF11; 50 lbs/600 yds WF14
Hand Retrieve: L or R
Line Weight: 1–3, 3–5, 5–7, 7–9, 9–11, 11–13, 11–13, 13–15
Features: A completely sealed and maintenance-free drag surface, impervious to salt water, dirt, grit, and other corrosive elements to last longer and hold up to real world abuse. A positive-click drag knob for accurate and repeatable drag settings. True large arbor performance picks up line fast to give you the edge over all fresh and salt water fish: from trout and panfish to bonefish, stripers, tarpon, tuna, marlin, and sails. Crafted of strong yet lightweight anodized 6061 T6 aluminum with a heavily-ventilated spool to shed weight yet keep its strength. Special handle shape reduces line from catching. Aggressive diamond knurling on knob for easier grasp and adjustment mid-battle. Quick release spool and easy conversion from left- to right-hand retrieve.
Price: . . . . **$425.00–$545.00**

PFLUEGER TRION
Model: 1934, 1956, 1978, 1990
Hand retrieve: L or R
Features: Ball bearings; instant anti-reverse bearing; forged, machined, and anodized aluminum frame and spool; central-disc drag system for total drag control; convertible left and right hand retrieve; large rosewood knob.
Price:. **$130.00**

SCIENTIFIC ANGLERS CONCEPT 2

Model: Model 58
Gear Ratio: 3.31
Weight: 4.3 oz
Spool Cap. (M): 20 lbs/200 yds WF5
Hand retrieve: L or R
Features: Durable, lightweight composite polymer graphite; perforated for lighter, easier handling; counter-balanced spool for vibration-free runs; heavy-duty compression disc drag; palming rim for added drag pressure; durable, corrosion-resistant graphite composition; no tools needed easy-change from right- to left-hand; easy-to-handle and built for bigger fish.

Price: **$33.95**

<u>SCIENTIFIC ANGLERS SYSTEM 4</u>

Model: 3/4, 5/6, 7/8
Gear Ratio: 3.125; 3.5; 3.75
Weight: 5.22 oz; 5.44 oz; 6.04 oz
Hand Retrieve: L or R
Line Weight: 3-8
Features: 6061-T6 proprietary aluminum alloy; Delrin 500AF with impregnated Teflon (space-age polymer that is durable, heat resistant, self-lubricating, and maintenance-free); Delrin 500AF to anodized aluminum interface (push frame friction disc drag system with redundancy radial pawl engagement and seamless transition between line-in and drag engagement [no startup friction]); fully machined, one-piece frame, one-piece spool with a Delrin pressed hub (manufactured on automated CNC machining centers); Delrin hub rotating on a stainless steel spindle (Sizes 3/4, 5/6), oil impregnated bronze bushing rotating on a stainless steel spindle (Size 7/8), quick-release locking spool, easy left-hand to right-hand retrieve conversion.
Price: . . . . **$200.00–$250.00**

TEMPLE FORK BVK SUPER LARGE ARBOR REEL

Model: 0, I, II, III, IV
Gear Ratio: 2.75; 3.30; 3.75; 4.10; 4.75
Weight: 2.1 oz; 4.6 oz; 4.9 oz; 5.2 oz; 8.7 oz
Spool Cap. (M): 20 lbs/50 yds WF1; 20 lbs/75 yds WF4; 20 lbs/200 yds WF6; 20 lbs/205 yds WF8; 30 lbs/275 yds WF12
Hand Retrieve: L or R
Features: BVK reels are precision machined from bar stock aluminum. The moss green anodized frames and spools are ported to eliminate excess weight. Equally at home in both fresh and salt waters, the super large arbor design provides faster line pick up and helps the maintenance free drag system work at a more constant pressure that standard arbor reels. Delrin/Stainless stacked discs make the drag silky smooth and the one way clutch bearing makes engagement instant and left to right hand conversion simple. BVK reels are available in moss green only.
Price: . . . . **$149.95–$299.95**

TEMPLE FORK HSR
Model: I, II
Gear Ratio: 2.875; 3.25
Weight: 4 oz; 4.5 oz
Spool Cap. (M): 20 lbs/75 yds WF5; 20 lbs/150 yds WF8
Hand Retrieve: L or R

Features: New for 2013, the HSR family of reels is sure to make a big splash. These reels are machined aluminum and anodized for use in fresh or salt water. They feature a sealed stainless steel and delrin drag system for maximum fish-stopping power without all the maintenance.
Price:. . . . . **$149.95–$159.95**

TEMPLE FORK NXT

Model: I, II
Gear Ratio: 3.10; 3.40; 3.75; 4.25
Weight: 6.2 oz; 7.5 oz; 8 oz; 9.2 oz
Spool Cap. (M): 20 lbs/100 yds WF6; 20 lbs/150 yds WF8; 20 lbs/250 yds WF8; 30 lbs/275 yds WF10
Hand Retrieve: L or R

Features: TFO Large Arbor reels are machined from 6061 aluminum and offer a state-of-the-art draw bar/carbon fiber disc drag. Three bearings give our reel its smooth as silk spin, and a one-way roller bearing makes it easily convertible from left- to right-hand retrieve. TFO 375 reels are now available in Black, Red, Gold, and Pewter.
Price:. . . . . **$249.95–$299.95**

TEMPLE FORK PRISM CAST LARGE ARBOR

Model: 3/4, 5/6, 7/8, 9/11
Gear Ratio: 2.75; 3; 3.38; 4.25
Weight: 4.9 oz; 5.5 oz; 5.8 oz; 8.7 oz
Spool Cap. (M): 20 lbs/80 yds WF3; 20 lbs/100 yds WF5; 20 lbs/150 yds WF8; 30 lbs/265 yds WF10
Hand Retrieve: L or R

Features: Consistent with TFO's tradition of offering high-performance gear at an affordable price, the new Prism Cast Large Arbor Reels are made from cast aluminum with a cork disc drag and a one-way clutch bearing for instant drag engagement. They feature quick change spools and easy LH/RH conversion.
Price:. . . . .**$84.95–$99.95**

HARDY FORTUNA X

Model: 1, 2, 3, 4
Gear Ratio: 4.01; 4.25; 4.57; 5.24
Weight: 7.8 oz; 8.4 oz; 12 oz; 13.9 oz
Spool Cap. (M): 20 lbs/200 yds WF8; 30 lbs/200 yds WF10; 30 lbs/275 yds WF12; 30 lbs/550 yds WF14
Hand Retrieve: L or R
Features: Low start-up inertia; largest sizes generate up to 32 pounds of top-end drag; large backing capacities; multi carbon disk brake system; top grade 6061 anodized bar stock aluminium; simple left- to right-hand wind change with tool supplied; secure, quick release; interchangeable spools; seven-pint sealed drag system; salt water safe; supplied with neoprene pouch.
Price: . . . . **$695.00–$845.00**

HATCH 5 PLUS FINATIC
Diameter: 3.625 in.
Weight: 6.5 oz
Hand Retrieve: L or R
Line Weight: 5W–7W

Features: We've used this workhorse surf fishing in So Cal, light steelheading in Oregon, chucking nasty streamers to ravenous browns in Montana, and stalking bones on the flats in Belize.
Price: **$500.00**

HATCH 7 PLUS FINATIC
Diameter: 4 in.
Weight: 8.6 oz
Hand Retrieve: L or R
Line Weight: 7W–9W

Features: If I was stranded on a desert island and had only one reel to bring, it would be the 7 Plus. We have sold more of these bad boys than any other size in the Hatch line up. From bonefish to permit, steelhead to carp, this reel has you covered.
Price: **$600.00**

HATCH 9 PLUS FINATIC
Diameter: 4.25 in.
Weight: 10.6 oz
Hand Retrieve: L or R
Line Weight: 9W–12W

Features: Where the rubber meets the road my friends! If you've been dreaming of a reel that has the look, feel and performance of a Ferrari, then look no further. Capable of running 9–12 weight lines, and your choice of mid or large arbor spools, this reel is one versatile hombre.
Price: **$750.00**

HATCH 11 PLUS FINATIC
Diameter: 4.625 in.
Weight: 11.1 oz
Hand Retrieve: L or R
Line Weight: 11W–12W

Features: The goal was to create a larger reel that bridged the gap between the 9 and 12 Plus models. We also wanted to make sure it had an oversized handle for greater grip control when fighting those big silver critters. The mid arbor option is also great for spey rods from 13.5–14.5 feet.
Price: **$825.00**

HATCH 12 PLUS FINATIC
Diameter: 5 in.
Weight: 15.6 oz
Hand Retrieve: L or R
Line Weight: 12W–16W
Features: Conventional wisdom says: Never take a knife to a gunfight. And when you're tackling big fish like the ones this reel was designed for, then I think that's really sound advice. GTs or tuna, just to name a few, can undo your average gear in a fraction of a second. You will not find a better fish-fighting tool on the market for these situations. Oh yeah, it's also great for big spey applications.
Price:. **$900.00**

OKUMA CEDROS

Model: 5/6, 7/8, 8/9
Gear Ratio: 3.2; 3.5; 3.7
Weight: 6 oz; 6.6 oz; 7.4 oz
Spool Cap. (M): 20 lbs/130 yds WF5; 20 lbs/150 yds WF7; 20 lbs/250 yds WF8
Hand Retrieve: L or R
Line Weight: 5-6; 7-8; 8-9

Features: Low start-up inertia; largest sizes generate up to 32 pounds of top-end drag; large backing capacities; multi carbon disk brake system; top grade 6061 anodized bar stock aluminium; simple left- to right-hand wind change with tool supplied; secure, quick release, interchangeable spools; seven-point sealed drag system; salt water safe; supplied with neoprene pouch.
Price:. . . . . $199.99–$219.99

TEMPLE FORK HSR
Model: I, II
Gear Ratio: 2.875; 3.25
Weight: 4 oz; 4.5 oz
Spool Cap. (M): 20 lbs/75 yds WF5; 20 lbs/150 yds WF8
Hand Retrieve: L or R

Features: New for 2013, the HSR family of reels is sure to make a big splash. These reels are machined aluminum and anodized for use in fresh or salt water. They feature a sealed stainless steel and delrin drag system for maximum fish-stopping power without all the maintenance.
Price:............................**$149.95–$159.95**

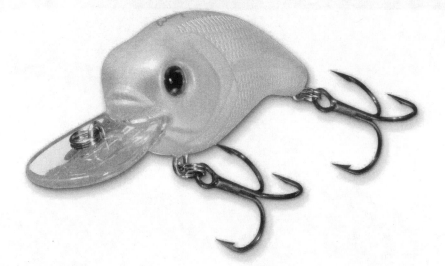

BASS PRO SHOPS CRAPPIE MAXX CRANK

Type: Crankbait
Color/Pattern: Pearl Shad, Chewing Gum, Lavender Shad, Midnight Fire, Chartreuse Shad, Watermelon Shad, Pinky Toe, Ole Miss, Albino Shad, Pearl Shad, Chewing Gum
Size: 1-5/8 in, 2 in

Weight: 3/16 oz, 1/3 oz, 5/16 oz, ¼ oz
Running Depth: 4 ft, 6 ft, 10 ft
Features: Hottest bait to hit crappie fishing in a long time; serious slab enticing features; tight wobble; highly detailed design; 3D lazer eyes; quality components; fiving depths up to 10'.
Price: **$4.29**

BASS PRO SHOPS EXTREME TOURNAMENT CRANKBAIT

Type: Crankbait
Color/Pattern: Chartreuse Silver, Ghost Spook, Baby Bass, Bone XXX Shad
Size: 2 ¾ in
Weight: ½ oz

Running Depth: 9 ft
Features: Tight-wiggling, lifelike baitfish action; quality components; 3D eyes
Price: **$2.29**

BASS PRO SHOPS XPS BALSA BOOGIE CRANKBAIT

Type: Crankbait
Color/Pattern: Firetiger, Homer, Pearl Red Eye, Red Crawfish, Blue Silver Shad, Orange Brown Crawfish, Plum Crazy, Fried Green Tomato, Texas Shad, Chrome XXX Shad, Gold XXX Shad, Bone XXX Shad, Chartreuse Green Craw
Size: 2 ¾ in

Weight: ½ oz
Running Depth: 4 ft
Features: Balsa body with precisely angled diving lip; rolling, vibrating action bass can't refuse; 3D laser eyes; loud internal rattles; VMC premium hooks
Price: **$5.99**

LURES

BASS PRO SHOPS XPS WHEEL N' DEAL
Type: Crankbait
Color/Pattern: Black/Orange, Black Shad, Pearl/White, Black Firetail, Black/Green, Black Frog, Dirty Duck
Size: 8 ¼ in
Weight: 2 ¼ oz
Running Depth: Topwater

Features: Twin chopper blade head section; single prop tail section; high-impact polystyrene body; 1.6 mm diameter through wire construction; 2 - 2/0 belly hooks; 1 - 3/0 tail hook
Price: **$19.99**

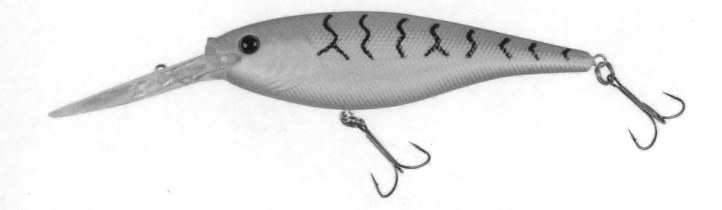

BERKLEY FLICKER SHAD

Type: Crankbait
Color/Pattern: Purple Cougar, Black Gold, Black Gold Sunset, Black Silver, Blue Tiger, Chartreuse Pearl, White Tiger, Red Tiger, Shad, Purple Tiger, Chrome Clown, Firetiger, Orange Tiger, Blue Scale Shad, Uncle Rico, Pearl White, Tennesse Shad, Dirty Craw, Chartreuse Growler, Blue Growler, Retro Shad, Perch
Size: 1 3/5 in; 2 in; 2 2/5 in; 2 ¾ in; 3 ½ in;

Weight: 1/8 oz, 3/16 oz, ¼ oz, 5/16 oz, ½ oz
Running Depth: 6 ft–8 ft, 9 ft–11 ft, 10 ft–12 ft, 11 ft–13 ft
Features: Designed by pros for optimal action, the Flicker Shad has a unique rattle and extra-sharp black-nickel hooks for solid hooksets. Ideal for trolling or cast and retrieve.
Price:............................. **$3.99–$5.99**

BERKLEY FLICKER SHAD PRO SLICK

Type: Crankbait
Color/Pattern: Slick Chartreuse Pearl, Slick Firetiger, Slick Green Pearl, Slick Mouse, Slick Purple Bengal, Slick Purple Candy, Slick Purple Pearl, Slick Racy, Slick Sunset
Size: 1 ½ in; 2 in; 2 ¼ in; 3 ¾ in
Weight: 1/8 oz, 3/16 oz, ¼ oz, 5/16 oz

Running Depth: 6 ft–8 ft, 9 ft–11 ft, 10 ft–12 ft, 11 ft–13 ft
Features: Berkley has worked with the Pros to design multiple sizes of Flicker Shads to match the hatch. The unique action creates a "Flicker" that imitates a fleeing baitfish.
Price: **$4.95**

BOMBER DEEP LONG A
Type: Stick bait
Color/Pattern: Fire River Minnow, Chrome Orange Belly Black Back, Fire Tiger Bass, Silver Flash Red Head, Silver Prism Blue Black, Gold Chrome, Silver Flash, Silver Flash Orange Belly, Chartreuse Flash Orange Belly, Pearl Black Orange, Baby Striper, Silver Flash Blue Black, Rainbow Trout, Gold Prism Black Back Bars
Size: 2 ½ in; 4 ½ in
Weight: 3/8 oz, ¾ oz
Running Depth: 10 ft–12 ft, 12 ft–15 ft

Features: Well-known as a big fish bait, the Bomber Deep Long A employs the original Long A's trademark action and adds a molded-in, deep-diving lip for extreme durability and out-of-the-package true- running performance. This deep-running version of the classic long A is especially effective when twitched for early season bass and can be trolled with precision for walleye, salmon, and striper.
Price: . . . . **$5.29–$5.99**

BOMBER LONG A

Type: Stick bait
Color/Pattern: Fire River Minnow, Chrome Orange Belly Black Back, Fire Tiger Bass, Silver Flash Red Head, Silver Prism Blue Black, Gold Chrome, Silver Flash, Silver Flash Orange Belly, Chartreuse Flash Orange Belly, Pearl Black Orange, Baby Striper, Silver Flash Blue Black, Rainbow Trout, Gold Prism Black Back Bars
Size: 3 ½ in; 4 ½ in
Weight: 3/8 oz, ½ oz

Running Depth: 2 ft–3 ft, 3 ft–4 ft
Features: You won't catch many pros without a jerkbait rigged, no matter the season. That's because the minnow imitator is well known as one of the single most versatile baits. The Long A is the best of the best when it comes to replicating a life- like swimming action. With a tight wiggle and castable design, the Long A is equally effective for largemouth, smallmouth, stripers, walleye, and pike.
Price: **$4.99**

LURES

BOMBER SWITCHBACK SHAD

Type: Crankbait
Color/Pattern: Hot Bream, Purple Darter, Red Crawfish, Sour Grape, Ghost Craw, Bama Shad, Foxy Phantom, Switchback Shad, Tennessee Special
Size: 2 ½ in; 3 in
Weight: ½ oz, ¾ oz
Running Depth: 4 ft–8 ft, 8 ft–14 ft, 10 ft–14 ft, 14 ft–18 ft
Features: It's easy to see why the Bomber Switchback Shad helped Tim win the 2007 Champion's Choice Elite event—it's action is so smooth! That day the fish were actively feeding on rock pile and Tim needed a subtle approach, not the reaction strike, and this bait proved to be the ticket. To further improve the design we incorporated a rattle you can turn on and off by locking the ball bearings in a chamber by simply rotating the crank until they're secure. It's very easy to do on the fly and adds a lot of versatility to your approach.
Price: **$7.99**

BOOYAH BUZZ

Type: Buzzbait
Color/Pattern: Black, White/Chartreuse Shad, Chartreuse Shad, Citrus Shad, Limetreuse Shad, Snow White Shad
Weight: ¼ oz, 3/8 oz, ½ oz
Features: The BOOYAH Buzz is made with premium hard coat paint, extra large 3D red eyes and flared red gills that illicit vicious strikes; the BOOYAH Buzz Bait planes quickly and runs true out of the package. The BOOYAH Buzz Bait clacker really attacks the blade to provide additional fish attracting vibration and the 55-strand Bio-Flex silicone skirt and a 5/0 Mustad Ultra Point hook seal the deal.
Price: **$3.99**

BOOYAH COUNTER STRIKE BUZZ

Type: Buzzbait
Color/Pattern: Alpine, Cortez Shad, Glowbee, Limesicle, Luna
Weight: ¼ oz, 3/8 oz, ½ oz
Features: The BOOYAH Counter Strike Buzz's counter-rotating blades deliver exceptional stability and offer a distinctive sound that fish have not heard, even in heavily fished waters. Designed with the unique triangle-shaped head, the Counter Strike Buzz will plane to the surface quickly and cut through amazingly thick cover. A multi-step painting process that creates realistic scales and eyes, silicone skirt, plated blades that maximize flash, and an XCalibur Tx3 hook combine with Counter Strike Technology to create the ultimate buzzbait.
Price:. **$7.99**

BOOYAH DOUBLE WILLOW BLADE

Type: Spinnerbait
Color/Pattern: Chartreuse, Chartreuse Perch, Chartreuse White Shad, Citrus Shad, Gold Shiner, Perch, Satin Silver Glimmer, Silver Shad, Snow White, White Chartreuse, Wounded Shad
Weight: 3/8 oz, ½ oz, ¾ oz, 1 oz
Features: The BOOYAH Double Willow Blade is a proven bass tournament winning spinnerbait. It's designed for maximum vibration, making it perfect for cool- or murky-water situations. The 55-strand Bio-Flex silicone skirt undulates like a baitfish and hides one of the toughest and sharpest hooks in the business.
Price: **$4.99**

LURES

BOOYAH MICRO POND MAGIC

Type: Spinnerbait
Color/Pattern: Alpine, Fire Ant, Lightning Bug, Locust
Weight: 1/8 oz
Features: The Booyah Micro Pond Magic is a unique, fish-catching bait in its own right. It's tough, durable, and catches fish in big lakes as well as ponds and streams. This 1/8 oz spinnerbait features a true-running "R" bend wire for incredible vibration and a single Colorado blade that provides the perfect amount of flash and water displacement. The 40 strand Bio-Flex silicone skirt features all of the baitfish and insect patterns available in the Pond Magic line. The head features realistic 3-D eye, a high-quality Mustad round-bend hook and a ball bearing swivel. Early season or any time fish are finicky, tie on a Micro Pond Magic.
Price: **$2.49**

BOOYAH MINI SHAD

Type: Spinnerbait
Color/Pattern: Chartreuse Gold Shiner, Golden Shiner, Pearl Shiner, Purple Glimmer Shad, Silver Chartreuse
Weight: 3/16 oz
Features: 3/16-ounce BOOYAH Mini Shad Spinnerbait A bait that was born in ultra clear water, the BOOYAH Mini Shad may be diminutive in stature but that doesn't mean it's not a big time, big fish bait. This spinnerbait has three willow blades, a 50-strand silicone skirt, amazing lifelike detail and it is capable of running true at high retrieve speeds, this is the bait to call them up.
Price: **$4.99**

LURES

BOOYAH PAD CRASHER
Type: Frog
Color/Pattern: Aqua Frog, Albino Frog, Bull Frog, Kuro Frog, Leopard Frog, Swamp Frog, Cricket Frog, Shad Frog, Dart Frog
Size: 2 ½ in
Weight: ½ oz
Running Depth: Topwater

Features: The BOOYAH Pad Crasher soft plastic is just the right consistency to ensure solid, consistent hook-ups while remaining weed and snag-free. The belly features "chines" that make "walking the frog" easy in open water, and it's just the right weight for pulling over slop or through the pads for big bass. Realistic decoration schemes and adjustable spinnerbait-style legs seal the deal for big bass.
Price: **$5.99**

BOOYAH POND MAGIC

Type: Spinnerbait
Color/Pattern: Craw, Firebug, Firefly, Grasshopper, Hornet, Junebug, Moss Back Craw, Nest Robber, Okie Craw, Shad, Sunrise Craw
Weight: 3/16 oz
Features: BOOYAH Pond Magic is specialized in color and blade combinations that have been hand selected to match the forage base of smaller waters. Small in size by spinnerbait standards but certainly not short on features. Premium components and 60-strand ultra fine silicone skirts make these every bit the quality of our BOOYAH Blades. Pick up a Pond Magic and you'll find out quickly that these are fish-catching machines.
Price: . . . . **$2.99–$3.99**

BOOYAH POPPIN' PAD CRASHER

Type: Frog
Color/Pattern: Aqua Frog, Bull Frog, Cricket Frog, Dart Frog, Leopard Frog, Shad Frog, Swamp Frog
Size: 2 ½ in
Weight: ½ oz
Running Depth: Topwater
Features: The Booyah Poppin' Pad Crasher is perfect for those times when you need more surface disturbance to get the fish to commit. Windy days, thick slop, and finicky fish that have seen other frogs all day long still will take the different action of the Poppin' Pad Crasher. It's great for fishing the slop but, with the cupped mouth also doubles as a popper/chugger in open water. This BOOYAH fishing lure is a great topwater lure, ideal for bass fishing.
Price: **$5.99**

BOOYAH SUPER SHAD

Type: Spinnerbait
Color/Pattern: Golden Shiner, Purple Glimmer Shad, Silver Chartreuse
Weight: 3/8 oz
Features: The BOOYAH Super Shad Spinnerbait is a bit larger than other spinners, but most of those don't sport four blades! Put the Super Shad in motion, and you'll swear you're looking at a pod of baitfish fleeing through the water. So will the bass and muskie. Combine the Super Shad's quad blades with its seductively undulating skirt, and you've got a Booyah big fish spinner in a class all by itself.
Price: **$5.69**

BOOYAH VIBRA-FLX

Type: Spinnerbait
Color/Pattern: AYU, Baby Bass, Blue Gill, Foxy Shad, Golden Shiner, Herring, Hitch, Kentucky Magic, Okie Shad, Shadtreuse
Weight: 3/8 oz, ½ oz
Features: BOOYAH Vibra-Flx spinnerbiat has added spinnerbait vibration, which means extra fish-attracting potency. The BOOYAH Vibra-Flx Spinnerbait apart of the BOOYAH Vibra-Flx fishing lures line. The BOOYAH Vibra-Flx Spinngerbait's frame is built from Vibra-Flx wire, which creates more vibration than standard stainless wire. In addition, Vibra-Flx wire offers flexible memory (meaning it stays tuned after several catches) and added toughness (twice as strong as standard stainless wire frames). Every BOOYAH Vibra-Flx Spinnerbait comes loaded with great features, including counter-rotating blades and a new Silo-Tek skirt, which undulates like flat rubber, but because it is silicone, it is much more durable.

Price: **$6.99**

CREEK CHUB SURFSTER

Type: Crankbait
Color/Pattern: Bone, Yellow Croaker
Size: 4 ½ in; 6 in; 7 in
Weight: 1 ½ oz, 2 ½ oz, 4 oz
Water Type: Saltwater

Features: Traditional stainless steel lip; super-tough stainless steel; ultra-realistic large pupil eyes; the perfect target for big predators; rugged heavy swivels; sturdy triple split rings; saltwater grade hooks.
Price: **$16.99; $19.99; $21.99**

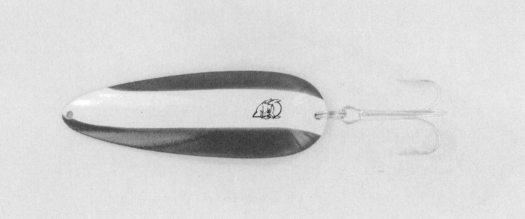

EPPINGER DARDEVLE SPOON
Type: Casting/trolling spoon
Color/Pattern: Nickel, Brass, Crackle Frog, Red/White, Black/White, Yellow/Black Diamond, Yellow/5 of Diamonds, Chartreuse/Orange Scale, Orange/Black Spots, Brown Trout, Pink Diamond, Glow Fluorescent Green Dot, Glow Fluorescent Orange Dot, Glow Green, Glow Blue, Glow Orange, Hot Firetiger/Black, Chartreuse/Lime, Grey Shad, Hot Shad, Rainbow Trout, Chartreuse/Red Spots, Orange/Green Perch Scale, Hammered Nickel/Blue, Hammered Nickel, Red/White Stripe, Fluorescent Orange/Black Spots, Yellow/Green Diamond
Size: 15/16 in–5 ½ in
Weight: 3/16 oz, ¼ oz, 2/5 oz, ¾ oz, 1 oz, 1 ¾ oz, 2 oz, 3 ¼ oz
Features: Only high-quality metal, durable enamels and strong steel hooks are used on a genuine Dardevle spoon; for nearly a century, these perfectly balanced spoons and their wobble action have helped land fish; made in USA.
Price:. . . . .**$3.79–$12.99**

HEDDON LUCKY 13

Type: Topwater bait
Color/Pattern: Baby Bass Red Gill, Bullfrog, Fluorescent Green Crawdad, Black Shiner Glitter, Red Head
Size: 2 5/8 in; 3 ¾ in
Weight: 5/8 oz
Features: The Lucky 13 produces a deep, resonating sound that drives gamefish crazy when it's chugged. Long considered one of the best lures made for catching schooling fish, the Lucky 13's size and action make it a true fresh- and saltwater multispecies bait (bass, pike, stripers, white bass, speckled trout, redfish, and other inshore species).
Price: **$6.29**

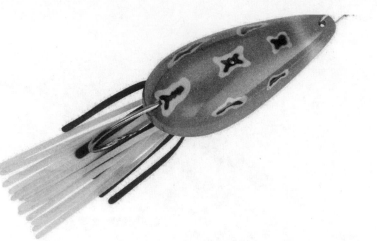

HEDDON MOSS BOSS

Type: Crankbait
Color/Pattern: Black Scale, Bullfrog, Chartreuse/Black Scale, White/Scale
Size: 2 1/5 in; 3 in
Weight: 3/8 oz, ¼ oz
Features: The Moss Boss is indeed the "boss" when it comes to tempting lunkers into striking from under the thickest moss, weed beds, and brush. The Moss Boss has been perfectly designed to glide easily over and through the heaviest of cover, the kind of cover that holds big muskie, bass, and northerns. When a lunker spies a Moss Boss sliding through the weeds overhead it makes for one of the most exciting strikes ever!
Price: **$4.69**

LURES

HEDDON ONE KNOCKER SPOOK

Type: Topwater bait
Color/Pattern: Blue Shad, Okie Shad, Baby Bass, G-Finish Shad, Ghost, G-Finish Bull Frog
Size: 4 ½ in
Weight: ¾ oz

Features: The One Knocker Spook thumps bass with a sound like no other topwater bait. The single tungsten rattle contained in a sound-intensifying chamber produces a loud thump that draws fish from long distances. Its positioning within the body of the lure makes walking-the-dog easier than ever. Fourteen color patterns and Mustad Triple Grip hooks take care of the rest.
Price: **$7.99**

LURES

HEDDON RATTLIN' SPOOK

Type: Topwater bait
Color/Pattern: Bone, Foxy Momma, Foxy Shad, Ghost, Okie Shad, Pearl Melon, Pearl Shad
Size: 4 ½ in
Weight: ¾ oz
Features: The Rattlin' Spook adds tremendous sound to your dog walking. A new rattle chamber containing tungsten BB's amplifies and intensifies the sounds of panicked and fleeing baitfish. This unique sound chamber also makes it easier to produce smooth walk-the-dog retrieves. Fourteen realistic color patterns and Mustad Triple Grip Hooks seal the deal when big bass crash the surface.
Price: **$6.99**

HEDDON SPIT'N IMAGE

Type: Topwater bait
Color/Pattern: Gizzard Shad, Threadfin Shad.
Size: 3 in; 3 ¼ in
Weight: 5/16 oz, 7/16 oz
Features: The Heddon Spit'n Image perfectly mimics the frantic antics of a fleeing shad—in fact, it's the Spit'n Image of one! When retrieved, the Spit'n Image moves from side to side; at rest, the tail sits low in the water. The Spit'n Image Jr. is a little more rounded and has a little more bounce than the original Heddon Spit'n Image.
Price: **$6.99**

HEDDON SUPER SPOOK

Type: Topwater bait
Color/Pattern: Nickel, Chartreuse, Black/Chartreuse/Gold Insert, Spectrum, Florida Bass, Lake Fork Shad, Bleeding Shiner, Clear, Oakie Shad, Clown, Foxy Shad, Bone.
Size: 5 in
Weight: 7/8 oz

Features: Often imitated, impossible to duplicate, the Super Spook is just as deadly as the original Zara Spook introduced decades ago. Oversized eyes and the trademark walk-the-dog action make everything from bass to redfish attack with a vengeance. Fish don't simply bite a Super Spook, they attack it. Per each.
Price: **$6.99**

HEDDON SUPER SPOOK JR.

Type: Topwater bait
Color/Pattern: Bone/Silver, Chartreuse/Black Head, Black/Chartreuse Gold, Spectrum, Golden Shiner, Red Head, Silver Mullet, Speckled Trout.
Size: 3 ½ in
Weight: ½ oz

Features: The Heddon Super Spook Jr. features the tough construction and good looks of the full-sized Super Spook in a smaller, but still explosive, fish-catching design. Rugged line ties and hooks ensure the Super Spook Jr. will hold up to opportunistic charges from schooling fish. Realistic finishes provide the proper look for virtually any topwater fishing situation.
Price: . . . . **$4.88–$6.99**

LURES

HEDDON TORPEDO

Type: Prop

Color/Pattern: Black Shiner, Natural Perch, Shad G-Finish, Leopard Frog, Clear, Bullfrog, Black Shore Minnow, Brown Crawdad, Baby Bass, Black Shiner, Natural Perch, Shad G-Finish, Leopard Frog, Bullfrog, Black Shore Minnow, Baby Bass, Black Shiner, Bullfrog, Baby Bass.

Size: 1 ½ in; 1 7/8 in; 2 ½ in; 3 5/16 in

Weight: 1/8 oz, ¼ oz, 3/8 oz, 5/8 oz

Features: The Heddon Torpedos have been the world's top-selling, top-producing spinner-equipped lures for generations. Their shape and weight allow anglers to cast these lures a little farther than many other prop-baits, allowing them to reach those special fish-holding spots quicker and easier. Torpedos create a wild splashing surface disturbance, making them the perfect lures for schooling fish. Use quick, short, and erratic twitches to make Torpedos perform at their best . . . producing explosive, heart-stopping surface strikes every time.

Price:.....................................**$5.99**

HEDDON ZARA SPOOK

Type: Topwater bait

Color/Pattern: Black Shiner, Red Head, Shad G-Finish, Leopard Frog, Blue Shad, Bullfrog, Flitter Shad, Baby Bass, Black Shiner, Red Head, Blue Shore Minnow, Shad G-finish, Leopard Frog, Blue Shad, Clear, Bullfrog, Fluorescent Green Crawdad, Flitter Shad, Baby Bass, Bone.

Size: 3 in; 4 ½ in

Weight: ¼ oz, ¾ oz

Features: The Zara Spook and Zara Puppy are the original walk-the-dog lures. Heavy-duty construction holds up to vicious strikes and casts like a bullet.

Price: . . . . **$6.49–$6.99**

LURES

PANTHER MUSKIE MARABUCK

Type: InLine Spinner
Color/Pattern: Electric Chicken, Gold/Black/Red, Gold/Firetiger, Silver/Red/Black, Silver/White/Red, White/Purple/Blue
Weight: 1 oz, 1-½ oz

Features: Genuine natural hand-tied marabou and bucktail; the famous convex/concave blades in gold and silver; super sharp and strong eagle claw treble hooks; oversized heavy weighted brass bodies; can be used as a true countdown lure.
Price: **$19.99; $21.99**

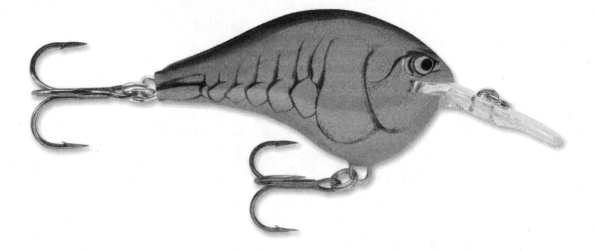

RAPALA DT (DIVES-TO) SERIES: 4, 6, 10, 14, 16

Type: Crankbait

Color/Pattern: Baby Bass, Bleeding Olive Shiner, Blue Shad, Bluegill, Chartreuse Brown, Dark Brown Crawdad, Firetiger, Helsinki Shad, Hot Mustard, Molting Blue Craw, Olive Green Craw, Parrot, Pearl Grey Shiner, Perch, Purple Olive Craw, Red Crawdad, Regal Shad, Shad, Silver, Yellow Perch

Size: 2 in, 2 ¼ in, 2 ¾ in

Weight: 5/16 oz, 3/8 oz, 3/5 oz, ¾ oz

Running Depth: 4 ft, 6 ft, 10 ft, 14 ft, 16 ft

Features: Quick-dive resting position; extra thin polycarbonate lip; perfect balance; 3D holographic or painted eyes; long-casting up to 150 ft; thin tail design; internal rattle chamber; VMC SureSet tail hook; VMC black nickel belly hook; balsa wood construction; 3D holographic eyes; hand-tuned and tank-tested.

Price: . . . . **$6.99–$7.59**

RAPALA ORIGINAL FLOATING MINNOW

Type: Stick bait
Color/Pattern: Silver, Gold, Hot Steel, Gold/Fluorescent Red, Blue, Perch, Firetiger, Silver Fluorescent/Chartreuse, Yellow Perch, Shiner, Brown Trout, Rainbow, Clown, Purpledescent, Bleeding Hot Olive, Bleeding Original Shad, Vampire
Size: 1 ½ in, 2 in, 2 ¾ in, 3 ½ in, 4 3/8 in, 5 ¼ in, 7 in
Weight: 1/16 oz, 1/8 oz, 3/16 oz, ¼ oz, 11/16 oz
Running Depth: 2 ft–4 ft, 3 ft–5 ft, 4 ft–6 ft, 6 ft–11 ft

Features: The lure that started it all is still the number one "go-to" lure. Whether twitched on top as a surface bait, retrieved as a shallow runner, weighted with a split shot for medium depth, or bottom walked off a three-way swivel or bottom bouncer, the wounded minnow action continues to be irresistible to fish everywhere. Premium black nickel VMC hooks; hand-tuned and tank-tested to ensure that world-renowned action straight from the box.
Price: . . . .**$7.99–$13.39**

SÉBILE ACAST MINNOW

Type: Crankbait
Color/Pattern: Chartreuse Holo, Natural Peacock, Natural White Perch, Natural Shiner, White Lady, Deep Red, Firetiger Gold, Craw Perch, Natural Rainbow Trout, Blue Althéa, Natural Golden Shiner
Size: 3 ¾ in; 5 in; 6 ½ in
Weight: 5/16 oz, 3/8 oz, ¾ oz, 7/8 oz, 1 ½ oz
Running Depth: 1 ft–2 ft, 2 ft–4 ft, 3 ft–5 ft, 4 ft–6 ft, 5 ft–8 ft, 12 ft–16 ft
Features: The ACAST Minnow's mass transfer system is designed to improve distance and accuracy on every cast. During the cast the weight of the lure moves to the tail of the bait guiding the lure to its target. Upon retrieve the weight chambers itself into position giving the lure perfect balance and movement. The sleek compressed design of the lure magnifies water displacement and vibration upon retrieve intensified by a series of sound beads. Brush runner/Jerk: Shallow runner produces excellent results under a steady retrieve as well as and erratic stop/start cadence. Its wide wiggle draws predator's attention and creates a visible profile for predators to attack. Long Bill Minnow: Dives quickly to its preferred depth and naturally suspends at rest. Extremely lifelike and has superior movement using a run and pause retrieve.
Price: . . . .**$12.19–$22.26**

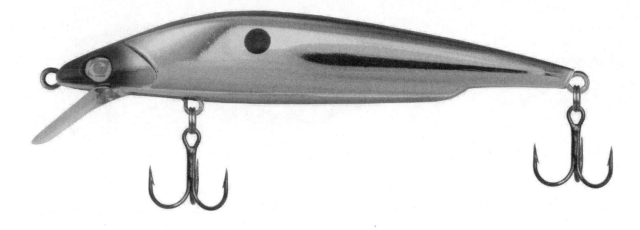

SÉBILE ACTION FIRST BULL MINNOW
Type: Jerkbait
Color/Pattern: Black Chrome, Black Gold, Bone Parrot, Chartreuse Tiger, Dark Blue Chrome, Eruption, Firetiger, Smokin' Black Shad', Smokin' Blue Chrome, Spotted Gray Shiner
Size: 4 in; 5 in
Weight: ½ oz, ¾ oz

Running Depth: 2 ft–5 ft, 3 ft–6 ft
Features: Low, external weight allows for a lower center of gravity, higher buoyancy potential, and better tracking stability; shape design as a noisy traditional floating jerkbait; one mass transfer bead allows for better casting and knocking noise.
Price: **$7.95**

SÉBILE ACTION FIRST RACER

Type: Crankbait
Color/Pattern: Black Chrome Gold Head, Blue Red Craw, Eruption, Firetiger, Golden Ghost, Greenback Ghost, Lime Ghost, Red Gold, Smokin' Black Shad, Smokin' Purple Pearl, Spotted Blue Lime, Spotted Mess
Size: 2 in; 2 ½ in; 3 in
Weight: 5/8 oz, ¾ oz

Running Depth: 6 ft–8 ft, 8 ft–12 ft, 10 ft–15 ft
Features: Low, external weight allows for a lower center of gravity, higher buoyancy potential, and better tracking stability; shape designed as a tighter action diving crank; long bill designed to go deep but little resistance on the rod tip making it easy to work all day.
Price: **$6.95**

LURES

SÉBILE BONGA JERK
Type: Jerkbait
Color/Pattern: Natural White Perch, Natural Golden Shiner, Natural Mullet, Natural Seatrout
Size: 3 ¾ in; 5 in; 6 ½ in
Weight: 7/8 oz, 2 oz, 4 oz
Running Depth: 1 ft–3 ft, 2 ft–4 ft
Features: Tall body allows for a large target for predator species; Power Keel technology increases suction and lowers the friction in the water to keep bait stable at high speeds with limited pull on the rod; at low speeds the power keel allows the bait to cut the water and make large gliding motion while jerking it; compact bait is less affected by the wind and casts are still accurate; bait will work in all water conditions from dead calm to very turbulent seas; larger models are full wire reinforced for larger fish.
Price: . . . .**$15.79–$37.10**

LURES

SÉBILE BONGA MINNOW

Type: Floating
Color/Pattern: Natural Shiner, Amber Fashion, Yellow Pepper, Perchy, Hollow Mullet, White Lady, Natural Dark Blue Black, Sea Chrome, Natural Mullet, Natural Red Drum, Natural Snook, Natural Seatrout, Natural Golden Shiner
Size: 3 in; 3 ¾ in
Weight: 3/8 oz, ¾ oz
Running Depth: Topwater

Features: The "Bonga" is a bait like no other. With its fat round head and narrow tail, the bait is extremely agile for its size. Easily moving through turbulent waters without compromising action. All components are re-enforced so the "Big One" wont get away. Great for use with super-lines, this bait is on the hunt for our next trophy! Subtle twitches of the rod tip will make the bait glide back and forth in a walking manner, while rips will send it plunging under with erratic darts.
Price: . . . .**$14.84–$15.79**

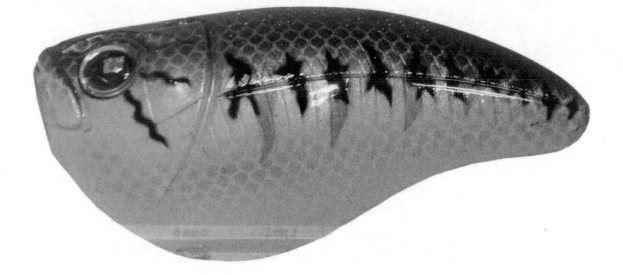

SÉBILE CRANKSTER

Type: Crankbait
Color/Pattern: Black Silver Eyes, Holo Greenie, Gold, Ghost Violet, Hot Lime, Craw Perch, Natural Blue Gill, Natural Shiner, Sea Chrome, Holo Greenie
Size: 1 ¾ in; 2 in; 2 1/8 in; 2 ½ in;
Weight: 1/8 oz, 5/16 oz, ½ oz, 5/8 oz, ¾ oz
Running Depth: Wake–6 in, 4 in–10 in, 6 in–1 ½ ft, 1 ft–2 ft, 2 ft–4 ft, 4 ft–6 ft

Features: Free bead mass transfer system designed for maximum distance and accuracy; single large bead createslow pitch rattle; lip created to deflect off cover to trigger reaction strikes (BMC); body shape contoured unlike other fat-bodied baits to optimize aerodynamics during cast; gap between lip and body allows for a faster response when lure is first retrieve; SR version is equipped with stronger hooks for heavy cover fishing application; MR version has glass beads in head to incorporate a high-pitch rattle as well.
Price: . . . .**$13.00–$16.11**

SÉBILE FLATT SHAD SNAGLESS
Type: Crankbait
Color/Pattern: Mat Brown/Red Crawdad, Holo Greenie, Gold Holo/Red/Chart, Hot Lime, Natural Blue Gill, Silver Liner
Size: 2 5/8 in
Weight: ½ oz, ¾ oz
Running Depth: 3 ft–5 ft, 4 ft–6 ft
Features: Ultimate lipless vibrating bait at any speed and technique with the addition of making it snagless; all the features and benefits of the original Flatt Shad Unique Sebile double hook design allowing the bait to swim through snags with minimum risk of hanging up; feather tail adds another aspect of attraction; hooking and landing efficiency actually increases on big fish because hook is bigger; only hardbait that can be used for pitching and flipping; special designed hook with welded ring vs slip-on double hook.
Price: . . . .**$15.64–$16.45**

LURES

SÉBILE GHOST WALKER
Type: Floating
Color/Pattern: Amber Fashion, Yellow Pepper, Perchy, Hollow Mullet, White Lady, Natural Dark Blue Black, Natural Shiner, Natural Snook, Natural Seatrout, Natural Shiner
Size: 3 ¾ in; 4 ¼ in
Weight: 5/8 oz, 1 oz

Running Depth: Topwater
Features: The contour and airfoil of this lure give it incredible action. Different retrieves such as zigzags, darts and pauses, and rock and rolls are easily created with a twitch of the rod tip to dictate the retrieve, and under heavier jerks it's also possible to plunge the lure or violently impact the surface with its head. The Ghost Walker 110 is fully wire-reinforced for big game fish.
Price: **$15.37; $17.49**

LURES

SÉBILE ONDUSPOON

Type: Spoon
Color/Pattern: Blue Shad, Orange Gold Black, White Shad
Weight: 5/16 oz
Running Depth: 2 ft–8 ft
Features: Casts very long distance because of high weigh tratio but still runs shallow; compact bait is less affected by the wind and casts are still accurate; short, squat body allows predatory fish to engulf the bait; wide head and tail's hydrofoil allows bait to cut water and creates a lot of swimming action even at slow speeds; flutters forward/backward on the fall for vertical fishing; oversized weedless single hook to hold big fish that are feeding on smaller prey; can be used as a perfect standard jig with natural baits.
Price:. **$13.00**

SÉBILE PROPPLER BUZZ

Type: Wire
Color/Pattern: Black Silver Eyes, Chartreuse Red Eyes, Gold, Natural White Perch, White Lady
Size: 3 in
Weight: 7/8 oz
Running Depth: Wake–3 in
Features: Designed to be fished in both finesse and everyday topwater conditions; lure combines the benefits of a top water frog and buzzbait; floating body filled with high pitch glass rattles for added noise; more than just a C&R buzzbait the bait can be stopped and twitched in heavy cover due to buoyant hollow body, allowing the skirt to pulse and attract fish; hook is oversized as compared to other buzzbait hooks on the market for better hooking efficiency; great bait to employ the dressed trailer hook for short striking fish.
Price: **$17.49**

SÉBILE PRO SHAD TROPHY

Type: Wire
Color/Pattern: Orange Gold Black, Hot Lime, Craw Perch, Natural Shiner
Weight: 1 oz, 1 3/8 oz
Running Depth: 6 in–8 ft
Features: Collapsible in-line swivel arm allows for morehook ups and helicopter/fluttering action on the fall; welded line tie allows the use of a snap; blade shape (asymmetric) lowers the resistance allowing the angler to cover more of the water column; blade and body are shad-shaped; oversized wide gap hook more efficient at hooking and landing fish; added skirt behind blade spirals and emits a large profile during the retrieve or fall; great bait to employ the dressed trailer hook for short, striking fish.
Price:............................ **$17.00; $17.75**

SÉBILE SPLASHER

Type: Floating
Color/Pattern: Holo Greenie, Natural White Perch, Natural Shiner, Sea Chrome, Holo Greenie, Natural Mullet, Natural Seatrout, Natural Shiner, Amber Fashion, Perchy, Hollow Mullet, White Lady, Natural Dark Blue Black
Size: 2 1/8 in; 3 in; 3 ½ in; 4 ¾ in; 6 in
Weight: 1/8 oz, 3/8 oz, 5/8 oz, 1 ½ oz, 2 ¾ oz
Running Depth: Topwater

Features: The specially designed concave face of the splasher make it superior to poppers and chuggers alike. Effortlessly the splasher will pop and throw water with the softest of twitches from the rod tip. A firm blow will cause the bait to chug and move water making its irritable presence noticeable in the roughest conditions. The special keel-on of the splasher causes the lure to lurch side to side in a zig-zag motion with rhythmic pops of the rod tip. The splasher is extremely versatile under all conditions.
Price: . . . .$12.19–$29.15

LURES

STORM ORIGINAL THUNDERSTICK

Type: Stick bait
Color/Pattern: Metalic Blue/Red Lip, Hot Tiger, Metallic Silver Black Back, Yellow Black Back, Chrome Yellow Perch, Black Chrome Orange, Blue Chrome Orange, Blue Steel Shad, Chartreuse Purple Shad, Chrome Clown, Metallic Gold/Chartreuse, Purple Fire UV, Blue Pink Fire UV, Green Fire UV, Orange Fire UV, Pink Fire UV
Size: 3 ½ in, 4 3/8 in

Weight: ¼ oz, ½ oz
Running Depth: 1 ft–5 ft, 2 ft–7 ft
Features: Original molds and components; original patterns and colors; original packaging style; rolling minnow action; premium VMC hooks, sizes 4 and 6; comes in Original, Deep, Deep Jr., and Jr. models.
Price: **$4.79**

STORM ORIGINAL WIGGLE WART

Type: Crankbait

Color/Pattern: Green Crawdad, Brown Scale Crawdad, Tennessee Shad, Phantom Brown Crayfish, Black/Glitter/Chartreuse, Naturistic Brown Crayfish, Naturistic Green Crayfish, Hot Tiger, Phantom Green Crayfish, Solid Fluorescent Pink, Metallic Blue/Black, Metallic Silver Fluorescent Red, Metallic/Silver/Chartreuse Lip, Metallic Blue Scale Red, Metallic Green Scale Red, Metallic Pink Black Lip, Metallic/Orange/Chartreuse, Black/Glitter/Fluorescent Red, Metallic Purple/Purple, Naturistic Red Crayfish, Watermelon, Tequila Glow, Black Chrome Orange, Blue Chrome Orange, Blue Steel Shad, Blazin' Pink UV, Blazin Red UV, Blazin' Green UV, Blazin Blue UV, Bluegill, Blue Back Herring, Green Fire UV, Orange Fire UV, Pink Fire UV, Firetiger, Honey Mustard, Shad, Ghost Shad, Texas Crawdad

Size: 2 in

Weight: 3/8 oz

Running Depth: 7 ft–18 ft

Features: A smaller version of the Mag Wart; original molds, components, patterns, and colors; classic "wart" rattle; side-to-side crayfish action; multi-species; premium VMC super-sharp hooks, size 4.

Price: **$4.79**

SÉBILE AT WORM

Type: Soft plastic
Color/Pattern: Hot Corn, Spicy Bubblegum, Green Peppercorn, Solid Milk, Black Watermelon, Tahiti Pearl, Aged Watermelon, Dark Cherry, Black Red Sparkle, Black Blue Sparkle, Violet Olive Oil, Clear Gold Red
Size: 5 in, 6 in, 7 in
Weight: ¼ oz, 5/16 oz, ½ oz
Quantity: 1

Features: Worm's full length is hollow; specifically designed holes to allow for multiple riggings; bottom of head is shaped like a "V" hull to raising bait off bottom when Carolina rigged and slide/swim action on Texas; ability to rig it backwards; perfect to use with Soft Weight System; "split tail" design allows for a lifelike motion on pull and drop; comes in both floating and sinking versions.
Price: **$7.00**

LURES

SÉBILE MAGIC SWIMMER—SOFT

Type: Soft plastic
Color/Pattern: Natural Shiner, Blue Black Herring, Ghostescent, Holo Greenie, Blue Gill, Electric Rainbow, Ayu, Golden Shiner, Brown/Red Craw, Perch, Fire Tiger
Size: 4 in, 5 in, 6-¼ in, 8 in
Weight: 3/8 oz, ¾ oz, 1 ¼ oz, 2 3/8 oz
Quantity: 1
Features: Can be rigged weedless due to large hollow slit that allows wide gap hook to fit nicely in body; longer lasting soft plastic due to hole in the nose and back allows the swimmer to slide on the leader once fish is hooked; soft body for fish to hold on longer; great for skipping under docks and trees; same quality of painting finish as the hard Magic Swimmer!; very easy to rig: open the belly's cut, slide the wide gap hook point into it through the back hole, then pull on the head and place hook eye from inside the head to outside's mouth; perfect to be used with Soft Weight System; different position of the tungsten rubber weights on the hook provides different actions to fit fishes and situations.
Price:. . . . .$15.95–$21.00

SÉBILE STICK SHADD HOLLOW

Type: Soft plastic
Color/Pattern: Translugreen, Trueblue, Orangee Bait, Menhy, Violet Silver, Transluclear
Size: 4 in
Weight: 5/8 oz
Quantity: 1
Features: Brings almost all of the advantages of the hard version with the added feature of being soft and hollow for all kinds of riggings, including weedless and jigs; streamlined shape very efficient for distance casts; wobble on the fall if used with a soft weight system wide gap hook; will outskip any other lure, hard, or soft; hollow body with thick walls allows the bait to be durable, but does not hinder the angler from setting a hook due to collapsible body; emulates a real fish's burst and movements under every jerk.
Price: **$13.78**

STORM KICKIN' GOBY

Type: Rigged plastic swimbait
Color/Pattern: Goby
Size: 4 in
Weight: 1 oz
Quantity: 1

Features: Segmented body with kicking tail; durable soft plastic body; life-like swimming action; single hook on back for snag-free presentation close to the bottom; holographic insert; holographic WildEye; polycarbonate lip.
Price: **$5.69**

LURES

STORM WILDEYE LIVE RAINBOW TROUT

Type: Rigged plastic swimbait
Color/Pattern: Ranbow Trout
Size: 2 in, 3 in, 4 in
Weight: 1/8 oz, ¼ oz, 5/16 oz
Quantity: 3
Features: Internally weighted body creates an incredibly life-like swimming; realistic color patterns and shape of the bait is backed up with 3D holographic WildEye, holographic swimmin' flash foil, and a tough yet soft outer body; swimbait has a rainbow trout body and color pattern and a back VMC needle point hook and a treble belly hook.
Price:. . . . . **$5.19–$6.19**

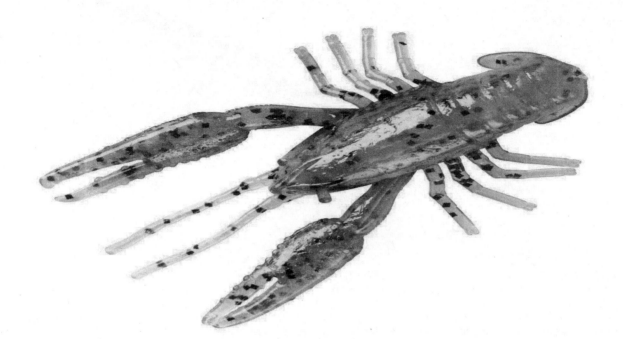

YUM F2 CRAWBUG

Type: Soft plastic
Color/Pattern: Watermelon Red Flake, Crawdad, Carolina Pumpkin, Green Pumpkin, Watermelon Seed, Black Blue
Size: 2 ½ in, 3 ¼ in
Quantity: 10, 8
Features: With incredible 3D detail and a specially designed hollow body, this is the ultimate soft-plastic crawfish; designed to accurately imitate a fleeing crawfish, the super-soft CrawBug is scent-infused with exclusive F2 Crawfish Formula plus salt that won't dry out or lose its effectiveness; however you fish it—flip, rig, or jip—it's sure to become your go-to bass bait in any condition.
Price: **$5.49**

YUM F2 DINGER

Type: Soft plastic
Color/Pattern: Black Blue Flake, Watermelon Candy, June Bug, Green Pumpkin, Black Blue Laminate, Chartreuse Pepper, Red Shad, Ozark Smoke, Smoke Red Pepper, Green Pumpkin Chartreuse Tail, Bumble Bee Swirl, Bubble Gum Lemon Swirl, Mardi Gras, Green Pumpkin Neon, Cajun Neon, Bama Bug, Bama Magic, Bream, Watermelon/Red Flake, Watermelon Seed

Size: 4 in, 5 in, 6 in, 7 in
Quantity: 7, 12, 15
Features: Infused with Yum's F2 bass attractant; subtle, lifelike; won't dry and shrivel up when left out of the package; great for wacky worming and Texas rigging; attract, enrage, engage!
Price: **$5.69**

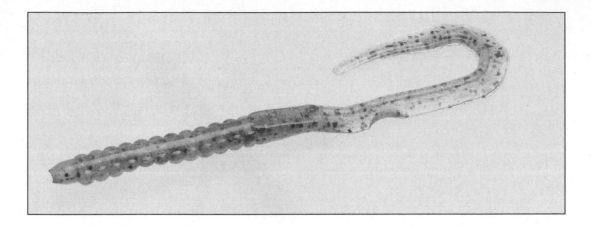

YUM F2 RIBBONTAIL
Type: Soft plastic
Color/Pattern: June Bug, Watermelon Seed, Red Shad, Tequila Sunrise, Red Bug, Green Pumpkin Purple Flake
Size: 7 ½ in

Quantity: 15
Features: Slithering action of the sinuous tail; integral F2 scent; standard ploy for catching big bass.
Price: **$4.49**

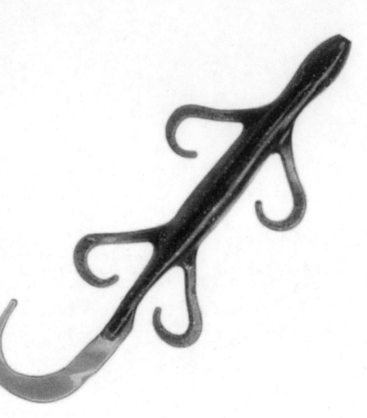

YUM F2 LIZARD
Type: Soft plastic
Color/Pattern: Watermelon Red Lake, Junebug, Green Pumpkin, Watermelon Seed, White, Carolina Pumpkin Chartreuse, Green Pumpkin Purple Flake, Black Neon, Carolina Pumpkin, Black Blue, Black Neon Chartreuse
Size: 4 in, 6 in
Quantity: 15

Features: The ultimate finesse lizard, it has everything an angler needs to fool big, finicky bass—curly legs that create motion and a long curly tail that pushes a lot of water; tough, durable plastic holds up to multiple fish, yet remains soft and supple even when fished in cold water.
Price: **$3.99**

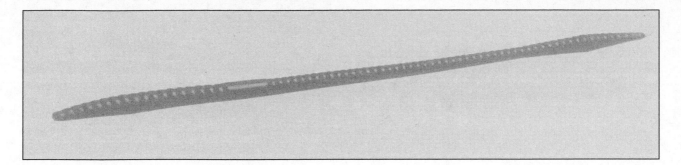

YUM F2 MIGHTEE WORM

Type: Soft plastic
Color/Pattern: Bama Bug, Blue Fleck, Grape Red Flake, Green Pumpkin, Junebug, Plum, Red Blood, Red Bug, Ultimate Craw, Virgo Blue, Watermelon Red Flake, Watermelon Seed
Size: 4 in, 6 in, 10 ½ in
Quantity: 5

Features: Big bass look at the Yum F2 Mightee Worm like a hungry pilgrim looks at Thanksgiving dinner; it presents a massive profile in the water, and with F2 attractant infused during the molding process, it gives of a strong scent trail that bass can't resist; created for power shaking on Edwin Evers' Yum Pumkin Ed Standup Jig Head, it's also a great choice on a Texas-rig, Carolina-rig, or even a Wacky-rig.
Price: **$4.79**

YUM F2 PANFISH WOOLY BEAVERTAIL
Type: Soft plastic
Color/Pattern: Firefly, Tail Light, Lemon Lime, Chartreuse, Limesicle, Belle Starr, Dutchess, Sunfish, Drum, Perch, Bluegill, Hot Shad
Size: 1 ½ in, 2 in

Quantity: 1
Features: Many lure designers gave up after the crappie tube was designed, but YUM engineers created the Wooly Beavertail, and it quickly pushed the tube aside; the big, flat tail can be used as is or split to provide more action; the perfect plastic for slow trolling.
Price: **$2.99**

YUM F2 WALLEYE GRUB
Type: Soft plastic
Color/Pattern: White, Red Bloodline, Lime Core, Chartreuse/Silver, Bumblebee, Chartreuse, Avocado Red/ Chartreuse, Pink Blush
Size: 3 in, 4 in

Quantity: 15
Features: F2 scent-infused technology makes fish hold on; unlike other scent-impregnated baits, it won't dry out and lose its effectiveness; long, wide tail produces plenty of fish-calling vibration.
Price: **$3.99**

LURES

YUM F2 WOOLY HAWGTAIL

Model: F2 Wooly Hawgtail
Type: Soft plastic
Color/Pattern: Watermelon/Red Flake, Green Pumpkin,
Red Shad, Green Flake, Black Blue, Dark Grasshopper,
Dark Watermelon

Size: 4 ½ in
Quantity: 8
Features: Big-time big-fish soft plastic bait; works well on a
Carolina rig, pitched, flipped, or a Texas rig; produces
massive action, F2 scent-infused.

YUM F2 YUMPHIBIAN
Type: Soft plastic
Color/Pattern: Black Neon, Watermelon/Red, Junebug, Green Pumpkin, Watermelon Shad, Red Shad, Green Pumpkin Neon, Big O Craw, Ultra Craw, Virgo Blue
Size: 4 ½ in, 5 ¼ in, 6 in
Quantity: 6, 8, 10

Features: With two small swimming arms at the top, a pair of longer curl tails at the end, and two big "flappers" at the midpoint, the YUM F2 YUMphibian never stops moving; customize by pinching off appendages to create less water disturbance for finicky or pressured fish; pitch it, flip it, or work it deep, the YUMphibian is a whole new species of creature bait.
Price: **$4.99**

YUM MONEY MINNOW
Type: Swimbait
Color/Pattern: Pearl, Pearl Black Back, River Shad, Hitch, Hologram Shad, Tennessee Shad, Foxy Shad, Pearl Chartreuse Back, Bluegill

Size: 2 ½ in, 3 ½ in, 5 in
Quantity: 4, 5, 8
Features: Lifelike finish; unique belly slot; rigging friendly; realistic action.
Price: **$9.79**

LURES

BASS PRO SHOPS CRAPPIE MAXX CAMO
Color: Camo
Length: 1420 yd, 1690 yd, 2040 yd, 3190 yd
Lb. Test: 4, 6, 8, 10
Diameter: 0.203mm–0.304mm

Features: Undetectable in any color water; fluorescent stripe easily seen above water; soft and supple; low memory for easy casting; high-abrasion resistance; excellent knot strength.
Price:. $7.99

BASS PRO SHOPS CRAPPIE MAXX SUPER VIS
Color: Super hi-vis
Length: 1420 yd, 1690 yd, 2040 yd, 3190 yd
Lb. Test: 4, 6, 8, 10

Diameter: 0.203mm–0.304mm
Features: Great for dawn, dusk, or night fishing; glows in low light conditions; can see even the lightest twitch.
Price:. $7.99

BASS PRO SHOPS EXCEL MONOFILAMENT—1 LB. SPOOL

Color: Clear, clear/blue fluorescent, green
Type: Monofilament
Length: 2250 yd, 2525 yd, 3240 yd, 4315 yd, 5065 yd, 6030 yd, 9000 yd

Lb. Test: 4, 6, 8, 10, 12, 14, 17
Diameter: 0.21mm–0.46mm
Features: Superior abrasion resistance; soft, smooth, and limp; limited stretch and high-impact shock strength.
Price: **$26.99**

BASS PRO SHOPS TOURNEY TOUGH MONOFILAMENT

Color: Clear, green
Type: Monofilament
Length: 275 yd
Lb. Test: 2, 4, 6, 8, 10, 12, 14, 17, 20, 25

Diameter: 0.18mm–0.52mm
Features: High-performance mono; copolymer construction; state-of-the-art extrusion; excellent knot strength and durability.
Price: **$3.99**

BASS PRO SHOPS XPS 8 ADVANCED BRAID

Color: Green
Type: Braid
Length: 150 yd
Lb. Test: 10, 20, 30, 50, 65, 80

Diameter: 0.18mm–0.44mm
Features: Bass Pro Shops' most advanced braided line yet; unparalleled strength and consistent roundness; woven from eight Dyneema fibers; enhanced color protection.
Price:.............................**$18.99–$22.99**

BASS PRO SHOPS XPS SIGNATURE SERIES FLUOROCARBON—FILLER SPOOL

Color: Clear
Type: Fluorocarbon
Length: 150 yd, 175 yd, 200 yd
Lb. Test: 6, 8, 10, 12, 14, 17, 20, 25

Diameter: 0.23mm–0.48mm
Features: Disappears in the water; twice as dense as monofilament; low stretch for increased sensitivity; low water absorption for superior knot strength.
Price:.............................**$19.99–$24.99**

BASS PRO SHOPS XPS SIGNATURE SERIES MONOFILAMENT

Color: Clear
Type: Monofilament
Length: 800 yd, 900 yd, 1000 yd
Lb. Test: 6, 8, 10, 12, 14, 17, 20

Diameter: 0.25mm–0.48mm
Features: Highest grade of monofilament; high abrasion resistance; superior tensile strength; locked-in knot-holding power; nearly frictionless surface for longer and smoother casts.
Price:............................. **$11.99–$16.99**

BERKLEY BIG GAME BRAID

Color: Low-vis green
Type: Braid
Length: 300 yd
Lb. Test: 6, 8, 12, 15, 17
Diameter: 0.009 in–0.017 in

Features: Uses Dyneema, the world's strongest gel-spun polyethylene fiber; ultra-sensitive, with virtually no stretch; transmits lure action and strikes directly to the rod tip and reel for instant and positive hooksets.
Price:............................. **$24.49–$38.49**

LINES

BERKLEY FIRELINE FUSED CRYSTAL
Color: Crystal
Type: Fused
Length: 125 yd, 300 yd, 1500 yd
Lb. Test: 2, 3, 4, 6, 8, 10, 14, 20, 30
Diameter: 0.005 in–0.015 in

Features: Combines the ultimate in low-visibility with all of the benefits of FireLine; incredibly thin diameter to work the tiniest micro bait; supple enough to handle the coldest weather; incredibly strong—three times stronger than mono; ultimate sensitivity to telegraph feel for structure and strikes.
Price: . . . . **$17.95–$37.49; 1500 yd: $176.99**

BERKLEY NANOFIL
Color: Clear mist, high-vis chartreuse, low-vis green,
Type: Uni-filament
Length: 150 yd, 300 yd
Lb. Test: 2, 3, 4, 6, 8, 10, 12, 14, 17
Diameter: 0.002 in–0.010 in

Features: Not a mono. Not a Braid. The Next Generation in Fishing Line. Unified filament technology provides the ultimate advantage against a wide variety of species; cast farther and feel everything with the ultimate spinning reel line; minimum diameter, maximum strength; zero memory virtually eliminates line tangles.
Price: . . . . **$19.95–$38.95**

BERKLEY SOLUTIONS CASTING

Color: Green mist
Type: Monofilament
Length: 250 yd
Lb. Test: 10, 12, 14, 17
Diameter: 0.014 in–0.017 in

Features: Targeted for anglers who want to take the guesswork out of choosing line for their reel and spend more time fishing; specifically designed for low-profile or round baitcasting reels; strong, trouble free, and easy to use; stacks and handles well on baitcast reels.
Price:. **$5.99**

BERKLEY SOLUTIONS SPINNING

Color: Green mist
Type: Monofilament
Length: 250 yd
Lb. Test: 4, 6, 8, 10
Diameter: 0.008 in–0.011 in

Features: Targeted for anglers who want to take the guesswork out of choosing line for their reel and spend more time fishing; specifically designed for open face or closed face spinning reels; strong, trouble free, and easy to use; resists tangles and hassles.
Price:. **$5.99**

LINES

BERKLEY TRILENE BIG CAT

Color: Solar green
Type: Monofilament
Length: 200 yd, 220 yd, 270 yd, 300 yd
Lb. Test: 15, 20, 30, 40
Diameter: 0.015 in–0.024 in

Features: High shock strength; controlled stretch adds fighting power for big cats; reflects sunlight or blacklight for high visibility; abrasion-resistant to stand tough against rough or sharp objects.
Price: **$7.29**

BERKLEY TRILENE COLD WEATHER

Color: Electric blue, fl. clear/blue
Type: Monofilament
Length: 110 yd
Lb. Test: 2, 3, 4, 6, 8, 10
Diameter: 0.005 in–0.011 in

Features: Improved formula is as flexible at 32°F as regular mono is at 70°F; extraordinary flexibility and low memory design to resist twists and tangles; available in electric blue color for maximum visibility against ice and snow.
Price: . . . . **$3.39–$4.19**

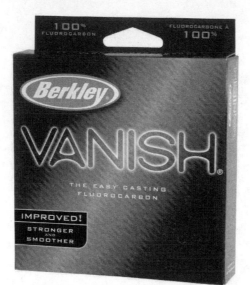

BERKLEY VANISH
Color: Clear
Type: Fluorocarbon
Length: 110 yd, 250 yd, 350 yd
Lb. Test: 2, 4, 6, 8, 10, 12, 14, 17, 20, 30, 40
Diameter: 0.006 in–0.022 in

Features: The most flexible, easiest casting fluorocarbon; best Vanish formula ever, with 20 percent better shock strength, improved knot strength and easier to handle; non-absorbing fluorocarbon maintains strength and abrasion resistance underwater.
Price:.............................**$5.99–$29.99**

CABELA'S DACRON PLANER BOARD LINE
Color: Fluorescent orange
Type: Braid
Length: 150 feet
Lb. Test: 135

Diameter: 0.135 in
Features: High-visibility orange line; low-stretch braided Dacron; resists kinks and tangles.
Price:......................................**9.99**

LINES

CABELA'S LEAD CORE

Color: 10 yd color changes
Type: Braid
Length: 100 yd, 200 yd
Lb. Test: 18, 27, 36, 45, 54
Diameter: 0.030 in–0.059 in

Features: Tightly braided, high-tenacity nylon multifilament yarn encapsulates a 99.9 percent pure lead core; smaller diameter than standard lead-core lines; color changes every 10 yards for accurate measurements of fishing depths without having to use a linecounter; great alternative to snapweights or divers; approximate sink rate is 1.25 feet with every 2 yards released, depending on speed.
Price: . . . . $15.99–$29.99

CABELA'S KING KAT

Color: Dirty green, hi-vis yellow
Type: Braid
Length: 200yd, 400 yd
Lb. Test: 20, 30, 50, 80
Diameter: 0.009 in–0.016 in
Features: A unique bi-component, small-diameter, braided superline with exceptional abrasion resistance and strength; made with Spectra fibers and a multifilament nylon tracer blended into the braid; nylon tracer increases the line's stretch by 5 percent so it's more forgiving when you set the hook; gives the line neutral buoyancy while hiding the line in the water with a mottled pattern; line is then permeated by a synthesized coating process that penetrates the braid.
Price: . . . . $16.99–$39.99

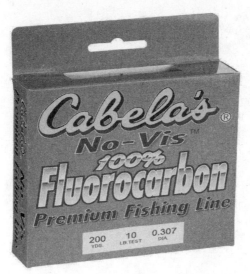

CABELA'S NO-VIS FLUOROCARBON LINE

Color: Clear
Type: Fluorocarbon
Length: 200 yd, 400 yd, 600 yd
Lb. Test: 4, 6, 8, 10, 12, 15, 20
Diameter: 0.007 in–0.016 in

Features: Virtually invisible under water, (only 100 percent Fluorocarbon comes close to matching the light refraction index of water); abrasion resistance, knot strength and tensile strength far exceeded expectations; extra-soft properties and minimal stretch.
Price: . 200 yd: $12.99–$16.99; 400 yd: $19.99–$26.99; 600 yd: $24.99–$39.99

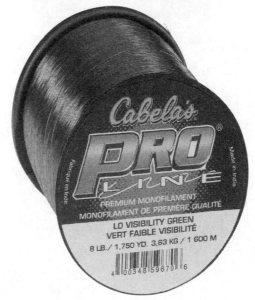

CABELA'S PROLINE

Color: Camo, clear, green, hi-vis yellow
Type: Monofilament
Length: 425 yds–3100 yds
Lb. Test: 4–30
Diameter: 0.008 in–0.022 in

Features: Controlled tensile strength enables ProLine to take the sudden shock and impact of bone-jarring hooksets with minimum stretch, while withstanding the runs and surges of any game fish; all of that in a small-diameter line with more than enough abrasion resistance to handle the toughest situations. Bulk spool also available.
Price: 9.99

CORTLAND 333+ FLOATING FLY

Color: Gecko green
Type: Fly DT, WF
Lb. Test: 3, 4, 5, 6

Features: The longer belly loads rods more quickly and allows you to carry more line in the air; durability and satin-smooth finish are second to none; floating double taper excels in tight casting conditions.
Price: **$32.99**

CORTLAND 333+ LS8 SINKING LEVEL FLY

Color: Dark brown/black
Type: Fly
Length: 150 feet
Diameter: 0.037 in

Features: Cortland Line Company's 333+ LS8 Sinking Level Fly Line is a level taper, 8-weight line (220 gr. at 30 ft. from tip). It has a diameter of .037" with a type 6 sink rate, 6.25-7" per second. Designed for trolling, it works well on an 8-weight rod.
Price: **32.95**

CORTLAND 444 CLASSIC FLY

Color: Brown, light brown, peach, peach/brown
Type: Fly DT, WF
Length: 90 feet
Lb. Test: 3, 4, 5, 6

Features: The built-in buoyancy and slick surface of the 444 lines allows for smooth pickups and efficient casts; precision tapers turn over your leaders for perfect fly presentations.
Price: **$62.00**

DAIWA SAMURAI BRAIDED

Color: Green
Type: Braid
Length: 150 yds, 300 yds, 1500 yds
Lb. Test: 15–150
Diameter: .18–.62
Features: Samurai line is unlike any other braided line on the market. Sure it's strong and sensitive, but it's also

noticeably thinner, softer, smoother, and more flexible than ordinary braids. That means less friction for better casts; reduced line noise on the retrieve; and a faster sink rate due to less current resistance. Available in 150-yard, 300-yard, and 1500-yard spools.
Price: . . . . **$24.95–$249.95**

LINES

DAIWA STEEZ FLUOROCARBON

Color: Green
Type: Fluorocarbon
Length: 125 yds
Lb. Test: 5–20
Diameter: .007–.016
Features: Finally, a green-colored, super soft, super strong 100 percent Fluorocarbon line with the flexibility and castability of regular monofilament. Formulated exclusively for Steez spinning and casting reels, it is highly resistant to abrasion and offers a faster sink rate than monofilament. Parallel winding on the filler spool prevents dents and inconsistency in roundness that can reduce casting efficiency.
Price:................................ $19.99–$26.99

L.L.BEAN STREAMLIGHT II

Color: Yellow
Type: Fly
Length: 90 feet

Lb. Test: 3–9
Features: Designed for beginning fly fishermen; short head allows for quick and easy loading of the fly rod.
Price:................................ $20.00

ORVIS ACCESS WF TROUT

Color: Mist green
Type: Fly
Length: 90 feet
Lb. Test: 3, 4, 5, 6, 7, 8
Features: Versatile freshwater floating trout fly line offering outstanding performance across a broad range of conditions; weight forward fly line with mid-length head for easy casting and mending; Orvis Line ID allows you to quickly and easily identify your line, with no more guessing; all of the lines are printed with the taper, weight, and functionality; Integrated Slickness additive is integrated throughout the PVC layer to provide lubrication for maximum distance, performance, and durability; new sleek and durable welded loop makes leader attachment quick and easy while holding up to repeated use—also helps to transfer energy more efficiently to the leader allowing better turnover; braided multifilament core provides excellent performance over a wide range of conditions; new paper pulp spool, made from recycled cardboard and kraft paper, is 100 percent compostable; mist green; line weights 3–8; length 90'; made in USA.
Price: **$59.00**

ORVIS CLEARWATER FLY

Color: Flourescent yellow
Type: Fly
Length: 90 feet
Lb. Test: 3, 4, 5, 6, 7, 8, 9
Features: An entry level fly line designed to aid the inexperienced caster; built a half-size heavy to help load the rod; Orvis Line ID allows you to quickly and easily identify your line, with no more guessing; all of the lines are printed with the taper, weight, and functionality; new sleek and durable welded loop makes leader attachment quick and easy while holding up to repeated use—also helps to transfer energy more efficiently to the leader allowing better turnover; Integrated Slickness additive produces high line slickness for longer casts and reduced friction, keeping lines cleaner longer to help with flotation and overall performance; braided multifilament core provides excellent performance over a wide range of conditions; new paper pulp spool, made from recycled cardboard and kraft paper, is 100 percent compostable; fluorescent yellow; line sizes 3–9; made in USA.
Price: **$39.00**

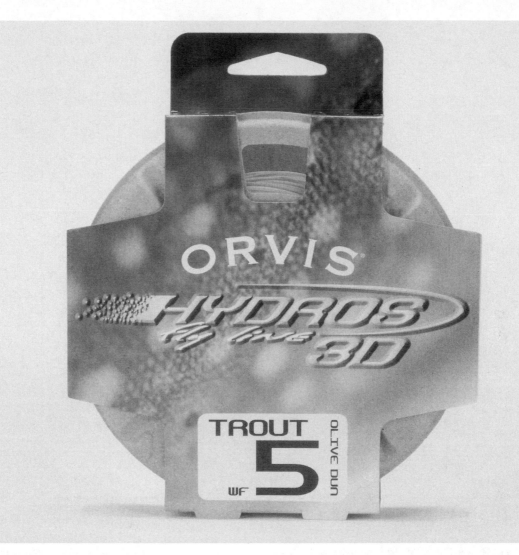

ORVIS HYDROS 3D WF

Color: Olive dun
Type: Fly
Length: 90 feet
Lb. Test: 4, 5, 6
Features: Textured fly line surface gives you incredible frictionless casting for most trout fishing situations; 3D Technology Microtexture surface reduces surface friction, improves flotation, and eliminates tangling; Hy-Flote Tip—highly specialized Micro-balloons concentrated in the front of the line to produce high floating tips; Integrated Slickness additive is integrated throughout the PVC layer to provide lubrication for maximum distance, performance, and durability; Orvis Line ID allows you to quickly and easily identify your line, with no more guessing; all of the lines are printed with the taper, weight, and functionality; new sleek and durable welded loop makes leader attachment quick and easy while holding up to repeated use—also helps to transfer energy more efficiently to the leader allowing better turnover; braided multifilament core provides excellent performance over a wide range of conditions; new paper pulp spool, made from recycled cardboard and kraft paper, is 100 percent compostable; in olive dun; 90'; line weights 4–6; made in USA.
Price: **$95.00**

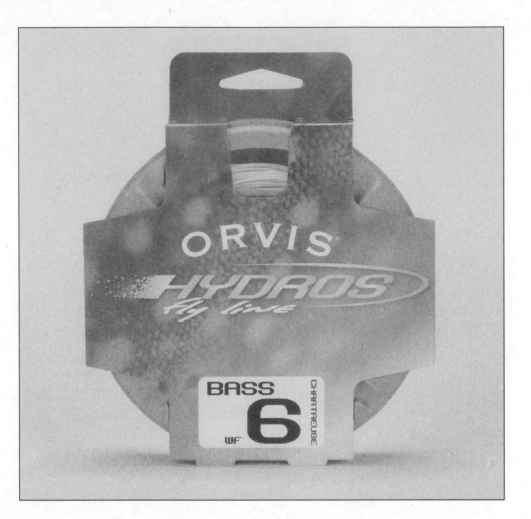

ORVIS HYDROS BASS/WARMWATER

Color: Chartreuse
Type: Fly
Length: 90 feet
Lb. Test: 5, 6, 7, 8, 9
Features: This bass fly line has a compact head and short front taper to turn over the big deer hair poppers and sliders with ease; drive flies into tight, heavy cover, under branches and back in holes where large bass lurk; latest generation of Wonderline coating is 20 percent slicker than the previous generation, resulting in the slickest fly lines on the market; casts farther with less effort, produces higher line speeds to cut through the wind and improve accuracy, repels dirt and grime, picks up off the water easier, improves flotation, and reduces tangles; Orvis Line ID allows you to quickly and easily identify your line, with no more guessing; all of the lines are printed with the taper, weight, and functionality; new sleek and durable welded loop makes leader attachment quick and easy while holding up to repeated use—also helps to transfer energy more efficiently to the leader allowing better turnover; braided multifilament core provides excellent performance over a wide range of conditions; new paper pulp spool, made from recycled cardboard and kraft paper, is 100 percent compostable; in chartreuse; 90'; line weights 5–9.; made in USA.
Price: **$79.00**

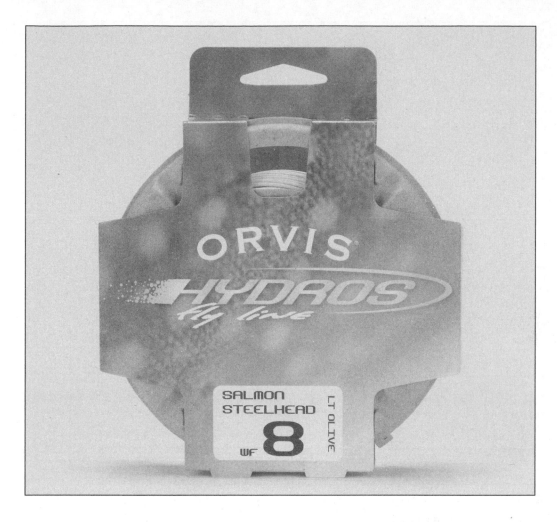

ORVIS HYDROS SALMON/STEELHEAD

Color: Light olive
Type: Fly
Length: 105 feet
Lb. Test: 7, 8, 9, 10
Features: Designed to handle the unique demands of salmon and steelhead fishing; super-long belly fly line body and rear taper (57' in an 8-wt.) provide a perfect platform for easy long-distance mending, roll casting, and singlehand Spey casting; latest generation of Wonderline coating is 20 percent slicker than the previous generation, resulting in the slickest fly lines on the market; casts farther with less effort, produces higher line speeds to cut through the wind and improve accuracy, repels dirt and grime, picks up off the water easier, improves flotation, and reduces tangles; Orvis Line ID allows you to quickly and easily identify your line, with no more guessing; all of the lines are printed with the taper, weight, and functionality; new sleek and durable welded loop makes leader attachment quick and easy while holding up to repeated use—also helps to transfer energy more efficiently to the leader allowing better turnover; braided multifilament core provides excellent performance over a wide range of conditions; new paper pulp spool, made from recycled cardboard and kraft paper, is 100 percent compostable; in light olive; made in USA.
Price: **$79.00**

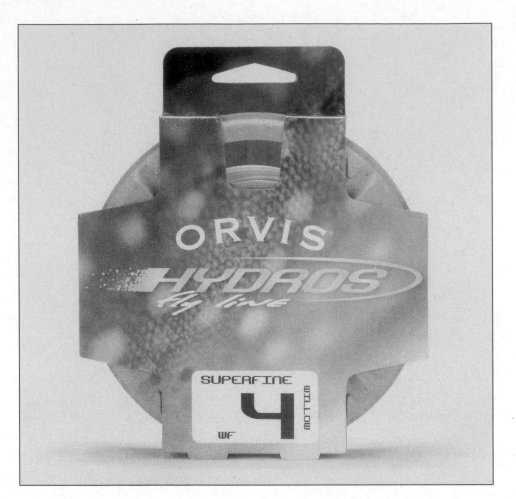

ORVIS HYDROS SUPERFINE
Color: Willow
Type: Fly
Length: 90 feet
Lb. Test: 1, 2, 3, 4, 5, 6
Features: An excellent fly line choice for spring creeks, slow moving, and clear water situations where stealth and technical expertise are at a premium; specially designed weightforward taper loads rods at short distances but still affords delicate presentations; latest generation of Wonderline coating is 20 percent slicker than the previous generation, resulting in the slickest fly lines on the market; casts farther with less effort, produces higher line speeds to cut through the wind and improve accuracy, repels dirt and grime, picks up off the water easier, improves flotation, and reduces tangles; Hy-Flote Tip—highly specialized Micro-balloons concentrated in the front of the line to produce high floating tips; Orvis Line ID allows you to quickly and easily identify your line, with no more guessing; all of the lines are printed with the taper, weight, and functionality; new sleek and durable welded loop makes leader attachment quick and easy while holding up to repeated use—also helps to transfer energy more efficiently to the leader allowing better turnover; braided multifilament core provides excellent performance over a wide range of conditions; new paper pulp spool, made from recycled cardboard and kraft paper, is 100 percent compostable; in willow; made in USA.

Price: **$79.00**

SHAKESPEARE MONOFILAMENT
Color: Clear
Type: Monofilmaent
Length: 700 yd
Lb. Test: 4–50

Features: 1/3 lb spool; excellent abrasion resistance; extremely affordable.
Price: **$2.99**

SPIDERWIRE EZ BRAID
Color: Moss green
Type: Braid
Length: 110 yds; 300 yds
Lb. Test: 10–50
Diameter: .007–.015

Features: Dyneema microfibers are 3X stronger than mono; diameters are 2 to 3X smaller than mono of the same weight test; super smooth for long, effortless casts; spider-sensitivity; near zero stretch to feel everything.
Price: . . . . **$9.95–$18.95**

SPIDERWIRE EZ FLUORO
Color: Clear
Type: Fluorocarbon
Length: 200 yds
Lb. Test: 2, 4, 6, 8, 10, 12, 15

Diameter: .006-.015
Features: 100 percent fluorocarbon for the key fluorocarbon benefits of virtual invisibility, sinking for less line between lure and reel and great wet strength; sensitive and abrasion resistant; good manageability, knot, and impact strength.
Price: . . . . $7.99–$8.99

SPIDERWIRE STEALTH GLOW-VIS
Color: Glow-Vis-Green Bulk
Type: Braid
Length: 125; 300 yds; 1500 yds
Lb. Test: 10–80
Diameter: .007-.016

Features: Fluorescent brighteners illuminate line above water; low-vis green disappears below water; enhances ability to watch line and detect bites that may not be felt.
Price: . . . 125, 300 yds: $14.99–$38.99; 1500 yds: $134.99–$184.99

SPIDERWIRE ULTRACAST 100% FLUOROCARBON

Color: Clear
Type: Fluorocarbon
Length: 200 yds
Lb. Test: 6, 8, 10, 12, 15
Diameter: .009-.014

Features: Thinner diameters than most competitive fluorocarbons allows lures to perform better; awesome performance on spinning reels (4–10 lb. test); disappears to fish as it is virtually invisible; spider-sensitivity transmits strikes and structure.
Price: . . . . **$14.99–$16.99**

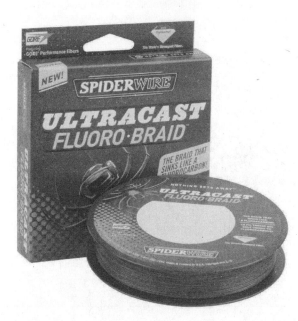

SPIDERWIRE ULTRACAST FLUORO-BRAID

Color: Moss green
Type: Braid
Length: 125; 300 yds; 1500 yds
Lb. Test: 10–80
Diameter: .008-.018

Features: Exceptionally high strength-per-diameter in a fluoro; thinner diameters than most competitive fluorocarbons allows lures to perform better; awesome performance on spinning reels (4–10 lb test); spider sensitivity transmits strikes and structure.
Price: . . . 125, 300 yds: $20.99–$49.99; 1500 yds: $187.49–$224.99

SPIDERWIRE ULTRACAST INVISI-BRAID

Color: Clear
Type: Braid
Length: 125; 300 yds; 1500 yds; 3000 yds
Lb. Test: 10–80
Diameter: .007-.022

Features: Ultra smooth 8 carrier braid; innovative coldfusion process; translucency for near invisibility; extremely high strength-per-diameter; amazingly thin and sensitive; high pick count for roundness and durability.
Price: . . . . . .125, 300 yds: $20.99–$49.99; 1500, 3000 yds: $187.49–$449.99

SPIDERWIRE ULTRACAST ULTIMATE MONO

Color: Clear; Brown recluse
Type: Monofilament
Length: 330 yds
Lb. Test: 4–20
Diameter: .006-.016

Features: Breakthrough strength-to-diameter co-polymer is 33 percent stronger than the average mono; unprecedented 15 percent stretch for incredible sensitivity and hook setting power; thin diameter allows exceptional bait action and high line capacity; excellent knot and shock strength—even when wet; optimized for baitcast reels, but still castable and manageable on spinning reels.
Price: . . . . $8.99–$11.99

SPIDERWIRE ZILLA BRAID

Color: Moss green
Type: Braid
Length: 125; 300 yds; 1500 yds
Lb. Test: 20–100
Diameter: .014–.038
Features: Dyneema provides unmatched strength; Cordura provides toughness; engineered with shock resistance for power baitcast techniques; dense braid creates a loading effect for longer casting distance; tough, durable and abrasion resistant; stretches 67 percent more than standard PE braid before failure; elastic—recovers to original length after stretch—maintains shock for life of the line.
Price:. . . 125, 300 yds: $14.99–$28.99; 1500 yds: $134.99–$219.99

STREN 100% FLUORO

Color: Clear/Blue flourescent
Type: Fluorocarbon
Length: 200 yds
Lb. Test: 6–20
Diameter: .01–.018
Features: Virtually invisible; maximum abrasion resistance.
Price:. . . . .$16.99–$23.99

STREN BRUTE STRENGTH

Color: Clear/Blue flourescent
Type: Monofilament
Length: 330 yds
Lb. Test: 6–20

Diameter: .01–.019
Features: Extra strong; extra tough; castable and manageable.
Price:. . . . .**$7.99–$10.99**

STREN FLUOROCAST

Color: Clear
Type: Fluorocarbon
Length: 100 yds; 200 yds
Lb. Test: 4-17
Diameter: .007–.016

Features: Easy to cast and handle; excellent know and shock strength; virtually invisible.
Price:. . . . . . . **100 yds: $4.99–$5.99; 200 yds: $8.99–$9.99**

STREN MAGNATHIN

Color: Clear
Type: Monofilament
Length: 330 yds; 2600 yds
Lb. Test: 4–30

Diameter: .007–.018
Features: Extra strong; extra tough; castable and manageable.
Price: . . . 330 yds: $9.49–$14.49; 2600 yds: $43.99–$76.99

STREN ORIGINAL

Color: Clear; Clear/Blue flourescent; Hi-Vis Gold; Clear/Blue flourescent; Lo-Vis Green
Type: Monofilament
Length: 100 yds; 330 yds; 1000 yds; 2400 yds
Lb. Test: 4–25

Diameter: .008–.02
Features: Superior knot strength; tough and abrasion resistant; low memory.
Price: . .100 yds: $2.99–$4.49; 330 yds: $6.99–$8.99; 1000 yds: $17.99–$21.49; $35.49–$62.49

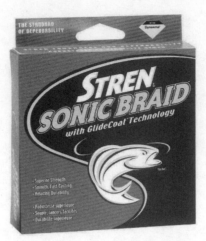

STREN SONIC BRAID

Color: Lo-Vis Green
Type: Braid
Length: 125 yds; 300 yds; 1500 yds
Lb. Test: 8-80
Diameter: .004-.014
Features: The only superline featuring GlideCoat technology, which produces a fast casting, super smooth, quiet, and wear-resistant braided line. GlideCoat treatment also holds color better than other superlines. Stren Sonic Braid is made with the highest strength Dyneema polyethylene (PE) fiber construction—stronger than steel. The round, full-bodied construction resists wind-knots and other handling problems found in ordinary braids. With unmatched knot strength for dependability.
Price: . . . .125,300 yds: $14.95–$39.95; 1500 yds: $152.95–$170.95

SUFIX 832 ADVANCED ICE BRAID

Color: Ghost, neon lime
Type: Braid
Length: 50 yd
Lb. Test: 4–30
Diameter: 0.004 in–0.011 in
Features: Most durable small diameter ice braid available; water-repellant protection to reduce freezing; GORE Performance Fiber adds incredible fray and abrasion resistance for durability.
Price: $11.29

SUFIX 832 ADVANCED SUPERLINE
Color: Camo, ghost, hi-vis yellow, low-vis green, neon lime
Type: Braid
Length: 150 yd, 300 yd, 600 yd
Lb. Test: 6–80
Diameter: 0.006 in–0.018 in

Features: 8 fibers (Featuring one GORE Performance Fiber and 7 Dyneema Fibers); 32 pics (weaves) per inch; R8 precision braiding technology; patent-pending construction; ultimate abrasion resistance; unbeatable strength; proven castability improvements; TGP technology enhances color retention.
Price: . . . .**$23.19–$440.59**

SUFIX CASTABLE INVISILINE 100% FLUOROCARBON
Color: Clear
Type: Fluorocarbon
Length: 100 yd, 200 yd
Lb. Test: 3–20
Diameter: 0.006 in–0.017 in

Features: Virtually disappears in the water for more natural presentation; low stretch; fast sinking; casts and handles like a premium monofilament; incredibly strong and abrasion resistant; resistant to ultra violet rays; performs great on casting and spinning reels; G² precision winding.
Price: . . . .**$14.09–$33.79**

LINES

SUFIX ICE MAGIC

Color: Clear, neon orange
Type: Monofilament
Length: 100 yd
Lb. Test: 1, 2, 3, 4, 6, 8
Diameter: 0.004 in–0.010 in

Features: Designed to stay manageable even in frigid water; special additives deter water absorption that causes ice build-up; fast sinking for more natural presentation.
Price: **$3.59**

SUFIX SIEGE

Color: Clear, camo, neon tangerine, smoke green
Length: 250 yd, 330 yd, 1000 yd, 3000 yd
Lb. Test: 4–35
Diameter: 0.008 in–0.022 in

Features: Superior casting distance with pinpoint accuracy due to its proprietary extrusion process; up to 15X greater abrasion resistance; exceptional knot strength and smooth handling; smooth, supple, handles beautifully—yet it is exceptionally strong; G² Precision Winding (330 yd spools) virtually eliminates line memory, even on spinning reels.
Price: . . . .**$9.09–$83.69**

LINES

BASS PRO SHOPS MAGIBRAID LEAD CORE TROLLING
Color: Metered
Type: Braid
Length: 100 yd
Lb. Test: 12, 15, 18, 27, 36, 45
Diameter: 0.61mm–0.89mm

Features: Manufactured with high tenacity, multifilament, Dupont nylon yarn tightly braided over a soft 99.9 percent-pure lead core; smaller-diameter line also allows more reel capacity than standard lead core lines; color metered every 10 yards with high visibility dye, this line enables the angler to determine depth at a glance.
Price: . . . .**$13.99–$16.99**

BERKLEY BIG GAME BRAID
Color: Low-vis green
Type: Braid
Length: 300 yd
Lb. Test: 6, 8, 12, 15, 17
Diameter: 0.009 in–0.017 in

Features: Uses Dyneema, the world's strongest gel-spun polyethylene fiber; ultra-sensitive, with virtually no stretch; transmits lure action and strikes directly to the rod tip and reel for instant and positive hooksets.
Price: . . . .**$24.49–$38.49**

LINES

BERKLEY FIRELINE FUSED CRYSTAL

Color: Crystal
Type: Fused
Length: 125 yd, 300 yd, 1500 yd
Lb. Test: 2–30
Diameter: 0.005 in–0.015 in
Features: Combines the ultimate in low-visibility with all of the benefits of FireLine; incredibly thin diameter to work the tiniest micro bait; supple enough to handle the coldest weather; incredibly strong—three times stronger than mono; ultimate sensitivity to telegraph feel for structure and strikes.
Price:.............**$17.95–$37.49; 1500 yd: $176.99**

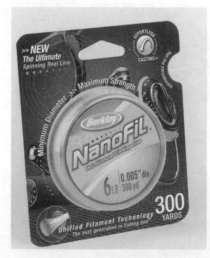

BERKLEY NANOFIL

Color: Clear mist, high-vis chartreuse, low-vis green,
Type: Uni-filament
Length: 150 yd, 300 yd
Lb. Test: 2–17
Diameter: 0.002 in–0.010 in
Features: Not a mono. Not a Braid. The Next Generation in Fishing Line. Unified filament technology provides the ultimate advantage against a wide variety of species; cast farther and feel everything with the ultimate spinning reel line; minimum diameter, maximum strength; zero memory virtually eliminates line tangles.
Price:...............................**$19.95–$38.95**

BERKLEY PROSPEC—1 LB. BULK SPOOL

Color: Fluorescent yellow, ocean blue
Type: Monofilament
Length: 800 yds–6000 yds
Lb. Test: 12–80
Diameter: 0.012 in–0.033 in

Features: Thin and supple with excellent knot and impact strength; premium co-polymer monofilament; built to withstand the abuse that professional saltwater anglers handle on a daily basis.
Price: **$49.95**

BERKLEY SOLUTIONS CASTING

Color: Green mist
Type: Monofilament
Length: 250 yd
Lb. Test: 10, 12, 14, 17
Diameter: 0.014 in–0.017 in

Features: Targeted for anglers who want to take the guesswork out of choosing line for their reel and spend more time fishing; specifically designed for low-profile or round baitcasting reels; strong, trouble free, and easy to use; stacks and handles well on baitcast reels.
Price: **$5.99**

LINES

BERKLEY SOLUTIONS SPINNING

Color: Green mist
Type: Monofilament
Length: 250 yd
Lb. Test: 4, 6, 8, 10
Diameter: 0.008 in–0.011 in

Features: Targeted for anglers who want to take the guesswork out of choosing line for their reel and spend more time fishing; specifically designed for open face or closed face spinning reels; strong, trouble free, and easy to use; resists tangles and hassles.
Price: **$5.99**

BERKLEY TRILENE BIG CAT

Color: Solar green
Type: Monofilament
Length: 200 yd, 220 yd, 270 yd, 300 yd
Lb. Test: 15, 20, 30, 40
Diameter: 0.015 in–0.024 in

Features: High shock strength; controlled stretch adds fighting power for big casts; reflects sunlight or blacklight for high visibility; abrasion-resistant to stand tough against rough or sharp objects.
Price: **$7.29**

BERKLEY TRILENE COLD WEATHER
Color: Electric blue, fl. clear/blue
Type: Monofilament
Length: 110 yd
Lb. Test: 2, 3, 4, 6, 8, 10
Diameter: 0.005 in–0.011 in

Features: Improved formula is as flexible at 32°F as regular mono is at 70°F; extraordinary flexibility and low memory design to resist twists and tangles; available in electric blue color for maximum visibility against ice and snow.
Price:. . . . . $3.39–$4.19

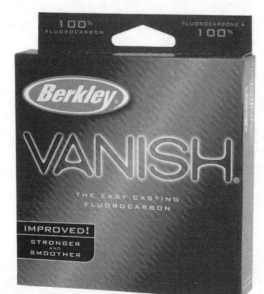

BERKLEY VANISH
Color: Clear
Type: Fluorocarbon
Length: 110 yd, 250 yd, 350 yd
Lb. Test: 2-40
Diameter: 0.006 in–0.022 in

Features: The most flexible, easiest casting fluorocarbon; best Vanish formula ever, with 20 percent better shock strength, improved knot strength and easier to handle; non-absorbing fluorocarbon maintains strength and abrasion resistance underwater.
Price:. . . . .$5.99–$29.99

CABELA'S 2008 CABELA'S PRESTIGE BRAIDED DACRON LINE

Color: Clear
Type: Braid
Length: 200 yd, 500 yd, 1200 yd
Lb. Test: 20, 30, 50, 80, 130

Features: Proven to be excellent for casting and trolling; perfect for muskie and saltwater bill fish; abrasion- and deterioration-resistant; mold- and mildew-resistant.
Price: . 200 yd: $8.99–$12.99; 500 yd: $14.99–$28.99; 1200 yd: $29.99–$61.99

CABELA'S DACRON PLANER BOARD LINE

Color: Fluorescent orange
Type: Braid
Length: 150 feet
Lb. Test: 135

Diameter: 0.135 in
Features: High-visibility orange line; low-stretch braided Dacron; resists kinks and tangles.
Price: $9.99

CABELA'S LEAD CORE

Color: 10 yd color changes
Type: Braid
Length: 100 yd, 200 yd
Lb. Test: 18, 27, 36, 45, 54
Diameter: 0.030 in–0.059 in
Features: Tightly braided, high-tenacity nylon multifilament yarn encapsulates a 99.9 percent-pure lead core; smaller diameter than standard lead-core lines; color changes every 10 yards for accurate measurements of fishing depths without having to use a linecounter; great alternative to snapweights or divers; approximate sink rate is 1.25 feet with every 2 yards released, depending on speed.
Price: . . . .**$15.99–$29.99**

CABELA'S KING KAT

Color: Dirty green, hi-vis yellow
Type: Braid
Length: 200yd, 400 yd
Lb. Test: 20, 30, 50, 80
Diameter: 0.009 in–0.016 in
Features: A unique bi-component, small-diameter, braided superline with exceptional abrasion resistance and strength; made with Spectra fibers and a multifilament nylon tracer blended into the braid; nylon tracer increases the line's stretch by 5 percent so it's more forgiving when you set the hook; gives the line neutral buoyancy while hiding the line in the water with a mottled pattern; line is then permeated by a synthesized coating process that penetrates the braid.
Price: . . . .**$16.99–$39.99**

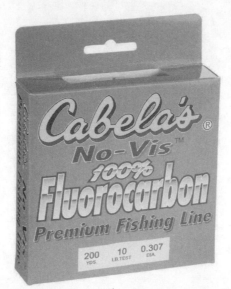

CABELA'S NO-VIS FLUOROCARBON LINE

Photo: IK-115174
Color: Clear
Type: Fluorocarbon
Length: 200 yd, 400 yd, 600 yd
Lb. Test: 4–20
Diameter: 0.007 in–0.016 in

Price: . . . . 200 yd: $12.99–$16.99; 400 yd: $19.99–$26.99; 600 yd: $24.99–$39.99
Features: Virtually invisible under water, (only 100 percent Fluorocarbon comes close to matching the light refraction index of water); abrasion resistance, knot strength, and tensile strength far exceeded expectations; extra-soft properties and minimal stretch.

CABELA'S PROLINE

Color: Camo, clear, green, hi-vis yellow
Type: Monofilament
Length: 425 yds–3100 yds
Lb. Test: 4–30
Diameter: 0.008 in–0.022 in
Features: Controlled tensile strength enables ProLine to take the sudden shock and impact of bone-jarring hooksets with minimum stretch, while withstanding the runs and surges of any game fish; all of that in a small-diameter line with more than enough abrasion resistance to handle the toughest situations. Bulk spool also available.
Price: $9.99

LINES

CABELA'S SALT STRIKER LINE – 1/4-LB. SPOOL

Color: Blue, chartreuse, clear
Type: Monofilament
Length: 400 yds–1350 yds

Lb. Test: 10, 15, 20, 25, 30
Features: Special UV additives; abrasion-resistant finish; low-stretch high-tensile strength; thinner-diameter copolymer line; also available in 1 lb. and 2 lb. spools.
Price: **$7.99**

CORTLAND LIQUID CRYSTAL FLY

Color: Crystal
Type: Fly Fused
Lb. Test: 8, 9, 10, 12
Features: Advanced composition of super-strong polyethylene and copolymers creates a line with twice the

strength of PVC lines PE+ jacket is naturally lighter than water, eliminating the need for microspheres or other agents for flotation; ultrasmooth, abrasion-resistant finish.
Price: **$80.00**

DAIWA SALTIGA BOAT BRAIDED

Color: Multi
Type: Braid
Length: 1800 meters
Lb. Test: 40–150
Features: Designed for deep drop fishing with Dendoh Style power assist reels, eight woven braids make it super-strong, yet one of the finest diameter braids available, less affected by currents for a straighter, more accurate drop. Its smooth surface means less friction and noise from guides on the retrieve. Color changes every ten meters, with five and one meter indicators, shows depth and line movement. Coded for quick programming into Dendoh reel memory for maximum readout accuracy.
Price: . . . . **$249.95–$379.95**

DAIWA SAMURAI BRAIDED

Color: Green
Type: Braid
Length: 150 yds, 300 yds, 1500 yds
Lb. Test: 15–150
Diameter: .18 in–.62 in
Features: Samurai line is unlike any other braided line on the market. Sure, it's strong and sensitive, but it's also noticeably thinner, softer, smoother, and more flexible than ordinary braids. That means less friction for better casts; reduced line noise on the retrieve; and a faster sink rate due to less current resistance. Available in 150-yard, 300-yard, and 1500-yard spools.
Price: . . . . **$24.95–$249.95**

DAIWA STEEZ FLUOROCARBON

Color: Green
Type: Fluorocarbon
Length: 125 yds
Lb. Test: 5–20
Diameter: .007 in–016 in
Features: Finally, a green colored, super soft, super strong 100 percent Fluorocarbon line with the flexibility and castability of regular monofilament. Formulated exclusively for Steez spinning and casting reels, it is highly resistant to abrasion and offers a faster sink rate than monofilament. Parallel winding on the filler spool prevents dents and inconsistency in roundness that can reduce casting efficiency.
Price:. . . . .$19.99–$26.99

L.L.BEAN STREAMLIGHT II

Color: Yellow
Type: Fly
Length: 90 feet
Lb. Test: 3–9
Features: Designed for beginning fly fishermen; short head allows for quick and easy loading of the fly rod.
Price:. $20.00

ORVIS ACCESS SALTWATER

Color: Mist green
Type: Fly
Length: 90 feet
Lb. Test: 6–10
Features: Orvis Line ID allows you to quickly and easily identify your line, with no more guessing; all of the lines are printed with the taper, weight, and functionality; Integrated Slickness additive is integrated throughout the PVC layer to provide lubrication for maximum distance, performance, and durability; new sleek and durable welded loop makes leader attachment quick and easy while holding up to repeated use—also helps to transfer energy more efficiently to the leader allowing better turnover; braided multifilament core provides excellent performance over a wide range of conditions; new paper pulp spool, made from recycled cardboard and kraft paper, is 100 percent compostable; made in USA.
Price:..................................... **$59.00**

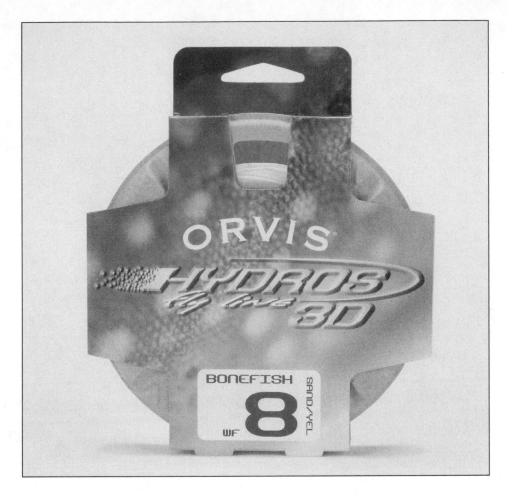

ORVIS HYDROS 3D BONEFISH

Color: Sand; yellow
Type: Fly
Length: 105 feet
Lb. Test: 7, 8, 9, 10
Features: Orvis Line ID allows you to quickly and easily identify your line, with no more guessing; all of the lines are printed with the taper, weight, and functionality; Integrated Slickness additive is integrated throughout the PVC layer to provide lubrication for maximum distance, performance, and durability; new sleek and durable welded loop makes leader attachment quick and easy while holding up to repeated use—also helps to transfer energy more efficiently to the leader allowing better turnover; braided multifilament core provides excellent performance over a wide range of conditions; new paper pulp spool, made from recycled cardboard and kraft paper, is 100 percent compostable; made in USA.
Price: **$95.00**

ORVIS HYDROS ALL ROUNDER SALTWATER

Color: Horizon blue
Type: Fly
Length: 100 feet
Lb. Test: 6–12
Features: The best-selling all-purpose floating line for saltwater or freshwater big game; works well for stripers and blues as well as bass and pike; allows for close-in or long-distance presentations, and turns over heavy flies in the wind; latest generation of Wonderline coating is 20 percent slicker than the previous generation, resulting in the slickest fly lines on the market; casts farther with less effort, produces higher line speeds to cut through the wind and improve accuracy, repels dirt and grime, picks up off the water easier, improves flotation, and reduces tangles; Orvis Line ID allows you to quickly and easily identify your line, with no more guessing; all of the lines are printed with the taper, weight, and functionality; new sleek and durable welded loops make leader attachment quick and easy while holding up to repeated use—also helps to transfer energy more efficiently to the leader allowing better turnover; saltwater lines have an enhanced rear loop as well for attaching to backing; braided multifilament core provides excellent performance over a wide range of conditions; new paper pulp spool, made from recycled cardboard and kraft paper, is 100 percent compostable; in horizon blue; 100'.
Price: **$79.00**

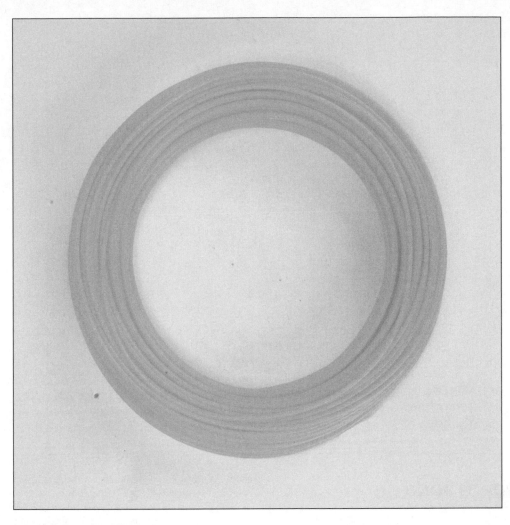

ORVIS HYDROS BLUEWATER

Color: Bright orange
Type: Fly
Length: 80 feet
Lb. Test: 14, 15
Features: Full-sinking specialty line designed to throw monster flies to sailfish, marlin, and sharks; sinks 4 ½"-5" per second to cut through the waves and keep your fly in the strike zone; has a 25' head to turn over big flies with ease; small diameter running line cuts through the water, helping to minimize break-offs; Integrated Slickness additive is integrated throughout the PVC layer to provide lubrication for maximum distance, performance and durability; Orvis Line ID allows you to quickly and easily identify your line, with no more guessing; all of the lines are printed with the taper, weight, and functionality; braided monofilament core offers outstanding performance in hot, humid saltwater environments; new paper pulp spool, made from recycled cardboard and kraft paper, is 100 percent compostable.
Price:. **$85.00**

ORVIS HYDROS BONEFISH

Color: Blue; sand
Type: Fly
Length: 105 feet
Lb. Test: 7–9
Features: Special weight-forward taper for quick, accurate presentations to fast-moving bonefish; trigger color change at 30' load point increases accuracy and eliminates unnecessary false casting; latest generation of Wonderline coating is 20 percent slicker than the previous generation, resulting in the slickest fly lines on the market; casts farther with less effort, produces higher line speeds to cut through the wind and improve accuracy, repels dirt and grime, picks up off the water easier, improves flotation, and reduces tangles; Orvis Line ID allows you to quickly and easily identify your line, with no more guessing; all of the lines are printed with the taper, weight, and functionality; new sleek and durable welded loops make leader attachment quick and easy while holding up to repeated use—also helps to transfer energy more efficiently to the leader allowing better turnover; saltwater lines have an enhanced rear loop as well for attaching to backing; an innovative weight forward taper combined with slightly larger line diameters produce a line that is ideal at close to medium range, but still capable of delivering at distance; braided monofilament core offers outstanding performance in hot, humid saltwater environments; new paper pulp spool, made from recycled cardboard and kraft paper, is 100 percent compostable.
Price: **$79.00**

ORVIS HYDROS REDFISH
Color: Sand
Type: Fly
Length: 105 feet
Lb. Test: 7–9
Features: A floating redfish fly line designed to work from a boat or while wading for redfish; short, heavy compact head aids in making quick, accurate deliveries while moderate front taper turns over the leader and fly easily; latest generation of Wonderline coating is 20 percent slicker than the previous generation, resulting in the slickest fly lines on the market; casts farther with less effort, produces higher line speeds to cut through the wind and improve accuracy, repels dirt and grime, picks up off the water easier, improves flotation, and reduces tangles; Orvis Line ID allows you to quickly and easily identify your line, with no more guessing; all of the lines are printed with the taper, weight, and functionality; new sleek and durable welded loops make leader attachment quick and easy while holding up to repeated use—also helps to transfer energy more efficiently to the leader allowing better turnover; saltwater lines have an enhanced rear loop as well for attaching to backing; braided monofilament core offers outstanding performance in hot, humid saltwater environments; new paper pulp spool, made from recycled cardboard and kraft paper, is 100 percent compostable.
Price: **$79.00**

ORVIS HYDROS STRIPER INTERMEDIATE

Color: Blue; stealth tip
Type: Fly
Length: 105 feet
Lb. Test: 8–10
Features: Gets your fly down just below the surface chop, helping you keep tight to the fly to detect subtle takes; great line for stripers, bluefish, false albacore, and other cool-water fish species; won't tangle when fishing from a stripping basket; Integrated Slickness additive is integrated throughout the PVC layer to provide lubrication for maximum distance, performance, and durability; Orvis Line ID allows you to quickly and easily identify your line, with no more guessing; all of the lines are printed with the taper, weight, and functionality; new sleek and durable welded loops make leader attachment quick and easy while holding up to repeated use—also helps to transfer energy more efficiently to the leader allowing better turnover; saltwater lines have an enhanced rear loop as well for attaching to backing; braided multifilament core provides excellent performance over a wide range of conditions; new paper pulp spool, made from recycled cardboard and kraft paper, is 100 percent compostable.
Price: **$85.00**

SHAKESPEARE MONOFILAMENT
Color: Clear
Type: Monofilmaent
Length: 700 yd
Lb. Test: 4, 6, 8,10, 12, 15, 20, 25,30, 50

Features: 1/3 pound spool; excellent abrasion resistance; extremely affordable.
Price: **$2.99**

SPIDERWIRE EZ BRAID
Color: Moss green
Type: Braid
Length: 110 yds; 300 yds
Lb. Test: 10–50
Diameter: .007–.015

Features: Dyneema microfibers are 3X stronger than mono; diameters are 2 to 3X smaller than mono of the same weight test; super smooth for long, effortless casts; spider-sensitivity; near zero stretch to feel everything.
Price: . . . . **110, 300 yds: $9.95–$18.95**

SPIDERWIRE EZ FLUORO

Color: Clear
Type: Fluorocarbon
Length: 200 yds
Lb. Test: 2–15
Diameter: .006–.015

Features: 100 percent fluorocarbon for the key fluorocarbon benefits of virtual invisibility, sinking for less line between lure and reel and great wet strength; sensitive and abrasion resistant; good manageability, knot, and impact strength.
Price:. . . . .$7.99–$8.99

SPIDERWIRE STEALTH GLOW-VIS

Color: Glow-Vis-Green Bulk
Type: Braid
Length: 125; 300 yds; 1500 yds
Lb. Test: 8–80
Diameter: .007–.016
Price:. . . . . .125, 300 yds: $14.99–$38.99; 1500 yds: $134.99–$184.99

Features: Fluorescent brighteners illuminate line above water; low-vis green disappears below water enhance ability to watch line and detect bites that may not be felt.

SPIDERWIRE ULTRACAST 100% FLUOROCARBON

Color: Clear
Type: Fluorocarbon
Length: 200 yds
Lb. Test: 6, 8, 10, 12, 15
Diameter: .009–.014

Features: Thinner diameters than most competitive fluorocarbons allows lures to perform better; awesome performance on spinning reels (4–10 lb. test); disappears to fish as it is virtually invisible; spider-sensitivity transmits strikes and structure.
Price: . . . .**$14.99–$16.99**

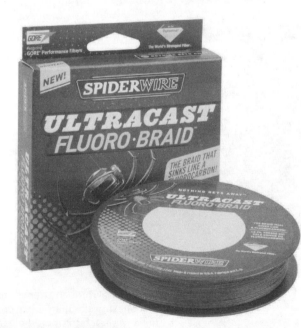

SPIDERWIRE ULTRACAST FLUORO-BRAID

Color: Moss green
Type: Braid
Length: 125; 300 yds; 1500 yds
Lb. Test: 10–80
Diameter: .008–.018

Features: Exceptionally high strength-per-diameter in a fluoro; thinner diameters than most competitive fluorocarbons allow lures to perform better; awesome performance on spinning reels (4–10 lb test); spider sensitivity; transmits strikes and structure.
Price: . . .125, 300 yds: $20.99–$49.99; 1500 yds: $187.49–$224.99

LINES

SPIDERWIRE ULTRACAST INVISI-BRAID

Color: Clear
Type: Braid
Length: 125; 300 yds; 1500 yds; 3000 yds
Lb. Test: 6–80
Diameter: .007–.022
Features: Ultra smooth 8 carrier braid; innovative cold-fusion process; translucency for near invisibility; extremely high strength-per-diameter; amazingly thin and sensitive; high pick count for roundness and durability.
Price:. . . . . 125, 300 yds: $20.99–$49.99; 1500, 3000 yds: $187.49–$449.99

SPIDERWIRE ULTRACAST ULTIMATE MONO

Color: Clear; Brown recluse
Type: Monofilament
Length: 330 yds
Lb. Test: 4–20
Diameter: .006–.016
Features: Breakthrough strength-to-diameter co-polymer is 33 percent stronger than the average mono; unprecedented 15 percent stretch for incredible sensitivity and hook setting power; thin diameter allows exceptional bait action and high line capacity; excellent knot and shock strength even when wet; optimized for baitcast reels, but still castable and manageable on spinning reels.
Price:. . . . .$8.99–$11.99

SPIDERWIRE ZILLA BRAID

Color: Moss green
Type: Braid
Length: 125; 300 yds; 1500 yds
Lb. Test: 20–100
Diameter: .014–.038
Features: Dyneema provides unmatched strength; Cordura provides toughness; engineered with shock resistance for power baitcast techniques; dense braid creates a loading effect for longer casting distance; tough, durable, and abrasion-resistant; stretches 67 percent more than standard PE braid before failure; elastic recovers to original length after stretch and maintains shock for life of the line.
Price: . . .125, 300 yds: $14.99–$28.99; 1500 yds: $134.99–$219.99

STREN 100% FLUORO
Color: Clear/Blue flourescent
Type: Fluorocarbon
Length: 200 yds
Lb. Test: 6–20

Diameter: .01–.018
Features: Virtually invisible; maximim abrasion resistance.
Price:.............................**$16.99–$23.99**

STREN BRUTE STRENGTH
Color: Clear/Blue flourescent
Type: Monofilament
Length: 330 yds
Lb. Test: 6–20

Diameter: .01–.019
Features: Extra strong; extra tough; castable and manageable.
Price:...........................**$7.99-–$10.99**

STREN FLUOROCAST
Color: Clear
Type: Fluorocarbon
Length: 100 yds; 200 yds

Lb. Test: 4–17
Diameter: .007–.016
Features: Easy to cast and handle; excellent know and shock strength; virtually invisible.
Price:. . . . . . 100 yds: $4.99–$5.99; 200 yds: $8.99–$9.99

STREN MAGNATHIN
Color: Clear
Type: Monofilament
Length: 330 yds; 2600 yds
Lb. Test: 4–16

Diameter: .007–.018
Features: Small diameter; super strong; advanced casting formula.
Price:. . . 330 yds: $9.49–$14.49; 2600 yds: $43.99–$76.99

LINES

LINES: Saltwater

STREN ORIGINAL

Color: Clear; Clear/Blue flourescent; Hi-Vis Gold; Clear/
Blue flourescent; Lo-Vis Green;
Type: Monofilament
Length: 100 yds; 330 yds; 1000 yds; 2400 yds
Lb. Test: 4–20

Diameter: .008–.02
Features: Superior knot strength; tough and abrasion
resistant; low memory.
Price: . . . **100 yds: $2.99–$4.49; 330 yds: $6.99–$8.99; 1000
yds: $17.99–$21.49; $35.49–$62.49**

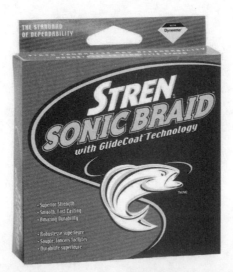

STREN SONIC BRAID

Color: Lo-Vis Green
Type: Braid
Length: 125 yds; 300 yds; 1500 yds
Lb. Test: 8–80
Diameter: .004–.014
Features: The only superline featuring GlideCoat
technology, which produces a fast casting, super smooth,
quiet, and wear-resistant braided line. GlideCoat treatment
also holds color better than other superlines. Stren Sonic

Braid is made with the highest strength Dyneema
polyethylene (PE) fiber construction—stronger than steel.
The round, full-bodied construction resists wind-knots and
other handling problems found in ordinary braids. With
unmatched knot strength for dependability.
Price: . . .**125, 300 yds: $14.95–$39.95; 1500 yds: $152.95–
$170.95**

SUFIX 832 ADVANCED ICE BRAID

Color: Ghost, neon lime
Type: Braid
Length: 50 yd
Lb. Test: 4–30
Diameter: 0.004 in–0.011 in

Features: Most durable small diameter ice braid available; water-repellant protection to reduce freezing; GORE Performance Fiber adds incredible fray and abrasion resistance for durability.
Price:. $11.29

SUFIX 832 ADVANCED SUPERLINE

Color: Camo, ghost, hi-vis yellow, low-vis green, neon lime
Type: Braid
Length: 150 yd, 300 yd, 600 yd
Lb. Test: 6–80
Diameter: 0.006 in–0.018 in

Features: 8 fibers (Featuring one GORE Performance Fiber and 7 Dyneema Fibers); 32 pics (weaves) per inch; R8 precision braiding technology; patent-pending construction; ultimate abrasion resistance; unbeatable strength; proven castability improvements; TGP technology enhances color retention.
Price:. . . . . $23.19–$440.59

LINES

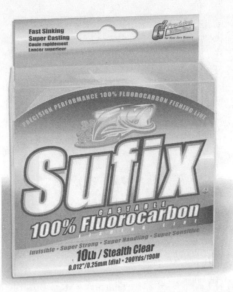

SUFIX CASTABLE INVISILINE 100% FLUOROCARBON
Color: Clear
Type: Fluorocarbon
Length: 100 yd, 200 yd
Lb. Test: 3–20

Diameter: 0.006 in–0.017 in
Features: Virtually disappears in the water for more natural presentation; low stretch; fast sinking; casts and handles like a premium monofilament; incredibly strong and abrasion-resistant; resistant to ultra violet rays; performs great on casting and spinning reels; G² precision winding.
Price:...............................$14.09–$33.79

SUFIX ICE MAGIC
Color: Clear, neon orange
Type: Monofilament
Length: 100 yd
Lb. Test: 1–8
Diameter: 0.004 in–0.010 in

Features: Designed to stay manageable even in frigid water; special additives deter water absorption that causes ice build-up; fast sinking for more natural presentation.
Price:...................................... $3.59

SUFIX SIEGE

Color: Clear, camo, neon tangerine, smoke green
Length: 250 yd, 330 yd, 1000 yd, 3000 yd
Lb. Test: 4–35
Diameter: 0.008 in–0.022 in
Features: Superior casting distance with pinpoint accuracy due to its proprietary extrusion process; up to 15X greater abrasion resistance; exceptional knot strength and smooth handling; smooth, supple, handles beautifully—yet it is exceptionally strong; G² Precision Winding (330 yd spools) virtually eliminates line memory, even on spinning reels.
Price: . . . .**$9.09–$83.69**

Directory of Manufacturers & Suppliers

ABU GARCIA
1900 18th Street
Spirit Lake, IA 51360
(800) 228-4272
abugarcia.com

BANDIT LURES INC.
444 Cold Springs Road
Sardis, MS 38666
(662) 563-8450
banditlures.com
customerservice@banditlures.
com

BASS PRO SHOPS
2500 East Kearney
Springfield, MO 65898
(417) 873-5000
basspro.com

BEAVERKILL ROD CO.
32 Andrea Lane
Scarsdale, NY 10583
(914) 490-3052
bkrod.com

**BERKLEY CUSTOMER
SERVICE**
1900 18th Street
Spirit Lake, IA 51360
(800) 237-5539
berkley-fishing.com

BIG BITE BAITS, INC
PO Box 1375
Eufaula, AL 36072
(877) 222-7429
bigbitebaits.com
bbbaits@bellsouth.net

BOMBER, PRADCO-FISHING
3601 Jenny Lind Road
Fort Smith, AR 72901
(479) 782-8971
lurenet.com

BOOYAH, PRADCO-FISHING
3601 Jenny Lind Road
Fort Smith, AR 72901
(479) 782-8971
lurenet.com

CABELA'S
One Cabela Drive
Sidney, NE 69160
(800) 2430-6626
cabelas.com

CORTLAND LINE CO.
3736 Kellogg Road
Cortland, NY 13045
(607) 756-2851
cortlandline.com
info@cortlandline.com

**CREEK CHUB, PRADCO-
FISHING**
3601 Jenny Lind Road
Fort Smith, AR 72901
(479) 782-8971
lurenet.com

DAIWA CORPORATION
11137 Warland Drive
Cypress, CA 90630
(562) 375-6800
daiwa.com
admail@daiwa.com

DAMIKI FISHING TACKLE
26017 Huntington Lane, Unit
D
Valencia, CA 91355
(661) 702-0506
damiki.com
daniel@damiki.com

**EAGLE CLAW FISHING
TACKLE CO.**
4245 East 46th Avenue
Denver, CO 80216
(303) 321-1481
eagleclaw.com
Info@eagleclaw.com

**FENWICK CUSTOMER
SERVICE**
1900 18th Street
Spirit Lake, IA 51360
(877) 336-7637
fenwickfishing.com
fenwick@purefishing.com

**GARY YAMAMOTO CUSTOM
BAITS**
849 Coppermine Road
Page, AZ 86040
(928) 645-9699
baits.com

HARDY & GREYS LIMITED
Willowburn
Alnwick, Northumberland, UK
NE66 2PF
01665-602-771 + OPTION 2
hardyfishing.com

HATCH OUTDOORS, INC.
1001 Park Center Drive
Vista, CA 92081
(760) 734-4343
hatchoutdoors.com

**HEDDON LURES, PRADCO-
FISHING**
3601 Jenny Lind Road
Fort Smith, AR 72901
(479) 782-8971
lurenet.com

KEITECH USA
6 Bonaparte Point Road
Hopatcong, NJ 7843
(973) 398-7608
keitechusa.com

LAMIGLAS, INC.
1400 Atlantic Avenue
Woodland, WA 98674
(800) 325-9436
lamiglas.com12
info@lamiglas.com

LEW'S
2253 E. Bennett
Springfield, MO 65804
(877) 470-5397
lews.com
info@lews.com

L.L.BEAN INC
15 Casco Street
Freeport, ME 04033-0001
(800) 441-5713
llbean.com

G.LOOMIS
1 Holland Drive
Irvine, CA 92618
(877) 577-0600
gloomis.com

NAUTILUS REELS
1549 NW 165th Street
Miami, FL 33169
(305) 625-3437
nautilusreels.com

**NORTHLAND FISHING
TACKLE**
1001 Naylor Drive SE
Bemidji, MN 56601
(218) 751-6723
northlandtackle.com
Sales@NorthlandTackle.com

OKUMA FISHING
2310 E Locust Street
Ontario, CA 91761
(909) 923-2828
okumafishing.com

THE ORVIS COMPANY
1711 Blue Hills Drive
Roanoke, VA 24012-8613
(888) 235-9763
orvis.com
customerservice@orvis.com

PANTHER MARTIN
19 N. Columbia Street
Port Jefferson, NY 11777
(800) 524-4742
panthermartincom
staff@panthermartincom

PRADCO-FISHING
3601 Jenny Lind Road
Fort Smith, AR 72901
(479) 782-8971
lurenet.com

**PENN FISHING TACKLE
COMPANY**
1900 18th Street
Spirit Lake, IA 51360
(800) 228-4272
pennreels.com

**PFLUEGER CUSTOMER
SERVICE**
7 Science Court
Columbia, SC 29203
(800) 554-4653
pfluegerfishing.com

POWER PRO
1 Holland Drive
Irvine, CA 92618
(877) 577-0600
powerpro.com

QUANTUM FISHING
6105 E. Apache
Tulsa, OK 74115
(800) 588-9030
quantumfishing.com
email.quantum@zebco.com

RIO PRODUCTS
5050 S. Yellowstone Hwy
Idaho Falls, ID 83402
(800) 553-0838
rioproducts.com